Applied Econometrics Association Series

General Editors: **Jean H.P. Paelinck**, Emeritus Professor, Erasmus University, Rotterdam; and **Henri Serbat**, University of Paris 2.

The vital importance of econometrics for understanding economic phenomena is increasingly recognized in every field of economics.

The discipline is based on 'scientific processes which aim to identify, explain and forecast economic phenomena using formalised tools to produce, measure, structure and model the information' (Gérard Duru and Henri Serbat, 1991).

The Applied Econometrics Association, established 1974, seeks to develop the use of econometric tools by regular updates on the state of the art and the progress made in each specific field, and so to further the transformation of unconnected facts into pertinent information for use in analysis and decision-making.

The series was conceived to form a set of working references for advanced students and researchers in each specific field, as well as a guide to development across the discipline more broadly.

This exchange of knowledge will be continued permanently by the opening of a debate site on the Internet (http://www.aea.fed-eco.org).

Titles include:

Françoise Bourdon and Jean Bourdon (*editors*)
WAGE ECONOMETRICS AND MODELLING

Fabrizio Carlevaro and Jean-Baptiste Lesourt (*editors*)
MEASURING AND ACCOUNTING ENVIRONMENTAL NUISANCES AND SERVICES

Arthur Getis, Jesús Mur and Henry G. Zoller (*editors*)
SPATIAL ECONOMETRICS AND SPATIAL STATISTICS

Siv S. Gustafsson and Danièle E. Meulders (*editors*)
GENDER AND THE LABOUR MARKET
Econometric Evidence of Obstacles to Achieving Gender Equality

Hans Heijke and Joan Muysken (*editors*)
EDUCATION AND TRAINING IN A KNOWLEDGE-BASED ECONOMY

Pavlos Karadeloglou (*editor*)
EXCHANGE-RATE POLICY IN EUROPE

Pavlos Karadeloglou and Virginie Terraza (*editors*)
EXCHANGE RATES AND MACROECONOMIC DYNAMICS

Sandrine Lardic and Valérie Mignon (*editors*)
RECENT DEVELOPMENTS ON EXCHANGE RATES

Benoît Mahy, Robert Plasman and François Rycx (*editors*)
GENDER PAY DIFFERENTIALS
Cross-National Evidence from Micro-Data

David Marsden and François Rycx (*editors*)
WAGE STRUCTURES, EMPLOYMENT ADJUSTMENTS AND GLOBALIZATION
Evidence from Linked and Firm-level Panel Data

Danièle Meulders, Robert Plasman and François Rycx (*editors*)
MINIMUM WAGES, LOW PAY AND UNEMPLOYMENT

Carine Peeters and Bruno van Pottelsberghe de la Potterie (*editors*)
ECONOMIC AND MANAGEMENT PERSPECTIVES ON INTELLECTUAL PROPERTY RIGHTS

Emile Quinet and Roger Vickerman (*editors*)
THE ECONOMETRICS OF MAJOR TRANSPORT INFRASTRUCTURES

Philippe Thalmann and Milad Zarin-Nejadan (*editors*)
CONSTRUCTION AND REAL ESTATE DYNAMICS

Applied Econometrics Association
Series Standing Order ISBN 978–0–333–91990–3 (hardback)
Series Standing Order ISBN 978–0–333–71460–7 (paperback)
(*outside North America only*)

You can receive future titles in this series as they are published by placing a standing order. Please contact your bookseller or, in case of difficulty, write to us at the address below with your name and address, the title of the series and the ISBN quoted above.

Customer Services Department, Macmillan Distribution Ltd, Houndmills, Basingstoke, Hampshire RG21 6XS, England

Wage Structures, Employment Adjustments and Globalization

Evidence from Linked and
Firm-level Panel Data

Edited By

David Marsden

and

François Rycx

Selection and editorial content © David W. Marsden and François Rycx 2010
Individual chapters © Contributors 2010

All rights reserved. No reproduction, copy or transmission of this publication may be made without written permission.

No portion of this publication may be reproduced, copied or transmitted save with written permission or in accordance with the provisions of the Copyright, Designs and Patents Act 1988, or under the terms of any licence permitting limited copying issued by the Copyright Licensing Agency, Saffron House, 6-10 Kirby Street, London EC1N 8TS.

Any person who does any unauthorized act in relation to this publication may be liable to criminal prosecution and civil claims for damages.

The authors have asserted their rights to be identified as the authors of this work in accordance with the Copyright, Designs and Patents Act 1988.

First published 2010 by
PALGRAVE MACMILLAN

Palgrave Macmillan in the UK is an imprint of Macmillan Publishers Limited, registered in England, company number 785998, of Houndmills, Basingstoke, Hampshire RG21 6XS.

Palgrave Macmillan in the US is a division of St Martin's Press LLC, 175 Fifth Avenue, New York, NY 10010.

Palgrave Macmillan is the global academic imprint of the above companies and has companies and representatives throughout the world.

Palgrave® and Macmillan® are registered trademarks in the United States, the United Kingdom, Europe and other countries.

ISBN: 978–0–230–25154–0 hardback

This book is printed on paper suitable for recycling and made from fully managed and sustained forest sources. Logging, pulping and manufacturing processes are expected to conform to the environmental regulations of the country of origin.

A catalogue record for this book is available from the British Library.

Library of Congress Cataloging-in-Publication Data

    Wage structures, employment adjustments and globalization: evidence from linked and firm-level panel data / edited by David Marsden and François Rycx.
      p. cm.—(Applied Econometrics Association series)
    Includes bibliographical references and index.
    ISBN 978–0–230–25154–0 (alk. paper)
    1. Wages. 2. Wage differentials. 3. Labor market. I. Marsden, David, 1950– II. Rycx, François, 1974–

HD4909.W262 2010
331.2′15—dc22
                                            2009048528

10 9 8 7 6 5 4 3 2 1
19 18 17 16 15 14 13 12 11 10

Printed and bound in Great Britain by
CPI Antony Rowe, Chippenham and Eastbourne

Contents

List of Figures	vii
List of Tables	viii
Foreword David Marsden and François Rycx	ix
Notes on Contributors	x
Introduction and Overview *David Marsden and François Rycx*	1

Part I Labour Turnover Flows and Mobility

1 Labour Turnover and Wage Mobility: The Impact of the Legal Setting and Institutions *Lorenzo Cappellari*	17
2 Job and Worker Flows at the Firm Level *Harald Dale-Olsen*	37
3 Summary of the Literature on Job Displacement in the US and EU: What We Know and What We Would like to Know *Till von Wachter*	64
4 Skill Mismatch in Europe *René Böheim, Iga Magda and Martina Zweimüller*	122

Part II Wages, Human Resource Strategies and Institutions

5 Variability of Wages across Sectors: How Much, Why and with What Consequences? *François Rycx*	155
6 Rent Sharing: A Survey of Methodologies and Results *Pedro S. Martins*	166
7 Union Effects on Wages *Alex Bryson*	174

8   Low-Wage Employment and the Role of the Firm:
    An Agenda for Data and Research   185
    Wiemer Salverda

9   Do Firms Compress the Wage Distribution?   202
    Ana Rute Cardoso

Part III Consequences of Globalization and Data Challenges

10 Labour Market Outcomes of Internationalization – What
    Have We Learnt from Analyses of Microdata on Firms and
    Their Employees?   221
    Tor Eriksson

11 Development of Linked Employer–Employee Data for
    EU Labour Market and Social Policy Analysis   244
    Tanvi Desai

Index   267

Figures

3.1	Measuring the cost of job displacement	69
3.2	Difficulties in estimating the cost of job loss	70
3.3	Estimate of the long-term earnings decline due to job displacement at mass layoffs using Jacobson, Lalonde and Sullivan's (1993) mass layoff sample	79
4.1	Distribution of educational groups in 2002, selected European countries	132
4.2	Distribution of educational groups for young workers in 2002, selected European countries	134
4.3	Extent of over- and undereducation for Spain, the Czech Republic, and Poland, 2002	135
4.4	Sensitivity of over- and undereducation, wage premium of at least 25 per cent	136
4.5	Distribution of university wage premiums, Poland, 1996 and 2002	136
4A.1	Distribution of high school graduates over occupational groups	149
4A.2	Distribution of university graduates in non-academic jobs over main occupational groups	149
8A.1	Incidence of low pay (%) with comprehensive coverage, five EU countries and US, 1973–2005	196

Tables

2.1	Cross-country job flow differences	41
2.2	Cross-country worker flow differences	43
3.1	Matrix of ideal estimates – study names and study counts by broad regions	71
3.2	Size of estimates of different studies by broad region and estimation method in the USA	73
3.3	Size of estimates of different studies by broad region and estimation method in EU member states	81
3.4	Summary of estimation methods used – study counts	93
3.5	Overview of selected data sets used and available in the USA	98
3.6	Overview of selected data sets used and available in EU member states	104
4A.1	Distribution of employees by skill group, Poland, 1996–2004	141
4A.2	Estimation results of the probability of over- and undereducation	141
4A.3	Estimation results of the probability of over- and undereducation, extended specification	142
4A.4	Estimates of over- and undereducation, Poland	143
4A.5	Estimates of over- and undereducation, with additional firm-level controls, Poland	144
4A.6	Estimates of the percentage of overeducated and undereducated workers	145
4A.7	Estimates of the percentage of overeducated and undereducated workers, with additional firm-level controls	146
4A.8	Estimates of the percentage of overeducated and undereducated workers, Poland	147
4A.9	Estimates of the percentage of overeducated and undereducated workers, with additional firm-level controls, Poland	148
7.1	Union membership wage premium from around the world	179
8A.1	Data sets to analyse low-wage employment	194
8A.2	Minimum wages in July 2008 and minimum-wage employment in 2004, 18 EU countries (nine EU15 and nine new member states) and the US	195
8A.3	Incidence of low pay (%) by year, 13 EU15 countries 1996–2000	196
8A.4	Incidence of low pay (%) with varying coverage in different data sets, four EU15 countries, 1996	197
11A.1	Microdata disseminated via LISSY (and other remote access systems) by EU member states	263

Foreword

The labour markets of Europe's national economies are becoming increasingly interdependent as the European economy integrates. National and European-level economic and monetary policy needs the analytical and statistical tools for informing and guiding its choices. Building a system of European labour market statistics that is both comparative across countries and capable of shedding light on the key policy areas is essential. A small adjustment of European interest rates based on inaccurate data can have far-reaching consequences for the citizens and businesses of the EU.

The papers in this book address a key aspect of this concern, namely the use of data sets that link the supply and the demand sides of labour markets, providing linked employer–employee data (LEED). By linking data that provide information on the characteristics of both individual employees and the organizations in which they work, one can gain a better understanding of the interaction between labour and product markets. By linking such data, one can hope to gauge the influence of profitability on pay, of business downsizing on employment, and of firms' human resource management practices on pay and jobs, for example. A number of pioneering studies have been undertaken at the national level, but there remain serious problems of comparability if we are to draw conclusions from experience in one country for policy in another. The European Commission and Eurostat have made major steps in this direction at both the policy and the statistical levels, but, as the papers in this book show, there is still much work to be done.

The work behind this book was funded by the European Commission and generously supported by Eurostat and the National Statistical Institutes of the EU. The project comprised two parts: a set of original reviews of the analytical and labour market policy issues published in this volume, and a number of statistical studies using the secure remote access system described in Chapter 11, based on the European Structure of Earnings Survey (ESES), which are to be published separately in academic journals.

The project was managed as a network, from LSE's Centre for Economic Performance. David Marsden had overall responsibility for the project, and Ana Cardoso, Tor Eriksson and François Rycx were responsible for each of the sets of analytical studies included in this volume. Tanvi Desai, working closely with Eurostat and Marc Cigrang, led the experimental secure remote access to ESES. Simone Moriconi provided excellent research assistance throughout. All members of the project team owe a special debt to Nigel Rogers and his administrative team at CEP.

DAVID MARSDEN AND FRANÇOIS RYCX

Contributors

René Böheim is an Associated Professor of economics at the Johannes Kepler University Linz, Austria. His research focuses on labour economics, family economics and applied microeconometrics. Recent projects are on the gender wage gap, atypical employment, job creation and the economic consequences of divorce.

Alex Bryson is a Senior Research Fellow at the National Institute of Economic and Social Research and a Research Fellow at the Centre for Economic Performance at the LSE. He is also an editor of the *British Journal of Industrial Relations*. His research interests include wage formation; the demand, supply and effects of trade unionism; determinants of worker well-being; and programme evaluation.

Lorenzo Cappellari is Associate Professor at the Catholic University in Milan and research fellow at the Institute for the Study of Labour (IZA, Germany) and the Center for Economic Studies (CESIfo, Germany). His research is concerned with empirical labour and education economics.

Ana Rute Cardoso is Associate Research Professor at the Institute for Economic Analysis of the Spanish Higher Council for Scientific Research (IAE-CSIC) in Barcelona, and Affiliated Professor of the Barcelona Graduate School of Economics (BGSE). She is a Research Fellow of the Institute for the Study of Labour (IZA) in Bonn, Germany and an elected member of the Executive Committee of the European Association of Labour Economists (EALE). Her research interests lie in labour economics and economics of inequality.

Harald Dale-Olsen is Senior Research Fellow at the Norwegian Institute for Social Research, Oslo. His research areas include job and worker flows, worker turnover and mobility, worker pay and compensation, health and sickness absence, and executive remuneration policies.

Tanvi Desai has worked in the data management field since 1999, building the LSE Research Laboratories data service from scratch. She has extensive experience of supporting international research groups with a need for comparable microdata, as well as of promoting academic access to data resources. Tanvi has advised the Australian and New Zealand Statistical Offices and Eurostat on remote access to data, and currently manages the only remote access system disseminating comparable linked employer–employee data.

Tor Eriksson is Professor of Economics at Aarhus School of Business at Aarhus University. His research deals with several aspects of labour markets, ranging from personnel economics to intergenerational mobility and the internationalization of workplaces and labour markets.

Iga Magda is a PhD student at the Warsaw School of Economics, Poland. Previously she has cooperated with the CASE Foundation in Warsaw and worked as a researcher in the Polish Ministry of Labour and Social Policy. She is author and co-author of publications on foreign trade and labour market.

David Marsden is Professor of Industrial Relations at the London School of Economics, and a Research Associate of the Centre for Economic Performance. He did his doctoral work at the Laboratoire d'Économie et de Sociologie du Travail (CNRS), Aix-en-Provence, where he developed his interest in the comparative study of labour markets and labour institutions, and how these affect the internal workings of organizations.

Pedro S. Martins is Professor of Applied Economics in Queen Mary, University of London, and Research Fellow at CEG-IST, Lisbon. His main research interests are in labour economics, including issues in education, personnel and international economics.

François Rycx is Associate Professor of economics at the Université Libre de Bruxelles (ULB) and Research Fellow at the Centre Emile Bernheim, DULBEA and the Institute for the Study of Labour (IZA, Germany). His research is concerned with labour and personnel economics, in particular the analysis of earnings inequalities and firm performance with linked employer–employee data (LEED) and firm-level panels. He is also doing research on the economics of gender, trade unions and international trade.

Wiemer Salverda (Dr) is Director of the Amsterdam Institute for Advanced Labour Studies (AIAS) of the University of Amsterdam. He is an active international research coordinator, and advisor to EU, OECD, ILO and Low Pay Commission. His interests concern wage and income inequality, including the role of employers and of institutions and policies, education and work, the workings of the Dutch 'Polder model', and the (gendered) labour market.

Till von Wachter is Associate Professor at Columbia University and research fellow at the National Bureau of Economic Research (USA), the Center of Economic Policy Research (UK), and the Center for the Study of Labour (IZA, Germany). His research is concerned with the long-term effect of temporary adverse labour market conditions on workers' earnings, careers and health outcomes.

Martina Zweimüller is a researcher at The Austrian Center for Labour Economics and the Analysis of the Welfare State (www.labornrn.at) at the Johannes Kepler University of Linz, Austria. Her research interests are the economics of education, health economics and labour economics.

Introduction and Overview

David Marsden and François Rycx

The development of firm-level panel data and linked employer–employee data (LEED) promises to shed light on many important areas of European labour market analysis which have previously been difficult to explore. This book examines the contribution of these data to the analysis of wage structures, employment adjustments and globalization. More precisely, it focuses on three key economic topics, namely labour turnover flows and mobility; the role of labour market institutions and firms' human resource strategies in relation to wages; and the labour market outcomes of internationalization. It also contains a methodological section where the development of linked and panel data sets for European labour market and social policy analysis is examined and discussed. The three central parts of the book and some of its main findings are briefly presented below.[1]

Labour turnover flows and mobility

Labour turnover, wage adjustments and job mobility are key processes in the way labour markets enable national economies to adjust to changing conditions. There has been a long debate as to whether they are sufficiently developed within the EU to enable the economies of member countries to adjust and to keep down unemployment, although it should be recognized that there are considerable differences among EU national economies. The needs for adjustment have been particularly great in the new member countries, which have experienced both a major change in their trading patterns and the transition from centrally planned to market economies.

The first part of this book deals broadly with labour market dynamics, and concentrates on four subthemes:

a. wage mobility and labour turnover (at the worker level), with special emphasis on the impact of the institutional background;
b. job and worker flows (at the firm level);
c. job displacement and its consequences;
d. skill mismatches in the labour market.

Within each theme, work has been directed towards identifying the major indicators used to quantify the phenomenon and the main stylized facts and policy conclusions emerging from the analysis, as well as the current data potential and constraints.

One of the key functions of labour markets in advanced industrial economies is to enable workers to find jobs that enable them to use their skills and abilities to their best advantage, and to enable firms to recruit the labour they need at wage levels that are mutually satisfactory. At a more macro level, labour markets play a key part in the adjustment of our economies: matching changing worker preferences to changing employer needs. Relative wages play an important part in this process of redirecting labour towards activities where it is most needed. Together with changing job opportunities, they also provide important signals to those in education and training as to the skills which will bring the best return. Because workers are concerned about many features of jobs apart from pay, such as proximity and fulfilling work, labour markets also are key providers of choice. For all these reasons, labour markets with a good level of turnover flows and mobility enhance citizens' welfare.

It is possible for turnover flows to be too high, and also for them to be too low. High rates of labour turnover may harm productivity and product quality, and they may reduce incentives to provide training and to acquire skills. They may also be disruptive for employees' personal lives. Flows may also be too slow, and a general consequence of this is that people who want to change jobs find it difficult to obtain suitable alternative employment, and those who have been laid off will usually find it harder to regain employment. It has been argued often that, compared with the United States, where job market flows are relatively higher, the slower flows in many EU countries have added to the duration of unemployment for those without work, and consequently they have also increased the numbers unemployed at any one time (e.g. Blau and Kahn, 2002).

Wage adjustments for individual workers have long been thought to play an important part in shaping the paths of labour mobility, attracting workers from lower to higher-paid jobs, at least within occupational segments of the labour market. Willingness to take lower-paid work when faced with unemployment has also been an issue. Do workers in fact often accept work at lower pay when they lose their jobs rather than remain unemployed, and do their earnings recover subsequently? To what extent should social insurance systems insure against loss of a job as opposed to loss of a particular level of pay?

In Chapter 1, Lorenzo Cappellari (Università Cattolica Milano) examines existing research on wage mobility and labour turnover. Some of the key findings are that a reduction in dismissal costs may lead to faster labour mobility flows, and ease the exit from unemployment. However, this beneficial outcome may be tempered if exit flows from jobs exceed entry flows into new jobs. Easier use of temporary jobs has been proposed as one means of reducing dismissal costs, but there is contrasting evidence from different member countries. In some cases they have functioned as stepping stones to permanent jobs, whereas in others conversion rates have been low. Evidence on flows out of unemployment suggests that the duration, but not the level, of benefits has an important effect on exit rates, which have been observed to rise sharply just before benefits expire.

Turning to wage mobility, that is, changes in individual workers' wages associated with job changes and across unemployment spells, it appears that differences across countries in labour market institutions have only a modest impact. However, as might be expected, transitory drops in wages, from which workers subsequently recover, are more common in countries with more flexible labour markets, whereas drops in wages tend to be more prolonged in more rigid labour markets. Nevertheless, firm-level bargaining arrangements may provide some compensating wage flexibility.

Job and worker flows are investigated in Chapter 2 by Harald Dale-Olsen (Institute for Social Research, Oslo). According to recent research, job and worker flows tend to be higher among small firms, and among younger firms, and to some extent lower for higher educational and skill levels, except where there are professional labour markets which enable highly educated workers to move easily between firms. On the whole, high-paying firms tend to have lower labour turnover.

Higher wage levels and starting wages, and steeper pay–seniority profiles, have been found to favour job and worker stability. However, the strength of the relationship varies from country to country, suggesting that firms may adopt different strategies on pay and employment stability in different institutional environments. One factor in this may be employment protection legislation (EPL), high levels of which have been found to reduce both worker and job flows. There has also been some indication that centralized bargaining may reduce job flows. These factors may well prove to be interrelated. For example, in an environment with strong employment protection, firms may well pursue employment strategies which build their distinctive capabilities on a stable workforce, adopting human resource policies to motivate their employees and develop their skills.

Owing to the scale and speed of economic change, developments in the transition economies provide a special opportunity to observe the effects of market reforms and trade internationalization on labour mobility, and on the processes of creation of new jobs and destruction of ones that are no longer economically viable. Evidence from these countries, and notably the new member states, suggests that strongly increased trade liberalization and product market competition increase both labour mobility and job reallocation. Job destruction has tended to precede the creation of new jobs. This may be expected, because increased import penetration is driven by the supply of goods and services from outside individual national economies where production facilities are already plentiful, whereas job creation depends upon organizing and expanding facilities to respond to new opportunities, which necessarily takes longer. Small firms and the emerging service sector have also played a key part in new job creation. The jury is still out on whether it is easier to balance job destruction and job creation by gradual as opposed to rapid transition.

In the third chapter, Till von Wachter (Columbia University) focuses on job displacement and its consequences. Worker displacement typically refers to the loss of a job due to slack work, job cuts or plant closures. The typical measure of the cost of job displacement focuses on the loss of workers' output as measured by their earnings. Ideally, such a measure would also capture any resultant loss of earnings over their remaining working lives. Thus, most of the economic literature on job loss has sought to evaluate short and long-term effects of displacement on earnings and employment.

Some of the key stylized facts in this domain relate to the US experience, where a picture emerges of large long-lasting unmitigated losses in earnings even for job losers of prime working age. There also appear to be significant differences in the costs of job loss among many groups of workers, with older workers, high-tenured workers, high-income workers and workers in certain industries more affected than others.

Institutional differences among European national labour markets make direct comparisons of estimates difficult, with those both from the US and from other European countries. In particular, the presence of more generous social insurance systems affects both the degree of associated income loss and the options open to those losing jobs.

Within the EU, although there is a reasonable number of studies, estimates are distributed over 12 countries, and concentrated on those with the best information (such as France, Germany, Denmark and Sweden). Other countries, such as Italy and Spain, are conspicuously absent from the list of studies compiled for this survey. Lack of data comparability also inhibits evaluation of the effect of different national policies on the cost of job loss.

Critical areas in which better information is needed relate to the long-term costs of job loss, and the size and duration of earnings and employment losses; differences therein by age, gender and education; and differences over time and between labour markets, industries and firms. In addition to this basic information, we should also like to know the effect of job loss by job tenure and firm characteristics, as well as its effects on other career and non-career outcomes.

In the US, data on job displacement are collected as a biannual Displaced Worker Survey that supplements the standard US labour force survey (the Current Population Survey). In Europe, there has traditionally been less focus on displaced workers, perhaps because widespread job loss was less of an issue due to lower turnover rates, more generous social insurance programmes, and large-scale programmes to address the plight of workers caught in industrial restructuring (such as early retirement schemes).

The fourth chapter, written by René Böheim (Johannes Kepler University, Linz), Iga Magda (Warsaw School of Economics) and Martina Zweimüller (Johannes Kepler University, Linz), addresses one of the outcomes of worker mobility, notably whether workers manage to find jobs whose requirements match their skills and education. It also addresses how effectively the education and training systems are producing the right mix and levels of skills to meet the needs of employers. Skill mismatches are a major concern. Workers in jobs that do not use much of their skill or education can feel frustrated, and there is potentially a waste of national resources. Similarly, workers in jobs for which they lack the necessary skills may be less productive or less able to work flexibly. Such 'mismatch' may be temporary, as workers take second-choice jobs while continuing to search for their first choice, or if they are hired into entry positions in organizations at the bottom of career ladders that will eventually lead to jobs that utilize their skills fully. However, it could also be long-term, if the education and training system is failing to respond adequately, and producing either too many or too few of the right skills. Of particular concern is the possibility that technical and economic change means that the educational requirements of the majority of jobs in advanced industrial countries are increasing, and the question of whether our educational systems are equipping workers and firms with the ability to compete in these markets.

Measuring skill mismatch, and whether workers are 'over' or 'under' educated for their jobs, is a complex operation because we lack good information on the requirements of jobs across the economy. Surveys of employer views which make no reference to price typically produce 'wish lists', and surveys of workers' views about how well their jobs use their skills can also be difficult to interpret. Detailed case studies may shed valuable light, but it is often hard to generalize their findings. Much of the existing research, therefore, has had to approach the question indirectly, using large-scale survey evidence on workers' education, their jobs, and their earnings in those jobs. It is possible to identify the typical educational levels of workers in particular kinds of jobs, and the other way round; what might be typical jobs, for example, for those with a university degree. It is then possible to compare the earnings of workers at different job levels to see whether they receive the same earnings as those with the typical level of education for those jobs. If they have a higher level of education than most workers at the same job level, but receive the same pay, then it could be argued that their additional education is not useful in these jobs, and that they are 'overeducated' for them. On the other hand, if their pay is much higher than that of less educated workers in the same job classifications, it is likely that their skills are being used. Nevertheless, caution is needed in interpreting such observations. Typically, job and educational classifications used are broad and group many diverse qualifications and types of work.

Although widely used in the literature, the terms 'over' and 'under' education can be misleading for public policy. They do not necessarily mean that the educational system is producing too many or too few graduates at different levels. They refer to the degree of match and mismatch of skills and jobs in the labour market. In other words, they tell us as much about the effectiveness of the labour market in allocating workers to the right jobs as about educational supply. As mentioned in the next section, labour markets take time to adjust, and during the matching process one would expect to find that many workers are temporarily in jobs which do not use all their qualifications. Moreover, the matching process need not take place only by means of job moves between employers. It may also take place within organizations as workers move from entry positions along career ladders. Typically, many university graduates are hired into quite junior positions, and their employers expect to develop them further before they enter managerial positions.

External and internal job matching processes can be affected by labour market institutions and firms' career development policies. If the matching requires people to move between organizations as they look for the right job for their skills, then 'mismatch' may persist for longer if job and labour turnover rates are slow than if they are relatively rapid. If the matching process takes place within organizations, for example, as highly educated recruits move up career ladders, then more stable employment would favour the matching process. Most economies need to achieve matches for both non-career and career jobs, although the balance between these two kinds will vary considerably from one economy to another. As the surveys in the first part of this book show, work on this question is still at a fairly early stage owing to data limitations, a particularly important one being the small number of suitable panel data sets. One notable finding is that the wage rewards and penalties for 'over' and 'under' education, respectively, tend to be smaller in the EU than in the US.

Wages, human resource strategies and institutions

The second part of this book examines five major issues relating to the role of labour market institutions and firms' human resource strategies in relation to wages. It deals with the following themes:

- inter-industry wage differentials,
- rent-sharing and wages,
- the effect of trade unions on wages,
- low-wage employment,
- wage-compression within firms.

The core theme running through this second part of the book can be summarized by what Melvin Reder (1969) once referred to as the 'competitive hypothesis': are the outcomes we observe in labour markets those of normal competitive processes, and so reflecting the best decisions of workers and firms? If so, then public policy interventions in labour markets may legitimately reflect social priorities, but they will come at the cost of distorting competitive outcomes. For example, our societies might consider that the market level of income from low-skilled work gives rise to socially undesirable levels of inequality. If the labour market is competitive, then a minimum wage policy to raise low-skilled pay could lead to higher unemployment for such workers, and so prove ineffective overall. In contrast, policies to raise low incomes by training or by tax changes might help low-paid workers without damaging their employment prospects.

Alternatively, if the 'competitive hypothesis' is not a good description of the real state of labour markets, then it could be argued that public policy should either seek to remove barriers to competition or seek ways of redressing market power imbalances. For example, in the case of trade unions and of professional organizations, there has been a long-running controversy over whether they seek to use collective power to boost the incomes of their members, or whether they provide fairer and more efficient ways of setting pay than by a myriad of individual negotiations, and whether they serve the customer by promoting common standards of service. Similar questions are sometimes raised about the effects of large employers in relation to their local labour markets. Many governments have taken the former view, and sought to restrict the power of unions and professional bodies. However, many others have taken the opposite view that the balance lay more in the direction of fairness and efficient administration. To some extent, their views reflect differences in where the balance has lain in their respective countries and at different time periods. One has also to be clear about the origins of non-competitive outcomes. For example, much of the debate about the effects of 'rent-sharing' on wages hinges, in fact, on the consequences of a lack of competition in product rather than in labour markets.

Chapters 5 and 6, written respectively by François Rycx (Université Libre de Bruxelles) and Pedro Martins (Queen Mary, University of London), refer to whether or not workers with the same productivity characteristics, such as skill and experience, are paid the same across different firms and industries. A chief source of firms' ability to pay wages above the competitive rate arises from their position of dominance in their main product markets. Such rents may be 'shared' in a number of ways. If such firms are unionized, then employees may bargain for a share in these rents. But they need not be unionized to benefit from rent-sharing. Managers in such firms may also concede higher pay in order to keep their employees happy and get a 'quiet life'. They may also use a part of these rents in order to develop policies to motivate their employees, or to build loyalty.

Thus, although the themes of Chapters 5 and 6, inter-industry wage differentials and 'rent sharing', may seem arcane, the reason they have generated so much research and debate is that they provide a major clue as to the diagnosis of many of our common labour market problems. Inter-industry wage differences can serve to reveal the underlying degree of competitiveness of labour markets, because economic theory tells us that in a competitive market the prices of the same kind of labour should converge over time towards the market-clearing level. In this situation, the observed differences at any time should either reflect part of the adjustment process, as firms with a strong demand offer higher wages in order to signal their labour needs to potential recruits, or possibly reflect wage supplements designed to compensate for difficult working or dangerous working conditions ('compensating differentials'). Two other important competitive causes of inter-industry wage differences relate to whether employers provide job training for transferable skills, in which case they might expect trainees to bear part of the cost because they retain the skill if they change employer, and whether employers offer higher pay as a part of their motivational or incentive policies. For example, some firms might offer profit-sharing to induce their employees to work harder or more flexibly than they otherwise would (sometimes called 'efficiency wage' policies).

In practice, very few, if any, labour markets are close to being perfectly competitive, so the question is not black and white. It is, rather, a question of how close or how distant they are from that ideal, and the scale of the trade-offs between interventions to support one policy goal as compared with those for another. This makes careful measurement essential, and explains why there is so much debate not just on whether or not there is rent-sharing or discrimination, but rather on *how much* there is. Is it small enough not to worry about, or is it so large as to necessitate public intervention?

Ideally, such analysis would focus on individual firms instead of industries, but researchers have been constrained by data availability: most wage statistics have been available by industry but not, until quite recently, by firm or establishment. To use industry data, one has to assume that firms in the same industry group tend to behave alike because they share common technologies, labour and product markets. They may also be members of the same industry-based trade and employer associations. Data problems have also made answering what is a very simple question quite complicated. For example, what is an 'identical' worker in a different firm or industry? Our statistical measures of occupational and educational or skill levels are quite broad, and those of personal characteristics rudimentary (most commonly age, firm tenure and gender). Firms spend large amounts of money every year on recruitment and selection, and on career development, reflecting their knowledge that a 'good' worker in the right job can be much more productive than a 'bad' worker. Lack of direct measures of worker quality helps to explain the large amount of statistical ingenuity shown in the literature. Panel data methods, which track the same firm over time, provide one such indirect method. Suppose 'Firm A' wishes to gain a reputation with its customers for a reliable high-quality service; then it might adopt recruitment and motivational policies designed to attract conscientious employees who like to take the initiative, factors that are not usually recorded in large-scale wage surveys. 'Firm B' might provide more standard 'cheap and cheerful' service, and be happy to recruit less dynamic workers who will work for less pay. If both firms stick to their policies over several years, then, by tracking the same firms over time, one can control for the effects of these statistically 'unobserved' but economically significant factors. In other words, the question shifts from one of levels to changes over time: from whether high-profit firms also pay high wages to whether the same firms raise wages more when profits increase.

Chapters 7 and 8, written respectively by Alex Bryson (National Institute of Economic and Social Research) and Wiemer Salverda (University of Amsterdam), extend the analysis by looking at the evidence on the effects of collective bargaining on wages, and at low-wage employment. A most important conclusion on the analysis of collective bargaining is that many of the models currently used in economic theory are based on US institutions where collective bargaining is primarily at company and plant level, is confined to non-managerial employees, and where the great majority of workers and plants are not covered. In contrast, in the majority of EU countries, owing to the presence of industry-level bargaining, high percentages of employees and plants are covered by collective agreements. Whereas employer and union negotiators have to consider only the immediate interest of a single firm and its workers when negotiating at company level, when they deal at industry level they have to consider the interests of all firms and their workers across the sector for which they are negotiating. Employers' associations, which are powerful in the EU but mostly weak or non-existent in the US, have a major influence on the outcomes of industry agreements, and the division of labour between industry and company-level bargaining. They are effectively bargaining coalitions of many different kinds of firms, and have to consider both those that are profitable and those facing hard times. They have also to consider the interests of both large and small firms. Likewise, unions have to consider their members across all of these different kinds of firms. Therefore, the key policy question in many EU countries has been not whether collective bargaining per se is good or bad, but what are the effects of different structures of collective bargaining: how much should be at industry level, and how much at company or establishment level, and what issues are best dealt with at each level?

Low-paid employment is the focus of Chapter 8. Since the publication of Card and Krueger's (1995) and Manning's (2003) studies of monopsony in low-wage labour markets, and the research of the Lower network, there has been a re-evaluation of previous received wisdom on regulation of low-wage employment. It had long been supposed that any increase in minimum wages would necessarily harm employment to a greater or lesser degree. Both the above studies brought new theory and much additional evidence on the nature of low-wage employment, and led to the conclusion that market power, and its lack for many low-paid workers, was a key factor contributing to the concentration of low pay on certain types of workers and in certain sectors. Notable among these are young workers, women and minorities, and retail trade, hotels and catering, agriculture and personal services.

In Chapter 9, Ana Cardoso (IAE-CSIC, Barcelona) first reviews the theoretical reasoning for the existence of wage-compression within firms. This refers to a situation where pay differences between workers in the same firm are compressed compared with the distribution of their respective productivity levels. The key factors highlighted by different theories to explain such wage-compression range from workers' preferences to the production technology, use of egalitarian pay systems to promote cooperation and information sharing, and frictions in the labour market. Next, Cardoso reviews empirical work that has used LEED to test theoretical predictions about the existence of firm-level wage-compression and its effects on worker and firm productivity and labour turnover.

Assuming that workers compare their wages with those of their co-workers when determining their level of effort, wage dispersion should influence this level and hence average firm performance. However, there is no clear theoretical consensus on the characteristics of this relationship. First, the 'tournament model' proposed by Lazear and Rosen (1981) stresses that more differentiated wage structures stimulate workers' effort by the incentive resulting from awarding the largest 'prizes' to the most productive workers. Their approach further suggests that the greater the pay dispersion, the higher the workers' optimal level of effort. In contrast, other theories argue that wage compression reinforces workers' productivity by improving workplace relations (Akerlof and Yellen, 1988), by sustaining and stimulating cohesiveness among the workforce (Levine, 1991), or by discouraging workers from engaging in costly rent-seeking activities instead of productive work (Milgrom and Roberts, 1990).

Cardoso shows that empirical evidence on the impact of wage-compression inside the firm on worker and firm performance is rather mixed, with results ranging from a positive impact to a negative one, and including a hump-shaped relationship or no significant relationship altogether. Pfeffer and Langton's comment thus remains pertinent: 'One of the more useful avenues for research on pay systems may be precisely this task of determining not which pay scheme is best but, rather, under what conditions salary dispersion has positive effects and under what conditions it has negative effects' (Pfeffer and Langton, 1993: 383). More research is also needed on the implications of firm wage-compression on worker and job flows. From a theoretical perspective, in general, morale and equity models suggest that firms with greater inequality would experience higher worker turnover, whereas labour market friction and monopsony models point to more restricted flows. However, the empirical evidence on this is rather scarce and provides conflicting results.

Consequences of globalization and data challenges

In the third part of the book (Chapter 10), Tor Eriksson (Aarhus School of Business) reviews the economic research on the employment and wage consequences of outsourcing and offshoring that makes use of firm-level data sets or linked employer–employee data.

In the past 20 years, international trade for European countries has been boosted by the Single European Market, and by major changes in the world economy, notably the rise of the Chinese and Indian economies, and the consequent increase in the world supply of labour they bring. Together with a revolution in information and communication technology (ICT), this has enabled firms to take a radical new look at their supply chains, and at the geographical location of different activities within these.

Until recently, the predominant focus of both international trade theory and much policy thinking has focused heavily on trade in *finished* goods. This remains important, and can have major employment consequences. Estimates initially from work in the United States, and broadly confirmed for Europe, indicate that unskilled jobs in high-wage countries have suffered, whereas skilled jobs have often benefited. It is not easy to disentangle the effects of increased international trade from those of skill-biased technical change, and, at least as concerns the organization of supply chains, the two are related. Nevertheless, US estimates for the decline of unskilled employment during the 1990s assign the major role to technical change, and about a quarter to increased international trade.

This could change. In the past, most world trade was between high-wage countries, so that its expansion would have had a neutral effect on employment by skill. Rapid economic growth of hitherto low-wage regions has altered this by increasing the potential impact on low-skill jobs in high-wage regions. Second, in the past, manufacturing bore the brunt of increased international trade for the advanced industrial countries, whereas the revolution in ICT has opened up the possibility for much greater trade in services which were hitherto more geographically bound. An eye-catching example has been the rapid growth and offshoring of call centres. According to US estimates, between a third and a half of service jobs do not depend on face-to-face contact, and so could potentially be handled from other regions in the world.

A third major change has been the growth in the share of international trade in *intermediate* goods, 'tasks', as opposed to *finished* goods. Recent estimates based on OECD countries, summarized in Eriksson's chapter, put this share at about one-third, and growing. In so far as this is associated with the global restructuring of firms' supply chains, this seems likely to increase. The focus on supply chains suggests that we need to consider an increasing share of international trade not in terms of purchases for final consumption, but in terms of how firms integrate their operations both within and across national borders. The most appropriate conceptual tools are those firms use for the 'make or buy' decision. Current employment costs are a part of this, but equally important is access to regional skill bases and to clusters of firms with particular organizational capabilities. Some European economies are well endowed with highly skilled labour markets, and organizations that have developed distinctive capabilities in certain activities. These could play a key role in certain supply chains, and so expect to benefit from their development, even though the point of final production may be in another region in the world. Some of the key management skills taught in business schools relate to how to reduce costs in supply chains, and how to identify key competencies that need to be bought-in. This suggests that the impact of internationalization on the demand for different skills is likely to be more selective within organizations than was previously thought. This is supported by a study of firms in Denmark.

The overall estimates of employment effects are mostly too broad-brush to discriminate between employment effects of global supply chains compared with those of trade in final goods because of data limitations. Indicative results outlined in Chapter 10 suggest that unskilled labour has been the main loser in manufacturing, and that skilled jobs have benefited, although the proportions vary considerably between countries. Firm-level as opposed to country-level studies suggest that there can be positive employment benefits from offshoring, although such studies are rather few in number and limited to certain regions. Studies in East Asia, of Hong Kong and Taiwan, indicate considerable benefits from offshoring in those cases.

One factor that makes international comparisons difficult is that patterns of wage inequality differ considerably between countries, even within the EU. For example, where there are big wage differences between firms within the same economy, this could reduce pressures to relocate activities.

A traditional measure of the benefits of internationalization, and notably of inward investment by multinational companies (MNCs), has been whether MNCs achieve higher levels of labour productivity than local firms, perhaps because of better management, newer technology or better integration into international markets. There has, therefore, been considerable effort to discover whether MNCs pay higher wages. As with the research on inter-industry differentials, a major problem has been to establish whether they employ the same kinds of labour, or whether they 'cream off' the local labour market so that higher pay and productivity simply reflect employment of more skilled and enterprising workers.

Increased international trade does represent increased competition within national markets. Thinking back to the work on rent-sharing, one might expect increased trade to reduce the rents individual firms can earn from dominance of their local, national, markets, and hence to reduce the rent-sharing component in workers' pay. This has been confirmed in one study based on France (Biscourp and Kramarz, 2007). It is worth also thinking back to the findings on worker and job mobility, and the impact of international trade. In high-wage countries, one can expect trade to lead to a restructuring of labour demand not just for skilled relative to unskilled labour, but also among skill categories. This places a premium on having sufficiently adaptive labour markets, and on labour relations and human resource systems that facilitate adjustments within firms.

The last chapter of this book, written by Tanvi Desai (London School of Economics), concerns methodological issues, namely the development of existing statistical resources, and how they might be better integrated in order to support EU policy analysis and in particular to improve our understanding of wage structures, employment adjustments and the socio-economic consequences of globalization.

The Lisbon treaty and its updating focus on labour market policy at the national level recognizes the great value of policy coordination, and of benchmarking practices and policies between member states. In many regards, this reflects the growing interdependence of European national labour markets as the single market and the single currency bring industrial and macroeconomic policies more into convergence. The spillover effects from one country's national economic and labour market policies onto its neighbours create the need for a good understanding of how the different national labour markets and their institutions function. This requires a good statistical system, which the EU has slowly been constructing with leadership from the European Commission and Eurostat, with contributions for wider comparability from other international bodies such as the ILO and the OECD.

A good illustration of the importance of good statistical indicators for European labour markets is provided by the decisions of the European Central Bank on interest rates. A small adjustment of as little as half a percentage point in interest rates can have a sizeable effect on business confidence and on final demand, and thus on employment and general prosperity. One of the ECB's chief targets has been to hold down inflation, for which it needs good information on the build-up, or otherwise, of inflationary pressures in different member countries' labour markets. This is hard to achieve without good-quality comparative information on wage movements in member countries, and the triggers within national labour market institutions which can cause increases to accelerate. It is easy to see that decisions based on inaccurate labour market data can have far-reaching economic and social consequences.

A repeated concern in the reviews associated with each of the preceding chapters of the book has been the lack of good-quality comparative data covering the whole of the EU. In its absence, it is hard to assess the scale of diversity of national experiences revealed by national studies and how far they reflect real underlying differences between the economies of member states, as opposed to problems of lack of comparability in the data used. Even when similar relationships are uncovered, it is hard to assess whether they are of similar size, and so whether they merit similar policy efforts.

In the last chapter of this book, Desai examines the legislation governing access to business microdata in the EU, and the availability of LEED sources. She also outlines some of the barriers to accessing LEED and to using national sources for comparative research. Moreover, strengths and weaknesses of strategies for secure access to confidential microdata are investigated from an academic researcher's point of view. Finally, Desai describes and discusses the development of researcher access to the microdata of the European Structure of Earnings Survey (ESES) as a test bed for more intensive use of European comparative microdata for research and policy purposes. She gives an account of the system for secure remote access by researchers, used as part of this project, and in which she has played a pioneering role in her position as the CEP's Data Manager. It is modelled on the system used by the Luxembourg Income Study. Many National Statistical Institutes (NSIs) are currently developing their own national schemes for research access to microdata, but, as highlighted in the previous chapters of this book, there is a pressing need for good-quality comparative studies spanning national data sets. Without these, it is hard to get a good grip on the relative scale of these labour market phenomena from one country to another.

Note

1. This book is the result of a research contract for the European Commission (DG Employment) (No. VT/2005/92) entitled 'Study and Conference on European Labour Market Analysis using Firm-level Panel Data and Linked Employer-Employee Data' (http://cep.lse.ac.uk/leed/). It has been coordinated by David Marsden (Centre for Economic Performance, London School of Economics). Ana Cardoso (Institute for Economic Analysis of the Spanish National Research Council), François Rycx (Université Libre de Bruxelles), Tor Eriksson (Aarhus School of Business) and Tanvi Desai (Centre for Economic Performance, London School of Economics) were responsible for Parts I–IV respectively, and for coordinating the tasks associated with them. The project also benefited from the active support of Eurostat and the National Statistical Institutes. The project comprised two sections, one based on the chapters presented in this book, and the other based on empirical studies using the secure remote access system to the European Structure of Earnings Survey described in Chapter 11. The views expressed in this book are those of the authors, and do not necessarily reflect those of the European Commission or Eurostat.

References

Akerlof, G.A. and Yellen, J. L. (1988) 'Fairness and Unemployment', *American Economic Review, Papers and Proceedings*, 78: 44–9.

Biscourp, P. and Kramarz, F. (2007) 'Employment, Skill Structure and International Trade: Firm-Level Evidence for France', *Journal of International Economics*, 72: 22–51.

Blau, F.D. and Kahn, L.L. (2002) *At Home and Abroad: US Labor Market Performance in International Perspective*, New York: Russell Sage Foundation.

Card, D. and Krueger, A. (1995) *Myth and Measurement: The New Economics of the Minimum Wage*, Princeton, NJ: Princeton University Press.

Lazear, E.P. and Rosen, S. (1981) 'Rank-Order Tournaments as Optimum Labor Contracts', *Journal of Political Economy*, 89: 841–64.

Levine, D.I. (1991) 'Cohesiveness, Productivity and Wage Dispersion', *Journal of Economic Behavior and Organization*, 15: 237–55.

Manning, A. (2003) *Monopsony in Motion: Imperfect Competition in Labor Markets*, Princeton, NJ: Princeton University Press.

Milgrom, P. And Roberts, J. (1990) 'The Efficiency of Equity in Organisational Decision Processes', *American Economic Review, Papers and Proceedings*, 80, 154–9.

Pfeffer, J. and Langton, N. (1993) 'The Effect of Wage Dispersion on Satisfaction, Productivity, and Working Collaboratively: Evidence from College and University Faculty', *Administrative Science Quarterly*, 38: 382–407.

Reder, Melvin (1969) A Partial Survey of the Theory of Income Size Distribution, in Soltow L. ed., Six Papers on the Size Distribution of Wealth and Income. Nber, Columbia University Press, New York.

Part I

Labour Turnover Flows and Mobility

1
Labour Turnover and Wage Mobility: The Impact of the Legal Setting and Institutions

Lorenzo Cappellari

1.1 Introduction

Understanding dynamics is a crucial task for labour economics. The incidence of certain adverse labour market states at a point in time, such as non-employment or low pay, is the object of concern for policymakers, but only looking at the factors determining individual dynamics across such states enables looking at their causes – not the symptoms – providing the information needed for policy design.

Initially, researchers have looked at this issue from a macro perspective, using time series data and studying facts such as the evolution of the unemployment rate and wage inflation. Subsequently, the increasing availability of longitudinal microdata (on individuals, firms or, more recently, on the match between the two) has spurred a wide field of research addressing micro-level concepts such as individual wage dynamics and mobility, unemployment transitions and labour turnover. Microdata allow researchers to correct for the compositional effects that may plague time series aggregates. When, in addition, data are longitudinal, they permit analysis of dynamics at the individual level, therefore tackling the issue of unobserved heterogeneity that may bias estimates of the processes of interest. Finally, a linked employer–employee structure of the data allows researchers to make important distinctions among the sources of heterogeneity, providing identification of worker–firm match effects separately from individual and firm idiosyncratic components.

In parallel, and increasingly more connected with applied research, developments have characterized the theoretical labour literature, which has moved towards micro-based theories of individual wage growth and labour turnover (human capital, job search and matching, personnel economics models). It is within this theoretical literature that questions about the role of institutions in shaping labour market outcomes and dynamics started to arise, at both the macro (Calmfors and Driffill, 1988; Layard et al., 1991) and the micro (Bertola, 1990; Lazear, 1990) levels. Such research questions have, in turn, stimulated empirical investigations of the links between labour market institutions and the dynamics of labour market outcomes.

The present paper provides a survey of the empirical literature on wage mobility, labour turnover and their relations with institutions. The focus of the paper is on studies that make use of longitudinal microdata. Broadly speaking, the two topics of wage mobility and labour turnover allow identification of two distinct strands of literature, while studies that combine analyses of the two phenomena within a unified framework are rather rare. Within these, papers that investigate the impact of institutions on individual labour market dynamics fall into two broad groups. On the one hand, there are cross-country studies based on internationally comparable panel data (such as the European Community Household Panel, ECHP), which enable the extent of institutional effects to be gauged by comparing results across countries characterized by different levels of regulations. On the other, single-country studies that perform policy evaluation exercises exploit the occurrence of labour market reforms to retrieve measures of the impacts of institutions on the labour market.

The survey is structured as follows. Section 1.2 provides an overview of the literature in terms of the definitions adopted, the variables utilized, the data and techniques employed. In Section 1.3, a summary of the results produced so far is provided, focusing on the impact of institutions on labour market dynamics. Section 1.4 discusses some possible improvements of wage mobility and turnover measures, while Section 1.5 identifies the more innovative work currently ongoing. Finally, Section 1.6 concludes by discussing the potential ahead in this research area.

1.2 Definition and extent of comparability across studies in variables, concepts, data sets, indicators, econometric techniques

1.2.1 Wage mobility

Wage mobility is typically defined as the change of individual positions within the wage distribution over time (*exchange mobility*). More rarely, it is defined as the absolute individual wage change between time periods (*structural mobility*). In this survey the focus will be predominantly on the first definition. Given its dynamic nature, mobility requires panel data on individual wage profiles for identification.

Wage mobility provides an important complement to static measures of wage inequality, since it assesses the extent of persistence of cross-sectional wage differentials. Less persistent distributions are seen as more egalitarian, as individuals in the low-wage tail succeed in climbing the wage ladder through time, thanks, for example, to human capital investments.

A first possibility for using panel data to measure mobility is to construct mobility indices based on the comparison between inequality measures of annual and lifetime earnings (the latter being some weighted average of individual earnings over time). Shorrocks (1978a) shows that the inequality of lifetime incomes may never exceed that of annual incomes, as some intertemporal redistribution is always going to take place as a result of mobility. Therefore, the more annual measures exceed lifetime measures, the more mobile the distribution. Such a measure has been applied by, among others, Buchinsky and Hunt (1999), using data from the National Longitudinal Survey of Youth (NLSY), and by Hofer and Weber (2002) on Austrian administrative records.

An alternative class of measures of mobility is that based on transition matrices. Given a partition of the cross-sectional wage distribution into classes, a transition matrix collects the probabilities that workers belonging to a certain wage class at the beginning of a time interval end up in a given wage class at the end of that period. Along the diagonal of such matrix there are the probabilities that the arrival class is equal to the starting class, measuring wage immobility. Cells above the diagonal measure the probability of upward mobility, whereas those below the diagonal measure downward mobility. The choice of classes to be used for partitioning the distribution is usually seen as relevant. Popular choices are quantiles of the distribution, or fixed proportions of the mean or median of the distribution.

A first possibility for analysing mobility using transition matrices is provided by the application of mobility indices. Shorrocks (1978b) provides an axiomatization of mobility indices and introduces an index of mobility, a negative function of the trace of the mobility matrix, which would have been widely applied in the literature of the following years. More recently, Dickens (2000b) has introduced an index of mobility based on the difference in the percentiles of the arrival and starting years, using administrative longitudinal records from the UK National Earnings Survey (see also Cardoso (2006) for an application of the same measure to Portugal using linked employer–employee panel data).

A second approach with mobility matrices is based on regression analysis for explaining the individual position within the matrix, or the arrival class as a function of the starting class. The limit of mobility indices resides in their descriptive nature. Descriptive measures cannot be given ceteris paribus interpretations, that is, they may suffer from compositional effects. Moreover, intertemporal wage persistence (and individual-level persistence in general) may be consistent with two alternative scenarios, called *unobserved heterogeneity* and *true state dependence*, and disentangling the two is informative about the causes of persistence. Observing that, for example, individuals remain trapped in low pay over time may mean that past low pay increases (in a causal sense) the probability of current low pay, that is, that there is dependence from past states, as could emerge in the presence of human capital deterioration or bad signalling (*scarring*) induced by low pay episodes. But it may also mean that individuals are heterogeneous in persistent attributes, such as unobserved (by researchers) productivity, which induce low wages.

Econometric models of wage mobility are the appropriate tool for overtaking the limitations of descriptive measures. As in all econometric applications involving individual-level dynamics, the presence of unobserved heterogeneity complicates the identification of persistence, and demands special treatment. When the outcomes investigated have a discrete nature, as is the case with mobility, the so-called *problem of initial conditions* can be solved by modelling transitions jointly with the determinants of the initial state (Heckman, 1981) or by conditioning individual specific effects on the initial state (Wooldridge, 2005). Stewart and Swaffield (1999) are the first to acknowledge these issues in the context of wage mobility models. Using survey data from the British Household Panel Survey (BHPS) to estimate low pay transitions and initial conditions jointly, they show that ignoring the issue leads to biased inference. The approach of Stewart and Swaffield has since been applied by other researchers working in the wage mobility field, including Cappellari (2002, 2007), using survey panel data from the Bank of Italy's Survey on Households Income and Wealth (SHIW); De Coulon and Zuercher (2004) on Swiss panel survey data; and Deding (2001) in a multi-country study.

Transitions into and out of wage classes over time may result from two distinct sources of wage dynamics. Wage may change because of dynamics induced by long-term wage determinants that drive individual wage careers, such as human capital accumulation on the job or the disclosure of match quality. On the other hand, there may be wage fluctuations that have more to do with transitory wage shocks such as those induced by changes in the degree of volatility characterizing the labour market. The two sources of mobility have opposite implications for welfare (see Cappellari (2004) and Raferzeder and Winter-Ebmer (2007) for discussions): while wage movements due to permanent characteristics may be seen as desirable, those due to volatility increase uncertainty and may be welfare-worsening, especially in the presence of liquidity constraints.

The distinction between permanent and transitory types of wage mobility can be investigated using stochastic models of the earnings process based on the distinction between permanent and transitory earnings components. A first generation of studies pioneered by Lillard and Willis (1978) estimated stochastic processes for individual earnings distinguishing between permanent and transitory components. However, it is only more recently that the implications of earnings decompositions for wage inequality and wage mobility have been deeply investigated, starting with the work of Moffitt and Gottschalk (1995). In their paper, they use the Panel Study of Income Dynamics (PSID) and first estimate the intertemporal covariance structure of wages, that is, the second moments of the wage distribution. Such statistics provide an alternative way to look at wage mobility: the more wage autocorrelations decline over time, the more individual mobility can be observed from one period to the next. Second, they specify a stochastic wage process composed of a permanent component (i.e. some unit root shock) and a transitory one (mean reverting shock), and estimate the process parameter by Generalized Method of Moments (GMM). This exercise enables them to decompose cross-sectional inequality into a permanent and a transitory component: the less permanent inequality there is, the more mobility we should observe in the wage distribution. The more transitory inequality there is, the more mobility should increase, at the cost of increased uncertainty.

The Moffitt and Gottschalk (1995) paper has been very influential in the field, and a literature focused on the decomposition of inequality into long-term and transitory components has developed in many countries. Studies include Haider (2001) for the US; Baker and Solon (2003) for Canada; Dickens (2000), Ramos (2003) and Alessie and Kalwij (2007) for the UK; Cappellari (2004) and Cappellari and Leonardi (2006) for Italy; Cervini and Ramos (2006) for Spain. One of the recurrent characteristics in these studies is the use of large administrative longitudinal archives on individual wage profiles, exceptions being Ramos (2003) on the BHPS and Cervini and Ramos (2006) on the ECHP.

1.2.2 Labour turnover

Labour turnover may be defined as the mobility of individuals across labour market states. Broadly speaking, such a definition embraces two different sets of movements: transitions between non-employment (or unemployment) and employment, and transitions between jobs. Following these two alternative definitions, it is possible to identify separate strands of literature, which, for convenience, we may label 'Employment dynamics' and 'Job mobility'.

1.2.2.1 Employment dynamics

The analysis of individual transitions between employment and unemployment or non-employment is a well-established tradition in empirical labour economics. Depending upon the econometric approach followed, it is possible to group papers into two broad areas: studies of (Markovian) transitions and studies of duration. While the former identify dynamics by relating current states to their lagged values, the latter are focused on the time it takes to exit from a certain labour market state. In the first case, transitions are identified by observing individual states in a panel sample; in the second, information on the spell length for these states is required. Both literatures are quite vast, and for reasons of space here we will survey only few representative papers.

Models of unemployment duration are a traditional tool for assessing the speed at which individuals exit from unemployment; see Lancaster (1990) and Nickell (1979) for early influential work in this area. The key object of analysis is the probability of leaving unemployment for those who have spent a certain amount of time in unemployment. Estimation of these models is enhanced by the availability of 'high frequency' data, which enable observation of transitions over intervals shorter than one year (typically quarters or months). Duration models are also solidly grounded in economic theory; specifically, the search and matching models of Burdett (1977) and Mortensen (1978) naturally lend themselves to a duration type of analysis – see, for example, van den Berg and Ridder (1998). Duration models have been estimated on a variety of data sources, ranging from household surveys (e.g. Tatsiramos (2009 on the ECHP)) to administrative data on unemployment benefit claimants (e.g. Kalwij (2001) on the Joint Unemployment and Vacancy Operating System – Juvos – data; Fitzenberger and Wilke, 2004). An interesting comparison of the two types of data sources for the estimation of duration models is provided by Biewen and Wilke (2005), who show the robustness of the conclusions derived in the two cases.

One concept of interest in duration analysis is duration dependence: to what extent the time spent in unemployment influences the probability of leaving such a state. Data are said to exhibit positive (negative) duration dependence if the exit probability increases (decreases) with elapsed durations. In the unemployment case negative dependence is typically found, and it is interpreted as the symptom of factors favouring long-term unemployment, for instance, human capital depreciation. However, as mentioned above while discussing the concept of state dependence, such dependence may be spurious, and due account has to be made for unobserved heterogeneity. With heterogeneous agents, those with a low inherent propensity to leave unemployment will remain unemployed over time, so that by widening the duration over which exits are considered the researcher will be comparing non-homogeneous groups. The observed dependence in that case will be induced by the different inherent propensity to exit from unemployment (e.g. search ability) across groups of individuals, not by the causal effect of time spent in unemployment within the same group. Duration models offer several possibilities of controlling for unobserved heterogeneity, thus providing unbiased estimates of duration dependence.

The alternative way of looking at employment dynamics is by means of Markovian models in which it is assumed that all the dependence between the present and the past may be captured by considering past states up to a certain lag, a popular choice being first order models. Heckman and Willis (1977) and Heckman and Borjas (1980) provide early contributions in this area. As for the transition models discussed in the section on wage mobility, due account has to be made for unobserved heterogeneity in order to disentangle genuine state dependence from spurious correlations, which is typically done using either the Heckman (1981) or Wooldridge (2005) approaches. These models are typically estimated using survey data at yearly intervals. In particular, survey data are necessary when applying the Heckman method to solve the initial conditions problem. In fact, such a method requires approximation of the initial condition of the process investigated using information pre-dating the start of the sample period, and the parental background information typically available in household surveys may serve the scope. A prominent recent example of this type of analysis is by Hyslop (1999), who analyses women's labour force participation dynamics using data from the PSID. A nice application to European data and the unemployment of men is provided by Arulampalam et al. (2000), using the BHPS and showing that state dependence accounts for between one and two-fifths of aggregate persistence, and increases with age. Applications of this type of approach are in current expansion. Michaud and Tatsiramos (2005) provide an application of the Wooldridge approach to initial conditions to the problem of employment dynamics for married women in Europe, using ECHP data. Interesting also is the study of Prowse (2005) on women's employment dynamics. She uses BHPS data and a trinomial partition of employment status into full-time employment, part-time employment and non-employment, while treating initial conditions via the Heckman approach. Besides the technical relevance of the model, Prowse's results seem to suggest that it is important to distinguish full- and part-time positions when studying women's dynamics.

1.2.2.2 Job mobility

According to the search/matching theory paradigm, job mobility is the fundamental mechanism through which even a labour market with frictions reaches equilibrium. These movements are essentially driven by a comparison between the actual wage and the wage offers that one can get outside the current firm. When the expected wage gain from changing job is positive, we should observe workers to change job voluntarily. On the other hand, job separations may be optimal for the firm, when, for some reason, the actual wage is higher than the worker's outside option. In this case, and assuming for simplicity no firing costs, we should observe involuntary changes, accompanied by wage losses.

Empirically, the distinction between voluntary and involuntary job mobility is rather difficult to identify. In the absence of explicit information about the nature of the move (which can be provided, for instance, by panel surveys), researchers typically identify layoffs as job changes that involve some intervening non-employment period.

The literature studying job mobility is rather vast, and here we will focus on empirical studies of the determinants of turnover and of the wage movements associated with such changes.

One example of these studies is Gottschalk (2001), who uses longitudinal data from the Survey of Income and Program Participation (SIPP) to estimate the wage growth of individuals within a job spell and between jobs, and shows that there is substantial heterogeneity in wage growth both within and between jobs. However, while within-job growth is always positive, job changes can be coupled with wage losses. Using the same data, Connolly and Gottschalk (2008) estimate a structural model in which it is optimal for workers to accept wage cuts upon a job change, as long as wage growth in the new job compensates for the initial earnings loss. Davia (2005) looks at a similar issue using ECHP data and focusing on young workers. She shows that wage gains associated with job mobility are decreasing in age, and that repeated job changes are associated with wage losses, rather than gains. Moreover, she provides evidence that the relationship may be blurred by spurious correlation. Finally, García Perez and Rebollo Sanz (2005) employ a similar ECHP-based approach but also consider the role of intervening unemployment spells, thus, indirectly, estimating the consequences of involuntary vs. voluntary moves. They find that involuntary moves imply a wage penalty, while quitters experience wage gains also with respect to job stayers.

The work of Cardoso (2005) is in a similar vein to those discussed above. However, this study devotes specific attention to wage ranks, in addition to wage levels, thus placing the focus of the paper on relative wage movements within wage hierarchies at the firm level. Using linked employer–employee administrative data for Portugal, she shows that movers are subject to slower rank progression than stayers. The larger the new firm compared with the old one, the larger the penalty. Moreover, faster rank progression is achieved by movers at the price of slower wage progression, suggesting the existence of a trade-off between wage and status.

While the ones above can be seen as attempts to look at the (wage) consequences of mobility, other focus on its causes. As discussed above, moves are induced by the difference between the actual wage and the worker's outside offers. Empirically, it is difficult to identify such a gap using wage data alone, due to the absence of counterfactual, that is, what the worker would earn outside the firm. Job satisfaction data may be helpful in this respect, to the extent that self-reported satisfaction is a function of that difference. This is clearly the case when data on satisfaction with pay are collected, but also data on non-pecuniary facets of the job may be useful. Clark et al. (1998) use data from the German Socio-Economic Panel (GSOEP) to examine the effect of wages and job satisfaction on workers' future quit behaviour. They show that workers who report dissatisfaction with their jobs are more likely to quit than those with higher levels of satisfaction. They also find evidence that wage changes are a better predictor of quits than wage levels. Kristensen and Westergård-Nielsen (2004) provide a cross-country study of these issues using the ECHP. They show that job satisfaction improves the model's ability to predict actual quit behaviour. In particular, satisfaction with type of work is found to be the best predictor of job mobility. Lévy-Garboua et al. (2005) show that job satisfaction can be interpreted as the experienced preference for the present job against available alternatives, and show that residuals from job satisfaction equations are better predictors of quits than the overall level of satisfaction.

1.2.3 Wage mobility and labour turnover

As we have seen above, the literature is quite vast on both wage mobility and workers' turnover. Rarer, however, are studies that look at the two concepts simultaneously. A relevant contribution in this direction is Stewart (2007), who proposes a model of joint unemployment and low pay dynamics, estimated using a variety of econometric techniques including the Heckman and Wooldridge's approaches to initial conditions, and data from the BHPS. He shows that state dependence effects act also cross-states, so that individuals in high-wage jobs experience significantly lower job loss probabilities compared with low-wage workers. He also shows that results are fairly robust to the choice of the method used for dealing with initial conditions.

Another contribution in this direction is Parent (2002), who estimates covariance structure models using the US National Longitudinal Survey of Youths and conditions the permanent earnings component upon job tenure, thereby linking a measure of earnings persistence (i.e. the variance of the permanent component) to an inverse measure of job mobility. He finds that the distribution of permanent wages shrinks (i.e. earnings persistence goes down) as tenure elapses, and interprets the result within an on-the-job training model. In a similar vein, Leonardi (2003) performs a permanent transitory decomposition of earnings inequality, distinguishing between job stayers and job changers. He uses the PSID and finds that the overall increase in transitory variance characterizing the US over the past few decades stems from the distribution of young job changers. Cappellari and Leonardi (2006) extend the Parent (2002) approach to include measures of on-the-job tenure also within the volatile earnings components, showing that tenure reduces instability to a meaningful extent.

1.3 Labour market laws and their impact on labour turnover and wage mobility

The link between labour market institutions and labour market outcomes has been the subject of several theoretical works. Confronted with the sluggish reaction of labour markets in Continental Europe to aggregate shocks in the early 1980s, analysts started investigating the differences with the US (and UK) settings, where (aggregate) post-shock unemployment rates converged to pre-shock levels more quickly. The main structural differences were found in the type and pervasiveness of labour market institutions. Stronger unions generating more compressed wage structures and firing restrictions were the feature in slow-responding economies, opposed to unemployment insurance schemes and an overall low level of institutional provisions in the UK and US. Bentolila and Bertola (1990) focused on the impact that firing restrictions may have on unemployment levels and flows, showing that it is the latter that are more sensitive to the degree of protection. Lazear (1990) clarified that the type of effect depends upon the type of firing restriction, and that with flexible wages the firm–worker transfer component of firing costs is neutral for job creation and destruction. Bertola and Rogerson (1997) showed that firing costs and labour unions/wage compression may have opposite effects on unemployment flows.

While the first attempts to test such predictions were based on aggregate data or descriptive statistics, more recent work perform microdata-based tests. The theoretical literature sketched out above yields predictions for the relationship between institutions and employment levels and flows, which are those most widely tested in the empirical papers. Much less developed, on the other hand, is the literature that investigates the relationship between institutional settings and wage mobility, and we start our review of findings from this latter literature. In what follows, results from papers that have looked at the relationship between institutions and the relevant outcomes are provided.

1.3.1 Labour market institutions and wage mobility

Economic models of the trade union predict that in the presence of union coverage average wages should increase compared with the benchmark of perfect competition; moreover, as long as wage-compression is among union objectives, the presence of unions should also reduce earnings inequality. Based on these considerations, part of the literature developed in the 1990s to analyse worldwide changes in the wage structure has identified the decline in union power and institutions in general as a relevant explanatory factor for increasing inequality (see Koeninger et al. (2007) for a recent piece of work looking at cross-country evidence). Economic models, however, are basically silent about the relationship one should expect between institutions and wage mobility, and the few empirical attempts aimed at quantifying such a relationship have essentially been based on the conventional wisdom (derived from models that do not investigate mobility per se, but rather inequality or employment patterns) that lower institutional protection and higher labour market flexibility should be associated with higher wage mobility.

The methodological approach followed for assessing the link between wage mobility and the legal setting in the labour market falls within the category of cross-country comparisons, in which the relationship of interest is inferred by comparing mobility levels across countries characterized by different degrees of institutional 'rigidities'. The first attempt of this kind can be found in the 1996 edition of the OECD Employment Outlook, in which comparable mobility indices based on transition matrices were computed for a number of countries, coming to the puzzling finding that mobility rates are very similar in countries that differ remarkably in their labour market institutions. A similar conclusion is reached by Burkhauser et al. (1997), who point to the remarkable similarity between the USA and Germany in terms of mobility levels and trend, discarding the hypothesis that countries with higher government intervention in the labour market and higher union influence will have lower wage mobility. The work of Deding (2002) compares low pay transitions in Denmark, Germany and the US using econometric models, and finds similarities across countries in the effects of individual characteristics on low pay transitions, again pointing towards a sort of neutrality of institutions for wage mobility. A cross-country comparison is, finally, provided by Cardoso (2006), who looks at percentile indices of wage mobility, comparing Portugal and the UK, two countries characterized by different degrees of institutional presence in the labour market. Her findings point towards remarkable similarities of wage mobility in the two contexts. The paper is based on linked employer–employee data, which enable a conclusion in favour of firm-level arrangements as a factor that, at the micro level, counteracts institutional rigidities.

Further insights upon the effects of institutions on wage mobility can be gained by considering results from the literature on the permanent and transitory components of earnings in a cross-country perspective. Even though each of these studies refers to a single country, the application of a rather homogeneous methodological framework in several countries offers the possibility to draw some tentative conclusions. Specifically, studies for the US (Haider, 2001; Moffitt and Gottschalk, 1995) and the UK (e.g. Dickens, 2000) find that the growth of earnings inequality witnessed by those countries received important contributions from the transitory components of earnings (the so-called 'earnings instability'), suggesting that 'flexible' labour markets favour short-term earnings fluctuations, so that wage mobility reflects earnings turbulence to a meaningful extent. Instead, studies for more 'rigid' labour markets find the role of transitory fluctuation to be negligible (see Cappellari (2004) for Italy), so that in those cases mobility reflects a low dispersion in the distribution of long-term earnings. Put another way, institutions may affect the sources of earnings mobility, setting the balance between transitory fluctuations and long-term earnings compression. Cappellari and Leonardi (2006) show that the degree of earnings instability is larger on temporary employment contracts relative to open-ended contracts, and that the level of instability doubles if workers on permanent contracts are compared with individuals who spend their entire career on temporary contracts. Cervini and Ramos (2006) provide indirect evidence in this direction for Spain, showing that earnings instability declined for younger cohorts in the late 1990s, after some restrictions in the use of temporary contracts were introduced.

1.3.2 Labour market institutions and labour turnover

Contrary to the case of wage mobility, the literature on institutions and labour turnover is rather vast and detailed. In particular, besides the cross-country approach, this literature is characterized by studies evaluating the impact of specific institutions on dynamic labour market outcomes, often exploiting the occurrence of reforms in a specific institution or legal setting to perform sharp evaluation exercises in the framework of quasi-natural experiments and difference-in-difference estimators.

One example of this approach is provided by the work of Kugler (1999), who examines the impact of the Colombian Labour Market Reform of 1990, which substantially reduced dismissal costs. The possibility to identify the effect of institutions (in this case dismissal costs) is provided by the availability of data on worker turnover for individuals who are exposed and not exposed to the reform, and with observations on the two groups before and after the reform. Essentially, this is the principle behind the so-called difference-in-difference estimator. Given an outcome of interest (in her case worker turnover), the impact of the institutional reform on the group of individuals exposed to the reform is identified by the variation of the outcome for this group before and after the reform (the first difference). Since such before–after comparison may also reflect other influences besides the reform (e.g. the economic cycle), a second difference in outcomes is estimated for individuals not exposed to the reform, and it is subtracted from the first difference. The result of this exercise provides the impact of the reform on outcomes net of any other economy-wide confounding factor. Specifically, Kugler (1999) exploited a reduction in severance payments and the existence of two different groups of workers, those in the formal sector – who are affected by the reform – and those in the informal sector, such as the self-employed, family workers, and domestic workers, all of whom are exempted from severance payments. Using household survey data with retrospective information on individual labour market transitions, she finds that the reform did indeed affect transitions in the direction predicted by the theoretical model, increasing both unemployment entries and exits. At the aggregate level, her estimates imply that the reform accounted for roughly one-quarter of the fall in the unemployment rate.

The work of Kugler and Pica (2008) is in a similar vein, in that it evaluates the effects of dismissal costs on worker turnover in Italy using a difference-in-difference approach. They exploit the reform of dismissal costs for small firms (fewer than 15 employees) that witnessed an increase in firing restrictions in 1990 relative to larger firms. They find that the increase in dismissal costs after 1990 decreased accessions and separations in small relative to big firms, again confirming theoretical predictions on the effect of firing costs on worker turnover.

The diffusion of flexible and temporary work contracts can be seen as a route for implementing an overall lower level of employment protection. However, the recent growth of temporary employment observed in many European countries has raised concerns that temporary jobs may be crowding out more stable forms of employment and thus creating an additional source of insecurity for workers. In this sense, it is feared that temporary jobs may amplify the dualism in the labour market between workers who are employed on a permanent basis and workers who are not, especially if workers experiencing temporary employment, particularly early in their careers, continue in a precarious condition for a long time before moving to a permanent contract. The main question, therefore, is the following: to what extent does a temporary job increase the probability of finding a permanent job?

In this context, Sciulli (2006) evaluates the effect of an overall labour market reform in Italy (the so-called *Treu package*, from the name of the Minister of Labour who signed the Law introducing it in 1997) aimed at increasing the flexibility of the employment relationship via the diffusion of flexible and fixed-term contracts. This time the research design is based not on a canonical difference-in-difference setup, but rather on the comparison of transition rates between job spells started before and after the exact day of implementation of the reform, with the sample restricted to young individuals, that is, those most likely to be interested in the new set of work contracts. He finds an increase in negative duration dependence for non-working state outflow, implying an amplification of the short-term unemployed – long-term unemployed duality. Also, previous atypical job experiences play a negative role in the probability of moving toward a stable job, but rather tend to lead to repeated atypical work. On the other hand, there is no evidence that the probability of finding a permanent contract is higher for workers who move from an atypical contract rather than from a non-working state.

While in Italy the move towards labour market flexibility is a relatively recent experience, reforms of this kind started in the 1980s in Spain. The effects on the unemployment rate were not unequivocal, but a more dynamic labour market has developed, with an increase of gross flows between unemployment and employment (Güell, 2003). However, the introduction of fixed-term contracts has generated some effects on other dimensions of the labour market. For example, Güell (2003) shows that these reforms have increased the duration dependence for unemployment spells, creating increased duality between short-term unemployed and long-term unemployed. Alba-Ramirez (1998) and Amuedo-Dorantes (2000) show that the probability of obtaining a permanent contract decreases after some previous atypical contracts. Güell and Petrongolo (2006) find that the conversion rate from temporary to permanent contract is rather low and concentrates close to the deadline of the temporary contract.

Evidence for other countries goes somewhat in the opposite direction and suggests that temporary employment may indeed act as a stepping stone into the labour market. Hagen (2003) investigates whether or not temporary work really increases the long-term employment prospects of unemployed people entering into temporary work in terms of future permanent employment relationships. In particular, the paper investigates the effects of the transition from unemployment to fixed-term jobs on an individual's future employment opportunities in the West German labour market, by using the GSOEP data set for the period 1991–2001. He finds that entering into temporary jobs increases the future employment probability for both temporary and permanent contracts, but this effect varies according to different time horizons, with a higher probability observed at the beginning for a renewal into a fixed-term job and later for a renewal into a permanent job. These findings are compatible with the hypothesis that temporary employment may be a stepping stone towards a permanent contract. For the UK,

Booth et al. (2002) use BHPS data and specify a model that relates the exit process to a number of individual and job-specific characteristics. The estimation is carried out separately for two different types of temporary jobs: fixed-term contracts and seasonal–casual contracts. Their results suggest that temporary employment is a viable route for accessing permanent employment, but this effect seems to be concentrated among women.

Employment protection legislation has its rationale in the need for providing insurance to workers against unemployment in the presence of missing insurance markets. The alternative legal setting traditionally designed for this purpose is the provision of unemployment benefits that help the unemployed cope with the income loss deriving from non-employment – an example of passive labour market policy. More recently, and due to the wrong incentives towards re-employment that unemployment insurance can generate, these provisions have increasingly been coupled with active policies such as training programmes. The literature evaluating the impact of such interventions on worker turnover is vast, and here we will provide a selective account of the main findings.

Early studies in this field were concerned with evaluating the impact of unemployment benefit generosity (in terms of both level and duration) on the speed at which benefit recipients leave unemployment. Meyer (1990) and Katz and Meyer (1990) find for US data that the exit rate from unemployment rises sharply just before benefits are exhausted. Such sharp increases are absent for non-recipients. For benefit recipients they find spikes around exhaustion points in both the new job finding rates and the recall rates. This suggest that unemployed people search harder just before the expiration of benefits, or they return to prearranged jobs just before they lose their benefits. Similar patterns were reported by Naredranathan and Stewart (1991) for Britain. These findings lend support to the idea that unemployment insurance acts as a disincentive in job search activity.

More recently, researchers have moved towards quasi-experimental evaluations based on changes in the degree of benefit generosity. There are several examples in this direction. Lalive et al. (2006) use an economy-wide reform in welfare generosity, which occurred in Austria, and find that welfare generosity has a disincentive effect that mostly stems from the duration, rather than the level, of benefits. Lalive (2008) exploits a sharper research design and studies an Austrian reform that affected only individuals above a certain age threshold and living in certain regions of the country, providing the framework for a regression discontinuity evaluation. His results still point towards a substantive disincentive effect of welfare payments, which increase the duration of unemployment.

A reform in unemployment benefit generosity for older workers in West Germany is studied by Fitzenberger and Wilke (2004), who find effects on transitions to non-employment but not on transitions into unemployment. They conclude that the conventional view that welfare generosity acts as a disincentive in search is not supported in their case.

Lalive et al. (2005) study the effect of benefit sanctions on unemployment duration. They employ Swiss administrative data and a bivariate duration model for the duration of sanctions and the duration of unemployment conditional on sanctions, which is identified thanks to the duration structure of the data. They find that sanctions are an effective tool for helping the unemployed back into work.

While all these studies are concerned with the disincentive effects of welfare provisions, a recent work by Tatsiramos (2009) highlights the possibility of positive effects on re-employment wages and duration. This is another corollary of the search model: since benefits allow longer search, the probability that the search ends with a good match is larger relative to the no-benefits case. The study uses ECHP data and studies unemployment and re-employment durations as a function of welfare receipts. The empirical results suggest that receiving unemployment benefits reduces significantly the hazard rate for leaving unemployment, which leads to longer unemployment duration. This confirms both the theoretical predictions and the extensive empirical literature on the effect of benefits on unemployment duration. Moreover, the effect of receiving benefits on unemployment duration is larger in countries with a more generous UI system, such as France and Germany.

Active labour market policies such as training schemes for the unemployed are the alternative institutional tool to provide 'insurance' against unemployment. Here the literature is rather extended, and results on the effectiveness of these policies tend to vary according to the programme considered, the country investigated and the groups targeted. Rather than going into the details of this literature, here we will refer to a recent study by Kluve (2006), who provides a meta-analysis in this field. He finds that the type of programme is the most important determinant of its success. The only institutional factor that appears to have an important effect on programme effectiveness is the presence of more restrictive dismissal regulations. Training programmes are found to have moderate effects, whereas private sector incentive programmes and Services and Sanctions show a significantly better performance. Direct employment in the public is by far the worst-performing policy.

1.4 How can we build better measures of labour turnover and wage mobility?

One of the goals that future research in this area should aim at is *completeness*. The literature reviewed in the previous sections tends to lack papers providing a joint assessment of labour turnover and wage mobility: most of the papers focus on either aspect, but studies of turnover and mobility are rare. Stewart (2007) is an important contribution in this direction. One first relevant advantage of such an integrated approach is the possibility of gaining a more complete picture of individual dynamics in the labour market. In turn, such a perspective is implicitly required by concepts of policy relevance such as the *flexicurity* promoted alongside the so-called Lisbon Strategy. Essentially, what is needed is a monitoring of individual trajectories within the labour market over the entire active working life, covering simultaneously spells of employment – distinguishing between low-paid and better-paid jobs – and non-employment. It is, for example, of relevance to understand what type of job unemployed people find, and whether it lasts for a long time or is followed again by other spells of unemployment. Second, this view can reveal to what extent legal interventions on one side of the problem, say the introduction of training programmes for the unemployed, have spillover effects on the other; for example, trained unemployed people are more successful than non-trained people in getting higher-paid jobs. Finally, the literature review highlighted that there are technical issues to be solved when dealing with models for labour market dynamics, and focusing, for example, on wage mobility alone leads researchers to overlook the underlying process for employment dynamics on which, necessarily, wage mobility depends. An integrated view has the virtue of highlighting such dependence and, possibly, of handling it with appropriate techniques, as is the case with the Stewart (2007) paper.

A second desirable property for turnover and mobility measures is being *model-based*. Summary statistics of transitions may result from a host of factors varying from compositional effects to spurious correlations over time. Better measures, and measures that convey quantities relevant for policy design, can be constructed as the predictions from correctly specified econometric models. Clearly, the costs of such an approach may be non-trivial, especially in the context of multi-country studies.

Third, there is the need for measures that *exploit labour market reforms for identification*. As long as they are unpredicted by agents, and the exposure to reforms affects circumscribed groups in the labour force, then the occurrence of reforms provides the sort of variation that can be used to estimate the effect of institutions and legal provisions on labour market dynamics. This approach is increasingly followed in the case of worker turnover, but examples in the wage mobility field are essentially absent, generating a gap of knowledge in the literature that needs to be filled.

Fourthly, measures should be *looking at the life cycle*. Most of the existing studies consider individuals at a specific point in time or over relatively short intervals, essentially for data limitations. Life cycle aspects of wage mobility and turnover are, therefore, inferred indirectly by comparing individuals from different cohorts. Such comparisons are necessarily biased, since different cohorts have entered the labour market in different periods, and this may affect their dynamic behaviour. Moreover, these indirect comparisons cannot reveal what is the impact of – say – early career episodes on later life outcomes. Recently, however, the data limitations preventing a more direct study of wage mobility and turnover throughout the individual career are increasingly less relevant. On the one hand, ongoing panel surveys now cover substantially long periods, as is the case with the German survey. But probably more promising is the exploitation of administrative archives from which entire working histories can be reconstructed at the individual level. Fostering the access of researchers to such administrative data sources is certainly one way of obtaining better measures of turnover and mobility.

Finally, measures of turnover and mobility should *derive from various types of data*. Administrative records, household surveys and linked employer–employee databases all have some specific advantages. For example, survey data enable individual dynamics in the labour market to be linked with family origins, whereas linked data allow the study of such dynamics while taking into account the role of firms. All this information is relevant for a better assessment of turnover and mobility.

1.5 Identification of more innovative work currently ongoing

The fundamental issue in empirical work is the identification of causal effects separately from the spurious associations induced by statistical correlation. In the case of labour market dynamics and institutions, identification requires researchers to uncover the impact that a certain legal setting has on individual mobility across states in the labour market. Essentially, this is the issue of finding a source of variation in the data (an *instrument*) that affects individuals' exposure to labour market institutions, but not individual labour market transitions.

A first possibility is provided by labour market reforms and difference-in-difference estimators. In all those circumstances in which the extent of labour market regulations changes over time for some groups of the workforce and not for others, it is possible to compare variations in outcomes between those affected by the reform and those not affected, providing a reliable estimate of the effect of interest. Examples of this approach in the field of labour market dynamics are Kugler (1999) and Kugler and Pica (2008).

In the absence of reforms, a second possibility is provided by an eclectic use of observable individual characteristics in the data, which goes under the labels of 'treatment effects models' and, more recently, 'regression discontinuity design'. Essentially, the idea consists of comparing outcomes across individuals who are 'identical' except for the exposure to some labour market institutional provision, and deriving an estimate of the effects of interest from such comparisons. This approach has rapidly become the workhorse in studies evaluating the effects of specific labour market programmes; see Kluve (2006).

Whenever exposure to labour market reforms or policies can be characterized by a duration, then an innovative suitable tool for estimating their impact on labour market transition is provided by multi-equation models of duration. Abbring and Van den Berg (2004) showed that, in such a context, the issue of identification is solved thanks to the duration structure of the data. Lalive et al. (2006) show an application of these ideas in the context of evaluation of the impact of unemployment subsidies on unemployment transitions.

Finally, a promising route for solving identification issues is provided by structural estimation, since in this case the parameters to be estimated are derived directly from a theoretical model. Applications of this approach in the context of turnover are still rare; Connolly and Gottschalk (2008) provide a nice example.

1.6 Directions for future research

Research on labour market dynamics and institution is in constant evolution, with some areas less investigated than others. One under-researched area is the impact of institutions on wage mobility. As we have seen in this survey, the questions have been addressed mainly by cross-country studies, but sharp evaluations within a country still do not exist. In principle, in all those contexts in which difference-in-difference evaluations of labour market reforms have been performed, the gap could be filled. In practice, this possibility may be hampered by data availability, say because of the lack of longitudinal sources on wages, or the lack of specific information on variables needed to identify dynamics.

A second aspect that is somehow unsatisfactory in the existing literature is the relative scarcity of studies that address simultaneously the endogeneity of dynamics and the endogeneity of exposure to institutional provisions. It is rare to find studies that perform sharp evaluations of institutional reforms within the framework of a properly specified dynamic model, and this is certainly one direction to pursue in the future.

Third, this survey has stressed that studies that look jointly at wage mobility and labour turnover are still rare, and this is certainly a fruitful route to follow in the future.

Finally, it should be stressed how research capacity is dependent on data availability, and this is even more true in the context of dynamic models, where longitudinal data are essential. In this respect, the access to longitudinal archives on both workers and firms seems a necessary condition for enhancing our knowledge of labour market dynamics.

Note

Paper written for the project 'European labour market analysis using firm-level panel data and linked employer-employee data'. I thank Gabriele Mazzolini for his invaluable assistance in finalizing the survey.

References

Abbring, J.H. and van den Berg, G.J. (2004) 'The Non-Parametric Identification of Treatment Effects in Duration Models', *Econometrica*, 71(5): 1491–517.

Alba-Ramirez, A. (1999) 'Explaining the Transitions Out of Unemployment in Spain: The Effect of Unemployment Insurance', *Applied Economics*, 31(2): 183–93.

Alessie, R. and Kalwij, A. (2007) 'Permanent and Transitory Wage Inequality of British Men, 1975–2001: Year, Age and Cohort Effects', *Journal of Applied Econometrics*, 22(6): 1063–93.

Amuedo-Dorantes, C. (2000) 'Work Transitions Into and Out of Involuntary Temporary Employment in a Segmented Market: Evidence from Spain', *Industrial and Labor Relations Review*, 53(2): 309–25.

Arulampalam, W., Booth, A.L. and Taylor, M.P. (2000) 'Unemployment Persistence', *Oxford Economic Papers*, 52(1): 24–50.

Baker, M. and Solon, G. (2003) 'Earnings Dynamics and Inequality among Canadian Men, 1976–1992: Evidence from Longitudinal Income Tax Records', *Journal of Labor Economics*, 21(2): 267–88.

Bentolila, S. and Bertola, G. (1990) 'Firing Costs and Labor Demand: How Bad is Eurosclerosis?', *Review of Economic Studies*, 57(3): 381–402.

Bertola, G. (1990) 'Job Security Employment and Wages', *European Economic Review*, 34(4): 851–79.

Bertola, G. and Rogerson, R. (1997) 'Institutions and Labor Reallocation', *European Economic Review*, 41(6): 1147–71.

Biewen, M. and Wilke, R.A. (2005) 'Unemployment Duration and the Length of Entitlement Periods for Unemployment Benefits: Do the IAB Employment Subsample and the German Socio-Economic Panel Yield the Same Results?' *ZEW*, 5(5).

Booth, A., Francesconi, M. and Frank, J. (2002) 'Temporary Jobs: Stepping Stones or Dead Ends?', *The Economic Journal*, 112(480): 189–213.

Buchinsky, M. and Hunt, J. (1999) 'Wage Mobility in the United States', *Review of Economics and Statistics*, 81(3): 351–68.

Burdett, K. (1977) 'Unemployment Insurance Payment as a Search Subsidy: A Theoretical Analysis', *Economic Inquiry*, 17(3): 333–43.

Burkhauser, R.V., Holtz-Eakin, D. and Rhody, S.E. (1997) 'Labor Earnings Mobility and Inequality in the United States and Germany During the Growth of the 1980s', *International Economic Review*, 38(4): 775–94.

Calmfors, L. and Driffill, J. (1988) 'Centralization of Wage Bargaining', *Economic Policy*, April.

Cappellari, L. (2002) 'Do the Working Poor Stay Poor? An Analysis of Low Pay Transitions in Italy', *Oxford Bulletin of Economics and Statistics*, 64(2): 87–110.

Cappellari, L. (2004) 'The Dynamics and Inequality of Italian Men's Earnings: Permanent Changes or transitory Fluctuations?', *The Journal of Human Resources*, 39(2): 475–99.

Cappellari, L. (2007) 'Earnings Mobility among Italian Low Paid Workers', *Journal of Population Economics*, 20(2): 465–82.

Cappellari, L. and Leonardi, M. (2006) 'Earnings Instability and Tenure', IZA Discussion Papers no. 2527.

Cardoso, A.R. (2005) 'Big Fish in Small Pond or Small Fish in Big Pond? An Analysis of Job Mobility', IZA Discussion Papers no. 1900.

Cardoso, A.R. (2006) 'Wage Mobility: Do Institutions Make a Difference?', *Labour Economics*, 13(3): 387–404.

Cervini, M. and Ramos, X. (2006) 'Permanent and Transitory Earnings Inequality in Spain, 1993–2000', paper presented at the 2006 conference of the European Association of Labour Economics, Prague.

Clark, A., Georgellis, Y. and Sanfey, P. (1998) 'Job Satisfaction, Wage Changes and Quits: Evidence from Germany', *Research in Labor Economics*, 17: 95–121.

Connolly, H. and Gottschalk, P. (2008) 'Wage Cuts as Investment in Future Wage Growth. Some Evidence', *Labour*, 22(1): 1–22.

Davia, M.A. (2005) 'Job Mobility and Wage Mobility at the Beginning of the Working Career: A Comparative View Across Europe', ISER Working Papers Number 2005–03.

De Coulon, A. and Zuercher, B. (2004) 'Low Pay Mobility in the Swiss Labor Market', in R. Plasman, F. Rycx and D. Meulders (eds) *Minimum Wages, Low Pay and Unemployment*, Basingstoke: Palgrave MacMillan.

Deding, M.C. (2002) 'Low Wage Mobility in Denmark, Germany, and the United States', The Danish National Institute of Social Research, Working Paper 33.

Dickens, R. (2000a) 'The Evolution of Individual Male Earnings Wages in Great Britain: 1975–95', *The Economic Journal*, 110(460): 27–49.

Dickens, R. (2000b) 'Caught in a Trap? Wage Mobility in Great Britain: 1975–94', *Economica*, 67(268): 477–97.

Fitzenberger, B. and Wilke, R.A. (2004) 'Unemployment Durations in West-Germany Before and After the Reform of the Unemployment Compensation System During the 1980s', ZEW Discussion Paper no. 04–24.

García Perez, J.I. and Rebollo Sanz, Y. (2005) 'Wage Changes through Job Mobility in Europe: A Multinomial Endogenous Switching Approach', *Labour Economics*, 12(4): 531–55.

Gottschalk, P. (2001) 'Wage Mobility within and between Jobs', mimeographed.

Güell, M. (2003) 'Fixed-Term Contracts and the Duration Distribution of Unemployment', IZA Discussion Papers No. 791.

Güell, M. and Petrongolo, B. (2006) 'How Binding are Legal Limits? Transitions from Temporary to Permanent Work in Spain', *Labour Economics*, 14(2): 153–83.

Hagen, T. (2003) 'Do Fixed-Term Contracts Increase the Long-Term Employment Opportunities of the Unemployed?', ZEW Discussion Paper no. 03–49.

Haider, S.J. (2001) 'Earnings Instability and Earnings Inequality of Males in the United States: 1967–1991', *Journal of Labor Economics*, 19(4): 799–836.

Heckman, J.J. (1981) 'The Incidental Parameters Problem and the Problem of Initial Conditions in Estimating a Discrete Time – Discrete Data Stochastic Process', in C.F. Manski and D. McFadden (eds) *Structural Analysis of Discrete Data with Economic Applications*, MIT Press, 179–95.

Heckman, J.J. and Borjas, G. (1980) 'Does Unemployment Cause Future Unemployment? Definitions, Questions and Answers from a Continuous Time Model of Heterogeneity and State Dependence', *Economica*, 47(187): 247–83.

Heckman, J.J. and Willis, R. (1977) 'A Beta-Logistic Model for the Analysis of Sequential Labor Force Participation by Married Women', *Journal of Political Economy*, 85(1): 27–58.

Hofer, H. and Weber, A. (2002) 'Wage Mobility in Austria 1986–1996', *Labour Economics*, September, 9(4): 563–77.

Hyslop, D. (1999) 'State Dependence, Serial Correlation and Heterogeneity in Intertemporal Labour Force Participation of Married Women', *Econometrica*, 67(6): 1255–94.

Kalwij, A. (2001) 'Unemployment Durations and the Pattern of Duration Dependence over the Business cycle of British males; *Empirical Economics*, forthcoming.

Katz, L.F. and Meyer, B.D. (1990) 'The Impact of the Potential Duration of Unemployment Benefits on the Duration of Unemployment', *Journal of Public Economics*, 41(1): 45–72.

Kluve, J. (2006) 'The Effectiveness of European Active Labor Market Policy', IZA Discussion Papers no. 2018.

Koeniger, W., Leonardi, M. and Nunziata, L. (2007) 'Labour Market Institutions and Wage Inequality', *Industrial and Labor Relations Review*, 60(3): 340–56.

Kristensen, N. and Westergård-Nielsen, N. (2004) 'Does Low Job Satisfaction Lead to Job Mobility?', IZA Discussion Papers no. 1026.

Kugler, A.D. (1999) 'The Impact of Firing Costs on Turnover and Unemployment: Evidence from the Colombian Labour Market Reform', *International Tax and Public Finance*, 6(3): 389–410.

Kugler, A.D. and Pica, G. (2008) 'Effects of Employment Protection and Product Market Regulations on the Italian Labour Market', *Labour Economics*, 15(1): 78–95.

Lalive, R. (2008) 'How Do Extended Benefits Affect Unemployment Duration? A Regression Discontinuity Approach', *Journal of Econometrics*, 142(2): 785–806.

Lalive, R., van Ours, J.C. and Zweimüller, J. (2005) 'The Effect of Benefit Sanctions on the Duration of Unemployment', *Journal of the European Economic Association*, 3(6): 1386–417.

Lalive, R., van Ours, J.C. and Zweimueller, J. (2006) 'How Changes in Financial Incentives Affect the Duration of Unemployment', *Review of Economic Studies*, 73(4): 1009–38.

Lancaster, T. (1990) *The Econometric Analysis of Transition Data*, Cambridge: Econometric Society Monograph Series.

Layard, R., Nickell, S. and Jackman, R. (1991) *Unemployment: Macroeconomic Performance and the Labor Market*, New York: Oxford University Press.

Lazear, E. (1990) 'Job Security Provisions and Employment', *Quarterly Journal of Economics*, 105(3): 699–726.

Leonardi, M. (2003) 'Earnings Instability of Job Stayers and Job Changers', IZA Discussion Papers no. 946.

Lévy-Garboua, L., Montmarquette, C. and Simonnet, V. (2005) 'Job Satisfaction and Quits', *Labour Economics*, 14(2): 251–68.

Lillard, L.A. and Willis, R.J. (1978) 'Dynamic Aspects of Earnings Mobility', *Econometrica*, 46(5): 985–1012.

Meyer, B. (1990) 'Unemployment Insurance and Unemployment Spells', *Econometrica*, 58(4): 757–82.

Michaud, P.C. and Tatsiramos, K. (2005) 'Employment Dynamics of Married Women in Europe', IZA discussion paper 1706.

Moffitt, R. and Gottschalk, P. (1995) 'Trends in the Covariance Structure of Earnings in the US: 1969-1987', Brown University working paper 9.

Mortensen, D.T. (1978) 'Specific Capital and Labor Turnover', *Bell Journal of Economics*, 9(2): 572-86.

Stewart, Mark B. (1993) 'How Does the Benefit Effect Vary as Unemployment Spells Lengthen?' *Journal of Applied Econometrics*, John Wiley & Sons, Ltd., October-December, 8(4): 361-81.

Nickell, S. (1979) 'Estimating the Probability of Leaving Unemployment', *Econometrica*, 47(5): 1249-66.

OECD (1996) 'Employment Outlook', Paris: OECD.

Parent, D. (2002) 'Matching, Human Capital, and the Covariance Structure of Earnings', *Labour Economics*, 9(3): 375-404.

Prowse, V. (2005) 'State Dependence in a Multi-State Model of Employment Dynamics', IZA Discussion Papers no. 1623.

Raferzeder, T. and Winter-Ebmer, R. (2007) 'Who is on the Rise in Austria: Wage Mobility and Mobility Risk', *Journal of Economic Inequality*, 5(1): 39-51.

Ramos, X. (2003) 'The Covariance Structure of Earnings in Great Britain: 1991-1999', *Economica*, 70(278): 353-74.

Sciulli, D. (2006) 'Making the Italian Labor Market More Flexible: An Evaluation of the Treu Reform', paper presented at IFAU/IZA Conference Labor Market Policy Evaluation, Uppsala.

Shorrocks, A.F. (1978a) 'Income Inequality and Income Mobility', *Journal of Economic Theory*, 19(2): 376-93.

Shorrocks, A.F. (1978b) 'The Measurement of Mobility', *Econometrica*, 46(5): 1013-24.

Stewart, M.B. (2007) 'The Inter-Related Dynamics of Unemployment and Low Wage Employment', *Journal of Applied Econometrics*, 22(3): 511-31.

Stewart, M.B. and Swaffield, J.K. (1999) 'Low Pay Dynamics and Transition Probabilities', *Economica*, 66(261): 23-42.

Tatsiramos, K. (2009) 'Unemployment Insurance in Europe: Unemployment Duration and Subsequent Employment Stability', *Journal of the European Economic Association*, forthcoming.

van den Berg, G.J. and Ridder, G. (1998) 'An Empirical Equilibrium Search Model of the Labor Market', *Econometrica*, 66(5): 1183-222.

Wooldridge, J. (2005) 'Simple Solutions to the Initial Conditions Problem for Dynamic, Nonlinear Panel Data Models with Unobserved Heterogeneity', *Journal of Applied Econometrics*, 20(1): 9-54.

2
Job and Worker Flows at the Firm Level
Harald Dale-Olsen

2.1 Introduction

The research on job and worker flows focuses on and explicitly analyses the dynamic environment of the labour market, analysing the creation and destruction of firms and jobs and reallocation of resources, as well as the voluntary and involuntary movement of workers between firms and how this is related to firm and worker characteristics.

Although some job and worker flow studies existed before the late 1980s, it is fair to say that the establishment of job and worker flows as a genre can be traced back to the late 1980s and early 1990s (e.g. Davis and Haltiwanger, 1992; Dunne et al., 1989). During the early 1990s, the works of Davis, Haltiwanger and Shuh (culminating in Davis et al., 1996) sparked a huge interest, generating a plethora of studies. Of course, these studies varied in focus. Some studies had a more narrow view, being satisfied by establishing job and worker flows for their country and for a specific time-period. Others chose a comparative approach, comparing job and worker flows at country level, thus drawing inference on institutions. Several studies sought to test different theories.

The earliest stages of this literature as well as studies conducted during the 1990s were surveyed by Davis and Haltiwanger (1999a). In their survey, for example, Davis and Haltiwanger discussed the cyclical characteristics of job and worker flows; they described cross-industry and cross-country differences; they established the relationship between the level of flows and size; and they even covered transition economy flows.

Let me briefly recapitulate some of their findings. High rates of gross job flows are pervasive, but there appear to be small cross-country differences. Roughly one in 10 jobs is destroyed annually, while one in ten jobs is created. Cross-country differences in worker flows appear greater. The US ranks as the country with highest mobility (a quarterly worker flow of over 40 per cent), Denmark scores as a typical high-turnover country in Europe (annual worker flow of 56 per cent), while Norway and Netherlands are low-mobility countries (annually 43 per cent and 32 per cent, respectively). Job flows diminish with employer size and age. From US manufacturing data, it is clear that job creation falls during recessions, while job destruction rises, but these changes are not symmetrical. Job destruction increases dramatically, while the reduction in job creation is smaller. Whether this cyclical pattern extends to other industries and other countries is not yet determined.

During the 2000s, with the tremendous changes in computer technology (storage capacity and speed) and data availability (for example, increased prevalence of linked employer–employee data sets – LEEDs), a huge number of studies have been conducted within the literature on job and worker flows and on labour mobility in general. This therefore merits a new survey. The new research studies extend many of the themes presented in Davis and Haltiwanger (1999a). We have seen increased emphasis on micro-based studies of institutional differences and changes. For many Eastern European countries the transition phase has ended, thus allowing more complete analyses of this process. The literature on worker flows and compensation issues, in particular, has evolved following the increased prevalence of LEEDs. In this survey I present the findings from a limited number of studies only, but I still hope to convey the main thoughts from the literature on job and worker flows, primarily covering studies conducted during the period 1999–2006.

After this introduction, the structure of the survey is as follows. Section 2.2 defines the job and worker flow measures. Aggregated cross-country differences in job and worker flows are described in Section 2.3. In Section 2.4 I discuss the relationship between worker flows and worker and firm characteristics. Section 2.5 covers the relationship between flows and business cycles, trends and productivity growth. Institutional aspects of job and worker flows are discussed in Section 2.6. Section 2.7 focuses on productivity, technology, organisational structure and flows. Transition economies are the focus of Section 2.8. Section 2.9 briefly points out some future research topics, and concludes.

2.2 Job and worker flow measures and data issues

2.2.1 Job and worker flow measures

Davis and Haltiwanger (1992, 1998, 1999a), Davis et al. (1996) and Burgess, Lane and Stevens (2000b, 2001) describe what have become the most common definitions of job and worker flows. Unfortunately there still exists some heterogeneity regarding these definitions.

The 'standard' definitions used in this survey are as follows. For each employer, *net job flow* ($JF = n_t - n_{t-1}$) is defined as employment growth during one year. If it is positive, we have *gross job creation* ($JC = |n_t - n_{t-1}|$ when $JF \geq 0$, otherwise $JC = 0$); if it is negative there is gross job destruction ($JD = |n_t - n_{t-1}|$ when $JF < 0$, otherwise $JD = 0$). *Gross job flow* ($AJF = |n_t - n_{t-1}|$) is the absolute value of net job flow. When aggregating over more than one establishment, AJF represents gross job reallocation, as both job creation and job destruction enter positively. *Excess job reallocation* is defined as the total gross job reallocation in an economy minus the absolute value of the net growth ($EJF = AJF - |JF|$ on the economy level), that is, the job reallocation over and above what is needed to accommodate the net growth.

Worker flow ($WF = h + s$) is defined as the sum of hires (h) and separations (s) during the year. *Churning flow* ($CF = WF - AJF = 2h$ if $JF < 0$, $CF = WF - AJF = 2s$ if $JF \geq 0$) is defined as the part of the worker flow that is not necessary to accommodate the job flow. Churning flow is thus the part of worker flow that would remain even in a stationary environment where each firm kept its stock of workers constant. In later studies the term 'accessions' is often used instead of 'hires'. Some authors define excess worker turnover as half the churning rate. The churning flow is sometimes referred to in later studies as excess worker reallocation. For example, Haltiwanger and Vodopivec (2003) define *excess accession* and *excess separations* as EXACC=h−|max(h−s,0)| (=s if JF≥0, otherwise EXACC=h) and EXSEP=s−|min(h−s,0)| (=h if JF<0, otherwise EXSEP=s), respectively.

Many studies do not differentiate between separations (which can be the voluntary or involuntary ending of an employment relationship) and quits (which are the voluntary ending of an employment relationship). Several studies focus on involuntary job separations, that is, displacements and lay-offs.

Each of these terms (net job flow, gross job creation and destruction, gross job reallocation, excess job reallocation, worker flow, churning flow, excess accession and excess separation) is made into rates by dividing by the average stock of workers during the year. When comparing job and worker flows between geographical regions (counties or municipalities) or between industries, one usually weights the flows by the employment share.

Studies based on labour force survey data calculate transition probabilities as the number of transitions divided on the level of employment at time t (and not the average level of employment from t to t+1 as is common in the literature on worker flows). Analysed at the level of the individual, labour turnover measures are often duration of job spell, seniority, or dummies for separation, quit, displacement or lay-off.

Finally, figures for job and worker flows depend on the sampling unit (firm vs. establishment), size thresholds for the unit population (for example, only firms with a minimum of 10 employees), sampling frequency (monthly, quarterly or annually) and identification procedures (for instance, if 50 per cent of the workforce in two units is identical, the units are the same). This is discussed, for instance, in Davis and Haltiwanger (1998, 1999a).

2.2.2 Data issues

The contributions in the literature on job and worker flows surveyed in this article are based on a wide range of data sources, from administrative registers comprising the complete population (universe) to small sample surveys of firms or establishments. I cannot provide a detailed discussion of each of these data sources. It is, however, important to recognise that data sources and data design matter for the results. Several studies in the last decade have discussed the pros and cons of register and survey data (for example, Abowd and Kramarz, 1999; Abowd et al., 2006b; Røed and Raaum, 2003). Administrative registers are designed for administrative purposes, which are seldom fully aligned with the researchers' interests. One typically needs to link several registers to create data sets comprising the desired (if possible) information. This creates the possibility of selection problems, validity and measurement problems. See, for example, the discussion on how to measure mergers and acquisitions, firm entry and exit in Benedetto et al. (2007).

Typically the administrative registers comprise the complete population (the universe) of the units, and the added costs to access the complete population instead of a sample are small. In some countries, huge surveys are conducted (e.g. the Portuguese Quadros de Pessoal and US JOLTS), providing similar information to that provided by these linked administrative registers. Surveys have the benefits of being designed to target specific questions; thus validity and measurement problems seldom occur. However, the units in a survey may change, causing similar problems to those for registers (see Benedetto et al., 2007). Surveys usually have more problems than administrative registers with non-respondents, but one should note that this problem actually exists there as well (e.g. employers stop reporting hiring or quits of employees). In some cases, respondents are asked about retrospective information (seen in, for example, labour force surveys), and this information is more likely to be affected by respondents' selective memory than similar information from administrative registers. Huge surveys and comprehensive register data make it possible to target small groups and minorities. Huge linked employer–employee data sets allow individual characteristics to be disentangled from firm/establishment characteristics. This opens up unique possibilities for analysing mobility issues (see Abowd et al., 2006b).

Finally, variation in the registers makes such data sources potentially very valuable. Røed and Raaum (2003) point out three sources of variation in register data that may be exploited to disentangle causal effects from unobserved characteristics of the individuals or units in their operating environment. Administrative registers have their own rules that may be considered exogenous from the individuals' decisions, they contain elements of random experiments, and these practices or rules may change.

2.3 Job and worker flows – cross-country differences

Cross-country comparisons of aggregate job and worker flow are not this article's main goals, since I concur with the objection of Davis and Haltiwanger regarding cross-country comparisons of aggregate job flows (Davis and Haltiwanger, 1999a: 2754). It is hard to draw strong policy conclusions from just comparing country figures, particularly since these represent very different economies, from different time periods and different institutional settings, and are derived from different kinds of data. The same is, of necessity, true for worker flows. Still, such numbers provide an introduction to job and worker flows. Tables 2.1 and 2.2 present the country average job and worker flows, respectively, taken from a number of studies. All figures are based on averages from series including, at least, 1997 or a more recent year. The tables show the large number of restrictions on data (e.g. size thresholds, population, frequency of sampling) that may affect the levels of flows.

On the one hand, the tables clearly indicate the need for harmonised cross-country databases (Gómez-Salvador et al. (2004) and Haltiwanger et al. (2006) are based on harmonised data). Comparing figures based on harmonised data with those arising from non-harmonised data is difficult. The levels of the job flows presented by Gómez-Salvador et al. are clearly low due to strict size thresholds in

Table 2.1 Cross-country job flow differences

Region	Year	Pop.	Freq.	Unit	JC	JD	JRR	Net	Source
Austria	1978–98	T[a]	Y	E	8.9	8.9	17.9	0.0	Stiglbauer et al. (2003)
Austria	1995–2000	T[b]	Y	F	4.6	3.4	7.9	1.2	Gómez-Salvador et al. (2004)
Argentina	1991–2001	M[c]	Q	F	5.3	9.4	14.6	-4.1	Sanchez and Butler (2004)
Belgium	1992–2000	T[b]	Y	F	5.2	3.8	9.0	1.3	Gómez-Salvador et al. (2004)
Brazil	1991–2000	P≥5	Y	F	16.0	14.9	30.9	1.1	Ribeiro et al. (2004)
Chile	1991–9	M	Y	E			23.2		Bergoeing et al. (2003)
Colombia	1993–9	M	Y	E			22.5		Medina et al. (2003)
Denmark	1996–2001	T[b]	Y	E	6.2	3.3	9.5	2.8	Gómez-Salvador et al. (2004)
Estonia	1996–2000	T	Y	F	12.4	12.3	24.7[d]	0.1[d]	Masso et al. (2006)
Finland	1997–2000	T[b]	Y	F	7.0	3.0	9.9	4.0	Gómez-Salvador et al. (2004)
France	1993–2000	T[b]	Y	F	5.1	3.2	8.3	1.8	Gómez-Salvador et al. (2004)
Germany	1994–2000	T[b]	Y	F	4.4	3.7	8.1	0.7	Gómez-Salvador et al. (2004)
Ireland	1994–2000	T[b]	Y	F	8.5	3.1	11.5	5.4	Gómez-Salvador et al. (2004)
Italy	1992–2000	T[b]	Y	F	8.2	4.1	12.3	4.1	Gómez-Salvador et al. (2004)
Latvia	1997–2001	T	Y	F	17.5	10.8	28.3[d]	6.7[d]	Masso et al. (2006)
Lithuania	1996–2000	T	Y	F	13.0	16.1	29.1[d]	-3.1[d]	Masso et al. (2006)
Mexico	1994–2000	M	Y	E			27.9		Kaplan et al. (2003)
Netherlands	1994–2000	T[b]	Y	E[c]	6.5	4.3	10.8	2.2	Gómez-Salvador et al. (2004)
Norway	1989–2004	T[e]	Y	F	12.5	11.5	24.0	1.1	This paper
Poland	1997–2004	P≥50	Y	F	10.6	12.8	23.4	-2.2	Rogowski and Socha (2008)
Portugal	1995–2000	T[b]	Y	F	4.9	3.5	8.4	1.5	Gómez-Salvador et al. (2004)
Russia	1991–9	M[f]	Y	F[g]	2.4	8.6	12.7	-8.0	Brown and Earle (2002)
Spain	1994–2000	T[b]	Y	F	8.6	3.6	11.7	4.5	Gómez-Salvador et al. (2004)
Sweden	1986–2002	T	Y	E	10.4	10.2	20.6	0.2	Gartell et al. (2007)

Continued

Table 2.1 Continued

Region	Year	Pop.	Freq.	Unit	JC	JD	JRR	Net	Source
Sweden	1998–2001	T[b]	Y	F	8.1	3.6	11.7	4.5	Gómez-Salvador et al. (2004)
Ukraine	1999–2000	T[b]	Y	F	4.3[d]	9.5[d]	13.8[d]	−5.2[d]	Konings et al. (2003)
UK	1992–2000	T[b]	Y	F	6.6	4.4	11.0	2.3	Gómez-Salvador et al. (2004)
US	2000–5	T	M	E[f]	1.5[h]	1.5[h]	3.0[h,d]	0[h,d]	Davis et al. (2006a)
US	1990–2005	P	Q	E[f]	7.9	7.6	15.5[d]	15.2[d]	Davis et al. (2006a)
OECD	1990s	T[i]	Y	F[i]	12.7	12.7	25.4	0.0	Haltiwanger et al. (2006)
LAC	1990s	T[i]	Y	F[i]	14.8	14.0	28.8	0.8	Haltiwanger et al. (2006)
Transition	1990s	T[i]	Y	F[i]	17.4	12.8	30.3	4.6	Haltiwanger et al. (2006)

Note: Pop.: T denotes total economy, P denotes private sector, and M denotes manufacturing. Number after letter code for population denotes size threshold. Freq.: Y, Q and M denote yearly, quarterly and monthly sampling frequency, respectively. Unit: E denotes establishment, ET denotes both firm and establishment, while F denotes firm. JC denotes gross job creation, JD denotes gross job destruction, and JRR denotes gross job reallocation, while NET denotes net job growth. [a] denotes excl. public sector, health, transport and missing sectoral label. [b] denotes the Amadeus firm database incorporating size thresholds (workforce, value of total assets or revenues). [c] denotes continuing units only. [d] denotes own calculation on published results. [e] denotes for Norway that establishments 1989–94 are defined by employer's PIN code, which until 1994 could, as an exception, be linked to a firm. [f] denotes that data incl. all manuf. enterprises with 100+ employees and those with fewer than 100 employees that are at least 25 per cent owned by other legal entities. [g] denotes large and middle-sized firms. [h] denotes that the figures are estimates. [i] denotes different size thresholds. [j] denotes that establishment sometimes is unit. The figures of Bergoeing et al. (2003) and Kaplan et al. (2003) are reported in Micco and Pagés (2004).

Table 2.2 Cross-country worker flow differences

Region	Year	Pop.	Freq.	Unit	H	S	WF	CF	Source
Finland	1988–97	P	Y	E[a]	27.1[b]	28.2[b]	55.2[b]	23.5[b]	Ilmakunnas and Maliranta (2003)
Norway	1989–2004	T	Y	E[a]	24.1	25.5	49.6	27.4	Dale-Olsen (2006d)
Portugal	1986–2000	M	Y	F	18.8	20.3	39.2	16.3	Martins (2008)
Russia	1990–9	M[c]	Y	F[d]	20.4[e]	26.9[e]	47.3[e]	35.8[e]	Brown and Earle (2003a)
Slovenia	1997–9	P	Y	E			32.0	12.3	Haltiwanger and Vodopivec (2003)
Sweden	1986–2002	T	Y	E	23.5	23.3	46.9	26.2	Gartell et al. (2007)
US	2000–5	T[f]	M	E	3.2[e]	3.1[e]			Davis et al. (2006a)

Note: Pop.: T denotes total economy, P denotes private sector, M denotes manufacturing. Freq.: Y, Q and M denote yearly, quarterly and monthly sampling frequency, respectively. Unit: E denotes establishment, while F denotes firm. H denotes hires, S denotes separations, WF denotes worker flow and CF denotes churning flow. [a] denotes for Norway that establishments 1989–94 are defined by employer's PIN code in the register of employer and employees, and that until 1994 this number could, as an exception, be linked to a firm. For Finland [a] denotes that the employer number could, as an exception, be linked to a firm. [b] denotes own calculation on published results. [c] denotes survey data. [d] denotes large and middle-sized firms. [e] denotes that the figures are estimates. [f] denotes that only continuing establishments are included.

the Amadeus database, but for cross-country comparisons the quality may nonetheless be better. Austria, Germany and France appear as countries with low job reallocation (around 8 per cent), while the Nordic countries, Netherlands and Spain experience high job reallocation (around 10–11 per cent). If the firm size distribution differs between countries, this ranking of countries is less reliable.

On the other hand, it is curious to note that, given that these job flow figures represent very different economies as well as reflecting the huge heterogeneity regarding data issues, the job flow rates are quite similar. Consider the Norwegian job flow figures and Gartell et al.'s figures for Sweden. These flows are calculated on very similar comprehensive data (equal population, unit and size threshold), and it is remarkable how similar the flows are. The levels of yearly gross job creation and destruction rates are slightly above 10 per cent, and the levels of gross job reallocation rates are around 20–5 per cent. These figures are similar to those observed by Haltiwanger et al. (2006) as the average flow figures for the OECD countries.

2.4 Worker flows – firm and worker characteristics

The main focus in this section is on worker flows, how they vary depending on firm and workforce characteristics, the relationship between these flows and pay. This complements Davis and Haltiwanger (1999a), who surveyed the job flows literature extensively.

2.4.1 Firm size and age, and workforce demographics

Davis and Haltiwanger (1999a) described gross job flows as pervasive. Burgess et al. (2000b) find, similarly, from Maryland UI data that churning flows are high, pervasive and highly persistent within establishment (employer). In France, Abowd et al. (1999) also show that hiring and separations occur simultaneously, even within skill groups.

Worker flows (hiring, separation, churning) decline (as job flows) with firm age, they vary across size groups and industries, and they depend on workforce composition, such as gender, age and educational qualifications. Hires and separations differ between employers, varying with employer size, average wage and industry (Burgess et al., 2001: 1). In Bauer et al. (2007) they appear to diminish with size using data from small German establishments. The churning flow declines with the age of establishments and it varies across industries (Burgess et al., 2000b). The evidence on the relationship between size and churning is mixed. Several studies report a declining churning rate with size (Burgess et al., 2000b; Hohti, 2000; Persson, 1999), but the opposite is also found. For example, Ilmakunnas and Maliranta (2005) observe that churning increases with size.

The relationship between churning flows and job flows is complex (Burgess et al., 2000b), and the evidence of within-firm job reallocation is mixed, while Bauer and Bender (2004), from German establishment data, reveal that internal worker flows explain only a small fraction of overall worker flows. In France, two-thirds of all hires and more than 50 per cent of the separations are on short-time contracts (Abowd et al., 1999).

Burgess et al. (2000a) establish that the worker flows vary with firm life cycle. They divide the firm population into four life-cycle phases: i) new firms exiting within 12 quarters, ii) continuing firms established for less than 12 quarters, iii) old firms where exiting will occur within the next 12 quarters, and iv) all remaining firms. Gross worker flow and churning flow decline from phase i) to iv), but the relative importance of the flow within each phase shows the opposite pattern.

What do we know of workforce composition and worker flows? As expected, worker and churning flows diminish with worker age (e.g., Haltiwanger and Vodopivec, 2003).

Several studies focus on worker flow differences between groups of workers having different skill levels or different educational qualification (level or kind). The evidence is rather mixed. Bauer and Bender (2004) observe only small churning flow differences between skilled and unskilled workers in Germany, while professionals and engineers experience slightly lower churning. Similarly, Abowd et al. (2006b) find in France that general educated workers separate more often than workers with a technical degree. In Norway, the hiring rate and the separation rate of highly educated workers in both manufacturing and financial sectors appear to be higher than those of lowly educated workers (Salvanes and Førre, 2003).

The evidence on gender worker flow differences is mixed. Haltiwanger and Vodopivec (2003) observe higher flows for men than for women in Slovenia. On Norwegian data, Barth and Dale-Olsen (2000) observe the contrary: gross worker and churning flows are higher for women than for men. Both men's and women's churning drops as the proportion of men in a workplace increases.

2.4.2 Worker flows and compensation

Several studies focus on the relationship between compensation and worker turnover. The aim is to understand how the average level of compensation affects turnover, as well as how the structure of compensation affects turnover. Firm seniority profiles, for example, may affect worker turnover. Most studies do not attempt to identify a *causal* impact of compensation on worker turnover, but report correlations.

There is a whole range of studies showing that higher firm wages in Western European countries imply lower worker turnover. Burgess et al. (2001) find a negative correlation between wages and churning. Higher wages in transition Slovenia reduce worker turnover as well (Haltiwanger and Vodopivec, 2003). More capital-intensive establishments also experience lower turnover.

Several studies find that relative wage premiums, starting wages and seniority profiles are important for separations. These usually observe a negative correlation between the level of wages, wage premiums, or wage growth and worker turnover. Barth and Dale-Olsen (1999) identify a turnover-reducing impact not only from an establishment's wage premium, but also from the seniority profile. Establishments paying a steeper seniority profile achieve lower turnover. These results are measured relative to the expected outside wage. Bingley and Westergaard-Nielsen observe that people tend to move if they can get a higher wage level in other firms, but workers on the 'fast track' are less likely to move than other employees (Bingley and Westergaard-Nielsen, 2006: 325). In addition, one observes a negative correlation between the individual starting-wage effect and separations, that is, good workers achieve longer tenures (Abowd et al., 2006b: F262). In a comparative study on data from seven countries, Lazear and Shaw (2009) observe that the negative relation between wages and separations is strong in the open economies, but in Sweden this relationship is weak and goes in the opposite direction.

The worker turnover of different groups of workers, for example different occupations or genders, may respond differently to wages. Christensen et al. (2005) find that skilled workers receive more job offers per job spell than unskilled workers, and, similarly, that search effort is highly sensitive to the expected return for skilled workers, but is less responsive for unskilled workers.

Based on Norwegian data, Barth and Dale-Olsen (2009) argue, when they find that women's turnover is less sensitive to wages than that of men, that this is evidence in line with what is predicted by the theory of monopsonistic discrimination. That women's turnover is less sensitive to wages than that of men is also found by Bingley and Westergaard-Nielsen (2006) on Danish firm data. This is in contrast to the received view (see Manning (2003: 207)).

The findings above present what appears as a homogeneous view of firms' pay policies. One should be aware that this impression is wrong. Abowd et al. (2006a, b) reveal what they call a daunting heterogeneity. In spite of this heterogeneity, since they observe that firms hire workers at all ages and more separations occur at the bottom of the age distribution, they argue that internal labour markets do not exist (Abowd et al., 2006b).

Furthermore, what should matter to workers is total compensation, where wages may be only one part (albeit in most cases, clearly the most important). Often a bundle of goods or a bundle of perks is offered by the employer in addition to wages. Similarly, when workers receive job offers, their preferences for different characteristics of the job matter as well. The impact of such non-wage characteristics on worker turnover has been analysed in several studies, for example Van Ommeren et al. (2000), which analyses commuting, Dale-Olsen (2006b), which studies injuries, and Dale-Olsen (2006c), which focuses on fringe benefits. These studies reveal strong worker preferences for the non-wage characteristics.

As pointed out above, most studies do not attempt to identify the causal impact of compensation on worker turnover. Studies that deal specifically with the causality problems are, for example, Abowd et al. (2006a, 2006b), Martins (2008) and the literature on adjustment costs surveyed in Section 2.4. Worker turnover and mobility may, of course, also affect compensation, that is, there is also a causal impact that goes in the opposite direction. The rich literature analysing the impact of turnover and mobility on pay, status and ranking will not be surveyed in this article.

While there are a multitude of studies focusing on how compensation or wages affect workers' probability of leaving a firm, the hiring policies of firms are less scrutinised. This should be important for several reasons. First, recent studies of the cyclical properties of job and worker flows (see next section) indicate that firms' hiring behaviour is very important for the observed cyclicality. Second, assumptions regarding firm hiring behaviour are important 'building blocks' in several theoretical frameworks. A related literature exists on how informal networks affect workers' job opportunities, wages and the subsequent job spell (Loury, 2006). Few works, however, have, for example, examined the relationship between recruiting processes and establishment size. Manning (2003: 284–92) finds no positive relationship between word-of-mouth recruiting and size, and interprets this as supportive of the random matching assumption (Burdett and Vishwanath, 1988). Dale-Olsen (2006a) studies the relationship between an estimated posting intensity and size and finds mixed results, but generally the notion of random matching is rejected. Differences in workers' attitude towards waiting – impatience – will also affect their separation and hiring probabilities. For example, DellaVigna and Paserman (2005) observe a negative correlation between search effort and measures of impatience.

2.5 Business cycle effects, shocks and trends

2.5.1 Business cycles

The literature focusing on how job and worker flows vary over the business cycle basically describes how job and/or worker flows for different countries change across the cycle for different countries, and sometimes differentiate between different groups of workers.

The counter-cyclical pattern of job destruction in the US manufacturing sector is fairly well established, while Davis et al. (2006a) present evidence that this is also seen, albeit more weakly, in the non-manufacturing sectors. Job creation moves more acyclically, and is remarkably high at all times. Davis et al. point out that the recovery of the US economy after the economic downturns of 1990–1 and 2000–1 was remarkably different. While job destruction peaks at the height of both recessions, the pace of job destruction is slow to decline after the first recession. After the last recession job destruction drops dramatically. In Europe the picture is slightly different. Messina and Vallanti (2007) find acyclical job reallocation in Europe, with the exception of UK and Spain, where the correlations turned negative. On Swedish quarterly data, Heyman and Arai (2004) observe acyclical job reallocation for permanent jobs in the private sector or non-manufacturing industries. In the manufacturing sector, job reallocation turns counter-cyclical.

The churning flow and gross worker flow are generally found to be pro-cyclical (for example, Burgess et al., 2000b). However, there are clear differences between the cyclical responses of the worker flows. On CPS data 1994–2003, Fallick and Fleischman (2004) identify strongly pro-cyclical job-to-job mobility. On JOLTS data, Faberman observes that 'Hires and quits are clearly pro-cyclical, though the latter are more related to unemployment than job growth. Layoffs, on the other hand, are counter-cyclical, but only with respect to job growth ...' (Faberman, 2005: 16). Similarly, Davis et al. (2006a) observe that the volatility of separations in the US is low across the cycle, since during recessions the number of quits falls while the number of lay-offs increases. Ascensions move markedly pro-cyclically. This is also observed by Bachman (2006) on German data and by Nagypál (2008) on CPS data. Nagypál points out that the increased flows into unemployment are caused by a decline in job-to-job mobility, and not a burst in separations. Finally, Davis et al. (2006b) observe that one-third of all hires occur without a vacancy posting. At the same time, not all vacant positions generate hires. They find the vacancy yield to be counter-cyclical and nonlinearly increasing in employment growth.

2.5.2 Shocks, propagation and business cycles

Davis and Haltiwanger (1999b) introduced the notion of two kinds of shocks (allocation shocks and aggregate shocks) in their study on quarterly job flow data. The former shocks disturb the current allocation of resources or input mix among firms or establishments. If the input mix was non-optimal, the shock makes the gap between realised and optimum even bigger. Davis and Haltiwanger claim that it is these shocks that drive the business cycles. Although they affect the total economy, aggregate shocks are less important for business cycles. Furthermore, both aggregate and allocation shocks affect incumbents' knowledge about technology and capital utilisation, and participate in making this knowledge obsolete (Davis et al., 1996; Blanchard and Kremer, 1997). The shocks may, of course, contribute to enforcing and propagating cyclical variations (den Haan et al., 2000). Often the shocks are lumpy, implying large changes (Cooper et al., 1999), and may follow from waves of innovations (Stein, 1997). On quarterly manufacturing data, Davis and Haltiwanger (2001) find that oil price and monetary shocks affect job creation and destruction differently, in that the short-run responses of job destruction are much more volatile. The former shocks are clearly more important than the latter, since these oil price shocks are twice as important as monetary shocks. Such oil price shocks generate reallocation of resources primarily expressed by excess reallocation. Capital-intensive production and producers of durable goods are hit particularly hard by oil price hikes, while the latter group is also hit hard by monetary shocks.

Several studies identify significant micro-level non-convex and convex costs associated with capital (Carlsson and Laséen, 2005; Cooper and Haltiwanger, 2006; Nielsen and Schiantarelli, 2003), convex and non-convex workforce level adjustment costs (Cooper et al., 2007; Ejarque and Portugal, 2007; Hamermesh, 1989, 1995; Nilsen et al., 2007) as well as convex (Dale-Olsen, 2006a) and non-convex worker turnover costs (Abowd and Kramarz, 2003; Hamermesh, 1995). Bingley and Westergaard-Nielsen (2004) relate hires and quits to profits. Ejarque and Portugal (2007) also identify important aggregate effects of the non-convex adjustment costs. A combination of fixed and linear adjustment costs works best in Cooper et al. (2007). In France, changing of workforce levels is achieved primarily through reduced hiring (entry) (Abowd et al., 1999). Finally, one should be aware of Caballero and Engel (2004) claiming that previous micro data studies underestimate the period needed for adjustment.

Therefore no established view exists about how long it takes for an economy to adjust to shocks, or about the aggregate costs of adjustments and the correct level of reallocation. This will probably vary between countries and over time within a country. Furthermore, the interpretation of the role of business cycles for flows is also mixed.

Cheaper alternative costs provide one motivation for why reallocation and liquidation should be beneficial consequences of recessions (Caballero and

Hammour, 1994, 1996), while Ramey and Watson (1997) point out the possible inefficiencies of the surge in job destructions during recessions. In contrast, Caballero and Hammour (2005) claim that a recession reduces restructuring and reallocation, and this is socially costly. The harmful effects of recessions are also advocated by Barlevy, who argues that during recessions the newly created jobs are low-paying and short-lived, thus creating an additional sullying effect (Barlevy, 2002) and that frictions in the credit market cause the survival of the least productive firms during recessions (Barlevy, 2003). Recessions thus cause increased reallocation, but of the wrong kind.

2.5.3 Trends in job and worker flows

There is not much evidence on the long-term trends in job and worker flows. In the US one observes a long-term fall in the overall magnitude of job flows (Davis et al., 2006b, 2007). In Norwegian data from 1989 to 2005, Dale-Olsen (2006d) identifies a positive trend for both worker flows and churning flows. The churning rate increases by 1 percentage point each year. This study does not take into account demographic changes.

Trend development is, however, an issue in literature on job stability discussing whether job stability is changing over time. This literature is relevant for worker flows. Reduced stability implies that it is more likely that workers quit or are fired, thus surfacing as increased worker flows. Several recent studies indicate reduced stability.

2.6 Institutional differences and the impact on flows

To study the impact of institutions on job and labour flows empirically, one must either conduct comparisons over time (for example, before and after the change of an institution) or conduct international comparisons. Since institutions do not change frequently, international comparisons are often the only way to study the impact of certain institutions.

The literature referred to in this section is related to studies of typical transition countries. Introduction of, for example, less strict employment protection legislation is one of the many deregulations the former planned economies introduced when establishing market economies. Flows in the transition countries in general are discussed in a later section of the article.

2.6.1 Employment protection legislation

The impact of employment protection legislation (EPL) on job and worker flows has been studied based on changes in EPL within a country and on cross-country comparisons of the relationship between the national flows and EPL. When it comes to worker flows, the literature presents an unambiguous picture of EPL. Stronger EPL is associated with reduced labour turnover (e.g., Kugler and Pica, 2008; OECD, 1999).

Earlier studies have problems identifying a strong impact of EPL on job reallocation (Bertola and Rogerson 1997; Boeri, 1999; OECD, 1999), but the consensus today is that stronger EPL causes reduced job reallocation.

The reason is two-fold. First, the earlier studies involved cross-country comparisons of the relationship between EPL and job reallocation, based on very heterogeneous data. Data comprised different units of observations, different time periods, different kinds of sources. It appears that, once cross-country data sources are improved and harmonised, analyses of the impact of EPL on job and worker flows show that stricter EPL reduces not only the worker flows but, more importantly, also the job flows.

Using data from 20 OECD countries for the period 1975–97, Nunziata (2003) finds that stricter employment protection regulations and looser working time arrangements are correlated with lower employment growth during expansions. Furthermore, evidence suggests that cyclical employment is primarily affected by permanent employment regulations.

Using harmonised 'Amadeus' data, Gómez-Salvador et al. (2004) examine job flows in the 1990s for 13 European countries. Applying regression techniques, they control for firm and sectoral effects, and find that employment protection legislation reduces job flows. Lower job flows are also a characteristic of countries with a more coordinated wage setting. In a follow-up study – also on 'Amadeus' data, but from 14 European countries for 1992–2001 – Messina and Valanti (2007), using regression techniques, reveal that employment protection legislation induces a positive co-movement of job turnover with the business cycle. This is mainly driven by job destruction. Firing restrictions reduce the volatility of job destruction during the cycle, having a milder effect on job creation.

Both Micco and Pagés (2004) and Haltiwanger et al. (2006) implement a difference-in-difference approach. Micco and Pagés analyse metadata from 18 different countries, of which 11 countries are to be considered developed, while Haltiwanger et al. utilise a new harmonised database incorporating job flow information from 16 industrial and emerging countries. The primary difference between Haltiwanger et al. (2006) and Micco and Pagés (2004) is that the former take into account sector-specific differences in the firm size distribution, and also study the impact of stringency of business regulations and the different degrees of enforcements of regulations.

Micco and Pagés find that stricter job security regulations slow down job reallocation, and that these effects are larger in sectors with higher demand for adjustment. They point out that EPL will thus have a different impact on job reallocation in different countries because countries' industry composition differs and different industries have different demand for flexibility. Once one controls for job security regulation, entry and exit regulations do not affect gross job flows significantly. Haltiwanger et al.'s analysis supports this, and they conclude that stringent hiring and firing costs reduce job turnover, especially in industries that demand flexibility. When controlling for enforcement, they find that 'more intrinsically volatile industries and size classically presents lower levels of gross job turnover, relatively to the less volatile industries, in countries with more stringent hiring and firing regulations' (Haltiwanger et al., 2006: 15). Regulations hit medium-sized and large firms more severely than small firms. Haltiwanger et al. explain this by small firms' better ability to circumvent regulations and by their being exempted from many regulations.

Finally, while later studies present convincing evidence of the negative impact of EPL on job flows, there are two studies using individual microdata in a difference-in-difference approach which do not support this notion. Neither Bauer et al. (2007) nor Martins (2009) finds any significant impact of changed dismissal protection on worker flows. Bauer et al.'s explanation for this result is that dismissal taxes are effectively smaller than legislation makes them appear, and that employment buffers are effectively unconstrained.

2.6.2 Trade liberalisation and product market competition

The literature on job and labour flows clearly indicates that trade liberalisation and product market competition increase job reallocation and favour creative destruction. In Europe this is seen in the transition countries. Increased import competition and a more competitive market structure in Poland increase job reallocation (Warzynski, 2003). Konings et al. (2003) find, in Ukraine, that stronger product market competition for firms engaged in world or EU trade reduces job reallocation. The exception is sectors with strong export links to the EU, which experience weak competition from the EU, where excess job reallocation is higher.

Although not a typical job flow study, Bertrand and Kramarz (2002) show that barriers to entry (regulations) in French trade industries increased concentration, reduced job creation and reduced employment growth.

From manufacturing and financial sector data from Norway and contingent on a wide range of controls, Salvanes and Førre (2003) establish a mixed impact of trade on gross job flows, since it depends on workforce educational attainment. For low or medium-educated workers, increased import penetration leaves job creation unaffected while job destruction increases. Increased export penetration affects job destruction positively. The contrary is found for highly educated workers.

The evidence of the positive impact of trade liberalisation and product market competition on job reallocation is not restricted to Europe only. In Japan, job creation and destruction associated with plant start-ups and closures were significantly sensitive to import competition (Tomiura, 2004). Import price fluctuation affected job creation in plants that altered their product mix during the Bubble period, 1988–90. However, job flows at plants that remained within the same industry were not affected.

In Latin America in general (Haltiwanger et al., 2004), Argentine (Sánchez and Butler, 2004) and Brazil (Ribeiro et al., 2004), trade liberalisation in the form of reduced tariffs increases job reallocation. In Brazil during 1991–2000, trade liberalisation and greater openness seem to have reduced the number of jobs though increased job destruction, with no effect on job creation. Neither on gross job reallocation nor on excess job reallocation are the impacts of import penetration significant.

2.6.3 Other legislations and institutions

Several studies observe increased employment when the exchange rate is lowered (Gourinchas, 1999; Ribeiro et al., 2004), that is, depreciations increase job creation and reduce job destruction. In Latin America depreciations are found to decrease job reallocation (Haltiwanger et al., 2004). On US data from 1973 to 1993, Klein et al. (2003) split the impact of the real exchange rate into a cyclical component and a trend component. They find that trend real exchange rates significantly affect job reallocation, but not net employment. On the other hand, cyclical real exchange rates affect net employment, but only through job destruction.

Only a few studies have empirically looked at how job and worker flows are affected by the level of centralisation in the wage-bargaining system (Gómez-Salvador et al., 2004; Salvanes, 1997; Serrano and Malo, 2002). A priori, the relationship between the level of centralisation in the wage-bargaining system and flows is ambiguous. Increased centralisation implies increased wage-compression and thus less room for wages to sort workers to more productive establishments. This reduces reallocation. On the other hand, increased centralisation in the wage-bargaining regime may increase the incentives for job creation, since the wage-compression increases the profits of the most productive firms. The empirical studies indicate that a more centralised wage-bargaining regime reduces gross job flows. In contrast, the related study of Haltiwanger and Vodopivec (2003) finds that higher wage-compression is associated with higher gross job flows and lower excess worker flows, that is, wage-compression leads to greater employment volatility. Wage-compression may also lead to less excess turnover of low-quality workers. They argue that 'wage compression creates excessive instability of jobs and thus both imposes additional dislocation costs and reduces firms' ability to achieve quality firm-worker matches' (Haltiwanger and Vodopivec, 2003: 255).

Minimum-wage legislation may theoretically improve or diminish social welfare. At the moment, it is also difficult to empirically judge whether or not minimum-wage legislation is beneficial (for example, see the controversy over minimum-wage legislation in New Jersey and Pennsylvania). The study of Portugal and Cardoso (2006), however, is particularly interesting and relevant for this survey due to its flow approach. In Portugal, a mandatory minimum wage was introduced in 1974 for workers 20 years or older. During 1987 and 1988 changes in the legislation caused significant wage increases for teenagers. The minimum wage legislation for teenagers reduced teenage hires but separations as well. Furthermore, Portugal and Cardoso find that the changes in the legislation made teenagers more likely than older workers to keep their jobs.

Gómez-Salvador et al. (2004) identify a negative impact of higher levels of unemployment benefits on job flows. A negative impact of unemployment benefits on job quits is also found in Light and Omori (2004) on NLSY data; thus they argue that, as these benefits rise, workers lose incentives to 'pre-empt' impending lay-offs by changing jobs.

Martins et al. (2006) study the impact of an increase in the Portuguese legal retirement age in 1993 using linked employer–employee data and a propensity score matching approach. They find that increasing the retirement age decreased job creation, increased job destruction and job reallocation, while both hires and separation diminished.

2.7 Technology, organisational structure and ownership

In this section we look more closely at how technological and organisational changes affect the labour market flows. As the frontier of technology moves, firms update and adopt new technologies and new ways of organising their workforces, which again affect productivity. The direction of causality between labour market flows and productivity is thus complex.

On German data, Bauer and Bender similarly observe that 'technological change leads to relatively lower employment rates for unskilled and professionals and engineers and to relatively similar growth rates for skilled worker if compared to the average firm' (Bauer and Bender, 2004: 278). From this they conclude that technological change does not appear to be skill-biased. However, they do observe higher hiring and separation rates as well as churning in establishments investing in IT. Thus incumbent workers are replaced.

In France, Askenazy and Galbis (2007), on survey data from 1993 and 1999, observe that the adoption of information technologies is positively correlated with blue-collar worker turnover. They explain this by the deterioration of these workers' relative productivity caused by the introduction of IT, as well as the disappearance of Tayloristic production systems.

When technology changes this often creates a need for firms to reorganise their workforce. Firms may also recognise that their current organisational structure is lacking in some dimensions, and may thus introduce organisational change without any previous technological change.

Salvanes and Førre (2003) observe a strong effect of substitution away from low-educated to highly educated or medium-educated workers both in manufacturing and in the high-skill financial sector. Gross job creation rates are different between educational groups, but job destruction rates are quite similar. 'Newly created jobs resulting from plant expansion and entry of plants is the driving force in the shift in employment composition' (Salvanes and Førre, 2003: 323). Salvanes and Førre argue that the changes are driven by changes in demand, and that vacant positions are not merely filled by more educated people as the workers' educational distribution changes over time.

Bauer and Bender (2004), on German establishment data from 1995–6, identify a strong positive impact of within-firm decentralisation of responsibility on job destruction and on worker flows (hires, separation and churning). However, this decentralisation seems to primarily affect the external separation rate and the internal promotion and demotion rates. The external hiring rate is not significantly affected. A reduction in hierarchy levels particularly drives up the separation rate, while self-managed teams lower the separation rate.

In contrast with technological change, which primarily affected blue-collar workers, organisational change positively influences managers' turnover (Askenazy and Galbis, 2007).

Several studies point out the relationship between reallocation of resources and productivity. The analysis of Foster et al. (2001) indicates that all the productivity growth in automotive repair industries occurs through net entry. Continuing plants achieve only modest changes in productivity, while primarily low-productivity plants exit. New plants, however, also have lower productivity than continuing plants. From Amadeus data for the period 1995–9, Warzynski (2003) observes that increased job reallocation yields higher productivity growth.

In Argentine, Sánchez and Butler (2004) find that intrasectoral and intersectoral reallocations contribute positively to productivity.

Ilmakunnas et al. (2005) identify positive correlation between the worker inflow rate and total factor productivity, while the worker outflow rate correlates negatively with productivity. They argue that churning speeds up productivity growth. It is, however, hard to see how to infer a causal impact from their regressions.

Very few studies have focused on financial ownership structure and how this may affect job and worker flows. Davis et al. (2007) observe that changes in the variations in job flows in publicly traded firms are offset by changes in the variation of similar job flows in privately held firms. Margolis (2006) studies how takeovers may affect the compensation policies of firms as well as their human resource management practices, and find that takeovers may be used as justification for undertaking a broader restructuring. Acquired firms do lay off workers more than the acquiring firms, but only in the short term.

2.8 Transition economies and job and worker flows

The dismantling of the Wall in 1989 marked the beginning of a period of rapid and dramatic changes in Eastern Europe, where the emerging new economies introduced market-based economies. For many of these countries, this transition period is still not ended. Since these economies originally showed signs of massive misallocation, the transition period usually implied a process of reallocating resources to new productive firms and industries. Generally this generated huge labour market flows. At the same time, the transition economies differed when it came to how quickly the reforms happened and how encompassing they were. Do 'gradualist' countries achieve better performance than countries adopting more rapid changes?

For researchers, these transition periods constitute huge social experiments, and they have sparked a number of studies. The greatest obstacle to these analyses is the lack of comprehensive administrative or survey databases, such as those that are found, for example, in the Nordic countries. Data quality and representativeness are clearly problematic issues for many of these studies. It is also difficult to compare the transition measures used in many analyses on Labour Force Surveys with the traditional job and worker flow measures.

Several countries introduced rapid reforms, for example Russia, the Czech Republic and the Baltic countries, while Ukraine, Croatia and Slovenia introduced reforms more gradually. It is, however, difficult to decide which approach is the better one. Rapid approaches to reforms seem possibly to yield higher flows than a gradual approach. During the early phases of the transition, job destruction dominates over job creation. Then job creation slowly catches up, and possibly surpasses job destruction.

Layard and Richter (1995) characterised Russia as a 'neoclassical economist's dream'. From 1992 to 1998, Russian worker flows were high, both before and during the transition period (Brown and Earle, 2002). The average annual hiring rate varied between 19 and 24 per cent each year. New and reorganised firms displayed larger flows than non-reorganised enterprises (Brown and Earle, 2003a). The gross job flows in Russia were smallish, but the reforms changed the usual pattern. Brown and Earle (2002) claim that the job destruction flow in Russia after the reform was higher even than the US flow, and that the persistence of the Russian job creation and destruction flows is equal to that of the US The 'post-reform reallocation rates are more than double the pre-reform rates, as are the rates of net decline' (Brown and Earle, 2002: 104). The problem is that such high levels of job destruction are not necessarily favourable for the economy. High job destruction rates could be taken as evidence of disorganisation (Konings and Walsh, 1999). Brown and Earle (2003a) conclude that, by focusing on flows only, one largely ignores many signs of institutional malfunctioning in Russia, and, like Earle and Sabirianova (2002), they are cautious about describing Russia as a 'neoclassical dream'. But, during the rapid liberalisation, the pace, heterogeneity and productivity effects of the flows have increased substantially (Brown and Earle, 2003b).

The Czech economy experienced one of the most rapid transitions to a market economy, by liberalising nearly all prices, and privatising much of the economy. In the Czech Republic, the transition involved significant movements into the finance, trade and tourism sectors, and out of the agricultural and industrial sectors. The restructuring in the Czech Republic was carried out relatively efficiently, since it occurred with lower incidence and duration of unemployment than in the other transition economies (Sorm and Terrel, 2000).

Polish firms were, before the transition period started, to some extent sensitive to market conditions (Basu et al., 1997). Konings et al. (1996) find high rates of job destruction at the start of the transition period, and argue that Polish state-owned enterprises were rapidly downsizing. From Amadeus data for the period 1995–9, Warzynski (2003) calculates an increasing job reallocation from 9 per cent in 1995 to nearly 19 per cent in 1999. The excess job reallocation rate fluctuates less, around 8–11 per cent. Rogowski and Socha (2008) find an average reallocation rate around 23 per cent during the period 1997–2004, with job creation exceeding 10 per cent and job destruction around 12 per cent. These values are quite comparable to many West European countries.

The Baltic countries introduced rapid reforms, which have had dramatic impacts on job and worker flows. According to Haltiwanger and Vodopivec (2002), before the reforms hiring and separation rates in Estonia were both around 10 per cent, while job creation and destruction rates hovered close to zero. During the transition period, hiring and separation rates increased to 25 per cent in 1994–5, while job destruction soared to 15 per cent in 1992–3 (with job creation lagging behind at 6 per cent), later to converge with job creation at 10 per cent in 1994–5. Close to 30 per cent of the excess job reallocation can be explained by between-sector shifts (Faggio and Konings, 2003). This picture of the reforms' impact on flows is slightly challenged by Masso et al. (2006), who argue that the gross job flows in the Baltic countries equalled that of the US, and they were synchronised, that is, job creation equalled job destruction. Masso et al. claim that their use of more representative register data (improved data on small businesses) provides a better picture, since the small firm sector is crucial for the high flexibility shown by the job flows.

The restructuring of the Estonian labour market was over by 2001, since a high proportion of the labour reallocation reflects shifts between industries following changes in the economy, and the worker flows then clearly dropped after 2001. Haltiwanger and Vodopivec (2002) claim that the massive restructuring in the 1990s has basically been successful, although Estonia has faced substantial restructuring costs in terms of foregone GDP.

Ukraine is one of the transition economies that have been lagging behind in reforms (Konings et al., 2003). Job destruction has been dominant, peaking at about 15.3 per cent in 1996, indicating possible evidence of disorganisation in the production process (Konings and Walsh, 1999). Compared, for example, with the Russian labour market, the Ukrainian labour market is less flexible (Brown and Earle, 2002), with lower pace, less heterogeneity and productivity effects (Brown and Earle, 2003b). In Ukraine, most of the dynamics after the reforms emerge from new private firms, while flows in privatised and state-owned enterprises are quite similar (Konings et al., 2003). Stronger product market competition for firms engaged in world or EU trade reduces job reallocation, but sectors with strong export links to the EU actually show higher excess job reallocation, while sectors with strong competition from EU imports still show lower reallocation.

Croatia and Slovenia also changed their market structure gradually. Rutkowski (2003a) notes that job creation and destruction remain low in Croatia, as well as tenures being very long. Haltiwanger and Vodopivec (2002) point out that the paths of job creation and destruction in Slovenia are much more synchronised than in Estonia. At the same time, the levels of job creation and destruction in Slovenia are much lower. During the recession early in the 1990s, the downturn in Slovenia was clearly less severe than in Estonia, but Estonia experienced higher growth rates of GDP after the recession. It may appear that the gradual approach of Slovenia has saved restructuring costs compared with the Estonian experience, but Haltiwanger and Vodopivec point out that it will be many years before these cases may truly be evaluated. Post-transition Slovenia experiences high excess job reallocation levels, while two-thirds of the worker flows are accounted for by job flows (Haltiwanger and Vodopivec, 2003). Job reallocation is mainly between firms (Haltiwanger and Vodopivec, 2003) and most of the reallocation of jobs occurs within sectors (Faggio and Konings, 2003).

2.9 Future topics for research

This paper has surveyed the recent contributions in the literature on job and worker flows. It has documented the tremendous research activity that is currently going on. The survey also points out directions for future research. In this section, we briefly point out some of the topics for future research. The survey clearly documents the need for cross-country analyses on harmonised data. As it is, only Gómez-Salvador et al. (2004), Messina and Vallanti (2007) and Haltiwanger et al. (2006) address cross-country policy issues such as, for example, EPL, unemployment insurance and centralisation in the wage-bargaining using harmonised data.

What do we not know? At the macro level it remains to establish the impacts of several important institutional characteristics on job and worker flows. The studies referred above identify reduced dynamics (job reallocation) from stricter EPL, and their approach must be considered state-of-the-art. However, it is difficult to see that they have solved the problem with interrelated institutional arrangement. By this we mean that a country's choice of institutions (e.g. bargaining regime, unemployment and sickness insurance, sick leave, EPL, market regulations, taxation regime) are related and have a joint impact on the labour market. This makes it very difficult to disentangle the separate impacts from the different institutions. And, even from the referred studies above, it remains to be seen whether this reduced dynamics caused by strict EPL is reflected in productivity losses.

From our perspective, these questions can also be related to the apparent success of the Nordic countries compared with Central European countries. How do the Nordic countries achieve and uphold well-functioning labour markets characterised by relatively low levels of unemployment at the same time as they provide the services and benefits of a generous welfare state? Workforce productivity is of course one answer, but surely not the only one. To elaborate slightly, in both Norway and Sweden, unions are strong, wage-bargaining is centralised, EPL is relatively strict (although less strict than in the Central European countries), a strict progressive labour taxation is established and generous welfare benefits are provided, so why do we not observe a stagnant labour market characterised by reduced dynamics?

Product market competition may affect job and worker flows, and should be studied to improve our understanding of the relationship between product and factor markets. While deregulations and increased competition appear to improve productivity, it remains to be seen how this affects job and worker turnover. In Argentina it appears that reduced non-wage labour costs primarily lead to smaller job destruction and increased net growth; that is, they work through the preservation of existing jobs. This is, to a certain extent, also seen in the transition economies, but this is difficult to generalise to the developed countries. One observes, for example, that nearly all of the productivity growth in US automotive repair industries occurs through net entry.

Even at a macro level, workers and firms may be considered heterogeneous, and changes in the institutions may have differential impact on different groups of workers and firms. Several economies experience problems associated with increased unemployment for 'weak' groups of workers, for example low-educated workers, the elderly and immigrants. While Dutch data do not support crowding-out of low-educated workers, it remain to be seen whether this will show up in data from other countries. The elderly and immigrants are important labour sources, and, with a diminishing labour force due to ageing, these groups become more important. Targeting these groups of workers for analyses will provide insights into how these groups of workers could be mobilised.

Trend development is clearly also an issue. From the US gross flow data, there appears to be a trend decline in level and volatility of job flows. Why do we observe this, and is this observation valid for Europe as well? What about trend development of the worker flows? Norwegian worker flows describe a positive trend development. Does this reflects changed labour market institutions (EPL, regulations, bargaining) or changed worker attitudes to employers? Do we observe this in other countries as well?

At the micro level it is clear that we still lack knowledge about firms' hiring and recruitment policies. The true cost of turnover is still an issue, particularly in relation to gross worker turnover. Several studies have tried to identify the costs associated with changing the workforce level, but very few studies have addressed hiring costs, training costs and separation costs associated with worker turnover. We still lack a good grasp of personnel policies, human resource management and profits, as well as the relationship between personnel policy and productivity. From an empirical point of view the problem is related to an issue of identification and causality. Mobility causes wage growth and wage growth causes mobility. Changes in firm wage policies following exogenous industry changes could be examined. While little support is found for internal labour markets in French data, this is relatively unexplored in other countries.

The relationship between labour demand, vacancies and hiring is relatively unexplored. Evidence on how changes of ownership, acquisitions and mergers affect job and worker flows is also just beginning to surface. Do takeovers by foreign firms imply, for example, changed personnel policies? How do takeovers affect firm productivity? In France, for example, it appears that acquiring firms use the takeover event as justification for undertaking a broader restructuring. Bargaining, communication and internal cooperation between worker organisations and firm management are still by and large unexplored issues, and may be important for the outcome of job reallocation processes.

Acknowledgements

Thanks to participants at the Linked employer–employee workshop in Brussels 2007, to Erling Barth at the Institute for Social Research, and to Anniken Hagelund for valuable comments and helpful suggestions. This work was financed by a contract of the European Commission to London School of Economics and Political Science, Contract No. VC/2006/0046, and the Norwegian Research Council under grant number 173591/S20.

References

Abowd, J.M. and Kramarz, F. (1999) 'The Analysis of Labor Markets Using Matched Employer-Employee Data', in O. Ashenfelter and D. Card (eds) *Handbook of Labor Economics*, Vol. 3B, Amsterdam and New York: Elsevier, 2629–710.

Abowd, J.M. and Kramarz, F. (2003) 'The Costs of Hiring and Separations', *Labour Economics*, 10: 499–530.

Abowd, J.M., Corbel, P. and Kramarz, F. (1999) 'The Entry and Exit of Workers and the Growth of Employment: An Analysis of French Establishments', *Review of Economics and Statistics*, 81: 170–87.

Abowd, J.M., Kramarz, F. and Roux, S. (2006a) 'Heterogeneity in Firms' Wages and Mobility Policies', in H. Bunzel, B.J. Christensen, G.R. Neumann and J.-M. Robin (eds) *Structural Models of Wage and Employment Dynamics*, Amsterdam and New York: Elsevier, 237–67.

Abowd, J.M., Kramarz, F. and Roux, S. (2006b) 'Wages, Mobility and Firm Performance: Advantages and Insights from Using Matched Worker-Firm Data', *Economic Journal*, 116: F245–F285.

Askenazy, P. and Galbis, E.M. (2007) 'The Impact of Technological and Orgnizational Changes on Labor Flows. Evidence on French Establishments', *LABOUR*, 21: 265–301.

Bachman, R. (2006) 'Labour Market Dynamics in Germany: Hirings, Separations, and Job-to-Job Transitions over the Business Cycle', SFB 649 Discussion papers.

Barlevy, G. (2002) 'The Sullying Effect of Recessions', *Review of Economic Studies*, 69: 65–96.

Barlevy, G. (2003) 'Credit Market Frictions and the Allocation of Resources Over the Business Cycle', *Journal of Monetary Economics*, 50: 1795–818.

Barth, E. and Dale-Olsen, H. (1999) 'The Employer's Wage Policy and Worker Turnover', in J.C. Haltiwanger, J.I. Lane, J.R. Spletzer, J. Theeuwes and K.R. Troske (eds) *The Creation and Analysis of Matched Employer-Employee Data*, Amsterdam and New York: Elsevier, 285–312.

Barth, E. and Dale-Olsen, H. (2000) 'Churning in the Norwegian Labor Market. Gender Differences in Job and Worker Mobility', in S. Gustafsson and D. Meulders (eds) *Gender and the Labour Market. Econometric Evidence on Obstacles in Achieving Gender Equality*, London: Macmillan, 149–87.

Barth, E. and Dale-Olsen, H. (2009) 'Monopsonistic Discrimination and the Gender Wage Gap', *Labour Economics* (forthcoming).

Basu, S., Estrin, S. and Svejnar, J. (1997) 'Employment and Wage Behaviour of Industrial Enterprises in Transition Economies: The Cases of Poland and Czechoslovakia', *Economics of Transition*, 5: 271–87.

Bauer, T. and Bender, S. (2004) 'Technological Change, Organizational Change and Job Turnover', *Labour Economics*, 11: 265–91.

Bauer, T., Bender, S. and Bonin, H. (2007) 'Dismissal Protection and Worker Flows in Small Establishments', *Economica*, 74: 804–21.

Benedetto, G., Haltiwanger, J., Lane, J. and McKinney, K. (2007) 'Using Worker Flows to Measure Firm Dynamics', *Journal of Business and Economic Statistics*, 25: 299–313.

Bergoeing, R., Hernando, A. and Repetto, A. (2003) 'The Effect of Policy Distortions on Aggregate Productivity Dynamics', Discussion paper, Santiago and Cambridge: Universidad de Chile and Harvard University.

Bertola, G. and Rogerson, R. (1997) 'Institutions and Labor Regulations', *European Economic Review*, 41: 1147–71.

Bertrand, M. and Kramarz, F. (2002) 'Does Entry Regulation Hinder Job Creation?', *The Quarterly Journal of Economics*, 117: 1369–413.

Bingley, P. and Westergaard-Nielsen, N. (2004) 'Personnel Policy and Profit', *Journal of Business Research*, 57: 557–63.

Bingley, P. and Westergaard-Nielsen, N. (2006) 'Job Changes and Wage Growth Over the Careers of Private Sector Workers in Denmark', in H. Bunzel, B.J. Christensen, G.R. Neumann and J.-M. Robin (eds) *Structural Models of Wage and Employment Dynamics*, Amsterdam and New York: Elsevier, 309–29.

Blanchard, O. and Kremer, G. (1997) 'Disorganization', *The Quarterly Journal of Economics*, 112: 1091–126.

Boeri, T. (1999) 'Enforcement of Employment Security Regulations, On-the-job Search and Unemployment Duration', *European Economic Review*, 43: 65–89.

Brown, J.D. and Earle, J.S. (2002) 'Gross Job Flows in Russian Industry Before and After Reforms: Has Destruction Become More Creative?', *Journal of Comparative Economics*, 30: 96–133.

Brown, J.D. and Earle, J.S. (2003a) 'The Reallocation of Workers and Jobs in Russian Industry', *Economics of Transition*, 11: 221–52.
Brown, J.D. and Earle, J.S. (2003b) 'Job Reallocation and Productivity Growth Under Alternative Economic Systems and Policies: Evidence from the Soviet Transition', Discussion paper no. 3796, London: CEPR.
Burdett, K. and Vishwanath, T. (1988) 'Balanced Matching and Labor Market Equilibrium', *Journal of Political Economy*, 96: 1048–65.
Burgess, S., Lane, J. and Stevens, D. (2000a) 'The Reallocation of Labour and the Lifecycle of Firms', *Oxford Bulletin of Economics and Statistics*, 62: 885–907.
Burgess, S., Lane, J. and Stevens, D. (2000b) 'Job Flows, Worker Flows, and Churning', *Journal of Labor Economics*, 18: 473–502.
Burgess, S., Lane, J. and Stevens, D. (2001) 'Churning Dynamics: An Analysis of Hires and Separations at the Employer Level', *Labour Economics*, 8: 1–14.
Caballero, R.J. and Engel, E. (2004) 'Adjustments is Much Slower than You Think', Working paper, Boston, MA: MIT and NBER.
Caballero, R.J. and Hammour, M.L. (1994) 'The Cleansing Effect of Creative Destruction', *American Economic Review*, 84: 1350–68.
Caballero, R.J. and Hammour, M.L. (1996) 'On the Timing and Efficiency of Creative Destruction', *The Quarterly Journal of Economics*, 111: 805–52.
Caballero, R.J. and Hammour, M.L. (2005) 'The Cost of Recessions Revisited: A Reverse-Liquidationist View', *Review of Economic Studies*, 72: 313–41.
Carlsson, M. and Laseén, S. (2005) 'Capital Adjustment Patterns in Swedish Manufacturing Firms: What Model Do They Suggest?', *Economic Journal*, 115: 969–86.
Christensen, B.J., Lentz, R., Mortensen, D.T., Neumann, G. and Werwatz, A. (2005) 'Job Separations and the Distribution of wages', *Journal of Labor Economics*, 23: 31–58.
Cooper, R.W. and Haltiwanger, J.C. (2006) 'On the Nature of Capital Adjustment Costs', *Review of Economic Studies*, 73: 611–33.
Cooper, R.W., Haltiwanger, J.C. and Powers, L. (1999) 'Machine Replacements and the Business Cycle: Lumps and Bumps', *American Economic Review*, 89: 921–46.
Cooper, R.W., Haltiwanger, J. and Willis, J. (2007) 'Search Frictions: Matching Aggregate and Establishment Observations', *Journal of Monetary Economics*, 54: 56–78.
Dale-Olsen, H. (2006a) 'Worker Turnover, Capital Dispersion and Matching', *LABOUR*, 20: 395–431.
Dale-Olsen, H. (2006b) 'Estimating Workers' Marginal Willingness to Pay for Safety Using Linked Employer-Employee Data', *Economica*, 73: 99–127.
Dale-Olsen, H. (2006c) 'Wages, Fringe Benefits and Worker Turnover', *Labour Economics*, 13: 87–106.
Dale-Olsen, H. (2006d) 'Økende mobilitet i det norske arbeidsmarkedet?', *Søkelys på arbeidsmarkedet*, 23: 3–11 (in Norwegian).
Davis, S.J. and Haltiwanger, J. (1992) 'Gross Job Creation, Gross Job Destruction, and Employment Reallocation', *The Quarterly Journal of Economics*, 107: 819–63.
Davis, S.J. and Haltiwanger, J. (1998) 'Measuring Gross Worker and Job Flows', in J.C. Haltiwanger, M.E. Mansner and R. Topel (eds) *Labor Statistics Measurements Issues*, Chicago, IL: University of Chicago Press, 77–120.
Davis, S.J. and Haltiwanger, J. (1999a) 'Gross Job Flows', in O. Ashenfelter and D. Card (eds) *Handbook of Labor Economics*, Vol. 3B, Amsterdam and New York: Elsevier, 2711–805.
Davis, S.J. and Haltiwanger, J. (1999b) 'On the Driving Forces Behind Cyclical Movements in Employment and Job Reallocation', *American Economic Review*, 89: 1234–58.
Davis, S. and Haltiwanger, J. (2001) 'Sectoral Job Creation and Destruction Responses to Oil Price Changes', *Journal of Monetary Economics*, 48: 465–512.
Davis, S.J., Haltiwanger, J. and Schuh, S. (1996) *Job Creation and Destruction*, Cambridge, MA: MIT Press.
Davis, S.J., Faberman, J. and Haltiwanger, J. (2006a) 'The Flow Approach to Labor Markets: New Data Sources and Micro-Macro Links', *Journal of Economic Perspectives*, 20: 3–26.

Davis, S.J., Faberman, J. and Haltiwanger, J. (2006b) 'The Micro-Level Behavior of Vacancies and Hiring', Manuscript, paper presented at the CAED 2006 in Chicago.

Davis, S., Haltiwanger, J. and Jarmin, R.S. (2007) 'Volatility and Dispersion in Business Growth Rates: Publicly Traded versus Privately Held Firms', *NBER Macroeconomics Annual*, 2006, 21: 107–80.

DellaVigna, S. and Paserman, M.D. (2005) 'Job Search and Impatience', *Journal of Labor Economics*, 23: 527–88.

den Haan, W. J., Ramey, G. and Watson, J. (2000) 'Job Destruction and Propagation of Shocks', *American Economic Review*, 90: 482–98.

Dunne, T., Roberts, M.J. and Samuelson, L. (1989) 'The Growth and Failure of U.S. Manufacturing Plants', *The Quarterly Journal of Economics*, 104: 671–98.

Earle, J.S. and Sabirianova, K.Z. (2002) 'How Late to Pay? Understanding Wage Arrears in Russia', *Journal of Labor Economics*, 20: 661–707.

Ejarque, J. and Portugal, P. (2007) 'Labor Adjustment Costs in a Panel of Establishments', IZA Discussion paper 3091, Bonn.

Faberman, R.J. (2005) 'Studying the Labor Market with the Job Openings and Labor Turnover Survey', Working paper 388, US Bureau of Labor Statistics, Washington.

Faggio, G. and Konings, J. (2003) 'Job Creation, Job Destruction and Employment Growth in Transition Countries in the 90s', *Economic Systems*, 27: 129–54.

Fallick, B. and Fleischman, C.A. (2004) 'Employer-to-Employer Flows in the U.S. Labor Market: The Complete Picture of Gross Worker Flows, Finance and Economics', Discussion Series 34, Board of Governors of the Federal Reserve System, Washington.

Foster, L., Haltiwanger, J. and Krizan, C.J. (2001) 'Aggregate Productivity Growth: Lessons from Microeconomic Evidence', in C.R. Hulten, E.R. Dean and M.J. Harper (eds) *New Developments in Productivity Analysis*, Chicago, IL and London: The University of Chicago Press, 303–63.

Gartell, M., Jans, A.-C. and Persson, H. (2007) 'The Importance of Education for the Reallocation of Labor: Evidence from Swedish Linked Employer-Employee Data 1986 – 2002', IFAU Working paper 2007: 14, Uppsala.

Gómez-Salvador, R., Messina, J. and Vallanti, G. (2004) 'Gross Job Flows and Institutions in Europe', *Labour Economics*, 11: 469–85.

Gourinchas, P.-O. (1999) 'Exchange Rates Do Matter: French Job Reallocation and Exchange Rate Turbulence, 1984–1992', *European Economic Review*, 43: 1279–316.

Haltiwanger, J. and Vodopivec, M. (2002) 'Gross Worker and Job Flows in a Transition Economy: An Analysis of Estonia', *Labour Economics*, 9: 601–30.

Haltiwanger, J. and Vodopivec, M. (2003) 'Worker Flows, Job Flows and Firm Wage Policies. An Analysis of Slovenia', *Economics of Transition*, 11: 253–90.

Haltiwanger, J., Kugler, A., Kugler, M., Micco, A. and Pages, C. (2004) 'Effects of Tariffs and Real Exchange Rates on Job Reallocation: Evidence from Latin America', *Journal of Policy Reform*, 7: 191–208.

Haltiwanger, J., Scarpetta, S. and Schweiger, H. (2006) 'Assessing Job Flows Across Countries: The Role of Industry, Size and Regulations', Manuscript, paper presented at the EALE 2006 conference in Prague.

Hamermesh, D.S. (1989) 'Labor Demand and the Structure of Adjustment Costs', *American Economic Review*, 79: 674–89.

Hamermesh, D.S. (1995) 'Labour Demand and the Source of Adjustment Costs', *Economic Journal*, 105: 620–34.

Heyman, F. and Arai, M. (2004) 'Temporary Contracts and the Dynamics of Job Turnover', *Economics Bulletin*, 10: 1–6.

Hohti, S. (2000) 'Job Flows and Job Quality by Establishment Size in the Finnish Manufacturing Sector 1980 – 1994', *Small Business Economics*, 15: 265–81.

Ilmakunnas, P. and Maliranta, M. (2003) 'The Turnover of Jobs and Workers in a Deep Recession: Evidence from the Finnish Business Sector', *International Journal of Manpower*, 24: 216–46.

Ilmakunnas, P. and Maliranta, M. (2005) 'Worker Inflow, Outflow, and Churning', *Applied Economics*, 37: 1115–33.
Ilmakunnas, P., Maliranta, M. and Vainiomäki, J. (2005) 'Worker Turnover and Productivity Growth', *Applied Economics Letters*, 12: 395–8.
Kaplan, D., Martínez, G. and Robertson, R. (2003) Worker and Job Flows in Mexico, ITAM, IMSS and Macalester College, Mexico City and St Paul.
Klein, M.W., Schuh, S. and Triest, R.K. (2003) 'Job Creation, Job Destruction, and the Real Exchange Rate', *Journal of International Economics*, 59: 239–65.
Konings, J. and Walsh, P. (1999) 'Disorganisation in the Process of Transition', *Economics of Transition*, 7: 29–46.
Konings, J., Lehmann, H. and Schaffer, M. (1996) 'Employment Growth, Job Creation and Job Destruction in Polish Industry, 1988–91', *Labour Economics*, 3: 299–317.
Konings, J., Kupets, O. and Lehmann, H. (2003) 'Gross Job Flows in Ukraine. Size, Ownership and Trade Effects', *Economics of Transition*, 11: 321–56.
Kugler, A. and Pica, G. (2008) 'Effects of Employment Protection on Worker and Job Flows', *Labour Economics*, 15: 78–95.
Layard, R. and Richter, A. (1995) 'How Much Unemployment Is Needed for Restructuring. The Russian Experience', *Economics of Transition*, 3: 35–58.
Lazear, E.P. and Shaw, K.L. (eds) (2009) *The Structure of Wages: An International Comparison*, Chicago, IL: University of Chicago Press.
Light, A. and Omori, Y. (2004) 'Unemployment Insurance and Job Quits', *Journal of Labor Economics*, 22: 159–88.
Loury, L.D. (2006) 'Some Contacts Are More Equal Than Others: Informal Networks, Job Tenure, and Wages', *Journal of Labor Economics*, 24: 299–318.
Manning, A. (2003) *Monopsony in Motion*, Princeton, NJ: Princeton University Press.
Margolis, D. (2006) 'Should Employment Authorities Worry About Mergers and Acquisitions?', *Portuguese Economic Journal*, 5: 167–94.
Martins, P. (2008) 'Worker Churning and Firms' Wage Policies', *International Journal of Manpower*, 29: 48–63.
Martins, P. (2009) 'Dismissals for Cause: The Difference That Just Eight Paragraphs Can Make', *Journal of Labor Economics* (forthcoming).
Martins, P., Novo, A. and Portugal, P. (2006) 'Retirement Age and Labour Market Outcomes', Manuscript, paper presented at the CAED 2006 in Chicago.
Masso, J., Eamets, R. and Philips, K. (2006) 'Job Flows and Worker Flows in the Baltic States: Labour Reallocation and Structural Changes', Manuscript, paper presented at the EALE 2006 conference in Prague.
Medina, P., Meléndez, M. and Seim, F. (2003) 'Productivity Dynamics of the Colombian Manufacturing Sector', Working paper, Bogota and Stanford, CA: Universidad de Los Andes and Stanford University.
Messina, J. and Vallanti, G. (2007) 'Job Flow Dynamics and Firing Restrictions: Evidence from Europe', *Economic Journal*, 117: 279–301.
Micco, A. and Pagés, C. (2004) 'Employment Protection and Gross Job Flows: A Difference-In-Difference Approach', Working paper no. 508, Inter-American Development Bank.
Nagypál, E. (2008) 'Worker Reallocation Over the Business Cycle: The Importance of Job-to-Job Transitions', Manuscript, Northwestern University, Evanston.
Nielsen, A. and Schiantarelli, F. (2003) 'Zeroes and Lumps in Investment: Empirical Evidence on Irreversibilities and Non-Convexities', *Review of Economics and Statistics*, 85: 1021–37.
Nilsen, Ø.A., Salvanes, K.G. and Schiantarelli, F. (2007) 'Employment Adjustment, the Structure of Adjustment Costs, and Plant Size', *European Economic Review*, 51: 577–98.
Nunziata, L. (2003) 'Labour Market Institutions and the Cyclical Dynamics of Employment', *Labour Economics*, 10: 31–53.
OECD (1999) 'Employment Protection Legislation', in *Employment Outlook*, June 1999, Organisation for Economic Co-Operation and Developments, Paris, 47–132.

Persson, H. (1999) 'Essays on Labour Demand and Career Mobility', PhD dissertation, Dissertation serie no. 40, Swedish Institute for Social Research, Stockholm.

Portugal, P. and Cardoso, A.R. (2006) 'Disentangling the Minimum Wage Puzzle: An Analysis of Worker Accessions and Separations', *Journal of the European Economic Association*, 4: 989–1013.

Ramey, G. and Watson, J. (1997) 'Contractual Fragility, Job Destruction, and the Business Cycle', *The Quarterly Journal of Economics*, 112: 873–911.

Ribeiro, E.P., Corseuil, C.H., Santos, D., Furtado, P., Amorim, B., Servo, L. and Souza, A. (2004) 'Trade Liberalization, the Exchange Rate and Job Flows in Brazil', *Policy Reform*, 7: 209–23.

Rogowski, W. and Socha, J. (2008) 'Business Demography, Job Flows and Productivity in the Enterprise Sector in Poland', *Gospodarka Norodowa*, 19: 1–23.

Rutkowski, J. (2003) 'Does Strict Employment Protection Discourage Job Creation? Evidence from Croatia', Policy Research Working paper no. 3104, World Bank, Washington.

Røed, K. and Raaum, O. (2003) 'Administrative Registers – Unexplored Reservoirs of Scientific Knowledge', *Economic Journal*, 113: F258–F281.

Salvanes, K.G. (1997) 'Market Rigidities and Labour Market Flexibility: An International Comparison', *Scandinavian Journal of Economics*, 99: 315–33.

Salvanes, K.G. and Førre, S.E. (2003) 'Effects on Employment of Trade and Technical Change: Evidence from Norway', *Economica*, 70: 293–330.

Sánchez, G. and Butler, I. (2004) 'Market Institutions, Labor Market Dynamics, and Productivity in Argentina during the 1990s', *Policy Reform*, 7: 249–78.

Serrano, C.G. and Malo, M.A. (2002) 'Worker Turnover, Job Turnover and Collective Bargaining in Spain', *British Journal of Industrial Relations*, 40: 69–85.

Sorm, V. and Terrell, K. (2000) 'Sectoral Restructuring and Labor Mobility: A Comparative Look at the Czech Republic', *Journal of Comparative Economics*, 28: 431–55.

Stein, J.C. (1997) 'Waves of Creative Destruction: Firm-specific Learning-by-Doing and the Dynamics of Innovation', *Review of Economic Studies*, 64: 265–88.

Stiglbauer, A., Stahl, F., Winter-Ebmer, R. and Zweimüller, J. (2003) 'Job Creation and Job Destruction in a Regulated Labor Market: The Case of Austria', *Empirica*, 30: 127–48.

Tomiura, E. (2004) 'Import Competition and Employment in Japan: Plant Start-Up, Shutdown and Product Changes', *The Japanese Economic Review*, 55: 141–52.

van Ommeren, J., van den Berg, G.J. and Gorter, C. (2000) 'Estimating the Marginal Willingness to Pay for Commuting', *Journal of Regional Science*, 40: 541–63.

Warzynski, F. (2003) 'The Causes and Consequences of Sector-Level Job Flows in Poland', *Economics of Transition*, 11: 357–81.

3
Summary of the Literature on Job Displacement in the US and EU: What We Know and What We Would Like to Know

Till von Wachter

3.1 Introduction

A large literature in the US and a growing literature in the EU examine the cost of worker displacement. Yet, despite the importance of the question, we have little systematic knowledge about the incidence and the cost of job loss, especially in European countries. This has been partly due to a lack of necessary data. Partly it is due to the inherent difficulty in studying the complex phenomenon of job loss and its causes and consequences. Yet it is also partially due to a lack of focus and coordinated effort to follow a more systematic approach yielding more comparable results between studies, over time, and between countries.

Worker displacement typically refers to the loss of a job due to slack work, the abolition of a job position, or a plant closing. The phenomenon of job loss on a large scale began to attract increasing attention in the US in part due to large declines in manufacturing employment in the course of deindustrialization in the 1970s and 1980s, and due to the high incidence of job loss among blue-collar workers traditionally in stable jobs in the 1982 recession. This phenomenon led, among other things, to the institution of the biannual Displaced Worker Survey as supplement to the standard US labour force survey (the Current Population Survey).[1]

In Europe, there has traditionally been less focus on displaced workers per se, perhaps because widespread job loss was less of a social and political issue due to lower turnover rates, more generous social insurance programmes, and large-scale programmes to address the plight of workers caught in industrial restructuring (such as early retirement schemes). Instead, the focus has traditionally been on the problem of long-term unemployment.[2] This emphasis appears to have been changing, which is partially attested by the recent surge in studies on displaced workers in European countries.

Since the early 1980s, an important and growing literature in the US has analysed the short and long-term effects of job loss on workers' earnings, careers, and other life outcomes. Thereby, the emphasis has been on three key questions. First, what is the overall cost of job loss for an affected worker? Second, what are the sources of these losses and the channels through which displaced workers recover? Third, what are the causes of job loss itself? Since then, the literature has made some progress in answering the first question, and this will be the focus of this literature review. There have also been some insights into the second question, which will be reviewed in passing below. There have been relatively few empirical insights into the third question. It should be stressed that the literature reviewed here typically does not analyse the macroeconomic consequences of job displacement, such as improved growth from restructuring or increased costs due to a rise in frictions in the course of the adjustment process.

The event of job displacement is a complex phenomenon, and many of the angles of job loss, its sources, and its costs have not yet been fully explored. This may in part arise because job loss itself is a puzzle for standard models of the labour market. In part, it may be due to the fact that some of the involved phenomena are hard to model in an economic framework, and some of the costs are hard to quantify at all. Yet even the most basic effects of job loss on such outcomes as earnings have not been fully understood, and the reasons will be explored in the following literature survey.

The typical measure of the cost of job displacement focuses on the lifetime loss of a job loser's earnings. As discussed in Section 3.2, available income might deviate from earnings, typically due to government transfers. However, in many cases lifetime earnings are likely to be a key indicator of individuals' long-term resources. Consequently, most of the economic literature on job loss has focused on the short and long-term effects of displacement on earnings and employment. While a final consensus has yet to be reached, it has become clear that for some groups of workers there are very large and long-lasting losses in annual earnings.

Clearly, there are additional costs of job loss, some of which have been explored as well. This has included analyses of the costs of relocation and retraining, or more recently on the effect of job loss on health and family outcomes. Similarly, a small literature has examined to what extent insurance programmes (such as unemployment insurance) help to alleviate some of the burden of the earnings loss. Related studies have evaluated the effects of training programmes targeted at displaced workers.

Overall, from the US literature a bleak picture emerges, with large long-lasting unmitigated losses in earnings even for job losers in prime working age. Job loss has been found to go hand-in-hand with losses in consumption, losses in health insurance coverage, increases in mortality, and reduced life-chances for the children of job losers.

There also appear to be significant differences in the costs of job loss among groups of workers, with older workers, high-tenured workers, high-income workers, and workers in certain industries more affected than others. Yet, no group appears to be fully exempt from persistent losses. Less is known regarding the channels of job loss, but multiple job loss, the loss of long-term jobs, and the loss of jobs in high-wage firms and industries have been found to matter.

While there have been several important insights, many open questions remain regarding even the core question of the overall cost of job loss. For example, the two main data sources underlying estimates of the cost of job loss in the US yield estimates of different magnitude. Important questions regarding the measurement of job loss and earnings concept, the methods of estimation, and the interpretation of the resulting numbers are left unresolved.

The state of information is worse in countries of the EU, and worse still in other European countries. A large increase in studies since the late 1990s, triggered in part by the availability of large administrative data sets and harmonized survey data, has started to fill this gap. From this young and active literature, it appears that the consequences of job loss for earnings in some European countries can be less detrimental and shorter-lived than in others. However, studies using different data sets and methodologies obtain different results even for the same country. Moreover, there are often important groups of workers bearing substantial costs, in particular in terms of lower employment.

Besides differences in research design, institutional features of European countries' labour market also make a direct comparison of estimates with those from the US and among each other difficult. In particular, in the presence of more generous social insurance systems, labour earnings may sometimes be a less informative measure than total income. Similarly, a higher incidence of non-employment among job losers implies that estimated effects of job loss for those lucky enough to work are not representative for the whole population.

Overall, much remains to be learned. There is lack of systematic evidence on the lifetime cost of job loss within and between countries. The available estimates are based on a wide range of different estimation methods, samples, time periods, data sources, and definitions of job loss. Oftentimes there are important differences in the degree of data access across countries, making the replication and extension of existing studies difficult.

Recent developments in terms of data access certainly give reasons to hope for a continuing increase in studies of displaced workers. However, other important obstacles remain, in particular in terms of choices of estimation methods and measurement of earnings, but also in the definition of job displacement, the key event under study. Similarly, to further achieve comparability among results in different countries, more emphasis on assessing the effect of different labour market institutions on the incidence and consequences of job loss will be helpful.

This survey will begin by briefly reviewing basic questions of measurement of the costs of job loss for different workers. Based on this overview, we will take stock of the basic facts that we would ideally like to know. Second, we will briefly review the empirical literature of the US. More extensive, it will serve as a benchmark for assessing what has been done, what issues have arisen, and what key substantive and methodological questions are outstanding. Third, we will compare these results with the available evidence from European countries. Thereby, we will mainly focus on EU member states. After we have summarized what we do actually know and what we still need to learn, the fourth section gives a concise introduction to the methodological issues involved when analysing the costs of job loss. There, we will also briefly address the question of comparability of estimates between different studies. The last section gives a brief overview over the available data in different countries, discusses the potential ahead, and suggests some concrete steps to be taken in terms of a common research strategy.

3.2 Measuring the cost of job loss

The vast majority of papers have focused on the reduction in earnings as a measure of the cost of job loss for the individual worker. In particular, most studies strive to estimate both the short and long-term losses in either annual earnings, or weekly (hourly) earnings and weeks (hours) worked. The explicit or implicit goal is typically to estimate the present discounted value (PDV) of the overall loss in earnings.

The focus on earnings (or employment and wages) has both practical and conceptual reasons. On the one hand, earnings are typically easier to measure than, say, consumption or total income. On the other hand, in a model where workers and their families optimally choose consumption given a budget constraint, all we need to know to assess welfare losses is the loss in overall resources available. Other outcomes, such as consumption, will be the result of workers' responses to the earnings loss and provide no additional information.

While in many cases earnings losses will indeed capture the reduction in resources available to a worker for consumption or saving, clearly in certain circumstances they will not adequately capture the welfare loss following a job displacement. For example, in countries with long-lasting and generous unemployment insurance schemes, the actual resources to the workers may be more accurately captured by disposable income. While in this case overall earnings losses may still index the overall loss in productive capacity, they do not reflect resources available to workers.

Even in the absence of welfare or unemployment insurance, the PDV of earnings may not capture welfare losses if job losses have direct effect on workers' lives that are unmitigated by workers' choices. For example, job loss may increase stress, imply a loss in social status, worsen physical or mental health, or affect the family.[3] More recent papers focusing on an extended set of outcomes will eventually give a richer picture of the circumstances and costs of job loss and may eventually lead to more complete modelling approaches.

Whether losses of earnings reflect a reduction in worker productivity depends on their sources. An important strand of literature suggests that earnings reductions are due to losses in industry, occupation, or firm-specific skills (e.g. Kambourov and Manovskii, 2009; Kletzer, 1989; Neal, 1995; Parent, 2000). However, earnings losses may also reflect losses in wage components that are related to unionization, job search (e.g. Burdett, 1978), contracts (e.g. Lazear, 1979), or wage rents paid at the firm or industry level (e.g. Abowd et al., 2002; Krueger and Summers, 1988; Oi and Idson, 1999). In this case, earnings losses may reflect not only a loss in productive capacity, but also a loss in rents workers had earned above their market wage (for evidence see Schmieder and von Wachter (2009)). Distinguishing the source of earnings losses thus becomes crucial on top of the question regarding worker welfare.

Implications of job loss for other outcomes are harder to draw and may require specification of workers' preferences. For example, if unemployment insurance does not perfectly smooth earnings losses, a simple model of consumption and leisure choice would suggest that permanent earnings losses lead to reductions in consumption, saving for retirement, health investments, or investments in children's education. Job loss may also have direct effects on health through losses in socio-economic status, due to heightened stress, or due to increased leisure. To make precise predictions, one would have to specify a more complete health production function that includes these components.[4] Similarly, there might be direct channels through which parents' economic success affects child outcomes (e.g. Oreopoulos et al., 2005). Along the same lines, spousal job loss may affect the stability of marriage or partners' labour supply.

3.3 What do we know about the cost of job loss?

3.3.1 Estimating the earnings effects of job loss

Figures 3.1 and 3.2 give a schematic overview of the main questions, goals, and difficulties that will be discussed in this review. Based in part on the discussion in the Introduction and the previous section, columns and rows of Table 3.1 give a basic overview of what we would like to know. This includes the size and duration of earnings and employment losses; differences therein by age, gender, and education; differences over time, between labour markets, industries, and firms. In addition to this basic information, we would also like to know the effect of job loss by job tenure and firm characteristics, as well as effects of job loss on other career and non-career outcomes.

In the present section we discuss mainly the effect of job loss on earnings and employment, since these estimates allow basic assessments of the present discounted value of annual earnings losses. This has been the focus of most studies. Later we will briefly summarize newer studies extending the scope of the effects and the costs of job loss. The entries in Table 3.1 give a snapshot overview of the extent of studies done on the different fundamental aspects of the costs of job loss. Panel A of Table 3.1 shows entries for the US. From this broad overview, it appears that a reasonably large number of studies have analysed the effects of job loss in the US. But already the breakdown by subgroups reveals we may know less than the overall number of studies suggests.

Most entries in the table come from studies doing some kind of comparison of earnings before and after a job loss. Basic estimates come from taking simple differences of wages or earnings over time. A key concern with this estimator is that it does not control for trends in earnings that may have occurred in the absence of the job loss. Another concern is that the trends of workers losing their job may be different from the overall population. The former issue has been typically addressed by comparing the wage change of job losers to wage changes of similar workers. Such a control group comparison (or difference-in-difference)

Summary of the Literature on Job Displacement 69

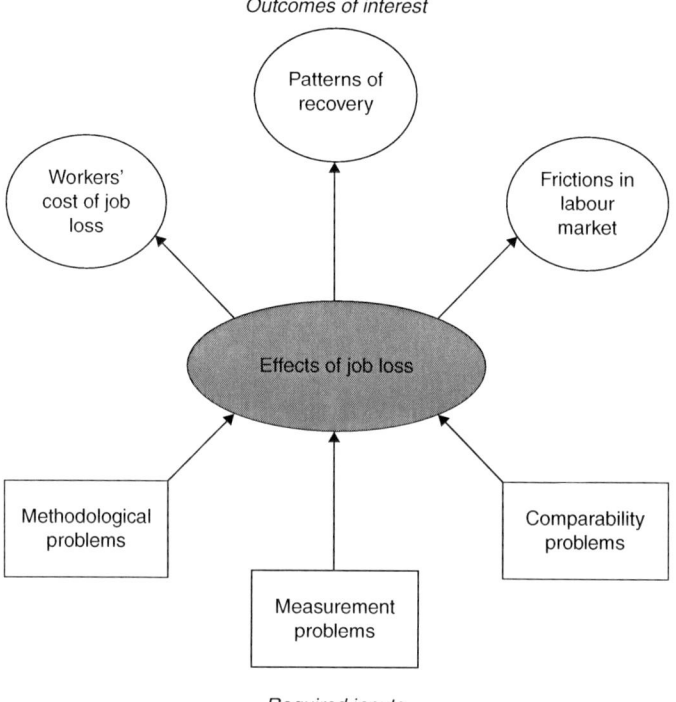

Figure 3.1 Measuring the cost of job displacement

can account for common underlying trends, related, say, to workers' industry or occupation, but does not automatically control for the problem of selective job displacement.

To address the question of whether job losers have been selected by the firm based on their productivity or based on their earnings potential, most studies control for worker characteristics prior to layoff. If time series observations on workers' earnings prior to a job loss are available, studies typically include fixed worker effects instead (this is equivalent to analysing earnings changes in short panels). Observable worker characteristics that change over time can be included as long as they are *not* affected by job loss (such as age).[5] For reasons discussed below, sometimes studies also include controls for characteristics of the displacing firm.

Many papers based on longitudinal data on workers' earnings estimate variants of the following distributed lag model:

$$y_{it} = \alpha_i + \gamma_t + \beta X_{it} + \sum_{k \geq -m,} \delta_k D_{it}^k + u_{it} \tag{1}$$

where the outcome variable y_{it} typically represents a measure of log annual earnings or another career outcome, the time dummies γ_t are identified by the presence

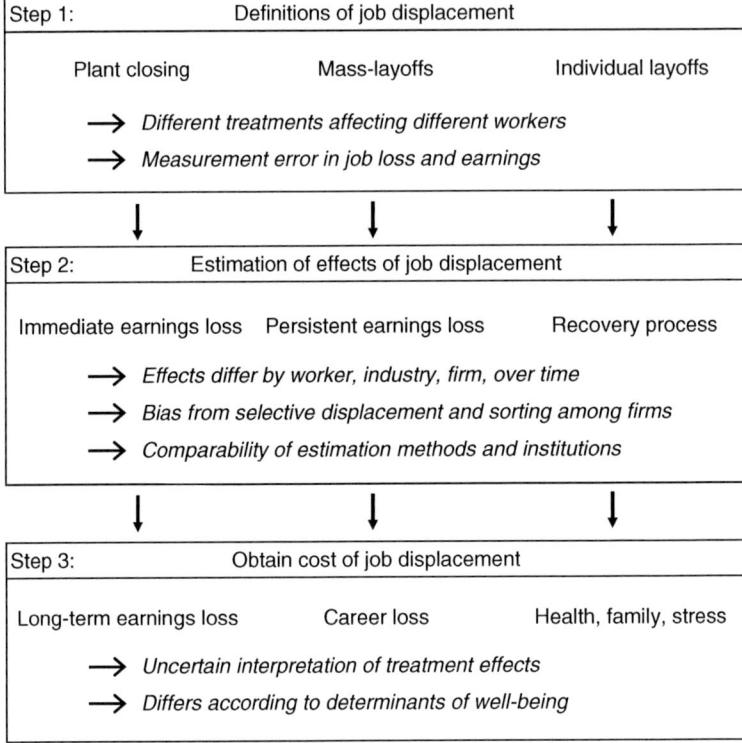

Figure 3.2 Difficulties in estimating the cost of job loss

of 'stayers' (i.e. workers not losing their jobs), and the error u_{it} represents truly random components affecting the outcome. The coefficients δ_k on the dummies indicating the k-th period before, during, or after job loss (D_{it}^k) measure the time path of earnings changes of job losers before and after a displacement relative to a baseline and the control group. The ability to estimate the dynamic effect of job loss is of particular interest since we are interested in the short- and long-term effects of job loss.

The displacement effect is identified by the inclusion of workers staying with their employers throughout the period under study (the control group). In an ideal world, the job loss would be random with respect to worker characteristics, and the model would identify a true causal effect of a job loss. Usually, a researcher has to assume that, conditional on worker fixed effects or conditional on included observable baseline characteristics, displaced workers are observationally equal to those workers in the control group. Whether this is a good assumption will depend on the particular definition of displacement, the time period, and the groups of workers under study.

As discussed in the methodology section below, several issues other than selective worker displacement affect a straightforward causal interpretation of the estimates

Table 3.1 Matrix of ideal estimates – study names and study counts by broad regions

Panel A: USA

Worker characteristic	Type of job loss		Time period			By industry	By region
	Plant closing	Layoff	1980s	1990s	2000s		
Overall	30	28	26	16	2	5	0
By age	12	12	9	8	2	2	0
By gender	14	14	11	10	2	3	0
By race/nationality	7	7	4	5	1	1	0
By education	11	11	9	7	2	1	0
By occupation	4	4	4	1	0	4	0
By job tenure	13	13	11	4	1	1	0
By job status	6	6	5	1	0	1	0
By work history	1	1	1	1	0	0	0
By firm size	1	1	1	0	0	1	0
By other firm characteristics	5	5	5	1	0	0	0

Panel B: EU

Worker characteristic	Plant closing	Layoff	1980s	1990s	2000s	By industry	By region
Overall	24	15	18	27	3	3	5
By age	6	2	5	5	1	2	0
By gender	7	4	6	7	1	2	1
By race/nationality	2	2	1	2	1	1	1
By education	3	3	2	4	1	2	1
By occupation	0	0	0	0	0	0	0
By job tenure	3	4	3	3	0	0	0
By job status	4	4	2	4	2	2	2
By income	2	2	2	2	0	0	0
By work history	0	0	0	0	0	0	0
By firm size	3	2	2	2	1	2	1
By other firm characteristics	1	1	1	0	0	0	0

that follow. Among others, the event of job loss is not always well defined; there are important measurement issues in both survey and administrative data; there is heterogeneity in the effect of job loss across workers; estimates are typically based on a potentially selected sample of workers with positive employment.

3.3.2 Summary of US estimates[6]

The two most common data sources in the US for studying the effect of job loss on earnings are the Displaced Worker Survey (DWS) and administrative earnings data from the unemployment insurance (UI) system. The DWS, available since 1984 on a biannual basis, is based on a random sample and asks workers who experienced a job loss in the three years prior to the survey date about the reason for job loss, and what their earnings at the lost job were. It also records other information on the lost and current job (if the worker is employed), and demographic information including education. The administrative UI data typically consists of quarterly earnings records with a worker and employer identification numbers, as well as basic demographic information such as age and gender. Sometimes the data contain regional and industry information.[7]

The estimates resulting from studies of cost of job loss in the US are summarized in detail in Table 3.2. In a series of papers, Farber (1997, 2003) has thoroughly analysed the incidence and the cost of job loss over time and for different workers using the DWS. A key drawback of the DWS is the lack of a detailed control group, so Farber imputes it based on group-level earnings trends of non-displaced workers from the CPS. The cost of job loss for the average in the DWS ranges from 7 to 15 per cent. The DWS does not allow going beyond a range of three years after a job loss, but estimates suggest that layoff effects tend to decline over time.

In contrast to estimates based on the DWS, Ruhm (1991b) finds, using the PSID, that job losses can have lasting effects. This is confirmed by results in Jacobson et al. (1993). Using data from the UI system, they confirm that initial earnings losses of workers losing jobs in mass layoffs in Pennsylvania in the early to mid-1980s can be as large as 50 per cent and that earnings losses even six years after a job loss are on average 20 per cent. Figure 3.3 displays the dynamic pattern of the cost of job loss for the same sample of workers in Pennsylvania, estimated in Sullivan and von Wachter (2009). That mass layoffs can have large and persistent losses has been confirmed in other states and time periods (e.g. Couch and Placzek, forthcoming; von Wachter et al., 2008; Schoeni and Dardia, 2003).

Both Farber (2003) and Jacobson et al. (1993) provide an overview of how the cost of job loss can differ across groups in the population. Other, more detailed analyses have shown that older workers tend to suffer large effects (e.g. Chan and Stevens, 2001). Similarly, high-tenured workers tend to have larger losses (Kletzer, 1989), specially if displaced workers switch industry (Neal, 1995; Parent, 2000). Interestingly, there are few in-depth studies of the effects of job loss for women or non-whites (though see Crossley et al., 1994; Madden, 1987; and recent papers by Hu and Taber (2008) and Kunze and Troske (2007)).

An important advantage of longitudinal data sets is that information on the evolution of careers after a job loss is available. The most common phenomenon

Table 3.2 Size of estimates of different studies by broad region and estimation method in the USA

					Main Estimate		
Method	Study	Study year	Country	Coefficient (S.E.)	Interpretation	Sample definition	Time period
Simple difference	Addison, John T. and Portugal, Pedro	1989	United States	−0.109 (0.019)	Effect of log unemployment duration on log weekly real wage change post vs. pre-displacement	DWS 1984, Male workers 20–65, economically active 1984	1979–83
	Carrington, W. and A. Zaman	1994	United States	−0.155 (0.013)	Change in log weekly real wages, here durable manufacturing	Male workers age 21–63	1979–88
	Couch, Kenneth A.	1998	United States	−11,200 (no S.E.)	US$ (in 1991) earnings loss for displaced workers	Workers age 51–61	1990–1
	De la Rica, Sara	1992	United States	−0.112 (0.012)	Pre-displacement log weekly earnings losses for displaced workers	Workers age 20–61	1984–5
	Farber, Henry S.	2003	United States	−0.152 (no S.E.)	Effect of displacement on log real weekly earnings among all full-time workers in the 1999–2001 period	Workers age 20–64	1981–2001
	Kletzer, Lori G.	1989	United States	−0.02155	Decline in weekly earnings returns to tenure on old job, between the pre- and post-displacement job	Workers age 20–60	1979–84

Continued

Table 3.2 Continued

Method	Study	Study year	Country	Coefficient (S.E.)	Interpretation	Sample definition	Time period
				Main Estimate			
	Magnani, Elisabetta	2001	United States	0.60 (0.18)	One Standard Deviation increase in risk of job loss increased the probability of intersectoral mobility by 10.5 per cent	Sample of household heads in PSID, CPS/DWS is used to calculate displacement risk for industry cells	1983–93
	Neal, Derek	1995	United States	industry switcher −0.019 (0.005) industry stayer −0.005 (0.005)	Effect of one year of pre-displacement tenure on change in log weekly wages	Workers who lost jobs due to establishment closings	1979–90
	Podgursky, Michael and Paul Swaim	1987	United States	men: 11.7 per cent (blue collar) 4.3 per cent (white collar)	Median full-time weekly earnings losses	Workers age 61 or younger who are displaced and reemployed full-time in 1984	1979–84
	Ruhm, Christopher	1991	United States	1.005 (0.376)	Effect on log weeks of joblessness after displacement (intercept)	Household heads age 21–50 in year of displacement	1972–6 (base years of displacement)
	Ruhm, Christopher	1994	United States	10 per cent	Difference in earnings between advance notified workers and non-notified workers	Workers age 25–60 at survey date	1983–90

Ruhm, Christopher	1991	United States	Unemployment: 8.73 (0.323) Log Wage -0.1149 (0.020)	Effect on Unemployment and Wages in year of displacement	Household Heads age 21-65 in base year	1969-82
Topel, Robert H.	1990	United States	Earnings 40 per cent Wage 20 per cent	Annual earnings loss for typical manufacturing worker	Men age 20-60	1968-85
Abbring et al.	2002	United States	Source of job loss: Plant closing 0.039 (0.043), slack work 0.12 (0.047)	Those displaced due to slack work gain relative to those losing jobs because of job closure	20-64 year old workers, focus on persons losing jobs that have lasted at least one year	1993-6
Difference in difference						
Chan, Sewin and Ann Huff Stevens	2001	United States	1.01 per cent	Increase in exit from work hazard for benchmark male-displaced worker relative to non-displaced worker	Workers age 50 and above in 1990	1992-6
Farber, Henry S.	1997	United States	-0.122 (0.005)	Effect of displacement on log real weekly earnings among all full-time workers in all years	Workers age 20-64	1981-95
Farber, Henry S.	2001	United States	-C.120 (0.019)	Effect of displacement on log real weekly earnings among all full-time workers in the 1997-9 period	Workers age 20-64	1981-99
Farber, Henry S.	2005	United States	-0.171 (no S.E.)	Effect of displacement on log real weekly earnings among all full-time workers in the 2001-3 period	Workers age 20-64	1981-2003

Continued

Table 3.2 Continued

Method	Study	Study year	Country	Coefficient (S.E.)	Interpretation	Sample definition	Time period
					Main Estimate		
	Gibbons, Robert and Lawrence F. Katz	1991	United States	−0.040 (0.017)	Coefficient on Layoff Dummy in Change in log earnings equations	Male workers age 20–61	1979–86
	Hamermesh, Daniel S.	1987	United States	–	Wage experience profiles of workers who are about to be laid off flatten out	Workers displaced or laid off	1977–81
	von Wachter et al.	2008	United States, CA	−12 per cent (lower bound) to −16 per cent (upper bound)	Change in log real weekly earnings	All displaced workers, age 20–64	1991–2000
	Jacobson et al.	2005	United States, Washington State	9 per cent	Quarterly earnings rate of return to one year of community college credits for men	Workers displaced	1987–95
	Jacobson et al.	2003	United States, Washington State	1.4 per cent (older men)	Quarterly earnings rate of return for one Academic Year of Retraining	–	1987–2000
	Kuhn, P. and A. Sweetman	1999	United States and Canada	–	High-tenure union members who are displaced lose more than high-tenure workers who are not union members	Men who lost full-time employment, age 20–64 and tenure less than 20 years	1987–96

Lefranc, A.	2003	United States	−0.1516 (0.0234)	Effect of losing job due to mass layoff on change in log weekly wages	Male heads of households aged 25–55 years old in t-2. Self-employed workers are excluded. The reference group of non-displaced workers is restricted to individuals who have stayed with the same firm, in the period studied	1983–92
Distributed lag model						
Couch, Kenneth A. and Data W. Placzek	2007	United States, CT	−6,022 (790)	Yearly Earnings loss (2000 $US) in fifth year	Workers with six or more years of tenure from large firms and strong labour force attachment	1999–2004
Jacobson et al.	1993	United States, PA	−6,611 (150)	Yearly Earnings loss (1987 $US) in fifth year	Workers with six or more years of tenure from large firms and strong labour force attachment	1980–7
Kletzer, Lori G. and R.W. Fairlie	2003	United States	−0.123 (0.045)	Log annual earnings loss five years after displacement relative to non-displaced workers	NLSY (cohort of 14–22-year-olds in 1979)	1984–93
Kodrzycki, Yolanda K.	2007	United States, MA	Job losers vs. non-separators: -0.24 Non-recalls vs. recalls: -0.11	Log annual earnings loss 7–10 years after displacement, recalled and non-recalled workers (2004 $US)	Workers with strong labour force attachment (no age, tenure, or firm restriction)	1995–2003

Continued

Table 3.2 Continued

Method	Study	Study year	Country	Main Estimate			
				Coefficient (S.E.)	Interpretation	Sample definition	Time period
	Schmieder Johannes and Till M. von Wachter	2009	United States	Min UR on lost job: 0.0214 (0.006) Unemployment Rate (UR) at job loss: 0.0252 (0.004)	Effect of different unemployment rates (UR) on loss in log annual earnings at displacement	DWS, Male workers 20–65	1984–2004
	Schoeni, R.F. and M. Dardia	2000	United States, CA	Long run: 17–25 per cent Short run: 60 per cent	Quarterly earning losses	Workers in California Unemployment Insurance system from firms > 50 employees	1989–94
	Stevens, A.H.	1997	United States	First displacement: 9 per cent Last displacement: 1 per cent	Average annual earnings reduced by 9 per cent after first displacement. Only 1 per cent if single displacement is isolated	Male household heads age 24–64	1968–88
	von Wachter et al.	2009	United States	With zeros: −12,000 Without zeros: −9,000	Year Earnings Losses 15 Years after Job Displacement (2000 $US)	Workers with six or more years of tenure from large firms and strong labour force attachment	1980–2004
Variance decomposition	Stevens, A.H.	2001	United States	–	In 1980s displaced workers (20 per cent of total) contributed to 40 per cent of transitory variance of earnings	Male household heads age 24–64	1968–92

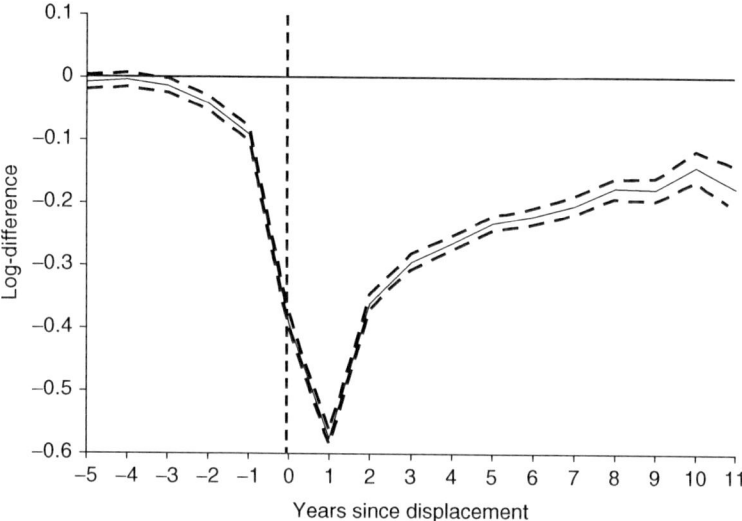

Figure 3.3 Estimate of the long-term earnings decline due to job displacement at mass layoffs using Jacobson, Lalonde, and Sullivan's (1993) mass layoff sample

Notes: Solid line represent coefficient estimates of the interaction of year effects and displacement dummies in a regression model of log quarterly earnings including year fixed effects, person fixed effects, and a quartic for age. Two standard error bands are drawn around main effects.
Source: Taken from Figure 1 of Sullivan and von Wachter (2007).

analysed after a job loss is the incidence of recurring job losses (e.g. Stevens, 1997). Another question that has attracted attention is the role of part-time jobs (e.g. Farber, 1999). Yet, overall, it is surprising how little is known about how workers try and catch up after a job loss. In particular, while administrative data sets often provide sample sizes large enough to analyse more detailed career outcomes, they have rarely been used to analyse the catch-up dynamics after a job loss.

Well-known studies of the effect of job loss on outcomes other than earnings and career outcomes have focused on the effect of job loss on consumption, and the role of unemployment insurance in mitigating the effect of job loss on well-being. This has been analysed by Gruber (1997) for the US, and by Browning and Crossley (2001) for Canada. From these studies, it appears job losses are not perfectly insured and lead to reductions in consumption.

More recently, researchers have begun to analyse the effect of job loss on family and health outcomes. Oreopoulos et al. (2005) have shown how the children of displaced fathers have themselves lower earnings in Canada. Sullivan and von Wachter (2009) have shown how workers losing their jobs during mass layoffs not only have long-term earnings declines but also experience increases in their probability of dying. For a middle-aged man losing his job in the early 1980s, this can lead to losses of life expectancy of up to two years.

This brief overview suggests that, even in the US literature, there are several open questions in the analysis of job loss.[8] First, there are important discrepancies in the size of the estimates of job loss effects between studies, and this is subject to ongoing research (von Wachter et al., 2008 (summarized below)). Second, knowledge on how different groups in the population are affected by job loss is incomplete. Among others, little is known about job losses from different type of firms and industries, or for women and non-white workers. Third, the effect of job loss on career patterns and other outcomes has generally received limited attention.

3.3.3 Summary of EU estimates

The second panel of Table 3.1 summarizes the available studies by different definitions of job loss, time period, and subgroup for countries within the EU. Overall, there appear to be a reasonable number of studies. However, the estimates are distributed over 12 countries, and some countries have noticeably more information than others (such as France, Germany, Denmark, and Sweden). Other countries, such as the UK, Italy, and Spain, have very few or no estimates of the cost of job loss. Moreover, as mentioned above, the majority of European studies are concentrated in the 1990s. The numbers also overstate the amount of information, since many of the studies surveyed do not provide comparable estimates of the effect of job loss on earnings, but analyse employment and other outcomes.

Table 3.3 gives a detailed overview of different studies of job loss in Europe.[9] Each row corresponds to a different study; each column summarizes core evidence pertaining to the analysis, such as definition of sample, the time period studied, and the interpretation of the main estimate (this is the table corresponding to Table 3.2 for US studies). The table groups studies by estimation method, and includes analyses of both earnings and employment outcomes. A closer look at Table 3.3 reveals that the first impression of Panel B in Table 3.1 may indeed have been erroneous. There are very few comparable studies of earnings losses in Europe. Those who do estimate the effect of job loss on earnings find quite different results even within countries.

For example, in France and Germany the estimated effects of job loss on earnings appear to be negligible in some studies and large in others. The discrepancies may arise because of differences in data and methodology. Similarly, there are substantial differences across countries. Job loss in Sweden seems to imply substantial losses (e.g. Eliason and Storrie, 2006), while in Norway losses appear small (e.g. Huttunen et al., forthcoming). We also know little about the persistence of earnings losses in most countries. Moreover, given differences in the data and study designs, it is hard to assess to what extent the numbers represent true differences in outcomes of displaced workers relating perhaps to countries' institutional or economic characteristics.

As in the case of the US, different groups in the labour force can experience substantial differences in earnings losses. There are some important interactions, such as the effect of firm size on earnings losses (e.g. von Wachter and Bender, 2006), or the importance of skill groups (e.g. Burda and Mertens, 2001). However, while interesting patterns appear, given the variety of approaches and outcomes, fewcomparisons of even approximate value can be made.

Something similar can be said about other outcomes of job loss. An interesting series of studies from Sweden and Denmark has used access to incredibly rich linked

Table 3.3 Size of estimates of different studies by broad region and estimation method in EU member states

					Main estimate				Other Estimates					
Method	Study	Study year	Country	Coefficient (S.E.)	Interpretation	Sample definition	Time period	By age	By gender	By education	By occupation	By industry	By region	By firm type
Simple difference	Albæk et al.	2002	Belgium and Denmark	Belgium: 0.587 (0.005); Denmark: 0.382 (0.054)	How does the wage in the previous job affect post-displacement wages? Belgium: Daily wage rates in 1981 Belgian Francs. Denmark: Hourly wage rates in 1988 Danish kroner	Exclude < 20 years. Look at displaced workers who are re-employed two years after displacement	B: 1978–85. Dismissal is considered from 1983 to 1984. D: 1980–91. Dismissal is considered from 1988 to 1989	1	1	0	0	0	1	1
	Boman, Anders	2006	Sweden	0.463 (0.049)	Effect of being foreign-born (excluding those born in other Nordic countries) on the probability of migrating after displacement	Individuals aged 25 to 55 in the year of displacement. Removed individuals with missing or erroneous data	1983–97	0	0	0	0	0	1	0

Continued

Table 3.3 Continued

				Main estimate						Other Estimates				
Method	Study	Study year	Country	Coefficient (S.E.)	Interpretation	Sample definition	Time period	By age	By gender	By education	By occupation	By industry	By region	By firm type
	Grund, Christian	2006	Germany	-0.026 (0.068)	Effects of collective dismissal on the probability of receiving severance payments	The sample is restricted to persons who were affected by an individual or collective dismissal (including plant closings). The sample includes only individuals who were full-time employees before the dismissal	1991–2002	0	1	1	0	1	1	1
	Frederiksen et al.	2006	Denmark	0.172 (0.024)	Effect of losing job due to closure on the probability of re-employment	Only look at males	Look at unemployment spells beginning in the period 1994-9	0	0	0	0	0	1	0
	Ibsen and Westergaard-Nielsen	2005	Denmark	0.1538 (0.0132)	Effect of losing job due to workplace closing on the probability of being re-employed immediately	Excludes (working students)	1980–2001	0	0	0	0	0	1	0

Method	Author	Year	Country	Estimate (SE)	Description	Sample	Period							
Difference-in-difference	Browning et al.	2006	Denmark	−0.04 (0.18)	The difference in hospitalization between the displacement group and matched control group one to four years after base year minus the difference in hospitalization two to five years before base year	Males. Use only 1986–96 as base years. Person is included if in t-1 employed full-time at a private sector plant with at least six employees and age 20–63	1981–99	0	0	0	0	0	0	0
	Abbring et al.	2002	Netherlands	−0.050 (0.038)	The effect of being displaced for an individual with at least one year of tenure, on his change in log real after tax monthly earnings	Focus on households where at least one person is between 15 and 51 years of age and is not a full-time student	1993–6	0	0	0	0	0	0	0
	Borland et al.	2002	Britain	−0.54 (0.27)	Effect of being displaced on change in wages (gross monthly pay – deflated by the retail price index into Sep 1995 prices)	Exclude those who report very low earnings, below £5 a week	1991–6	0	1	0	0	0	0	0
	Orazem et al.	2005	Slovenia	−0.122 (0.029)	Effect of displacement on log wages (hourly deflated wages)	–	1987–93	0	1	1	0	0	0	0

Continued

Table 3.3 Continued

			Main estimate				Other Estimates						
Method	Study	Study year	Country	Coefficient (S.E.)	Interpretation	Sample definition	Time period	By age	By gender	By education	By occupation	By industry	By region	By firm type
	Burda and Mertens	2001	Germany	−0.0216 (0.0033)	Effect of displacement on wage growth (four years after displacement)	Full-time male workers	1985–94	0	0	0	0	0	0	0
	Lehmann et al.	2005	Estonia	0.040 (0.100)	Change in real net monthly wages between 1992 and 1994, for someone who was displaced between 1992 and 1994, vs. someone who stayed in the same job	Exclude individuals who work abroad and outliers having wages below 100 EEK and above 10,000 EEK	1992–4	0	0	0	0	0	0	0
	Carneiro and Portugal	2006b	Portugal	−0.933 (0.012)	Marginal effect of predicted probability of displacement on log of real monthly wage = −0.892	Full-time workers aged between 18 and 64 in the year prior to displacement	Looks at workers who were displaced between 1994 and 1996	0	0	0	0	0	0	0
	Gallo et al.	2001	Germany	0.06 (0.04)	Effect of being displaced on change in self-assessed health		1994–6	0	0	0	0	0	0	0

84

Eliason and Storrie	2004	Sweden	Effect of being displaced on labour market status	Figures: The difference in probability of being employed between displaced and matched non-displaced workers decreases about 8 per cent in the year of displacement. The gap narrows afterwards.	Workers aged between 21 and 50 years in 1987	1983–2000	1	0	0	0	0	0	0
Ohlsson and Storrie	2007	Sweden	Effects of policy measures for displaced workers	Figure: Earnings decrease in the year of job loss, but seem to recover quickly	Exclude those who have reached retirement age 65 in 1999	People displaced in 1983 (LKAB) and 1985 (Uddevalla) and the control groups are followed until 1999	0	0	0	0	0	0	0
Grund, Christian	1999	Germany	Effect of layoffs on change in wages, relative to displacement	−0.008 (0.032)	Full-time male employees between 20 and 60	1991–6	0	0	0	0	0	1	0

Continued

85

Table 3.3 Continued

				Main estimate				Other Estimates						
Method	Study	Study year	Country	Coefficient (S.E.)	Interpretation	Sample definition	Time period	By age	By gender	By education	By occupation	By industry	By region	By firm type
	Lefranc, A.	2003	France	−0.1212 (0.0118)	Effect of losing job due to mass layoff on change in log weekly wages	Male heads of households aged 25–55 years old in t-2	1990–7	0	0	1	0	0	0	0
	Winter-Ebmer, Rudolf	2001	Austria	−0.010 (0.001)	Marginal effect of ln (firm size) on probability of displacement	Male workers. Eliminate observations of persons with a monthly income below $300	1972–91	0	1	0	0	0	0	0
Distributed lag model	Schmieder et al.	2009	Germany	Year of displacement: 8000 Euros, 5 years after displacement 4000 euros, 15 years after displacement 3500 euros	Workers who separate from stable firm because of mass-layoff suffer earnings losses of 15 per cent lasting 15–20 years	Men, age 25–53 in 1979, job displacements in 1980–5	1975–2005	–	–	–	–	–	–	–

Author	Year	Country	Results	Description	Sample	Period									
Bender et al.	2002	France and Germany	France: five years before D: −0.0917 (0.0068); five years after D: −0.0250 (0.0115); Germany: five years before D: 0.0023 (0.0142); five years after D: −0.0103 (0.0118)	France: Workers who separate because of firm closure earn 8.8 per cent (exp(beta)-1) less than continuously employed workers five years prior to the actual separation. Dep. Var = log average real daily earnings. Germany: Effect of displacement on yearly earnings five years before and five years after displacement, relative to their average earnings in the year before closure	F: Men aged 26–50 years in 1984. G: Male 25–50 in 1984	F: 1984–9. G: 1984–90	0	0	0	0	0	0	0	0	0
Couch, Kenneth A.	2001	Germany	Dip (three years before): 1,141 (1,037), Drop (year of displacement): −6,995 (1,405), Recovery (two years after): −5,147 (1,458)	The effect of displacement on annual earnings (in real 1996 DM)	Individuals 25–55 years old	1988–96	1	1	1	0	1	1	0	1	

Continued

Table 3.3 Continued

Method	Study	Study year	Country	Main estimate					Other Estimates						
				Coefficient (S.E.)	Interpretation	Sample definition	Time period	By age	By gender	By education	By occupation	By industry	By region	By firm type
	Dahlberg, Matz and Anders Forslund	2005	Sweden	Training program: −0.114 (0.150); −0.662 (0.147) Subsidized employment	Effect of labour market programs on displacement/ employment	Drop municipalities with missing observations	1987–96	0	0	0	0	0	0	0
	Carneiro, Anabela and Pedro Portugal	2006b	Portugal	0.04 (0.02)	Effect of displacement on real hourly earnings four years after displacement for men in 10th wage quantile	Full-time workers, aged 18–59 in the year prior to displacement	Looks at workers who were displaced between 1994 and 1996	0	1	0	0	0	0	
	Eliason, Marcus and Donald Storrie	2006	Sweden	Figures: Earnings drop in the year of displacement, most of the drop seems persistent	Effect of being displaced on (long time) annual earnings	Workers aged between 21 and 50 years in 1986. Exclude people working in the construction sector or a sector not adequately defined	1983–99	1	0	0	0	0	0	

| Eliason, Marcus and Donald Storrie | 2005 | Sweden | Figures: increased risk over the first four years (almost 50 per cent higher for displaced men); five years later the cumulative risk at same level; during the last four years the risk of dying was actually higher among non-displaced men | Effect of displacement on mortality risk | Workers between the ages of 20 and 65 in the end of year t-1 | 1983–2000 | 0 | 0 | 1 | 0 | 0 | 0 | 0 | 0 |

Continued

Table 3.3 Continued

				Main estimate				Other Estimates						
Method	Study	Study year	Country	Coefficient (S.E.)	Interpretation	Sample definition	Time period	By age	By gender	By education	By occupation	By industry	By region	By firm type
	Eliason, Marcus (2005a)	2005	Sweden	Indication of positive impact from job loss on the risk of divorce. Immediate effects are not significant. Seems to go slightly up four to five years after displacement	Effect of displacement on the probability of divorce	Only couples who were married in 1986 were included	1983–99	0	1	0	0	0	0	0
	Eliason, Marcus (2005b)	2005	Sweden	-0.035 (P-value 0.709)	Effect of man's displacement on his wife's annual earnings three years after displacement	Use couples where both spouses were between 26 and 50 years at the end of 1986	1985–98	0	0	0	0	0	0	0

Author	Year	Country	Method/Estimate	Effect	Sample	Period								
Hijzen et al.	2005	UK	Matched on characteristics (different estimates when matched on wages): three years before: 0.0131 (P-value: 0.685); year of displacement: 0.0041 (P-value: 0.898); three years after: -0.1001 (P-value: 0.008)	Effect of displacement on log real weekly earnings	Workers aged 25–55	1994–2003	1	0	0	0	0	1	0	0
Other methods														
VAR model Pehkonen, Jaakko	1997	Finland	20–24 years old: -1.11 (0.83)	Effect of job-creation programs directed at young people on youth displacement	Workers aged 20–24 years old	1981–95	1	0	0	0	0	0	0	0
VAR model Skedinger	1995	Sweden	-0.410 (0.34)	How participation in t-1 effects youth employment in year t	16–24-year-old workers	1971–91	0	0	0	0	0	0	0	0

data sets to study the effect of job losses on health and family outcomes. These confirm a potential effect of job displacement on mortality, but suggest effects on other outcomes, such as hospitalization or divorce, may be harder to detect. Since these countries' social welfare systems are very different from those of the US and other European countries, comparative studies should yield interesting results.

Overall, although an increasing number of studies examine the consequences of job loss in Europe, many of them do not study the effect of earnings or income. An important number study the effect on employment. As mentioned at the outset, given the presence of more complete insurance in Europe, this may be a relevant focus, and indeed many studies find important employment effects. The scope of these studies remains similar in nature, since the loss in employment can be thought of as a proxy for losses in productivity. In addition, these studies move towards a broader assessment of the social costs of job loss through an implicit or explicit concern with the increasing costs of transfer programmes. However, large employment effects also raise the concern of sample selection, an issue that is rarely addressed but may be particularly relevant in European countries.

The next section will discuss the problems in estimating the effect of job loss in more detail. We will then come back in the last section to discuss the potential ahead for European studies of job losers and how some of the issues of comparability and consistency across studies could be addressed.

3.4 Methodology and threats to validity

3.4.1 Selection within and sorting between firms

Tables 3.2 and 3.3 have shown a substantial number of alternative samples, approaches, and outcomes with sometimes significant differences in results even for the same countries and time periods. Table 3.4 gives an overview of the large number of studies using alternative estimation methods in the US and the EU. Often, the choice of methods is driven by the data, and most studies strive to address potential threats to the validity of their research design in various ways. Figures 3.1 and 3.2 gives a broad schematic overview of the potential pitfalls involved when estimating the costs of displacement.

To understand when these efforts are successful and why, consider the following basic stylized statistical model of the determinants of log earnings:

$$y_{it} = (a_i - \bar{a}^f) + \bar{a}^f + \delta_t D_{i0} + \beta X_{io} + \varepsilon_{it},$$

where a_i indexes individuals' unobserved skills, X_{io} captures observed productivity differences in a baseline period, D_{i0} is a dummy for involuntary mobility (a job loss) at a given time zero, and ε_{it} is captures purely random component of earnings. Time-varying exogenous characteristics, such as age, are omitted for simplicity. The model is written such that individual ability a_i enters as deviation from a firm-specific component $\bar{a}^f$. The firm-specific component is simply the average ability at the firm the worker was at the time of displacement ($t = 0$). It is straightforward to include additional fixed firm-specific wage components. The parameter δ_t is the effect to be estimated.

Table 3.4 Summary of estimation methods used – study counts

Panel A: USA

Estimation method	Without controls	With controls	Dynamic estimates	Breakdown by Worker characteristics	Other
Simple difference	11	12	1	11	5
Difference-in-difference	10	11	5	9	2
Distributed lag model	7	7	7	7	4
Breakup of estimates by plant closing/Layoff	7	9	3	7	3

Panel B: EU Member States

Estimation method	Without controls	With controls	Dynamic estimates	Breakdown by Worker characteristics	Other
Simple difference	3	5	1	3	2
Difference-in-difference	6	11	2	6	1
Distributed lag model	5	5	8	6	2
Breakup of estimates by plant closing/layoff*	2	3	0	3	2

Note: *Papers that include both separations because of plant closing and because of layoffs but report separate estimates for the two categories.

It is well known that job losers and other workers differ in terms of their observable characteristics. Job losers are typically younger, lower-skilled, and have lower pre-displacement wages. Thus, most studies comparing the wages of job losers and job stayers control for observable worker characteristics. Clearly, if in addition there are components of skill observed by the market and not by the statistician, a_i, they may correlate with the mover dummy as well as earnings. This leads to a bias from omitted variables and will overstate the earnings effects of job losses.

The omitted variable bias arises from two components. First, the firm is likely to displace the least able workers. Second, firms with higher job loss rates are also likely to attract less able workers. Thus, even in the absence of selection *within* firms, there will be sorting *between* firms. This sorting will again lead movers and stayers to be of different ability and invalidate a simple control group comparison.

To exclude the bias from unobserved omitted components of the wage correlated with job loss, studies based on panel data include worker fixed effects. However, it is important to realize that individual worker fixed effects *only* take care of omitted variable bias from selection if wages before displacement were a function of worker skills *and* if workers only differ in their average earnings. In this case, if the time series is long enough, the average worker-specific component of wages may be absorbed by fixed effects.

However, there are important cases where wages are not fully a function of workers' skills. For example, this occurs in the presence of asymmetric information (Gibbons and Katz, 1991). It may also be relevant for young workers for whom the markets have not learned their true ability. Similarly, it can arise in the case when wages are affected by internal labour markets, collective wage bargains, or other labour market institutions.

Similarly, it is likely that workers' earnings profiles differ by more than just earnings levels. For example, workers may have different trends in earnings (e.g. arising from different rates of human capital accumulation), or there may be correlated occupation-specific earnings shocks. It is possible to control for selective displacement based on these additional earnings components by conditioning on a richer set of career characteristics. If sample sizes are sufficiently large, this could be implemented in a matching framework.

3.4.2 Firm-level estimates

An alternative approach that more directly addresses the role of selection is to analyse the effect of job loss at the firm level. This approach divides workers into groups based on their employer at the beginning of the study period. Average wages at the firm level are then compared before and after, say, a mass layoff event. To account for sorting as well, such an approach would include firm fixed effects. Thus, it amounts to a comparison over time of workers within the same firm.

In econometric terms, this amounts to using interactions between firm dummies and mass layoff dummies as instruments for job loss in an earnings equation. A straightforward and easier way to implement this approach is to estimate earnings losses directly at the firm level.[10] To do so, in a first step one obtains average earnings for each year at the firms from which workers are displaced, possibly controlling for worker characteristics.[11] In a second step, one estimates a model of the form

$$\bar{y}_{ft} = \gamma_t + \psi_f + \sum_{k \geq -m,} \delta_k D_{ft}^k + u_{ft} \qquad (2)$$

where the coefficients of interest are again the parameters (δ_k) on the distributed lag dummies (D_{ft}^k) capturing the periods before and after a mass layoff. This model is equivalent to the model in equation (1), but does not rely on worker fixed effects to eliminate selection bias.

Von Wachter and Bender (2006) use a related research strategy in which wages of workers exiting the same firm in different years are compared after the job loss. Variation in the layoff rate at the firm level allows them to identify the true effect of job loss. In the context of year-to-year fluctuations in the layoff rate, it makes sense to assume that the firm-level shock only affects displaced workers, and not those remaining at the firm. However, in the event of strong employment reductions – such as in the case of mass layoffs – those staying at the firm may see earnings reductions as well. In this case, an intent-to-treat estimator at the firm level will estimate the effect of the firm-level shock on all affected workers, whether they leave or stay at the firm (von Wachter et al., 2009).

Thinking about sorting at the firm level also helps to address a common misconception about the benefit of using plant closing to get rid of selection effects. While in the case of plant closing the effect of selection within firms is reduced (all workers have to leave; however, typically plants die gradually enough that there is ample opportunity for selective exit prior to the actual day of plant closure), typically the plants that close are smaller. Smaller plants tend to pay lower wages and also attract less able workers. Thus, one cannot simply compare workers laid off in plant closings with other workers in the economy (Krashinsky, 2002). More generally, comparisons between firms risk being between apples and oranges due to average wage differences, sorting, and differences in layoff and closing rates.

Some studies use no control group and look at simple differences in earnings over time. Clearly, in addition to the same selection problems (in the form of classic sample selection in this case), there is also the problem of common underlying trends. It may be that workers losing jobs have had wage declines anyway, or that wage declines are overstated due to an overall decline in labour market conditions. Alternatively, they may be understated because they occur in periods of high wage growth, such as for young workers. Yet, clearly, it is not often straightforward to choose the appropriate control group. Should it be similar workers at the same firm? If yes, should one constrain these 'stayers' to continue working for same the firm over a longer period, or only not to be laid off on the same day? These questions influence the final result of the study, and cannot be decided on econometric grounds alone. Clearly, large data sets with detailed information on employer, previous and current earnings histories will allow researchers to use detailed control groups and compare relevant alternatives. However, better data alone will not alleviate the need for a careful research design tackling the questions of control groups, sorting, and selection.

3.4.3 Measurement error in job loss and earnings

An additional important concern that has received little attention in both the US and European literature is the role of measurement error. Measurement error in the study of job loss is particularly troublesome since it arises from two sources, both of which can potentially introduce a bias in the results. First, there is recall bias in survey data, especially if workers have to remember earnings on jobs lost several years prior to the survey date.

Second, in both survey and administrative data the event of a job loss can be measured with error. This leads to misclassification bias. On the one hand, workers misunderstand the question in a survey. On the other hand, in administrative data the job loss event has to be imputed, typically using changes in overall firm employment. Clearly, not all workers leaving at the time of a downsizing or a plant closure would call themselves displaced.

The literature, therefore, has settled on a few basic approximations, the most common being to consider a worker displaced if he or she leaves a firm whose employment is 30 per cent below a baseline employment level. While the estimates are roughly robust around this definition (von Wachter et al., 2008), clearly there is a certain degree of arbitrariness. This is important, since the size of the layoff and the type of firm will affect which workers are laid off and what type of event they are subject to. This is likely to influence the costs of job loss and will therefore affect interpretation of the resulting estimates.

Measurement error from imperfect recall of past earnings is innocuous unless it is correlated with workers' observable characteristics. If this is the case, the error will load these characteristics onto the estimates. It may thereby also affect the estimates of the cost of job loss. Typically, older and low-income workers tend to overstate past earnings, thereby leading to underestimates of earnings losses. Misclassification bias, if it is random, leads to an attenuation bias parallel to that of classical measurement error. Thus, this would tend to lead to understatements of the cost of job loss. However, often the misclassification does depend on worker characteristics, as shown by von Wachter et al. (2008). In this case, more complicated corrections are in order.

von Wachter et al. (2008) take these different sources of measurement error into account and revisit the discrepancy in estimates using the DWS and the UI data in the US. They find that both data sets are subject to significant measurement error, but that the DWS tends to underestimate the costs of job loss. The final estimates tend to be closer to estimates based on the UI data.

There is no study assessing the role of measurement error in estimates of the effects of job loss in Europe. Some of the questions we would like to know are: what do the firm events in the administrative data actually measure? How are workers to be displaced chosen, and do they receive advance notification? What do they receive in terms of severance pay? What are their total earnings, including bonuses and overtime pay?

3.4.4 Heterogeneous effects of job loss

A last question concerns the interpretation of resulting estimates even if they are generally believed to be free of bias. We would expect the response to job loss to be heterogeneous, and this is confirmed by the findings reported in Tables 3.3 and 3.5. Since there is likely to be remaining heterogeneity even within, say, demographic group, this begs the question for which workers the estimated coefficients represent causal responses.

Within our simple statistical model of earnings, we are interested in the interpretation of our estimates in the presences of heterogeneous coefficients on the job loss dummy, that is,

$$y_{it} = a_i + \delta_{it} D_{i0} + \varepsilon_{it},$$

where for simplicity the firm-specific component and baseline worker characteristics have been dropped. The average treatment effect (ATE) is typically defined as the unconditional mean of the earnings loss $\bar{\delta}_t = E\{\delta_{it}\}$.

Given results in the literature on programme evaluation, it is unlikely that the estimated effects are average treatment effects. The necessary condition requires that the correlation between the event in question (the job loss) and the heterogeneous response (the effect of job loss) is unaffected by the dimension of our control–treatment comparison (i.e. the instrument). In other words, we have to assume that the particular nature of the firm level event we use to proxy for involuntary layoff does not affect the degree of correlation between job loss and the sensitivity to job loss.[12] However, it is very likely that layoffs of different size lead to either a declining or an increasing correlation. This might occur because of differences in self-selection – different workers choosing to leave the firm at different degrees of restructuring. It may also be due to the way firms select which workers to lay off.

If such selection based on the individual treatment effect takes place, it is more reasonable to consider whether the estimates obtain the local average treatment effect. This is the average response to a job loss of workers induced to lose their jobs in the particular event considered $\bar{\delta}_t = E\{\delta_{it} \mid Z_{io} = 1\}$ (e.g. those workers losing their jobs during a mass layoff). This estimate is a valid causal effect for that group, but may not generalize to other groups in the population.

While this interpretation is intuitive and yields estimates for populations of intrinsic interest (i.e. those most at risk for a mass layoff), it does not attain without an additional assumption. The requirement for the estimates to obtain such a local average treatment effect is to assume that no worker who would have left the firm in the absence of a mass layoff now stays. That is, there can be no workers switching their behaviour due to mass layoffs (this is sometimes referred to as the 'monotonicity' condition).

One can easily imagine situations during which this assumption fails in the present context. For example, it may that a worker would have left the firm in the absence of the mass layoff, but decides to stay because leaving the firm at time of a restructuring sends a bad signal to the market. In this case, the resulting

Table 3.5 Overview of selected data sets used and available in the USA

Name of data set	Country	Type (survey, administrative, matched)	Time period	Sample size	Worker or firm level observations (or both)	Key worker characteristics	Measure of earnings and hours	Worker career history	Information about job loss	Firm characteristics	Study used	Type of access
Administrative data from California Unemployment Insurance System	United States, CA	Administrative, Panel	1989 to 1994 (Schoeni and Dardia), 1991 to 2000 (von Wachter et al., 2008)	830,000 workers (All in Aerospace and 20 per cent of other workers)	Worker level	Age, sex and ethnicity only available for subset of workers (non-random)	Quarterly earnings	Panel	Employer indicator, changes indicate job change. Many job losses at an establishment interpreted as displacement/involuntary job loss	Firm size, industry	Schoeni and Dardia (2000), von Wachter et al. (2008)	Contact: http://www.ces.census.gov/ces.php/home

98

Current Population Survey (CPS), Displaced Worker Survey (DWS)	United States	Monthly Survey, Repeated Cross Section	1940 to today	About 60,000 households each month	Worker level	Extensive information on workers' background. Workers are asked about displacement, reasons for job loss, pre-displacement wage and hours etc.	Weekly hours and wages	Tenure and information about pre-displacement jobs	Workers are asked whether they were ever displaced during the previous three years, and if so detailed information about pre-displacement job is collected	Occupation, industry	Addison and Portugal (1989) Abbring et al. (2002) Carrington and Zaman (1994) Couch and Fairlie (2005) Di la Rica (1992) Farber (1993, 1997, 1999, 2001, 2003, 2005) Gibbons and Katz (1991) von Wachter et al. (2008) Jacobson et al. (2005) Kletzer (1989) Kuhn et al. (1999) Magnani (2001) Neal 1995) Podgursky and Swaim (1987) Ruhm (1994)	Data available from http://www.census.gov/cps/ and http://www.nber.org/data/cps_basic.html
Health and Retirement Study (HRS)	United States	Survey, Panel (Biennal)	1992 to present	About 20,000 individuals over the age of 50.	Worker level (Household information)	Extensive information on worker's background. Focus especially on health related issues and work history	Detailed variables for earnings, wages, assets, pensions, hours and weeks worked	Detailed work history also for time before Panel starts	Information about job losses and reasons for job loss	Occupation, industry	Chan and Stevens (2001), Couch (1998)	Data available from http://hrsonline.isr.umich.edu/

Continued

Table 3.5 Continued

Name of data set	Country	Type (survey, administrative, matched)	Time period	Sample size	Worker or firm level observations (or both)	Key worker characteristics	Measure of earnings and hours	Worker career history	Information about job loss	Firm characteristics	Study used	Type of access
National Longitudinal Survey of Youth 1979 (NLSY79)	United States	Survey, Panel (Annual until 1994, Biennial after 1994)	Representative sample of individuals age 14 to 22 in 1979.	Original sample 12,686	Worker level	Extensive information on workers' background.	Weekly hours and wages	Panel study, detailed work history	Individuals are asked about reasons for leaving a job	Occupation, industry, size of employer, covered by collective bargaining	Holzer and LaLonde (1999) Kletzer and Fairlie (2003)	Data available on the web: http://www.bls.gov/nls/nlsy79.htm
Panel Study of Income Dynamics (PSID)	United States	Survey, Panel	1968 to present	In total more than 65,000 individuals	Worker level (most studies use only household heads)	Wide variety of information about both families and individuals. Substantial detail on income sources and amounts, employment and residence. In some years also information about achievement motivation, job training, retirement plans, education and wealth	Hourly earnings of head and wife, work hours, unemployment, taxable income. Information more precise for household heads	Panel study, detailed work history as people are followed over time and earnings and hours are available throughout the sample period	Household heads are asked what happened to their last job if they are unemployed or their job tenure is less than a year	Job characteristics and some employer characteristics	Magnani (2001) Hamermesh (1987) Ruhm (1991) Stevens (1997, 2001) Topel (1990)	Data available from http://psidonline.isr.umich.edu/

Pennsylvania Administrative Data (Unemployment Insurance and Tax Records)	United States, PA	Administrative, Panel	1974 to 1986 (time period used in Jacobson et al. 1993)	5 per cent sample of all workers	Worker and Firm level (workers are matched to firms)	Gender, birthdate	Quarterly earnings	Work history due to Panel Structure	Employer indicator, changes indicate job change. Many job losses at an establishment interpreted as dis-placement/involuntary job loss	Firm size, industry	Jacobson et al. (1993)	Contact Pennsylvania Department of Labor and Industry: http://www.dli.state.pa.us/
Washington State Administrative Data (Unemployment Insurance, College Transcripts)	United States, Washington State	Administrative, Panel	Unemployment Insurance 1990–4 Wage Records 1987–2000 Community College Transcripts 1989–1996	About 60,000 after some sample restrictions are applied	Worker level	Education, age, minority, region, gender, detailed information on community college from merging with transcripts.	Quarterly earnings	Detailed history due to Panel Structure	Information about employer changes and unemployment benefits receipt	Industry	Jacobson et al. (2003 and 2005)	Contact Washington State Training and Coordinating Board: http://www.wtb.wa.gov/
Ontario Ministry of Labor Survey (OML)	Canada, Ontario	Survey, Cross Section	1982	21 firms with mass layoffs (50 or more workers each)	Worker and firm level (workers are matched to firms)	Tenure, education, marital status, years since displacement, age	Pre- and Post-displacement Wage	Tenure and information about pre-displacement jobs	Only displaced workers, information about previous and current job	Union status (covered by collective bargaining)	Kuhn and Sweetman (1999)	Contact Ontario Ministry of Labour: http://www.labour.gov.on.ca

Continued

Table 3.5 Continued

Name of data set	Country	Type (survey, administrative, matched)	Time period	Sample size	Worker or firm level observations (or both)	Key worker characteristics	Measure of earnings and hours	Worker career history	Information about job loss	Firm characteristics	Study used	Type of access
Canadian Displaced Worker Survey (CDWS)	Canada	Survey, Cross Section	1986 (asking for job loss 81–5)	about 1200 displaced workers	Worker level	Tenure, education, marital status, years since displacement, age	Pre- and Post-displacement Wage	Tenure and information about pre-displacement jobs	Only displaced workers, information about previous and current job	Union status (covered by collective bargaining), establishment size	Kuhn and Sweetman (1999)	Data available from http://www.statcan.ca/english/Dli/Data/Ftp/dws/dws1986.htm
Canadian Out-of-Employment Panel (COEP)	Canada	Survey, Cross Section	1993, workers interviewed 3 times	About 10,000 workers (about 900 displaced)	Worker level	Tenure, education, marital status	Pre- and Post-displacement Wage	Tenure and information about pre-displacement jobs	Only displaced workers, information about previous and current job	Union status (covered by collective bargaining)	Kuhn and Sweetman (1999)	Data available from http://www.statcan.ca/english/Dli/Data/Ftp/coep/coep1995.htm

estimates will be biased, and the bias can be bounded as suggested by Angrist et al. (1996).

3.5 Available data, comparability and the road ahead

The difficulty in comparing studies within the US is partially driven by differences in data sources. This difficulty is magnified in the EU, with different statistical agencies granting access to different databases. The recent surge of papers in this area is an encouraging sign of increasing access to large administrative data sets and sometimes new survey data.

Table 3.5 and Table 3.6 document the wide range of data sets in the US and the EU, respectively. The tables provide information on time periods covered, information available, and in some cases sample sizes of selected data sources. The recent increase in the availability of large administrative data sets is a phenomenon unique to some European countries. This represents a great opportunity to move beyond some of the measurement problems and design problems afflicting analyses with smaller data sets. The ongoing active research activity in Europe in this field indicates the potential ahead.

Yet, part of the difficulty in comparing outcomes from different studies both within and between countries arises from differences in research designs that try to deal with threats to validity in different ways. Moreover, different samples of workers covering different time periods can often lead to different estimates. Studies also tend to analyse alternative outcomes, making a more direct comparison difficult. More worryingly, studies often consider different definitions of job loss events that may lead to estimates that are not comparable even when considering the same outcomes. As suggested above, alternative definitions of job loss events do not only represent differences in treatments, but will also induce different groups of workers to move, and thus obtain different local average treatment effects. Similarly, differences in labour market institutions may affect the incidence of job loss.

Some of these differences are an integral part of the determinants of the cost of job loss (e.g. differences in institutional arrangements in the labour market), and should be part of a careful comparative analysis. However, there are differences in the choice of method, sample, and definitions that could be alleviated.

In particular, future studies could focus on obtaining estimates free of biases from selection for a comparable event and a comparable group of workers. To do so, the method chosen should be both reliable and easy to understand and to implement. As discussed in the previous section, a proposal for a set of empirical studies aiming at obtaining comparable estimates of the cost of job loss would then be to analyse the effect of a common event (e.g. a 30 per cent drop in employment with respect to a baseline) on a single outcome (e.g. annual earnings) for a common group of workers (e.g. prime age men and women) over a similar period of time (e.g. 1995–2000) with similar sample specifications regarding pre-job loss tenure or ensuing labour market participation. The method used would be a dynamic difference-in-difference (distributed lag) model at the worker-year or firm-year level.

Table 3.6 Overview of selected data sets used and available in EU member states

Name of data set	Country	Type (survey, administrative, matched)	Time period	Sample size	Worker or firm level observations (or both)	Key worker characteristics	Measure of earnings and hours	Worker career history	Information about job loss	Firm characteristics	Study used	Type of access
Austrian social security records	Austria	Administrative	Since 1972	–	Both	Age, gender	–	Detailed day-by-day information of all employment and unemployment spells	–	–	Winter-Ebmer (2001)	–
Administrative data from the Belgian social security system	Belgium	Administrative	–	All Belgian workers, except tenured employees of the federal government	Worker (and firm-based)	Age, sex, blue collar/white collar	Wage, number of days worked	Observe employee and firm histories; get censored measure of tenure	Observe separation from job, but not the reason for the separation	–	Albæk et al., (2002)	–
BHPS	Britain	Survey	Since 1991	Around 5,500 households	–	–	Information on gross monthly pay and hours	–	Respondents are asked why they left their previous employment	–	Borland et al. (2002)	–
CCP version of the IDA database maintained by Statistics Denmark	Denmark	Administrative	1980–2001	Information about all individuals aged 15–74	Matches individuals and workplaces	Demographic characteristics, education, labour market experience, tenure and earnings	–	–	–	–	Ibsen and Westergaard-Nielsen (2005); Fredriksen et al. (2006)	Data may be approached at CCP with the permission of Statistics Denmark

Danish register data collected by Statistics Denmark	Denmark	Administrative	1981–99	10 per cent random sample of the Danish adult population	Individual (and plant-based)	Tax forms, visits to the doctor or hospital, interactions with the welfare system, schooling, work status, registration of residence	–	–	The data set contains variables connecting individuals to firms and plants	Browning, Dano and Heinesen (2006); Albæk et al. (2002)	Available for research purposes – subject to stringent controls to maintain confidentiality
Estonian Labor Force Surveys	Estonia	Survey	1995, 1997, 1999	10,000 (1995); 5,000 (1997) and 12,000 (1999) working individuals	Individual	Gender, nationality, age, education, job tenure, occupation, industry, sector	Gross monthly wages	Individuals give labour market history (info. on income and labour market status) in previous years (first survey gives history since Jan 1989)	The survey makes it possible to distinguish between job losses because of plant closure, of personnel reductions, and of dismissal or privatization. (Can also identify people who leave their job for parental leave, retirement, etc.)	–	Lehmann et al. (2005)	–

Continued

Table 3.6 Continued

Name of data set	Country	Type (survey, administrative, matched)	Time period	Sample size	Worker or firm level observations (or both)	Key worker characteristics	Measure of earnings and hours	Worker career history	Information about job loss	Firm characteristics	Study used	Type of access
Annual Social Data Reports (DADS)	France	Administrative	1976–96 (excl. 1981, 1983 and 1990)	Random 1/25 sample of the French population	Information on workers and employers	Sex, age, occupation, region, full- or part-time, sector	Info. earnings, full-time vs. part-time, but not hours	–	–	–	Bender et al. (2002)	–
Permanent Dynamic Sample (EDP)	France	Administrative	–	–	Worker	Date of birth, marriage, death and birth/death/marriage of parent or child	–	–	–	–	Bender et al. (2002)	–
Unified System of Enterprise Statistics (SUSE)	France	Administrative	–	–	Firm	–	–	–	–	–	Bender et al. (2002)	–

106

French Employment Surveys (FES) – conducted by the French national statistics institute (INSEE)	France	Survey	–	approx. 60,000 hh	Households – Individuals	Age, education, region of residence, industry of job, seniority	Monthly wage, hours worked	–	If individual is unemployed, the survey distinguishes between voluntary quits, end of contract, individual out of labour force, workers on 'collective' permanent layoff and workers on 'individual' permanent layoff	–	Lefranc (2003)	–
IAB, three components: Beschäftigungsstichprobe (BS), Histcrikdatei (HD), and Leistungsempfängerdatei (LD)	Germany	Administrative	BS covers 1975–90	BS: 1 per cent sample from the overall employees' statistics; HD estimated to cover 79 per cent of total labour force	Worker. Every individual in HD is associated to an establishment by an establishment identifier.	Gender, nationality, educational attainment	Gross earnings over the past employment spell	HD: contains continuous employment history for each employee covered by the social security system. Contains information on interruptions in employment, such as maternity leave, or obligatory military and civil service	LD contains information on unemployment benefits, unemployment assistance, and payments while participating in training and retraining programs	Plant size, educational structure of the work force, industry information	Bender et al. (2002)	–

Continued

Table 3.6 Continued

Name of data set	Country	Type (survey, administrative, matched)	Time period	Sample size	Worker or firm level observations (or both)	Key worker characteristics	Measure of earnings and hours	Worker career history	Information about job loss	Firm characteristics	Study used	Type of access
German Socio-Economic Panel (GSOEP)	Germany	Survey	Started 1984	In 1996: 6,525 households and 12,729 individuals	Individual	Age, year of education, gender, self-assessed health	Measure of annual labour earnings constructed by the survey staff	–	If individual changes job, he or she is asked why	Firm size, industry	Couch (2001); Burda and Mertens (2000); Gallo et al. (2001); Grund (2006); Grund (1999)	–
Social Insurance File (IAB)	Germany	Administrative		1 per cent public use panel of the universe of dependent status employed workers in West Germany	Employees	–	–	–	–	–	Burda and Mertens (2001)	–

108

First Employment data set (FE)	Netherlands	Administrative	1992–6	2,000 firms/ 26,000 workers per year	Firm–worker	Worker transitions into and out of firms, tenure, separations, reasons for separations, variety of individual and job characteristics	–	–	Layoffs and separations from shrinking firms	–	Abbring et al. (1999)	–
UI data set – provided by the Dutch Social Security Council	Netherlands	Administrative	1992–3	209,478 cases	Worker	Information on unemployment spells of all workers entering UI in 1992. Information on sector, municipality and month entering UI	–	–	–	–	Abbring et al. (2002)	–
Labor Force Survey (LFS) – provided by the Netherlands Organization for Strategic Labor Market Research	Netherlands	Survey	1985–90	2,132 hh/4,020 individuals in the first wave	Household–Individual	–	Information on earnings	Full labour market histories	Layoffs/ Reasons for layoffs	–	Abbring et al. (2002)	–

Continued

Table 3.6 Continued

Name of data set	Country	Type (survey, administrative, matched)	Time period	Sample size	Worker or firm level observations (or both)	Key worker characteristics	Measure of earnings and hours	Worker career history	Information about job loss	Firm characteristics	Study used	Type of access
Data derived from administrative registers and prepared for research by Statistics Norway	Norway	Administrative	1988–98	Covers all Norwegian residents 16–74 years old	Worker–Firm/Plant	Employment relationships, labour income, education, labor market status, gender, age, experience, marital status	Annual earnings	–	–	Can see if firm/plant is downsizing or closing down	Huttunen, Møen and Salvanes (forthcoming)	–
Annual mandatory employment survey collected by the Portuguese Ministry of Employment – obtained from Quadros de Pessoal (QP)	Portugal	Administrative	–	Covers virtually all firms employing paid labour	Firms–Workers	Gender, age, education, skill, occupation, tenure, earnings and duration of work	Real monthly wage	–	–	Location, economic activity, employment, sales, legal framework	Carneiro and Portugal (2006a): IZA 1926; Carneiro and Portugal (2006b): IZA 2289	–

Merged official Slovenian datasets on unemployment and on work history	Slovenia	Administrative	–	12,923 individuals	–	–	The Slovenian Pension and Invalid Fund collects data on hours and earnings	Data on employment spells, unemployment spells, and time out of labour force	Quits and displacements due to layoffs or bankruptcy	Private ownership, foreign ownership, firm profits, differential layoff costs, cause of unemployment	Orazem et al. (2005)	–
Register from Statistics Sweden (RAMS) + information from the National Labour Market Board	Sweden	Administrative	Since 1985	–	Worker	Employment by industry, age group, municipality, information on participation in labour market programs	–	–	–	–	Dahlberg and Forslund (2005)	–

Continued

Table 3.6 Continued

Name of data set	Country	Type (survey, administrative, matched)	Time period	Sample size	Worker or firm level observations (or both)	Key worker characteristics	Measure of earnings and hours	Worker career history	Information about job loss	Firm characteristics	Study used	Type of access
Procedures: Developed by Statistics Sweden	Sweden	Administrative	1983–99	–	Links establishment data to employee data	Age, sex, number of children, marital status; if married, information on spouse, region of birth	Labour income	–	–	Births, deaths, mergers, ownership changes, industry sector, composition of work force, number of employees, location	Eliason and Storrie (2004, 2005, 2006), Eliason (2005a, 2005b)	–
Data collected from various registry data sources (The Principal registers used are, The Register Based Labour Market Statistics,	Sweden	Administrative	Observe individuals 1987–97	The original data set covers all individuals in Sweden who were displaced through closures or substantial cutbacks of	Workers	Detailed information on demographic, family and labour market variables	–	–	–	–	Boman (2006)	–

The Income and Wealth Register, and the Longitudinal Register of Education and Labour Market Statistics)				establishments with 10 or more employees, which occurred in 1987 or 1988			
Register data from Statistics Sweden and the Swedish National Board of Health and Welfare	Sweden	Administrative	1983–99	–	Individuals, firms and establishments	Birth year, sex, birth country, education, number of children	Working hours (for 1990), annual income	–	Can identify if individual is working in closing and downsizing establishment	Firm size, age structure, gender structure, sector, municipality, number of employees	Ohlsson and Storrie (2007)	–
Statistics Sweden: Labour Force Surveys, Labour Market Statistics and unpublished statistics	Sweden	Survey and administrative	–	–	–	–	–	–	–	–	Skedinger (1995)	–

Continued

Table 3.6 Continued

Name of data set	Country	Type (survey, administrative, matched)	Time period	Sample size	Worker or firm level observations (or both)	Key worker characteristics	Measure of earnings and hours	Worker career history	Information about job loss	Firm characteristics	Study used	Type of access
New Earnings Survey (NES) linked with the New Earnings Survey Panel Dataset (NESPD)	UK	Survey	1994–6, 1998 onwards	Random sample of 1 per cent of employees who are part of the PAYE tax scheme	Employees	–	–	–	–	–	Hijzen et al. (2005)	–
Ukrainian Longitudinal Monitoring Survey (ULMS)	Ukrainia	Survey	Survey first undertaken in 2003	4,000 hh and approx. 8,500 individuals	Households– Individuals	Demographic structure of hh, its income and expenditure patterns, living conditions	Gross monthly wages	Survey records month and year of every labour market transition since end of 1997	Makes it possible to distinguish between job loss because of plant closure, firm reorganization, bankruptcy, privatization, dismissal and personnel reduction	–	Lehmann et al. (2006)	–

Such an approach has been taken by Schmieder et al. (2009), who have replicated the approach taken by Jacobson et al. (1993) and von Wachter et al. (2009) for the United States with similar data for Germany. Using administrative data covering 30 years Schmieder et al. (2009) used the same definitions of time period, sample, mass-layoff, job separation and methodology. The estimates can be easily compared across the studies; the striking finding is that mass-layoffs during the recession of the early 1980s had similarly large and persistent effects in both countries.

Ideally, such an approach would go hand-in-hand with continued developments towards general access to administrative data sources for researchers from all countries without restrictions in access by institutional affiliation or nationality. This would help to foster new research projects, replication of existing studies, and rapid progress of our understanding of the causes and consequences of job displacement.

Notes

Contact: vw2112@columbia.edu. I would like to thank Johannes Schmieder and Herdis Steingrimsdottir for excellent financial support from the National Science Foundation (grant 0453017).

1. Alternative data sources and their properties will be discussed in more detail below.
2. Consistent with the notion of low rates of job loss and low hiring rates, long-term unemployment has been often found to be caused by low outflow rates rather than high inflows into unemployment.
3. Note that worsening health due to lower earnings would not be added separately to the total cost of job loss if they represent outcomes of individuals' optimal responses.
4. For a comparison of the implications of models of health investments and socio-economic status for the correlation of earnings and health see Deaton (1999).
5. Variables that are affected by job loss itself, such as tenure at current job or current firm size, should be analysed as outcome variables. Since they are likely to be correlated with unobservable characteristics that also affect earnings, including them as explanatory variables is likely to bias the coefficient on the displacement indicators.
6. For more detailed earlier surveys, see Fallick (1996) and Kletzer (1998).
7. Other longitudinal data sets used are the Panel Study of Income Dynamics (PSID), the National Longitudinal Study of Youth (NLSY), and the Health and Retirement Survey (HRS).
8. Several other papers analyzing different aspects of job displacement are summarized in the tables. In addition, recently, Farber (2007) and Bowlus and Vilhuber (2002) have studied the incidence and timing of job loss. Jacobson et al. (1999, 2003, 2005) have studied the role of retraining, while Kletzer (2000, 2001, 2002, 2004) has analyzed the role of trade in explaining the incidence and cost of job loss; Olson (1992), Lin (2005) and Simon (2005) have studied the effect of job loss on health insurance, while Gallo et al. (2000), Catalano et al. (1993), and Dew et al. (1992) have studied job loss and various aspects of health. From early studies such as Topel (1991), to more recent ones such as Couch and Placzek (2009), numerous other studies have analyzed the effect of job displacement on earnings.
9. Several other papers analyzing different aspects of job displacement are summarized in the tables. In addition, Margolis (1999) has studied the effect of job loss on earnings and employment in France, Ichino et al. (2007) and Schwerdt et al. (2008) in Austria; Pfann (2006) in the Netherlands; von Wachter and Bender (2008) and Schmieder von

Wachter and Bender (2009) in Germany; and Arulampalam et al. (2001), and Hijzen et al. (2006, forthcoming) in the UK.
10. To obtain estimates corresponding to instrumental variable regression, the coefficients from this reduced form can be divided by the layoff rate. The 'reduced form' at the firm level is the 'intention to treat' estimate.
11. The first step regression is an ordinary least squares model of log earnings on firm-year dummies controlling for fixed worker characteristics and age (note that controlling for the former is not strictly necessary, since worker characteristics are held constant at the level of the firm experiencing layoffs; age controls will eliminate wage changes due to experience growth):

$$y_{it} = \beta X_{i0} + \sum_{t}\sum_{f} \phi_{tf} D_i \left(firm = f, year = t\right) + u_{it};$$

the averages used in a second step are the coefficients on the year-firm-dummies. Note that, without additional characteristics, these are just firm-year averages.
12. If we have a measure of individual job loss and we estimate its effect on earnings loss by ordinary least squares, we have to assume that $cov(\delta_{it}, D_{i0})$ is equal to zero. Often, administrative data is used to find proxies for involuntary job loss using employment flows at the firm level. If we compare workers losing their jobs in a mass layoff ($Z_{i0}=1$) with those staying at the same firm ($Z_{i0}=1$), we have to assume that $cov(\delta_{it}, D_{i0} \mid Z_{i0})$ is independent of Z_{i0}.

References: Displacement Literature Europe

Abbring, J.H., van den Berg, G.J., Gautier, P.A., van Lomwel, A.G.C., van Ours, J.C. and Ruhm, C.J. (2002) 'Displaced Workers in the United States and the Netherlands', in P. Kuhn (ed.) *Losing Work, Moving On: Work Displacement in International Perspective*, Kalamazoo, MI: Upjohn Institute, 105–94.

Albæk, K., Van Audenrode, M. and Browning, M. (2002) 'Employment Protection and the Consequences for Displaced Workers: A Comparison of Belgium and Denmark', in P. Kuhn (ed.) *Losing Work, Moving On: Work Displacement in International Perspective*, Kalamazoo, MI: Upjohn Institute, 471–511.

Bender, S., Dustmann, C., Margolis, D. and Meghir, C. (2002) 'Worker Displacement in France and Germany', in P. Kuhn (ed.) *Losing Work, Moving On: Work Displacement in International Perspective*, Kalamazoo, MI: Upjohn Institute, 375–470.

Boman, A. (2006) 'Internal Migration of Natives and Immigrants Following Job Displacement', Working Papers in Economics 192, Göteborg University.

Borland, J., Gregg, P., Knight, G. and Wadsworth, J. (2002) 'They Get Knocked Down. Do They Get Up Again?', in P. Kuhn (ed.) *Losing Work, Moving On: Work Displacement in International Perspective*, Kalamazoo, MI: Upjohn Institute, 301–74.

Bowlus, A. and Vilhuber, L. (2002) 'Displaced Workers, Early Leavers, and Reemployment Wages', Technical Papers 2002–18, Longitudinal Employer-Household Dynamics, Center for Economic Studies, US Census Bureau.

Browning, M., Dano, A.M. and Heinesen, E. (2006) 'Job Displacement and Stress-Related Health Outcomes', *Health Economics*, 15(10): 1061–75.

Burda, M.C. and Mertens, A. (2001) 'Estimating Wage Losses of Displaced Workers in Germany', *Labour Economics*, 8(1): 15–41.

Carneiro, A. and Portugal, P. (2006a) 'Wages and the Risk of Displacement', IZA Discussion Papers 1926, Bonn.

Carneiro, A. and Portugal, P. (2006b) 'Earnings Losses of Displaced Workers: Evidence from a Matched Employer-Employee Data Set', IZA Discussion Papers 2289, Bonn.

Couch, K.A. (2001) 'Earnings Losses and Unemployment of Displaced Workers in Germany', *Industrial and Labor Relations Review*, 54(3): 559–72.

Dahlberg, M. and Forslund, A. (2005) 'Direct Displacement Effects of Labour Market Programmes', *The Scandinavian Journal of Economics*, 107(3): 475–94.

Eliason, M. (2005a) 'Lost Jobs, Broken Marriages', Economic Studies 144: Individual and Family Consequences of Involuntary Job Loss, Göteborg University.

Eliason, M. (2005b) 'Displaced Workers, Added Workers, and Family Income', Economic Studies 144: Individual and Family Consequences of Involuntary Job Loss, Göteborg University.

Eliason, M. and Storrie, D. (2004) 'The Echo of Job Displacement', ISER Working Papers 2004-20, Essex.

Eliason, M. and Storrie, D. (2005) 'Does Job Loss Shorten Life?', Economic Studies 144: 'Individual and Family Consequences of Involuntary Job Loss', Göteborg University.

Eliason, M. and Storrie, D. (2006) 'Lasting or Latent Scars: Swedish Evidence on the Long-Term Effects of Job Displacement', *Journal of Labor Economics*, 24(4): 831–56.

Frederiksen, A. and Westergaard-Nielsen, N. (2007) 'Where Did They Go?', *Labour Economics*, 14(5): 811–28.

Frederiksen, A., Ibsen, R., Rosholm, M. and Westergaard-Nielsen, N. (2006) 'Labour Market Signalling and Unemployment Duration: An Empirical Analysis Using Employer-Employee Data', IZA Discussion Papers 2132, Bonn.

Gallo, W.T., Bradley, E.H. and Kasl, S.V. (2001) 'The Effect of Job Displacement on Subsequent Health', *Vierteljahrshefte zur Wirtschaftsforschung/Quarterly Journal of Economic Research*, 70(1): 159–65.

Grund, C. (1999) 'Stigma Effects of Layoffs?: Evidence from German Micro-Data', *Economic Letters*, 64(2): 241–7.

Grund, C. (2006) 'Severance Payments for Dismissed Employees in Germany', *European Journal of Law and Economics*, 22(1): 49–71.

Hijzen, A., Upward, R. and Wright, P. (2005) 'The Earnings Costs of Business Closure in the UK', GEP Research Paper no. 2005/31, Nottingham, UK.

Hijzen, A., Upward, R. and Wright, P. (2006) 'Using Linked Employer-Employee Data to Estimate the Earnings Costs of Business Closure', in A. Bryson, J. Forth and C. Barber (eds) *Making Linked Employer-Employee Data Relevant to Policy*, London: Department of Trade and Industry, 134–53.

Hijzen, A., Upward, R. and Wright, P. (forthcoming) 'The Income Losses of Displaced Workers', *Journal of Human Resources*.

Huttunen, K., Møen, J. and Salvanes, K.G. (forthcoming) 'How Destructive is Creative Destruction? The Costs of Worker Displacement', *Journal of the European Economic Association*.

Ibsen, R. and Westergaard-Nielsen, N. (2005) 'Job Creation and Destruction over the Business Cycles and the Impact on Individual Job flows in Denmark 1980–2001', *Allgemeines Statisches Archiv*, 89(2): 183–207.

Ichino, A., Schwerdt, G., Winter-Ebmer, R. and Zweimüller, J. (2007) 'Too Old to Work, too Young to Retire?', IZA Discussion Paper No. 3110, Bonn.

Lefranc, A. (2003) 'Labor Market Dynamics and Wage Losses of Displaced Workers in France and the United States', William Davidson Institute Working Paper 614, Ann Arbor, MI.

Lehmann, H., Philips, K. and Wadsworth, J. (2005) 'The Incidence and Cost of Job Loss in a Transition Economy: Displaced Workers in Estonia, 1989 to 1999', *Journal of Comparative Economics*, 33(1): 59–87.

Lehmann, H., Pignatti, N. and Wadsworth, J. (2006) 'The Incidence and Cost of Job Loss in the Ukrainian Labor Market', *Journal of Comparative Economics*, 34(2): 248–71.

Margolis, D.N. (1999) 'Part-Year Employment, Slow Reemployment and Earnings Losses: The Case of Worker Displacement in France', Papers 9904, *Institut National de la Statistique et des Etudes Economiques*.Ohlsson, H. and Storrie, D. (2007) 'Long Term Effects of Public Policy for Displaced Workers in Sweden – Shipyard Workers In the West and Miners in the North', Uppsala Universitet Department of Economics Working Paper No. 2007:19, Uppsala

Orazem, P.F., Vodopivec, M., and Wu, R. (2005) 'Worker Displacement During the Transition: Experience from Slovenia', *The Economics of Transition*, 13(2): 311–40.

Pehkonen, J. (1997) 'Displacement Effects of Active Labour Market Policy: The Youth Labour Market in Finland', *Empirica*, 24(3): 195–208.

Pfann, G. (2006) 'Downsizing and Heterogeneous Firing Costs', *The Review of Economics and Statistics*, 88(1): 158–70.

Schwerdt, G., Ichino, A., Ruf, O., Winter-Ebmer, R. and Zweimüller, J. (2008) 'Does the Color of the Collar Matter? Firm Specific Human Capital and Post-Displacement Outcomes', IZA Discussion Paper No. 3617, Bonn.

Skedinger, P. (1995) 'Employment Policies and Displacement in the Youth Labour Market', *Swedish Economic Policy Review*, 2(1): 135–71.

Tatsiramos, K. (2007) 'The Effect of Job Displacement on the Transitions to Employment and Early Retirement for Older Workers in Four European Countries', IZA Discussion Paper No. 3069, Bonn.

von Wachter, T. and Bender, S. (2006) 'At the Right Place at the Wrong Time: The Role of Firms and Luck in Young Workers' Careers', *American Economic Review*, 96(5): 1679–705.

von Wachter, T. and Bender, S. (2008) 'Do Initial Conditions Persist between Firms?: An Analysis of Firm-Entry Cohort Effects and Job Losers using Matched Employer-Employee Data', in S. Bender, J. Lane, K. Shaw, F. Andersson and T. von Wachter (eds) *The Analysis of Firms and Employees: Quantitative and Qualitative Approaches*, Chicago, IL: University Chicago Press.

Winter-Ebmer, R. (2001) 'Firm Size, Earnings, and Displacement Risk', *Economic Inquiry*, 39(3): 474–86.

References: Displacement Literature US

Addison, J.T. and Portugal, P. (1989) 'Job Displacement, Relative Wage Changes, and Duration of Unemployment', *Journal of Labor Economics*, 7(3): 281–302.

Arulampalam, W., Gregg, P. and Gregory, M. (2001) 'Unemployment Scarring', *Economic Journal*, 111: F577-F584.

Browning, M. and Crossley, T.F. (2001) 'Unemployment Insurance Levels and Consumption Changes', *Journal of Public Economics*, 80(1): 1–23.

Browning, M. and Crossley, T.F. (2008) 'The Long-Run Cost of Job Loss as Measured by Consumption Changes', *Journal of Econometrics*, 145(1–2): 109–20.

Carrington, W. and Zaman, A. (1994) 'Interindustry Variation in the Costs of Job Displacement', *Journal of Labor Economics*, 12(2): 243–76.

Catalano, R., Dooley, D., Wilson, G. and Hough, R. (1993) 'Job Loss and Alcohol Abuse: A Test Using Data from the Epidemiologic Catchment Area Project', *Journal of Health and Social Behavior*, 34(3): 215–25.

Chan, S. and Stevens, A.H. (2001) 'Job Loss and Employment Patterns of Older Workers', *Journal of Labor Economics*, 19(2): 484–521.

Couch, K.A. (1998) 'Late Life Job Displacement', *The Gerontologist*, 38(1): 7–17.

Couch, K. and Fairlie, R. (2005) 'Last Hired, First Fired? Black-White Unemployment and the Business Cycle', Working Paper Series 2005–50, University of Connecticut.

Couch, K.A. and Placzek, D.W. (forthcoming) 'The Earnings Impact of Job Displacement Measured with Longitudinally Matched Individual and Firm Data', *American Economic Review*.

Couch, K.A. and Placzek, D.W. (2007) 'Earnings Losses of Displaced Workers in Connecticut', Occasional Paper Series 2007–1.

Couch, K.A., Jolly, N.A. and Placzek, D.W. (2009) 'Earnings Losses of Older Displaced Workers: A Detailed Analysis with Administrative Data', *Research on Aging*, 31(1): 17–40.

Crossley, T.F., Jones, S.R.G. and Kuhn, P. (1994) 'Gender Differences in Displacement Cost: Evidence and Implications', *Journal of Human Resources*, 29(2): 461–80.

De la Rica, S. (1992) 'Displaced Workers in Mass Layoffs: Pre-Displacement Earnings Losses and Unions Effect', Industrial Relations Section, Working Paper No. 303, Princeton University.

Dew, M.A., Bromet, E.J. and Penkower, L. (1992) 'Mental Health Effects of Job Loss in Women', *Psychol Med*, 22(3): 751–64.

Fallick, B.C. (1996) 'A Review of the Recent Empirical Literature on Displaced Workers', *Industrial and Labor Relations Review*, 50(1): 5–16.

Farber, H.S. (1993) 'The Incidence and Costs of Job Loss: 1982–91', *Brookings Papers on Economic Activity: Microeconomics*, 1: 73–132.

Farber, H.S. (1997) 'The Changing Face of Job Loss in the United States 1981–1995', *Brookings Papers on Economic Activity. Microeconomics*, 1997: 55–28.

Farber, H.S. (1999) 'Mobility and Stability: The Dynamics of Job Change in Labor Markets', in O. Ashenfelter and D. Card (eds) *The Handbook of Labor Economics*, Vol. 3, North Holland: Elsevier Science, 2439–83.

Farber, H.S. (2001) 'Job Loss in the United States 1981–1999,' Industrial Relations Section, Working Paper No. 453, Princeton University.

Farber, H.S. (2003) 'Job Loss in the United States 1981–2001', NBER Working Paper 9707, Cambridge, MA.

Farber, H.S. (2005) 'What Do We Know about Job Loss in the United States? Evidence from the Displaced Workers Survey, 1984–2004', Industrial Relations Section Working Paper No. 498, Princeton University.

Farber, H.S. (2007) 'Job Loss and the Decline in Job Security in the United States', Industrial Relations Section Working Paper 520, Princeton University.

Gallo, W.T., Bradley, E., Siegel, M. and Kasl, S.V. (2000) 'Health Effects of Involuntary Job Loss Among Older Workers', *The Journals of Gerontology Series B: Psychological Sciences and Social Sciences*, 55: S131–S140.

Gibbons, R. and Katz, L.F. (1991) 'Layoffs and Lemons', *Journal of Labor Economics*, 9(4): 351–80.

Gruber, J. (1997) 'The Consumption Smoothing Benefit of Unemployment Insurance', *American Economic Review*, 87(1): 192–205.

Hamermesh, D.S. (1987) 'The Cost of Worker Displacement', *Quarterly Journal of Economics*, 102: 51–75.

Hamermesh, D.S. (1989) 'What Do We Know About Worker Displacement in the U.S.?', *Industrial Relations*, 28(Winter): 51–9.

Hildreth, A.K.G., von Wachter, T.M. and Handwerker, E.W. (2008) 'Estimating the "True" Cost of Job Loss: Evidence using Matched Data from California 1991–2000', CES Working Paper.

Holzer, H. and LaLonde, R.J. (1999) 'Job Change and Job Stability Among Less-Skilled Young Workers', JCPR Working Papers, 80, Northwestern University/University of Chicago Joint Center for Poverty Research.

Hu, L. and Taber, C. (2008) 'Displacement, Asymmetric Information and Heterogeneous Human Capital', Working Paper No. 2008–02, Federal Reserve Bank of Chicago.

Jacobson, L.S., LaLonde, R.J. and Sullivan, D.G. (1993) 'Earnings Losses of Displaced Workers', *The American Economic Review*, 83(4): 685–709.

Jacobson, L.S., LaLonde, R.J. and Sullivan, D.G. (1999) 'Measures of Program Performance and the Training Choices of Displaced Workers', Working Paper Series WP-99-28, Federal Reserve Bank of Chicago.

Jacobson, L.S., LaLonde, R.J. and Sullivan, D.G. (2003) 'Should We Teach Old Dogs New Tricks? The Impact of Community College Retraining on Older Displaced Workers', Working Paper Series WP-03-25, Federal Reserve Bank of Chicago.

Jacobson, L., LaLonde, R. and Sullivan, D.G. (2005) 'Estimating the Returns to Community College Schooling for Displaced Workers', *Journal of Econometrics*, 125(1–2): 271–304.

Kambourov, G. and Manovskii, I. (2009) 'Occupational Specificity of Human Capital', *International Economic Review*, 50(1): 63–115.

Kletzer, L.G. (1989) 'Returns to Seniority after Permanent Job Loss', *The American Economic Review*, 79(3): 536–43.

Kletzer, L.G. (1998) 'Job Displacement', *Journal of Economic Perspectives*, 12(1): 115–36.

Kletzer, L.G. (2000) 'Trade and Job Loss in U.S. Manufacturing, 1979–94', in R.C. Feenstra (ed.) *The Impact of International Trade on Wages*, Chicago, IL: University of Chicago Press, 349–96.

Kletzer, L.G. (2001) *Job Loss from Imports: Measuring the Costs*, Washington, DC: Institute for International Economics.

Kletzer, L.G. (2002) *Imports, Exports, and Jobs: What Does Trade Mean for Employment and Job Loss?*, W.E. Upjohn Institute for Employment Research, Kalamazoo, MI.

Kletzer, L.G. (2004) 'Trade-Related Job Loss and Wage Insurance: A Synthetic Review', *Review of International Economics*, 12(5): 724–48.

Kletzer, L.G. and Fairlie, R.W. (2003) 'The Long-Term Costs of Job Displacement Among Young Adult Workers', *Industrial and Labor Relations Review*, 56(4): 682–98.

Kodrzycki, Yolanda K. (2007) 'Using Unexpected Recalls to Examine the Long-Term Earnings Effects of Job Displacement'. Federal Reserve Bank of Boston Working Paper W07-2.

Krashinsky, H. (2002) 'Evidence on Adverse Selection and Establishment Size In the Labor Market', *Industrial and Labor Relations Review*, 56(1): 84–96.

Kuhn, P. and Sweetman, A. (1999) 'Vulnerable Seniors: Unions, Tenure, and Wages Following Permanent Job Loss', *Journal of Labor Economics*, 17: 671–93.

Kunze, A. and Troske, K.R. (2007) 'Comparative Advantage or Discrimination? Studying Male-Female Wage Differentials Using Displaced Workers', IZA Discussion Paper No. 3052, Bonn.

Lin, E.Y. (2005) 'Health Insurance Coverage And Reemployment Outcomes Among Older Displaced Workers', *Contemporary Economic Policy*, 23(4): 529–44.

Madden, J. (1987) 'Gender Differences in the Cost of Displacement: an Empirical Test of Discrimination in the Labor Market', *American Economic Review*, 77(2): 246–51.

Magnani, E. (2001) 'Risk of Labor Displacement and Cross-Industry Labor Mobility', *Industrial and Labor Relations Review*, 54(3): 593–610.

Neal, D. (1995) 'Industry-Specific Human Capital: Evidence from Displaced Workers', *Journal of Labor Economics*, 13: 653–77.

Olson, C. (1992) 'The Impact of Permanent Job Loss on Health Insurance Benefits', Industrial Relations Section Working Paper No. 305, Princeton University.

Oreopoulos, P., Page, M. and Stevens, A. (2005) 'The Intergenerational Effects of Worker Displacement', *Journal of Labor Economics*, 26(3): 455–83.

Parent, D. (2000) 'Industry-Specific Capital and the Wage Profile: Evidence from the National Longitudinal Survey of Youth and the Panel Study of Income Dynamics', *Journal of Labor Economics*, 18(2): 306–23.

Podgursky, M. and Swaim, P. (1987) 'Job Displacement Earnings Loss: Evidence from the Displaced Worker Survey', *Industrial and Labor Relations Review*, 41(October): 17–29.

Ruhm, C. (1991a) 'Displacement Induced Joblessness', *The Review of Economics and Statistics*, 73(3): 517–22.

Ruhm, C. (1991b) 'Are Workers Permanently Scarred by Job Displacements?', *The American Economic Review*, 81(1): 319–23.

Ruhm, C. (1994) 'Advance Notice, Job Search, and Postdisplacement Earnings', *Journal of Labor Economics*, 12(1): 1–28.

Schmieder, J. and von Wachter, T. (forthcoming) 'Does Wage Persistence Matter for Employment Fluctuations? Evidence from Displaced Workers', *American Economic Journal, Applied Economics*.

Schmieder, J., von Wachter, T. and Stefan Bender (forthcoming) 'The Long-Term Impact of Job Displacement in Germany During the 1982 Recession on Earnings, Income, and

Employment', Columbia University, Department of Economic, Discussion Paper No. 0910–07.

Schoeni, R.F. and Dardia, M. (2003) 'Estimates of Earnings Losses of Displaced Workers using California Administrative Data', PSC Research Report No. 03–543, Population Studies Center, University of Michigan.

Simon, K. (2005) 'Displaced Workers and Employer-Provided Health Insurance: Evidence of a Wage/Fringe Benefit Tradeoff?', *International Journal of Health Care Finance and Economics*, 1(3–4): 249–71.

Stevens, A.H. (1997) 'Persistent Effects of Job Displacement: The Importance of Multiple Job Losses', *Journal of Labor Economics*, 15: 165–88.

Stevens, A.H. (2001) 'Changes in Earnings Instability and Job Loss', *Industrial Labor Relations Review*, 55(1): 60–78.

Sullivan, D. and von Wachter, T. (2009) 'Mortality and Job Displacement: An Analysis using Administrative Data', *Quarterly Journal of Economics*, 124 (3), 1265–306.

Topel, R.H. (1990) 'Specific Capital and Unemployment: Measuring the Costs and Consequences of Job Loss', *Carnegie Rochester Conference Series on Public Policy*, 33(1): 181–214.

von Wachter, T.M., Handwerker, E.W. and Hildreth, A.K.G. (2008) 'Estimating the "True" Cost of Job Loss: Evidence using Matched Data from California 1991–2000', CES Working Paper 09–14.

von Wachter, T., Song, J. and Manchester, J. (2009) 'Long-Term Earnings Losses due to Mass-Layoffs During the 1982 Recession: An Analysis Using U.S. Administrative Data from 1974 to 2004', Mimeo, Columbia University.

Other References

Abowd, J., Creecy, R. and Kramarz, F. (2002) 'Computing Person and Firm Effects Using Linked Longitudinal Employer-Employee Data', Cornell, mimeo.

Angrist, J., Imbens, G. and Rubin, D. (1996) 'Identification of Causal Effects Using Instrumental Variables', *Journal of the American Statistical Association*, 91(434): 444–55.

Burdett, K. (1978) 'A Theory of Employee Job Search and Quit Rates', *American Economic Review*, 68(1): 212–20.

Deaton, A. (1999) 'Inequalities in Income and Inequalities in Health', in F. Welch (ed.) *The Causes and Consequences of Increasing Inequality*, Chicago, IL: University of Chicago Press.

Krueger, A. and Summers, L. (1988) 'Efficiency Wages and the Inter-Industry Wage Structure', *Econometrica*, 56(2): 259–93.

Lazear, E. (1979) 'Why is there Mandatory Retirement?', *Journal of Political Economy*, 87(6): 1261–84.

Oi, W.Y. and Idson, T.L. (1999) 'Firm Size and Wages', in O. Ashenfelter and D. Card (eds) *Handbook of labor economics*, Vol. 3B, Amsterdam, New York, and Oxford: Elsevier Science.

Topel, R. (1991) 'Specific Capital, Mobility, and Wages: Wages Rise with Job Seniority', *Journal of Political Economy*, 99(1): 145–76.

4
Skill Mismatch in Europe
René Böheim, Iga Magda and Martina Zweimüller

4.1 Introduction

Since the expansion of higher education in the 1970s, the supply of high-skilled workers has increased substantially in the OECD. There is evidence that the demand for skilled labour has been increasing in Europe for (at least) the last decade, and Goldin and Katz (1998) argue that the demand for skilled labour has been increasing since industrialization. If demand for skilled labour increases faster than the supply, wages for skilled workers will increase in competitive markets and lead to more inequality between skilled and unskilled workers. In labour markets where wages are rigid, the employment levels of skilled labour will rise, employment of unskilled labour will fall, and aggregate unemployment rates will, in all probability, rise.

4.1.1 Over- and undereducation

Although technological change demands a highly educated workforce, concern has been raised whether all workers can fully utilize their skills or hold positions for which less education would suffice. The literature on educational mismatch provides some answers to questions concerning the incidence, duration and wage effects of overeducation and undereducation as well as the effects on job satisfaction and productivity (Tsang, 1987; Tsang et al., 1991).

Comparing estimates of the incidence of over- and undereducation from different studies over time, Hartog (2000) shows that the proportion of overeducated workers rose and the proportion of undereducated workers fell in the Netherlands (1960–95), in Spain (1985–90) and in Portugal (1982–95). In contrast, Daly et al. (2000) report a decrease in the incidence of overeducation and an increase in undereducation in the United States between 1976 and 1985. Comparing estimates for the United States and Germany in the mid-1980s, they find that the phenomenon of educational mismatch was less common in Germany.

4.1.2 Skill mismatch

Manacorda and Manning (2007), using data for five European countries and the US, show that the relative demand for skills has increased more than the relative supply in the US and in the UK in the 1980s, but not in the other European countries. In the 1990s, the relative demand for high-skilled labour outpaced the relative supply in Italy and in the Netherlands. For Germany and France they do not find evidence of an increase in the skill mismatch, and conclude that there is little evidence to support the view that the high unemployment rates in these countries are caused by an increase in the skill mismatch, coupled with rigid wage structures.

We address skill mismatch empirically, investigating the extent of overeducation and undereducation by looking at the highest two groups of formal education. We do this at three different levels. First we investigate the extent of over- and undereducation at the aggregate level, that is, for a specific country. We then address the question of how workers' personal characteristics are related to the probability of being overeducated or undereducated. The unique structure of the available data, namely matched employer–employee surveys, permits the analysis of firms and the extent to which they use educational mismatch. We aggregate for each workplace the workers' characteristics to obtain characteristics of the firm and relate these indicators to the number of overeducated (undereducated) workers in the workplace.

Our results for Poland, the Czech Republic and Spain show that there is evidence of overeducation, that is, university graduates who work in non-academic occupations; however, undereducation, that is, high-school graduates who work in academic occupations, is more common.

There are personal characteristics that make a worker more likely to be undereducated (overeducated); however, these differ between countries. For example, in the Czech Republic, women are less likely to be undereducated and more likely to be overeducated, these associations are the reverse for Spain.

Similarly, the characteristics of firms who hire undereducated (overeducated) workers differ by country. We cannot point to a typical firm that is likely to employ overeducated or undereducated workers. For example, in the Czech Republic, the higher the share of female workers, the higher the number of overeducated workers, but we do not find this association for Spanish firms. Our results suggest that institutional settings, such as the access to education or the transition from school to work, influence the incidence and the extent of skill match.

4.2 The wage effects of skill mismatch

From a theoretical perspective, the wage effects of a skill mismatch are fairly straightforward and depend on the rigidity of wages. If wages are fully flexible, demand that exceeds supply will, ceteris paribus, lead to higher wages and in consequence to more wage inequality between skill groups. Over time, as the supply of skills changes, wage levels will adjust and reflect marginal productivity. In labour markets where wages are not fully flexible, for example where minimum wages are in operation, a relatively high demand for high-skilled workers will cause the employment level of the low-skill group to fall, possibly leading to an increase in overall unemployment.

Much of the empirical literature on educational mismatch has focused on whether or not workers who have more or less education than required for a certain occupation receive the same returns to education as their co-workers with exactly the required amount of education. Although the estimated returns differ in size, there is general agreement that returns to years of overeducation are smaller than to required education and that undereducation involves a penalty (Hartog, 2000). Few studies have investigated whether the demand for high skilled workers has risen more than the supply of high-skilled workers. A recent example is Manacorda and Manning (2007), who have used data for the US and the UK, which they see as countries with relatively flexible labour markets, and France, Germany, Italy and the Netherlands, representing more rigid labour markets. In their analysis, they use a simple index of skill mismatch μ which is based on labour force shares and wages by educational group. The central observation for the construction of their index is that, in a situation where demand for a skill group is greater than the supply, the rate of return to education relative to the standard deviation of schooling will increase. Their empirical results for the 1980s and 1990s indicate that the mismatch of skills was greater in the US and in the UK than in the four other countries. The US and the UK show an increase in the skill mismatch throughout the 1980s, levelling off in the 1990s. Continental European countries exhibit a more varied pattern: Italy and Germany show some upward trend in the skill mismatch throughout the 1980s, it increases for the Netherlands in the 1990s, but there is no trend in the 1980s, and there is no trend discernible for France throughout these years. Manacorda and Manning (2007) conclude their analysis with the observation that the high unemployment experienced by continental European countries in the 1980s and 1990s was not primarily caused by an increase in the skill mismatch in the presence of rigid labour markets.

4.2.1 Measuring educational requirements

The literature has followed different approaches concerning the measurement of educational requirements within occupations and the resulting classification of workers as adequately educated, overeducated or undereducated. Required education can either be derived from job analysis (e.g. Rumberger, 1987), self-assessment (e.g. Duncan and Hoffman, 1981) or realized matches (e.g. Kiker et al., 1997; Verdugo and Verdugo, 1989).[1] In a job analysis the level of required education is specified for each occupation by professional job analysts. The method of self-assessment makes use of survey questions that explicitly ask for the education required for a worker's job. The method of realized matches uses the mean or mode of the distribution of attained education levels within a certain occupation as a measure of required education. The measure of educational mismatch is then obtained by relating the worker's attained education level to the estimate of required education for his or her occupation.

A major drawback of these definitions of over- and undereducation concerns the way they reflect the supply of labour and its attributes. In other words, when we analyse skill mismatches we want to quantify the extent to which the characteristics of the workers, in particular their schooling level, deviate from those required to properly perform the tasks of the job. Ideally, the definition of the required level of schooling involved in a job or occupation relies strictly on the requirements of the job, taking into consideration, for example, the type of technology used and its degree of development.

However, the concepts used in the literature take a different approach, which is probably best explained with examples. For instance, in a country that experiences a severe recession, that is, a country with a high unemployment rate, skilled workers may be forced to accept jobs which require fewer skills than they have (the traditional example being university graduates working as taxi drivers). If the recession were severe enough, a naïve researcher who analyses overeducation might conclude that a university degree is the 'required' level of education to become a taxi driver. Workers' self-assessment of under- or overeducation could also lead to a biased estimate of the extent of over- or undereducation as the assessment might be influenced by the educational levels of the workers' co-workers. Similarly, the description of job contents by job analysts may change over time, adapting to the actual distribution of skills in a particular job. Yet another case forces us to be cautious when interpreting analyses on over- and undereducation. Consider a country whose educational system has been clearly unable to supply enough workers with a certain level of schooling for the prevailing demand. For example, almost 60 per cent of the working population in Portugal in 2000 had at most six years of education (MSST, 2000), a result of the explicit neglect of investment in education during the dictatorship that prevailed until the mid-1970s. In such a country, the definition of the 'right' or 'required' level of schooling to perform a job is bound to reflect the constrained supply – if there are hardly any workers with a certain (high) level of schooling, the job will be performed by lower-educated workers, possibly not even poorly, but with low productivity.[2]

4.2.2 Specifications of the wage function

In the literature, two different specifications of the wage function can be distinguished, depending on whether years of over- and undereducation or dummy variables indicating whether a worker is over- or undereducated are included as explanatory variables. The first approach follows Duncan and Hoffman (1981), who use a Mincer-type wage function (Mincer, 1974) and decompose education into years of required education, overeducation and undereducation:

$$\ln W_i = \beta_r E_i^r + \beta_o E_i^o + \beta_u E_i^u + \gamma X_i + \varepsilon_i \quad \text{with} \quad E_i^a = E_i^r + E_i^o - E_i^u, \tag{1}$$

where E_i^r measures years of required education, E_i^o and E_i^u measure years of over- and undereducation, X_i includes other explanatory variables such as work experience or tenure and ε_i is the error term. In this specification, the earnings effects of educational mismatch are conditional on required education, that is, workers with different levels of attained education are compared within a certain occupation. Since required education, overeducation and undereducation are all measured in years, the return to required education can be compared to the return to attained education. Furthermore, earnings effects can be computed conditional on required education (i.e. within occupation) and attained education (i.e. between occupations).

The second specification, introduced by Verdugo and Verdugo (1989), includes the level of attained education and makes use of dummy variables to account for over- and undereducation. In their model, a worker is defined as overeducated or undereducated if his or her education level is more than one standard deviation higher or lower than the mean education level within the respective occupation, that is, the unobserved required education level for a certain occupation is approximated by the mean of the distribution of observed education levels. The returns to education are then estimated by including these measures of educational mismatch in a wage regression:

$$\ln W_i = \beta_a E_i^a + \beta_{od} OD_i + \beta_{ud} UD_i + \gamma X_i + \varepsilon_i, \qquad (2)$$

where E_i^a denotes years of attained education, and OD_i and UD_i are dummy variables indicating whether a worker is over- or undereducated. In contrast to the Duncan and Hoffman (1981) specification, the effects of over- and undereducation are conditional on attained education, that is, workers having the same education level are compared across occupations. Since over- and undereducation are measured as binary indicators, their coefficients cannot be compared to the return to attained education and therefore the return to required education cannot be computed. It follows that the wage effects can only be estimated conditional on attained education (i.e. between occupations) and not conditional on required education (i.e. within occupation).

4.2.3 Theoretical considerations

Depending on the theoretical assumptions concerning the determinants of individual earnings, different signs for the estimated parameters (the β's) are expected. According to human capital theory (Becker, 1975), wages are determined by the marginal productivity of a worker depending on his or her human capital, such as education, work experience and training. It follows that wages are independent of the level of required education, and thus independent of occupations, because occupations are characterized by certain educational requirements. Therefore, in the DH specification, the parameters of the variables measuring years of required education (β_r), overeducation (β_o) and undereducation (β_u) are expected to be equal in absolute terms, whereas in the VV specification the coefficients of the dummy variables measuring overeducation (β_{do}) and undereducation (β_{du}) should be zero.

In contrast, the job competition model (Thurow, 1975) offers a demand-side explanation of the wage determinants by assuming that marginal productivity is independent of the worker's human capital, but is related to his or her occupation. In this model, workers compete for jobs with fixed wage rates and employers choose workers according to their level of attained education, which is taken as a predictor of potential training costs. Therefore, any educational mismatch, whether over- or undereducation, should only affect the employment probability, not wages. It follows that the coefficients of the educational mismatch variables (β_o, β_u) in the DH specification should be zero. In the VV specification the coefficient of the overeducation dummy (β_{od}) should be negative and the coefficient of the undereducation dummy (β_{ud}) should be positive, because, compared with workers with the same level of attained education, overeducated (undereducated) workers are in occupations with lower (higher) educational requirements and receive lower (higher) wages.

4.2.4 Empirical evidence

Hartog (2000) summarizes previous studies on the incidence and earnings effects of educational mismatch in the United States, the Netherlands, Spain, Portugal and the United Kingdom. Based on the DH specification of the wage function, but using different measures of required education derived from job analysis, self-assessment and realized matches, these studies share the following results:[3] years of overeducation yield a positive return ($\beta_o > 0$), whereas years of undereducation yield a negative return ($\beta_u < 0$). The return to required education is greater than the return to overeducation ($\beta_r > \beta_o$) and the penalty to undereducation is smaller (in absolute terms) than the rewards for overeducation ($|\beta_u| < \beta_o$). It follows that overeducated (undereducated) workers have lower (higher) earnings than they would have at a job requiring their education level (i.e. conditional on attained education) and higher (lower) earnings than workers at the same job whose education level meets the requirements of the job (i.e. conditional on required education). Similar conclusions are drawn by Rubb (2003a), who includes more recent studies in a meta-analysis on the returns to educational mismatch.[4] He shows how different study designs, particularly different measures of required education, influence the estimated returns by comparing the estimates of the returns to required education, over- and undereducation (based on a DH specification). The results of the meta-analysis suggest that studies using the modal definition of required education estimate greater returns to overeducation and larger penalties for undereducation and studies using required education derived from self-assessment estimate lower returns to required education than studies which use a measure of required education that is derived from job analysis.[5]

Compared with US studies, European studies find smaller returns to required education and overeducation, and also smaller penalties for undereducation. Since the 1980s, the return to required education has increased significantly, whereas the return to overeducation was greater in the 1980s than before 1980 and the 1990s.

Empirical evidence based on the VV specification is provided by Alba-Ramirez (1993) for Spain, Kiker et al. (1997) for Portugal, Cohn and Kahn (1995) and Sicherman (1991) for the United States and Bauer (2002) for Germany, which all show a negative wage effect of overeducation and a positive wage effect of undereducation. As mentioned above, the results may reflect wage differentials across different job levels or occupations because conditioning is on attained education.

All in all, the empirical results support neither the pure human capital model nor the job competition model, because both supply-side and demand-side characteristics determine wages. Rather, they are in line with the assignment theory (Sattinger, 1993), which states that the performance of a worker depends on the job; thus both the individual human capital (i.e. the supply side) and the job requirements (i.e. the demand side) determine wages.

Since most empirical studies use cross-sectional data to explore the wage consequences of educational mismatch, the results may be biased due to unobserved heterogeneity if, for example, educational mismatch reflects a lack of motivation or ability. As Bauer (2002) and Chevalier (2003) argue, some workers may appear to be overeducated because they need more formal education to compensate for a lack of ability. Assuming that low-ability workers are more likely to be overeducated and high-ability workers are more likely to be undereducated, the difference in returns are expected to disappear or at least become smaller when using panel data methods that account for unobserved heterogeneity. This is what Bauer (2002) finds for both specifications of the wage function with random and fixed effects models using German panel data. Chevalier (2003) provides evidence for the importance of unobserved skill differences among UK graduates. Using a measure of job satisfaction, he distinguishes between genuinely and apparently overeducated workers and finds that genuinely overeducated workers earn between 22 and 26 per cent less than adequately educated workers, whereas apparently overeducated workers are only paid 5 to 11 per cent less than those adequately educated. Since apparently overeducated workers account for two-thirds of the group of overeducated workers, previous estimates of the wage penalty for overeducated UK graduates (Battu et al., 1999; Dolton and Vignoles, 2000) are deemed misleading because they ignore heterogeneity within the group of overeducated workers. In a recent study, Green and Zhu (2007) report that in the UK there has been a substantial growth in the proportion of graduates who are overqualified for their jobs between 1992 and 2006. Women graduates have been experiencing a particularly large rise in the incidence of overqualification, which is estimated to have increased from 23 to 32 per cent between 2001 and 2006.

Robst (1995) explores the link between college quality and the incidence of overeducation for a sample of US workers. Using different quality measures and controlling for individual ability, he shows that the probability of being overeducated is lower for workers with a degree from a high-quality college.

4.2.5 Why do over- and undereducation exist?

Besides estimating the incidence and wage effects of educational mismatch, the literature attempts to explain the reasons for its existence and whether it is a short-run or a long-run phenomenon. The following hypotheses are found in the literature. Educational mismatch may simply reflect a bad match due to imperfect information in the labour market (e.g. matching models by Johnson (1978) or Jovanovic (1979)), or, from a human capital perspective, may be due to an investment decision or a trade-off between different forms of human capital (Hartog, 2000; Sicherman, 1991). Another explanation focuses on the role of technological change and adjustment cost and questions the view of human capital theory that firms immediately respond to a changing supply of labour by adapting their production technologies (e.g. Kiker et al., 1997; Oliveira et al., 2000).

If the existence of overeducation and undereducation is due to imperfect information, different mobility patterns for overeducated and undereducated workers will be expected. Since overeducation can be seen as a bad match from the worker's perspective, high occupational and firm mobility should be observed for overeducated workers. In contrast, undereducation reflects a good match, and undereducated workers should be less mobile between firms and occupations. Although undereducation may reflect a bad match for the firm, empirical evidence does not suggest a higher incidence of dismissals for undereducated workers (Sicherman, 1991).

From a human capital viewpoint, undereducated workers may simply compensate for the lack of formal education with other forms of human capital such as work experience, training or unobserved ability, whereas the opposite is true for overeducated workers (trade-off hypothesis). Thus, overeducation can be seen as an investment opportunity to acquire general and specific human capital and to gain access to higher-level occupations (career mobility hypothesis; Sicherman, 1991). Indeed, empirical evidence for the United States (Sicherman, 1991) suggests that undereducated workers have more work experience and training than overeducated and adequately educated workers. The fact that undereducated workers have more work experience may simply reflect a cohort effect or may be due to measurement error if experience is proxied by age, because overeducated individuals may have already worked during their education. However, these findings are also consistent with the matching hypothesis (Hartog, 2000). Occupational and firm mobility is highest among overeducated workers, but undereducated workers are also more likely to change occupations than adequately educated workers. Since undereducated workers with more training are less likely to change firms than undereducated workers with little training, Sicherman (1991) claims that there is some support for the trade-off hypothesis.

Büchel and Mertens (2000) use German data to explore the career prospects of over- and undereducated workers. They claim that Sicherman's (1991) results are caused by inadequately controlling for a worker's occupational choice. Since overeducated workers by definition work in occupations with lower requirements than adequately educated workers, the observed higher mobility of overeducated workers merely reflects the difference in their occupational choices. Using wage growth as an indicator for upward mobility and controlling for the initial wage, they find the opposite result, that is, undereducated workers have higher wage growth and overeducated workers have lower wage growth than adequately educated workers.

Based on Spanish cross-sectional data, Alba-Ramirez (1993) presents evidence that, when changing firms, overeducated workers are more likely to change occupations than undereducated workers. This finding is consistent with the view that overeducated workers use their job to acquire general human capital to increase their probability of finding a better-paying occupation, whereas undereducated workers acquire more occupation-specific human capital, which lowers the returns to changing occupations.

According to the trade-off hypothesis, the wage effects of an educational mismatch should vary with the level of general and specific human capital. Since different types of human capital are complements, undereducated workers with more experience and training are expected to suffer from lower wage penalties from undereducation than undereducated workers with less experience and training.

The wage effects may be more ambiguous for overeducated workers because, on the one hand, higher levels of both general and specific human capital may be associated with a lower wage gap between overeducated and adequately educated workers (Kiker et al., 1997), but, on the other hand, neither workers nor firms may be willing to invest into firm-specific human capital because overeducated workers are expected to leave earlier than workers who are adequately educated. Therefore, the wage effect of increased tenure need not be positive for overeducated workers (Oliveira et al., 2000).

Kiker et al. (1997) use Portuguese data to test the trade-off between education and tenure (experience) by interacting years of required education, over- and undereducation with tenure (experience). They find some evidence for the importance of interaction effects. Using the same data and methods, Oliveira et al. (2000) explore whether rapid technological change and adjustment cost are responsible for the incidence and the wage effects of educational mismatch. Since technological change induces employers to increase hiring standards, new entrants are perceived as overeducated compared with the existing workforce. At the same time, undereducated workers become even less desirable to employers because they lack certain formal skills. Employers are less willing to provide training to undereducated workers, and experience and tenure should not, therefore, be associated with a lower wage penalty, but the opposite should be true for overeducated workers. Oliveira et al.'s (2000) empirical results are consistent with such a view and they conclude that there is no evidence for the validity of the trade-off hypothesis.

Gottschalk and Hansen (2003) test the hypothesis that US college graduates were forced to work in non-college jobs due to the increased supply of highly educated workers in the 1980s and 1990s. Using a classification of jobs into college and non-college jobs based on the estimated wage premium that workers with college education receive, they show that the proportion of college graduates employed in non-college jobs has decreased between 1983 and 1994. This result may reflect the impact of skill-biased technological change within this period. Using the same framework, Cardoso (2007) finds similar results for Portugal.

Both the matching and the human capital hypothesis lead to the conclusion that overeducation may be a temporary situation, whereas undereducation is likely to be lasting. Using matched CPS data for the recession years 1991–2 and the expansion years 1995–9, Rubb (2003b) estimates the percentage of overeducated workers who – within one year – obtain a job for which they are adequately educated. Consistent across economic conditions, gender, age and ethnic groups, some 20 per cent of the overeducated workers find an adequate job–education match within one year, suggesting overeducation is not a short-run phenomenon. Dolton and Vignoles (2000) find that the incidence of overeducation among UK graduates decreased from 38 to 30 per cent between 1980 and 1986. Furthermore, they test whether the returns to overeducation vary with the quality of degree and the competitiveness of the labour market. They find no empirical support for the hypothesis that individuals with a better degree are more productive and earn higher wages. Overeducated workers in the public sector may face a higher wage penalty than in the private sector, because wages are more rigid in the public sector. The authors find no evidence for the validity of this hypothesis.

Daly et al. (2000) compare the incidence and wage effects of educational mismatch within the United States over time as well as between the United States and Germany. The authors provide evidence that the wage effects of educational mismatch did not change in the United States between 1976 and 1984, a period characterized by structural changes in the labour market and rising wage inequality. Furthermore, pooled regression results for Germany and the United States show that there is little difference in the wage effects of over- and undereducation between these two countries. The authors conclude that differences in the wage effects of educational mismatch are not correlated with institutional differences such as differences in the educational system or differences in labour market flexibility, thus supporting a 'universalistic view of labor markets' (Daly et al., 2000). Apart from this study there seems to be little evidence on cross-country differences in the incidence and wage effects of educational mismatch using comparative data.[6]

4.3 Data

We use data from the European Structure of Earnings Survey (ESES) 2002 to document the extent of skill mismatch in Europe. The ESES is a linked employer–employee survey with data at both unit level and the employee level. Employees can be linked to their places of work via a unique identifier. The aim of the ESES was to provide accurate and harmonized data on earnings in EU member states. The ESES 2002 covers enterprises with at least 10 employees in the areas of economic activity defined by sections C-K of NACE. The inclusion of sections L-O was optional for 2002, as was the inclusion of enterprises with fewer than 10 employees.[7]

Data were obtained only for countries that have agreed to provide access to their data via the LEED-LISSY system. These countries are the Czech Republic, Italy, Latvia, Lithuania, the Netherlands, Norway, Portugal, Slovakia and Spain.[8] Unfortunately, the sample sizes for most countries are too small to be used in our estimates (we require at least 100 observations for each 3-digit SOC occupation); we therefore only use data for the Czech Republic and Spain for our estimations of over- and undereducation. Data from other countries are used to provide descriptive cross-sectional background. Although data for Italy and Spain are also available for 1995, the occupational information is aggregated to a 2-digit SOC classification and we cannot use these data for our estimates.

In Figure 4.1 we plot the distribution of educational groups by gender in 2002 for European countries, where data were available through the LEED-LISSY system. The distribution of educational groups varies drastically across countries; in the Mediterranean countries (Portugal, Spain, Italy) the fraction of low-skilled workers is much greater than in the other countries, most noticeably the Baltic countries. The fraction of highly skilled workers is also higher in the Baltic countries, but Spain also has a considerable fraction, some 21 per cent, of highly skilled

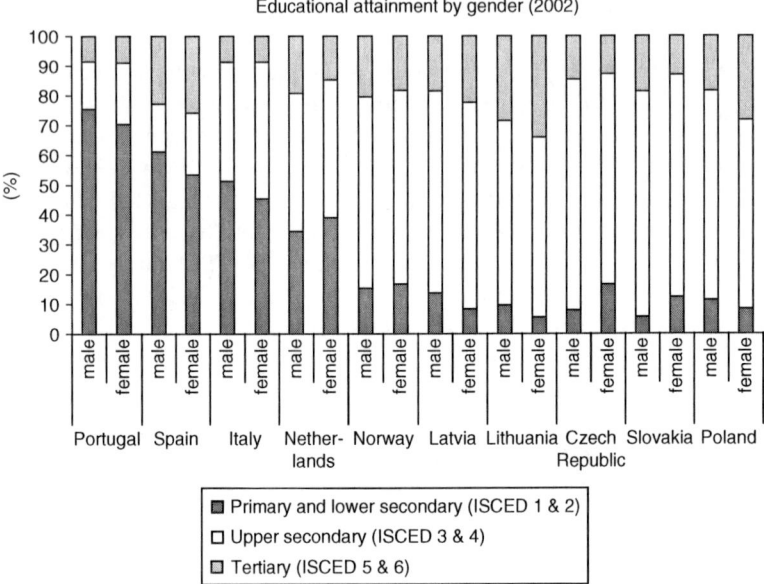

Figure 4.1 Distribution of educational groups in 2002, selected European countries

Note: Workers in enterprises with at least 10 employees in the areas of economic activity defined by sections C-K of NACE. Own calculations from the ESES 2002.

workers. Italy and Portugal have the lowest relative numbers of workers with tertiary education.

For one country, Poland, we have repeated cross-sectional data, collected in the Polish Structure of Earnings Survey, for the years 1996, 1998, 1999, 2001, and 2002.[9] Poland did undergo economic changes and is thus an illustrative example of how skill mismatch changed over time. After a period of economic transformation, which was marked by rising unemployment, the Polish economy experienced fast growth and a gradual improvement of the labour market between 1995 and 1998. In 1999, the employment rate decreased by 4 percentage points and unemployment rose to 15.3 per cent in the last quarter. The slowdown that followed in 2001 and 2002 contributed to a further increase of the unemployment rate, which exceeded 20 per cent in 2003. The economy improved since 2004 and employment has been rising since then; however, some 1.2 million jobs were lost between 1996 and 2002.

Between 1996 and 2002, the number of workers with tertiary education increased by more than 0.5 million.[10] A significant share of low-skilled workers was pushed out of the labour market, and employment of workers with, at most, primary education fell by more than 40 per cent. The demand has shifted towards sectors which employ high-skilled workers, and the large job losses in manufacturing, mining and construction were accompanied by the creation of jobs in the service industry, particularly in real estate and hotels and restaurants. The share of workers with tertiary education rose considerably in the market services – by 4 percentage points to 14 per cent in 2002. Labour market developments were also marked by changes in the demographic structure of the labour force. Owing to a large inflow of labour market entrants, the share of younger cohorts (those aged 15–34) increased from 31 per cent in 1996 to 39 per cent in 2002.

At the same time, wage inequalities increased substantially. For example, the decile ratio (i.e. the ratio of the 90th percentile of the wage distribution to the 10th percentile, p90/p10) increased from 3.39 to 3.98. The earnings distribution has widened at the tails; however, the increases in inequality were greater in the bottom of the distribution.

As research of MPiPS (2007) shows, the university wage premium increased only slightly in this period. The enrolment rates have increased for both secondary and tertiary levels. Between 1994/95 and 2005/2006 the net enrolment rate in secondary education increased from 24.8 to 43.1 per cent; in tertiary education from 15.6 to 30.8 per cent. As a result, the average educational level of Polish workers has risen, particularly among the younger cohorts. See Table 4A.1 for a distribution of the employment of skill groups and the changes between 1996 and 2004. For example, the proportion of workers with tertiary education has increased from 15.2 per cent in 1996 to 27 per cent in 2004.

The educational system underwent important structural reforms, which changed ownership of schools and the fields of education. The state's monopoly in higher education was abolished (1991), which led to an increase in the share of students enrolled in private schools. Up to one-third of students in 2005/2006 were enrolled in a private school (UNDP, 2007). The reforms also led to an increase in the share of part-time students (by 28 percentage points to 51 per cent between 1990 and 2005) and an increase in extramural studies.

How did the labour market accommodate the substantial inflow of young university graduates? If the labour market cannot absorb them, we should observe an increasing fraction of university graduates in non-university jobs. If, on the other hand, skill-biased technological change leads to an upgrading of jobs, thus making university graduates more productive and raising their wage premium, we should observe a decreasing fraction of university graduates in non-university jobs (cf. Gottschalk and Hansen (2003) for the USA and Cardoso (2007) for Portugal). However, given the possible fall in the quality of education resulting from reforms and any mismatch between the demand and supply of skills, as pointed out by, for example, MGiP (2005), we might expect that more graduates do not possess the qualifications needed by the employers and decide to take up jobs for which they seem overeducated.

4.4 Empirical strategy

Following Gottschalk and Hansen (2003) and Cardoso (2007), we estimate the extent of overeducation of young university graduates and the extent of undereducation of young high school graduates using microdata from the ESES for Poland, the Czech Republic and Spain. Our sample of young workers consists of workers with 10 years' or less potential experience (age – years of education – age at school entry) working in enterprises with at least 10 employees in the areas of economic activity defined by sections C–O of NACE.

In Figure 4.2 we plot the distribution of educational groups for young workers (as defined above) by gender for Spain, the Czech Republic and Poland in 2002. Again, the distribution varies across countries; in Spain the fraction of low-skilled workers is much greater than in the Eastern European countries, but Spain also has a higher fraction of highly skilled workers, although some 55 per cent of young Polish women are also highly skilled.

Since we estimate the extent of overeducation of young university graduates and the extent of undereducation of young high school graduates, we remove from our sample all workers with educational attainments below the higher secondary education level (ISCED 3). For classification purposes, we group workers with higher secondary and post-secondary education (ISCED 3 and 4) into the 'non-academic' group of workers and those with the first and second stage of tertiary education (ISCED 5 and 6) into the 'academic' group. We drop all observations from our sample if they contain fewer than 100 observations in each 3-digit SOC group.

Our indicator for overeducation is the percentage of workers with an academic degree who work in non-academic occupations. Similarly, we use the percentage of non-academics who work in academic occupations as an indicator of undereducation. We class the occupational groups (at the 3-digits ISCO level) into academic and non-academic occupations and label an occupation as academic if more than 90 per cent of the workers in that occupation have a university degree. For occupations in which fewer than 90 per cent are university graduates, we

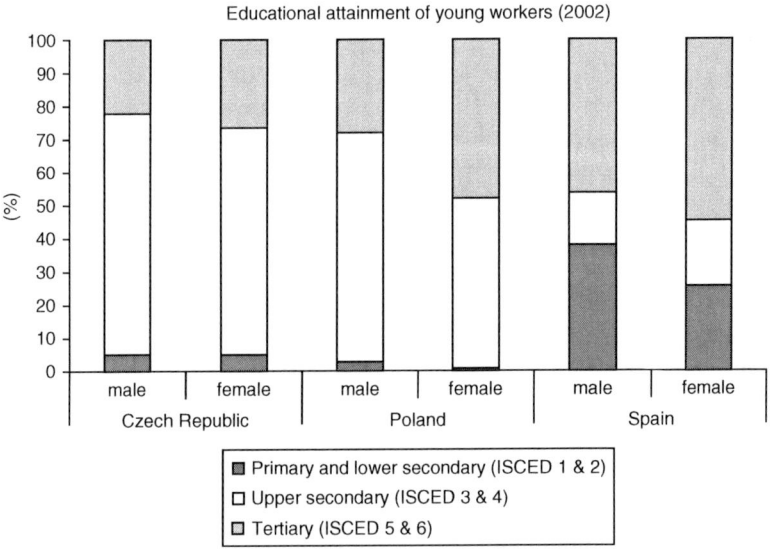

Figure 4.2 Distribution of educational groups for young workers in 2002, selected European countries

Note: Workers with 10 years or less potential experience in enterprises with at least 10 employees in the areas of economic activity defined by sections C-K of NACE. Own calculations from the ESES 2002.

estimate for each occupational group a wage regression where we include gender, experience and its square, and a dummy variable indicating whether or not the worker has a university degree. The estimated coefficient on this dummy variable, that is, the estimated wage premium, is used to further class occupational groups as 'academic' if the estimated coefficient is statistically significant at least at a 10 per cent level and if the coefficient is greater than 0.15. We also use a cut-off of 0.25 and the 25th percentile of the distribution of estimated wage premiums to check the sensitivity of our results to the arbitrarily chosen cut-off.[11] Figure 4.3 shows the estimated extent of over- and undereducation in Spain, the Czech Republic and Poland in 2002. (Figures 4A.1 and 4A.2, in the Appendix, provide a graphical breakdown of over- and undereducation across occupational groups.)

Figure 4.4 plots the results when the underlying threshold for the classification of an occupation as academic is raised from 15 per cent to 25 per cent.[12] In all four countries we see an increase in overeducation and a decrease in undereducation. This is an expected result, as a higher threshold requires us to class fewer occupations as academic. However, we see a dramatic increase in overeducation and a decline of undereducation in Spain. This indicates that the distribution of academic wage premiums has more observations at lower levels in Spain than in the other two countries, and increasing the threshold leads to fewer occupations being classified as academic.

Figure 4.5 shows the distribution of estimated wage premiums (significant at the 10 per cent level) for Poland in 1996 and 2002. Over this period, the mean of the distribution has shifted to the left, indicating that the average university wage premium has decreased. This finding is consistent with the view that an

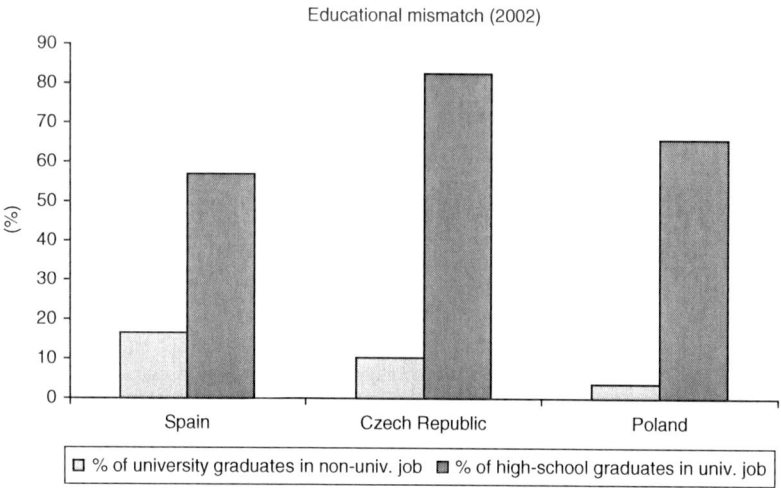

Figure 4.3 Extent of over- and undereducation for Spain, the Czech Republic, and Poland, 2002

Note: Academic occupations are those with an academic wage premium of at least 15 per cent. Own calculations based on ESES 2002.

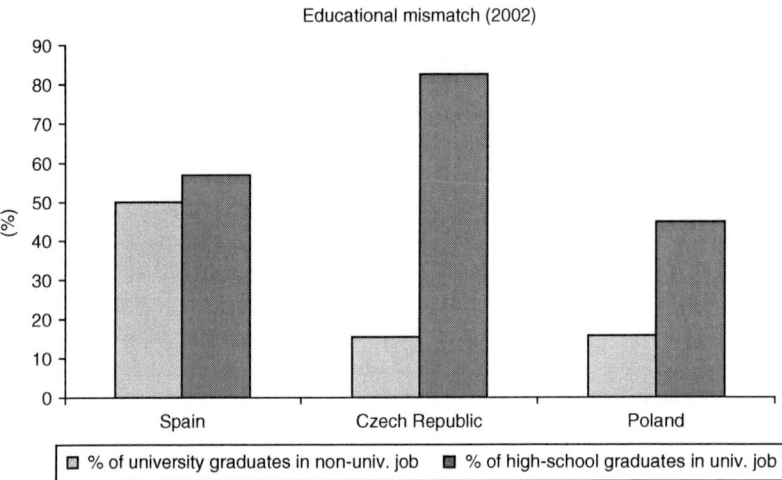

Figure 4.4 Sensitivity of over- and undereducation, wage premium of at least 25 per cent

Note: Academic occupations are those with an academic wage premium of at least 25 per cent. Own calculations based on ESES 2002.

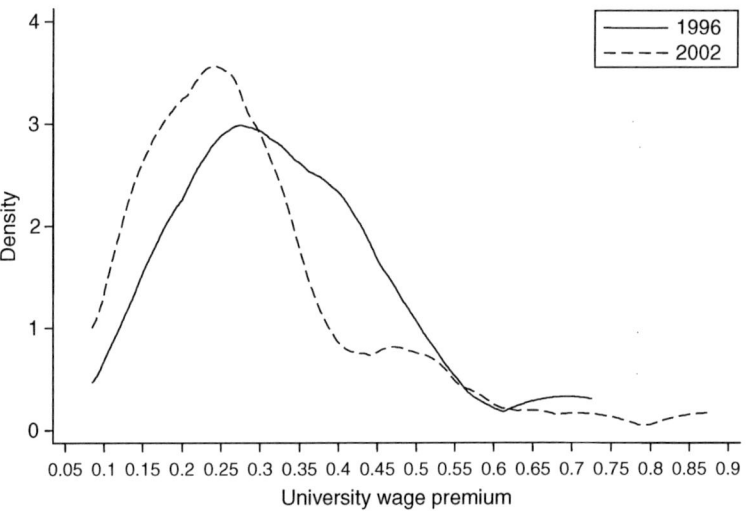

Figure 4.5 Distribution of university wage premiums, Poland, 1996 and 2002

Note: Only for occupations with fewer than 90 per cent university graduates, only wage premiums that are significant at the 10 per cent level.

increase in the supply of workers with university education has decreased their wage premium.[13]

In a next step, we estimate the probability of a worker with (without) a university degree to work in a non-academic (academic) occupation. We estimate probit models of the probability that a university graduate holds a non-university job. The sample consists of all university graduates; the dependent variable is whether the university graduate holds a university job (0) or a non-university job (1). Similarly, we use the sample of workers without a university degree and estimate the probability that a non-academic worker works in an academic occupation. We use gender, experience (squared) and a part-time dummy as explanatory variables. We estimate two specifications which differ by the inclusion of indicators for firm size, industry and public sector effects to evaluate differences in skill requirements by firm and industry.

Our estimates, which use the Polish data (repeated cross-sections), include as explanatory variables the gender and experience (squared) of the worker, the unemployment rate for graduates, and dummy variables for the year of the survey. A second specification also includes industry indicators, an indicator for the public sector and the (log of) firm size. In order to account for changes in the skill premiums over time, we compare the results from two different cut-offs that are used for the classification of the occupation into academic and non-academic. The first specification uses a 15 per cent threshold for wage premiums and the second specification uses 25 per cent as a threshold.

The linked employer–employee data allow an analysis of over- and undereducation at the firm level. For this, we calculate the number of over- or undereducated workers per firm and relate this 'intensity' of educational mismatch to firm characteristics to provide more information on which firms tend to mismatch workers. Firm characteristics are the share of female workers, the share of young workers, the share of older workers, the share of part-time employees, the share of manual workers, and the share of low-skilled workers in the firm. In addition, we relate the educational mismatch to the firm's size, the firm's industry (1-digit NACE) and whether it operates in the public or the private sector.

We estimate two different specifications of the extent of overeducation and undereducation where we combine different groups of firms' characteristics to present the robustness of the empirical associations.

4.5 Results

Estimates of the probability of over- and undereducation are presented in Tables 4A.2 and 4A.3. Presented are marginal effects, evaluated at the mean of the explanatory variables, and their standard errors. The marginal effects of our first specification for the Czech Republic and Spain show that women are more likely than men to be overeducated, and less likely to be undereducated, in the Czech Republic. The situation is different in Spain, where women are less likely to be overeducated than men, and more likely to be undereducated.

Workers in the Czech Republic are less likely to be overeducated when they are experienced, but are more likely to be undereducated. In Spain, there is no significant association between experience and overeducation, but experienced workers are more likely to be undereducated.

Part-time workers in the Czech Republic are less likely than full-time workers to be undereducated; the association between part-time work and overeducation is not statistically significant. In Spain, part-time workers are more likely to be overeducated, but we do not find a significant association between part-time work and undereducation.

The inclusion of firm size and industry fixed effects indicates that in Spain there is considerable segregation of male and female workers in different firms and/or industries. This can be deducted by the change in the marginal effects when these indicators are included in the estimations. When we include these indicators in our regressions, the association between female workers and the likelihood of being overeducated is much lower for the overeducation results, mirroring the association in the other two countries.

Firms' demand for skilled workers is, according to our estimates, clearly related to the size of the firm. Workers in small firms are, ceteris paribus, more likely to be overeducated, and this pattern can be seen in all three countries and may indicate different recruiting costs for small and large firms.

In Tables 4A.4 and 4A.5 we present our estimates using the Polish repeated cross-sectional data. Comparing the specifications, we see that there is considerable segregation by gender, as the association between gender and the likelihood of skill mismatch varies according to whether or not industry controls are used in the estimations. The specification in Table 4A.5 controls, in addition to the variables presented in Table 4A.4, also for industry indicators, a public sector dummy variable, and (log of) employment. Specification I uses a threshold for the wage premiums of 15 per cent and specification II uses 25 per cent.

The association of the business cycle, measured by the unemployment rate, and the likelihood of the skill mismatch indicates that the probability of being overeducated is greater when unemployment is higher. This could be explained by highly skilled workers crowding out lower-skill workers in times of tight labour markets.

When we consider the evolution of the probability of a skill mismatch, we see that in all likelihood skill mismatches are declining in this period; the size of this decline depends on the chosen definition of overeducation (the cut-off value in the distribution of wage premiums). These estimates show that the spectacular increase in higher education in Poland did not result in a great imbalance of supply and demand of skills. Judging from these results, the imbalance was reduced in recent years, and there appears to be less overeducation than in 1996. The estimates for undereducation are, in contrast, sensitive to the chosen cut-off: the less restrictive cut-off (15 per cent, specification I) indicates an increase of undereducation over time; the more restrictive cut-off (25 per cent, specification II), however, does not permit such an interpretation.

4.5.1 Firm-level analyses

For each firm, we calculate the share of mismatched workers (distinguishing between over- and undereducated workers) and regress this share on a number of firm characteristics. The results from these regressions are presented in Tables 4A.6 to 4A.9. Specification 1 includes only characteristics of the workers in the firm, such as the share of female workers. In our preferred specification we also control for firm size, industry and the share of manual workers. (Regressions are weighted with the firm's probability of being sampled to address differences in size and industry.)

In the Czech Republic, the fewer undereducated and the more overeducated workers a firm employs, the more women are employed in the firm. This association is somehow less pronounced once we control for industry and size of the firms, which is evidence for labour market segregation by gender, that is, the (self-) selection of women and men into gender-specific occupations or industries.

While there is no association between a young workforce and the number of undereducated workers, there is some indication that the more older workers are employed in a firm, the fewer undereducated workers are employed. The firm characteristics that are mainly related to the employment of undereducated workers appear to be the occupational organization of firms. A higher share of manual workers is associated with a lower share of undereducated workers.

We do not find an association between the number of women and the number of undereducated workers for Spanish firms. A young workforce tends to be associated with more undereducated workers. We find for Spanish firms that the more highly skilled workers are hired, the more overeducated workers are employed.

The higher the share of female workers, the higher the number of overeducated workers – however, we only find this association for Czech firms, not for Spanish firms. There is no clear pattern between overeducation and the size of firms. The public sector in the Czech Republic tends to hire more overeducated workers than the private sector, whereas in Spain the public sector tends to hire fewer overeducated workers.

The repeated cross-sections for Poland permit an additional view on whether the skill mismatch increased or decreased over time. The estimation results presented in Tables 4A.8 and 4A.9 indicate that overeducating seem to have decreased between 1996 and 2002, the exact amount depending, again, on the chosen cut-off levels in the wage premium distributions. In contrast, undereducation appears to have increased since 1996. These two developments indicate that Polish firms demanded high-skilled workers, as fewer high-skilled workers worked in occupations with lower average skill levels and more low-skilled workers worked in occupations with higher average skill levels. This is a surprising finding, given that Poland did increase the supply of high-skilled workers dramatically in this period. In addition, the business cycle indicator points to a counter-cyclical evolution of overeducation and a pro-cyclical evolution of undereducation.

The number of female workers is associated with a lower share of overeducated workers, whereas the association with the share of undereducated workers depends on the chosen cut-off level. However, the more younger workers are employed, the more over- and undereducated workers are employed in the firm. This is a result which is consistent with a high degree of uncertainty about a young worker's productivity; such mismatches should be reduced as the productivity of the worker is revealed over time.

The more low-skilled workers are employed in a firm, the higher is the number of overeducated workers and the lower the number of undereducated workers. The more manual workers are employed in a firm, the lower the extent of overeducation and undereducation – these firms have most likely an exceptionally homogeneous workforce. The larger the firm, the more likely is skill mismatch; however, this is estimated to decline for very large firms.

4.6 Conclusion

There is wide evidence that the demand for high-skilled workers is increasing – and European countries face this challenge by promoting and facilitating education and training, of which the Lisbon strategy is one prominent example. An impressive push for higher qualifications has been seen in the new member states of the European Union, where educational levels, most often following a fundamental restructuring of the institutional framework, have drastically increased. However, some observers (e.g. Gray and Chapman, 1999) worry that the investment is misspent money if the created human capital is not fully utilized, that is, if these highly trained workers work in jobs that require less education than was paid for. Such a form of skill mismatch might be accompanied by the opposite, that is, workers who work in jobs for which they have too little formal education.

Concerns of this sort are not easily addressed because there is a scarcity of consistent time-series data, but evidence from meta-analysis (Rubb, 2003a) indicates that overeducation is less severe than previously feared.

Our efforts in this study focused on describing the European background, using a new source of data, the European Structure of Earnings Surveys from the year 2002. This harmonized survey provides detailed data on firms, workers and their working conditions throughout Europe. While these data are not optimal for addressing the question of how any skill mismatch has evolved, they allow a rich picture of the current state of educational attainments in Europe, including the employment, incomes and occupational sorting of workers according to their educational attainments.

The data indicate that there is skill mismatch in European labour markets; however, the number of workers who – according to scientific conventions – are underqualified is much greater than the number of workers who appear overqualified.

We characterize the evolution of the skill mismatch by looking at Poland's development over the last decade. The longitudinal evidence from Poland points to an increase of skill mismatch for lower educational levels, which is maybe not surprising given the effort the country has spent on increasing the number of highly skilled workers. Unfortunately, we are not in the position to contrast this evidence with new data from other European countries.

Our estimates on the probability of over- and undereducation suggest that there are no clear patterns for the European countries analysed. While we find for each country statistically significant and economically important associations between characteristics and the likelihood of over- or undereducation, these associations cannot be generalized across these countries. We do not find personal characteristics that make employment as an overeducated (undereducated) worker more or less likely in each of these countries, nor can we classify the typical firm that is likely to employ overeducated or undereducated workers. These results suggest that institutional settings, for example, the access to education or the transition from school to work, influence the incidence and the extent of skill match. The association between institutions and the skill mismatch requires further research; this research should also focus on how governments' attempts to increase skill levels differ.

Green and Zhu (2007) state in their analysis of the British skill mismatch that any evidence for a skill mismatch is no justification for reducing government efforts to increase the levels of formal education. Such intervention is warranted if the social returns of the investment in human capital are greater than the private returns, which is likely the case.

Our results indicate that there is mismatch, and that this mismatch is greater for the lower-skilled. Further research is needed to investigate how, for example, these mismatches evolve over time, how firms that hire over- or undereducated workers fare over time, and what careers such mismatched workers experience.

Appendix

Table 4A.1 Distribution of employees by skill group, Poland, 1996–2004

Education level	1996	1998	1999	2001	2002	2004
Tertiary	15.2	17.6	18.6	22.0	23.2	20.9
Secondary	6.7	6.9	5.8	5.9	5.6	6.1
	30.1	30.9	25.8	26.4	25.8	24.9
			7.0	7.1	7.2	7.0
	30.8	30.2	29.7	27.8	28.2	27.2
Primary	17.0	14.2	12.8	10.7	9.7	7.8
Less	0.2	0.2	0.2	0.1	0.2	

Note: Tertiary are ISCED categories 5 and 6, Secondary consists of ISCED 3a, 3c, and 4c, Primary are ISCED 1(2), and Less is ISCED category 0.

Table 4A.2 Estimation results of the probability of over- and undereducation

	Czech Republic		Spain	
	OE	UE	OE	UE
	Marginal effects (SE)			
Female	0.10970	−0.04083	−0.05349	0.09475
	(0.00707)	(0.00599)	(0.00632)	(0.01474)
Experience	−0.00632	0.02098	−0.00212	0.02323
	(0.00345)	(0.00518)	(0.00387)	(0.01183)
Experience squared	0.00083	−0.00143	−0.00026	−0.00067
	(0.00036)	(0.00044)	(0.00036)	(0.00098)
Part-time	0.01161	−0.04084	0.06239	0.02399
	(0.01148)	(0.01103)	(0.01194)	(0.01933)
Observations	58,412	166,276	26,952	9,368

Note: OE is overeducated, that is, graduates working in non-academic occupations. UE is undereducated, that is, non-graduates working in academic occupations. Marginal effects from probit-estimates, evaluated at the means of the explanatory variables.

Table 4A.3 Estimation results of the probability of over- and undereducation, extended specification

	Czech Republic		Spain	
	OE	UE	OE	UE
	Marginal effects (SE)			
Female	0.04813	−0.03864	−0.02844	0.10877
	(0.00509)	(0.00544)	(0.00613)	(0.01689)
Experience	−0.00404	0.01935	−0.00079	0.01872
	(0.00228)	(0.00423)	(0.00376)	(0.01289)
Experience squared	0.00040	−0.00139	−0.00026	−0.00010
	(0.00023)	(0.00036)	(0.00035)	(0.00107)
Part-time	−0.03074	−0.05922	0.08786	0.02110
	(0.00416)	(0.01077)	(0.01334)	(0.02255)
Size				
1–49	0.05578	−0.04564	0.01705	−0.00537
	(0.01244)	(0.01192)	(0.00940)	(0.02408)
50–249	0.03896	−0.01012	0.00525	−0.01805
	(0.00495)	(0.00493)	(0.00925)	(0.02370)
250–499	0.05372	−0.03184	−0.00261	0.04047
	(0.00765)	(0.00405)	(0.01185)	(0.02740)
500–999	0.00128	0.02302	−0.02417	−0.00972
	(0.00371)	(0.00333)	(0.00975)	(0.02881)
Public sector	0.06691	−0.05809	−0.10050	0.10541
	(0.00867)	(0.01072)	(0.00828)	(0.03877)
Industry indicators	yes	yes	yes	yes
Observations	58,412	166,276	26,952	9,368

Note: OE is overeducated, that is, graduates working in non-academic occupations. UE is undereducated, that is, non-graduates working in academic occupations. Marginal effects from probit-estimates, evaluated at the means of the explanatory variables.

Table 4A.4 Estimates of over- and undereducation, Poland

	Specification I		Specification II	
	OE	UE	OE	UE
	Marginal effects (SE)			
Female	−0.00486	0.20742	−0.09667	0.00297
	(0.00171)	(0.00236)	(0.00399)	(0.00285)
Experience	−0.00049	−0.00594	−0.00509	−0.01123
	(0.00034)	(0.00067)	(0.00073)	(0.00075)
Experience squared	0	0.00034	−0.00008	0.0008
	(0.00003)	(0.00005)	(0.00006)	(0.00006)
Unemployment rate	0.00226	−0.07604	0.05216	−0.00728
	(0.00089)	(0.00160)	(0.00190)	(0.00182)
1998	0.02717	0.00352	−0.02284	0.01273
	(0.00207)	(0.00212)	(0.00310)	(0.00231)
1999	−0.00442	0.02572	−0.05687	0.02795
	(0.00182)	(0.00281)	(0.00338)	(0.00325)
2001	−0.00513	0.18813	−0.07568	0.01537
	(0.00294)	(0.00344)	(0.00536)	(0.00567)
2002	0.00291	0.18949	−0.11354	−0.09117
	(0.00449)	(0.00495)	(0.00672)	(0.00801)
Observations	222,259	493,670	222,259	493,670

Note: OE is overeducated, that is, graduates working in non-academic occupations. UE is undereducated, that is, non-graduates working in academic occupations. Specification I uses a threshold for the wage premiums of 0.15, specification II uses a threshold of 0.25. Marginal effects from probit-estimates, evaluated at the means of the explanatory variables. 1996 is the omitted year.

Table 4A.5 Estimates of over- and undereducation, with additional firm-level controls, Poland

	Specification I		Specification II	
	OE	UE	OE	UE
	Marginal effects (SE)			
Female	0.00393	0.17814	−0.03599	0.03869
	(0.00118)	(0.00249)	(0.00358)	(0.00311)
Experience	−0.00045	−0.00318	−0.00652	−0.00381
	(0.00023)	(0.00066)	(0.00065)	(0.00078)
Experience squared	0.00004	0.00021	0.00027	0.00047
	(0.00002)	(0.00005)	(0.00005)	(0.00006)
Employment (log)	0.00057	0.01908	0.00718	0.0052
	(0.00021)	(0.00048)	(0.00060)	(0.00062)
Unemployment rate	0.0004	−0.07863	0.04043	−0.02285
	(0.00064)	(0.00157)	(0.00171)	(0.00189)
1998	0.02517	0.00329	−0.02514	0.00818
	(0.00183)	(0.00213)	(0.00277)	(0.00240)
1999	−0.00119	0.02341	−0.05538	0.03335
	(0.00138)	(0.00277)	(0.00291)	(0.00339)
2001	0.00045	0.17998	−0.07111	0.03609
	(0.00232)	(0.00330)	(0.00451)	(0.00585)
2002	0.00802	0.18169	−0.09773	−0.07343
	(0.00369)	(0.00469)	(0.00577)	(0.00831)
Public sector	−0.00311	0.00139	−0.02179	0.02053
	(0.00095)	(0.00217)	(0.00263)	(0.00257)
Industry indicators	yes	yes	yes	yes
Observations	222,259	493,670	222,259	493,670

Note: OE is overeducated, that is, graduates working in non-academic occupations. UE is undereducated, that is, non-graduates working in academic occupations. Specification I uses a threshold for the wage premiums of 0.15, specification II uses a threshold of 0.25. Marginal effects from probit-estimates, evaluated at the means of the explanatory variables. 1996 is the omitted year.

Table 4A.6 Estimates of the percentage of overeducated and undereducated workers

	Czech Republic		Spain	
	POEF	PUEF	POEF	PUEF
	Coefficients (SE)			
Share of female workers	0.31593	−0.42782	−0.03229	−0.00391
	(0.03930)	(0.04987)	(0.02065)	(0.02497)
Share of young workers (<34)	−0.07766	0.10138	0.09211	0.23635
	(0.05317)	(0.10820)	(0.02246)	(0.02902)
Share of old workers (>54)	0.16475	−0.35105	0.03322	−0.06062
	(0.09220)	(0.16166)	(0.05481)	(0.06383)
Share of part-time workers	0.12529	−0.37597	0.05207	−0.08879
	(0.08035)	(0.13205)	(0.02726)	(0.03297)
Share of low-skilled workers	0.04873	−0.09029	−0.00393	0.00145
	(0.07864)	(0.13763)	(0.01585)	(0.02196)
Constant	−0.06529	0.96348	0.11122	0.11111
	(0.03080)	(0.05745)	(0.01633)	(0.02204)
Observations	2,277	2,277	12,273	12,273

Note: POEF is the percentage of overeducated workers, that is, graduates working in non-academic occupations within a firm. PUEF is the percentage of undereducated workers, that is, non-graduates working in academic occupations within a firm. Estimations are based on a threshold for the wage premiums of 0.15. Coefficients from OLS regressions with robust standard errors in parentheses.

Table 4A.7 Estimates of the percentage of overeducated and undereducated workers, with additional firm-level controls

	Czech Republic		Spain	
	POEF	PUEF	POEF	PUEF
	Coefficients (SE)			
Share of female workers	0.12881	−0.26279	0.04632	0.03402
	(0.03287)	(0.06616)	(0.02042)	(0.02920)
Share of young workers (<34)	0.04542	0.02692	0.06011	0.19672
	(0.05145)	(0.10993)	(0.02269)	(0.02970)
Share of old workers (>54)	0.01027	−0.21104	0.02390	−0.02111
	(0.08725)	(0.16193)	(0.05501)	(0.06328)
Share of part-time workers	−0.08475	−0.19711	0.02474	0.02292
	(0.08113)	(0.12566)	(0.02804)	(0.03251)
Share of low-skilled workers	0.12085	−0.05215	−0.15752	0.03463
	(0.07976)	(0.14741)	(0.02163)	(0.02845)
Share of manual workers	−0.02538	−0.17035	0.25331	−0.11741
	(0.02689)	(0.06356)	(0.02443)	(0.03083)
Size				
1–49	0.02507	−0.13325	0.02535	−0.06086
	(0.01608)	(0.03004)	(0.01160)	(0.01986)
50–249	0.02191	−0.03516	0.02271	−0.03711
	(0.01298)	(0.02160)	(0.01235)	(0.02070)
250–499	0.03132	−0.01035	0.05645	−0.00812
	(0.01198)	(0.02129)	(0.02278)	(0.03085)
500–999	0.01706	0.01599	0.00065	−0.04784
	(0.01298)	(0.02043)	(0.01704)	(0.03022)
Public sector	0.06378	−0.05755	−0.06448	−0.00459
	(0.02770)	(0.04280)	(0.01662)	(0.02457)
Constant	−0.07120	1.10770	0.03209	0.21292
	(0.03446)	(0.08744)	(0.02307)	(0.03176)
Industry indicators	yes	yes	yes	yes
Observations	2,277	2,277	12,273	12,273

Note: POEF is the percentage of overeducated workers, that is, graduates working in non-academic occupations within a firm. PUEF is the percentage of undereducated workers, that is, non-graduates working in academic occupations within a firm. Estimations are based on a threshold for the wage premia of 0.15. Coefficients from OLS regressions with robust standard errors in parentheses. Firm size of 1000 employees and more is the omitted category.

Table 4A.8 Estimates of the percentage of overeducated and undereducated workers, Poland

	Specification I		Specification II	
	POEF	PUEF	POEF	PUEF
	Coefficients (SE)			
Share of female workers	−0.07314	0.00726	−0.12480	−0.00834
	(0.00581)	(0.00167)	(0.00575)	(0.00351)
Share of young workers (<34)	0.26102	0.00562	0.23145	0.02759
	(0.00843)	(0.00247)	(0.00847)	(0.00517)
Share of old workers (>54)	0.25348	0.08319	−0.09903	0.23232
	(0.02839)	(0.00918)	(0.02641)	(0.01745)
Share of low-skilled workers	−0.39449	-0.03199	−0.27865	−0.18518
	(0.01387)	(0.00390)	(0.01356)	(0.00789)
Unemployment rate	−0.02049	0.00050	−0.01425	0.00313
	(0.00212)	(0.00072)	(0.00196)	(0.00159)
1998	−0.01749	0.01616	−0.01951	0.00254
	(0.00442)	(0.00142)	(0.00460)	(0.00239)
1999	−0.05528	0.00212	−0.02381	0.01115
	(0.00530)	(0.00152)	(0.00517)	(0.00321)
2001	0.00640	0.00430	−0.07619	0.05702
	(0.00771)	(0.00252)	(0.00744)	(0.00557)
2002	−0.11006	0.01654	−0.19574	0.10026
	(0.01025)	(0.00348)	(0.00962)	(0.00753)
Constant	0.73671	0.00597	0.60046	0.06378
	(0.00789)	(0.00245)	(0.00766)	(0.00516)
Observations	72,541	72,541	72,541	72,541

Note: POEF is the percentage of overeducated workers, that is, graduates working in non-academic occupations within a firm. PUEF is the percentage of undereducated workers, that is, non-graduates working in academic occupations within a firm. Specification I uses a threshold for the wage premia of 0.15, specification II uses a threshold of 0.25. Coefficients from OLS regressions with robust standard errors in parentheses. 1996 is the omitted year.

Table 4A.9 Estimates of the percentage of overeducated and undereducated workers, with additional firm-level controls, Poland

	Specification I		Specification II	
	POEF	PUEF	POEF	PUEF
	Coefficients (SE)			
Share of female workers	−0.14406	0.01386	−0.15112	−0.00455
	(0.00706)	(0.00237)	(0.00691)	(0.00463)
Share of young workers (<34)	0.18563	0.02112	0.09512	0.08051
	(0.00862)	(0.00268)	(0.00869)	(0.00552)
Share of old workers (>54)	−0.09055	0.04420	−0.28494	0.04710
	(0.02738)	(0.00894)	(0.02620)	(0.01704)
Share of low-skilled workers	0.04303	−0.04686	0.12749	−0.08247
	(0.01575)	(0.00460)	(0.01554)	(0.00864)
Share of manual workers	−0.42994	−0.03082	−0.35485	−0.11834
	(0.00788)	(0.00332)	(0.00797)	(0.00566)
Unemployment rate	−0.01106	0.00083	−0.00917	0.00668
	(0.00196)	(0.00069)	(0.00185)	(0.00150)
1998	−0.00412	0.01811	−0.01263	0.01151
	(0.00420)	(0.00139)	(0.00438)	(0.00232)
1999	−0.05345	0.00305	−0.02402	0.01650
	(0.00490)	(0.00148)	(0.00490)	(0.00306)
2001	−0.00720	0.00481	−0.08203	0.05615
	(0.00725)	(0.00244)	(0.00707)	(0.00531)
2002	−0.12972	0.01695	−0.20687	0.09889
	(0.00956)	(0.00337)	(0.00906)	(0.00716)
Employment (log)	0.07547	0.00892	0.05015	0.02577
	(0.00593)	(0.00202)	(0.00599)	(0.00394)
Employment (log) squared	−0.00403	−0.00054	−0.00441	−0.00052
	(0.00059)	(0.00021)	(0.00060)	(0.00041)
Public sector	−0.03054	0.00386	−0.01873	0.00855
	(0.00448)	(0.00158)	(0.00455)	(0.00327)
Constant	0.71906	−0.00636	0.65497	−0.01331
	(0.01762)	(0.00602)	(0.01770)	(0.01161)
Industry indicators	yes	yes	yes	yes
Observations	72,541	72,541	72,541	72,541

Note: POEF is the percentage of overeducated workers, that is, graduates working in non-academic occupations within a firm. PUEF is the percentage of undereducated workers, that is, non-graduates working in academic occupations within a firm. Specification I uses a threshold for the wage premiums of 0.15, specification II uses a threshold of 0.25. Coefficients from OLS regressions with robust standard errors in parentheses. 1996 is the omitted year.

Skill Mismatch in Europe 149

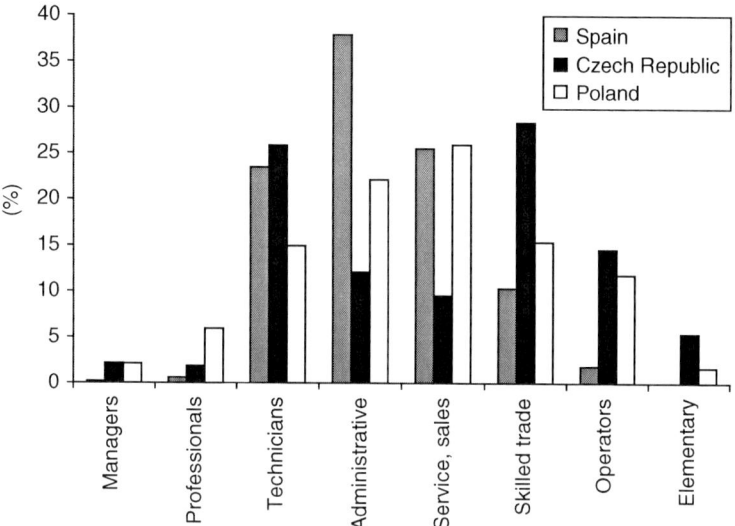

Figure 4A.1 Distribution of high school graduates over occupational groups

Note: The height of a bar gives the percentage of high school graduates who work in the occupational group and who are underqualified according to the definition in the text. Own calculations based on ESES 2002.

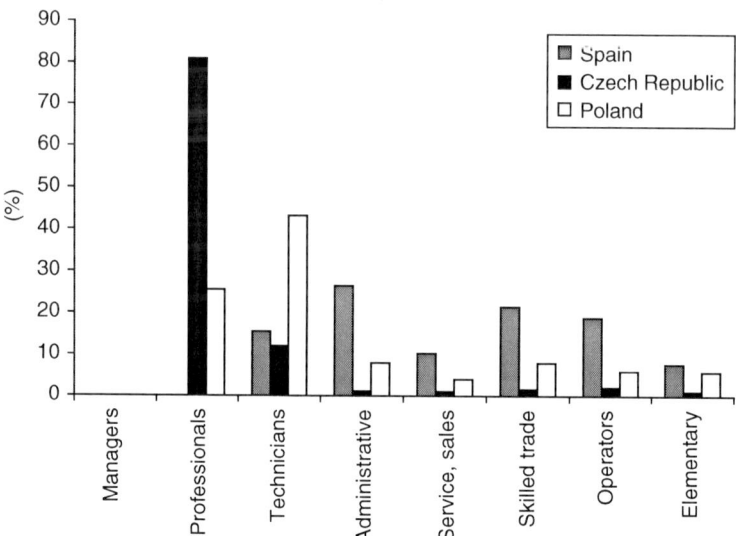

Figure 4A.2 Distribution of university graduates in non-academic jobs over main occupational groups

Note: The height of a bar gives the percentage of graduates who work in the occupational group and who are overqualified according to the definition in the text. Own calculations based on ESES 2002.

Notes

We would like to thank Alex Bryson, Ana Rute Cardoso, David Marsden, Pedro Martins and participants at the LEED conferences for discussions and valuable suggestions. Tanvi Desai was extremely helpful with all questions relating to data management.

1. See Hartog (2000) and Kiker et al. (1997) for a detailed description including pros and cons of different measurement methods.
2. We thank Pedro Martins for initial discussions on this issue.
3. Cited studies include Duncan and Hoffman (1981), Hartog and Tsang (1987), Rumberger (1987), Sicherman (1991) and Cohn and Khan (1995) for the United States, Alba-Ramirez (1993) for Spain, Kiker et al. (1997) for Portugal, Hartog and Oosterbeek (1988) and Oosterbeek and Webbink (1996) for the Netherlands, and Groot and Maassen van den Brink (1995) and Sloane et al. (1995) for the United Kingdom (cf. Hartog 2000, Tables 3–5).
4. The additional studies are Bauer (2002) for Germany, Daly et al. (2000) for Germany and the United States, and Kiker et al. (1997) for Portugal, amongst others (cf. Rubb (2003b), Table 1).
5. Similar results are obtained by Kiker et al. (1997).
6. Hartog (2000) and Rubb (2003b) provide surveys of existing studies from different countries.
7. The ESES are intended to provide information on the situation of employees and do not sample the unemployed or those out of the labour force. We cannot use these data to calculate indices of skill mismatch as in Manacorda and Manning (2007).
8. Restrictions in data processing prevent the presentation of summary statistics such as means, standard deviations, and minimum and maximum values for these countries.
9. We would like to thank the Polish Ministry of Labour and Social Policy for the access to the data.
10. Polish Labour Force Survey data.
11. We also experimented with a lower cut-off, such as 10 per cent. However, using these thresholds did not discriminate sharply between academic and non-academic occupations, as the wage premiums are typically above these values.
12. Figures 4.5 and 4.6 show the distribution of undereducated workers (high-school graduates in academic jobs) and overeducated workers (university graduates in non-academic jobs) over occupational groups.
13. The use of the 25th percentile of the wage premium distribution as a cut-off to classify occupations into academic and non-academic occupations should account for the fact that the wage premium for academic occupations has decreased. In contrast, fewer occupations are classified as academic when using a fixed cut-off of 0.25.

References

Alba-Ramirez, A. (1993) 'Mismatch in the Spanish Labor Market: Overeducation?', *Journal of Human Resources*, 28(2): 259–78.

Battu, H., Belfield, C.R. and Sloane, P.J. (1999) 'Overeducation among Graduates: A Cohort View', *Education Economics*, 7(1): 21–38.

Bauer, T.K. (2002) 'Educational Mismatch and Wages: A Panel Analysis', *Economics of Education Review*, 21(3): 221–9.

Becker, G.S. (1975) *Human Capital: A Theoretical and Empirical Analysis, with Special Reference to Education*, Chicago, IL: University of Chicago Press.

Büchel, F. and Mertens, A. (2000) *Overeducation, Undereducation, and the Theory of Career Mobility*, Humboldt Universitaet Berlin, Sonderforschungsbereich, 373.

Cardoso, A.R. (2007) 'Jobs for Young University Graduates', *Economics Letters*, 94(2): 271–7.

Chevalier, A. (2003) 'Measuring Over-Education', *Economica*, 70(279): 509–31.
Cohn, E. and Khan, S.P. (1995) 'The Wage Effects of Overschooling Revisited', *Labour Economics*, 2(1): 67–76.
Daly, M.C., Büchel, F., Duncan, Greg J. (2000) 'Premiums and Penalties for Surplus and Deficit Education: Evidence from the United States and Germany', *Economics of Education Review*, 19(2): 169–78.
Dolton, P. and Vignoles, A. (2000) 'The Incidence and Effects of Overeducation in the U.K. Graduate Labour Market', *Economics of Education Review*, 19(2): 179–98.
Duncan, G.J. and Hoffman, S.D. (1981) 'The Incidence and Wage Effects of Overeducation', *Economics of Education Review*, 1(1): 75–86.
Goldin, C. and Katz, L.F. (1998) 'The Origins of Technology-Skill Complementarity', *Quarterly Journal of Economics*, 113(3): 693–732.
Gottschalk, P. and Hansen, M. (2003) 'Is the Proportion of College Workers in Noncollege Jobs Increasing?', *Journal of Labor Economics*, 21(2): 449–71.
Gray, J. and Chapman, R. (1999) 'Conflicting Signals: The Labor Market for College-Educated Workers', *Journal of Economic Issues*, 33(3): 661–75.
Green, F. and Zhu, Y. (2007) 'Overqualification, Job Dissatisfaction, and Increasing Dispersion in the Returns to Graduate Education', MHRL Discussion Paper Series (November 2007).
Groot, W. and Maassen van den Brink, H. (1995) 'Allocation and the Returns to Overeducation in the United Kingdom', Universiteit van Amsterdam, Tinbergen Institute Discussion Paper TI 3-95-205.
Hartog, J. (2000) 'Over-Education and Earnings: Where Are We, Where Should We Go?', *Economics of Education Review*, 19(2): 131–47.
Hartog, J. and Oosterbeek, H. (1988) 'Education, Allocation and Earnings in the Netherlands: Overschooling?', *Economics of Education Review*, 7(2): 185–94.
Hartog, J. and Tsang, M. (1987) 'Estimating, Testing and Applying a Comparative Advantage Earnings Function for the Us 1969–1973-1977', Research Memorandum 8709, Universiteit van Amsterdam, Department of Economics.
Johnson, W.R. (1978) 'A Theory of Job Shopping', *Quarterly Journal of Economics*, 92(2): 261–78.
Jovanovic, B. (1979) 'Job Matching and the Theory of Turnover', *Journal of Political Economy*, 87(5): 972–90.
Kiker, B.F., Santos, M.C., de Oliveira, Mendes M. (1997) 'Overeducation and Undereducation: Evidence for Portugal', *Economics of Education Review*, 16(2): 111–25.
Manacorda, M. and Manning, A. (2007) 'Shifts in the Demand and Supply of Skills in the OECD: A Single-Index Model with a Continuous Distribution of Skills', *Oxford Bulletin of Economics and Statistics*, 69(5): 635–66.
MGiP (2005) *Employment in Poland 2005*, Warsaw: Ministry of Economy and Labour.
Mincer, J. (1974) *Schooling, Experience and Earnings*, New York: NBER Press.
MPiPS (2008) *Employment in Poland 2007*, Warsaw: Ministry of Labour and Social Policy.
MSST (2000) *Quadros de Pessoal 2000*, Lisbon, Portugal: Ministério da Segurança Social e do Trabalho.
Oliveira, d.M.M., Santos, M.C., Kiker, B.F. (2000) 'The Role of Human Capital and Technological Change in Overeducation', *Economics of Education Review*, 19(2): 199–206.
Oosterbeek, H. and Webbink, D. (1996) 'Over scholing, overscholing en inkomen', *Economisch-Statistische Berichten*, 81(4049): 240–1.
Robst, J. (1995) 'College Quality and Overeducation', *Economics of Education Review*, 14(3): 221–8.
Rubb, S. (2003a) 'Overeducation in the Labor Market: A Comment and Re-analysis of a Meta-analysis', *Economics of Education Review*, 22(6): 621–9.
Rubb, S. (2003b) 'Overeducation: A Short or Long Run Phenomenon for Individuals?', *Economics of Education Review*, 22(4): 389–94.

Rumberger, R.W. (1987) 'The Impact of Surplus Schooling on Productivity and Earnings', *Journal of Human Resources*, 22(1): 24–50.

Sattinger, M. (1993) 'Assignment Models of the Distribution of Earnings', *Journal of Economic Literature*, 31(2): 831–80.

Sicherman, N. (1991) '"Overeducation" in the Labor Market', *Journal of Labor Economics*, 9(2): 101–22.

Sloane, P.J., Battu, H. and Seaman, P.T. (1996) 'Overeducation and the Formal Education/ Experience and Training Trade-Off', *Applied Economics Letters*, 3(8): 511–15.

Thurow, L.C. (1975) *Generating Inequality*, New York: Basic Books.

Tsang, M.C. (1987) 'The Impact of Underutilization of Education on Productivity: a Case Study of the U.S. Bell Companies', *Journal Economics of Education Review*, 6(3): 239–54.

Tsang, M.C., Rumberger, R.W. and Levin, H.M. (1991) 'The Impact of Surplus Schooling on Worker Productivity', *Journal Industrial Relations*, 30(2): 209–28.

UNDP (2007) Edukacja dla pracy. *Raport o rozwoju społecznym Polska 2007*, Warsaw.

Verdugo, R.R. and Verdugo, N.T. (1989) 'The Impact of Surplus Schooling on Earnings: Some Additional Findings', *Journal of Human Resources*, 24(4): 629–43.

Part II

Wages, Human Resource Strategies and Institutions

5
Variability of Wages across Sectors: How Much, Why and with What Consequences?

François Rycx

5.1 Introduction and background

According to the standard Walrasian (competitive) model of the labour market, where the equilibrium wage is determined through marginal productivity, two agents with identical productive characteristics necessarily receive the same wages. However, so-called compensating differences may occur between similar individuals placed in different working conditions. Indeed, the disutility undergone by one individual following the performance of a task in an unfavourable situation may lead to wage compensation. This simple description of the wage determination process has been challenged by the pioneering observations of Slichter (1950) and more recently by Dickens and Katz (1987), Krueger and Summers (1987, 1988), and Katz et al. (1989). These authors demonstrated that pay differentials existed in the US between workers with the same observable individual characteristics and working conditions employed in different sectors.

In recent years, comparable results have been obtained for a large number of countries (Araï et al., 1996; Ferro-Luzzi, 1994; Hartog et al., 1997; Lucifora, 1993; Rycx, 2002, 2003; Vainiomäki and Laaksonen, 1995). Accordingly, the existence of sectoral effects on workers' wages has become an accepted fact in the economic literature. There is, moreover, a large agreement on the fact that these effects are quite persistent (Du Caju et al., 2008; Helwege, 1992), strongly correlated between countries[1] (Magda et al., 2008; Zanchi, 1992) and on a variable scale in the industrialized countries (Gannon et al., 2007).[2] A number of studies, except that of Björklund et al. (2007), suggest in addition that sectoral effects are significantly weaker in strongly corporatist countries, regardless of the period studied (Edin and Zetterberg, 1992; Gannon et al., 2007; Hartog et al., 2000; Kahn, 1998; Zweimüller and Barth, 1994). Teulings and Hartog (1998), for example, report that from the most to the least corporatist country the dispersion in industry wage premia increases roughly at a ratio of 1:4.[3]

Overall, the existence of sectoral wage premia increasingly casts doubt on the assumption of a perfectly competitive labour market. Indeed, they suggest that individual wages are not solely determined by personal productive characteristics and task descriptions but also by the features of the employers in each sector. Nevertheless, many uncertainties remain.

5.2 The unobserved ability hypothesis

One of these derives from the fact that the unobserved quality of the labour force might not be randomly distributed among industries. In other words, high-paying industries might simply be those in which the unmeasured labour quality is the highest. Almost all studies examining the unobserved quality explanation rely on panel data. They compute industry wage premia on the basis of a wage equation estimated in first-differences so as to control for time-invariant unobserved individual ability. Results arising from these studies are mixed. Krueger and Summers (1988), for example, show for the US that the magnitude of the industry wage differentials is almost undiminished when estimating wage equations in first-differences rather than in levels. A similar result has been reported by Gibbons and Katz (1992) on the basis of US data from plant closings. In contrast, Abowd et al. (1999), Goux and Maurin (1999) and Murphy and Topel (1990) show that individual fixed effects explain a large fraction of the estimated industry wage differentials in the US and France, respectively. Using longitudinal data from the British Household Panel Survey, Benito (2000) and Carruth et al. (2004) also provide strong evidence in favour of the unobserved quality explanation.

Longitudinal data make it possible to control for fixed unobserved individual characteristics. This is a major advantage with respect to cross-sectional data. Yet, the use of panel data generates specific problems that are not encountered with cross-sectional data. Indeed, first-difference estimates may be biased if: (i) the number of workers changing industry is small, (ii) workers who switch industry have non-random characteristics, and (iii) the unobserved labour quality is not equally valued among industries. Fixed effects estimations are also more affected by measurement errors (i.e. errors in reporting changes in workers' sectoral affiliation) since they exclusively focus on individuals switching industry. A final issue concerns the return-to-tenure component of the wage equation (Björklund et al., 2007). Indeed, it is argued that fixed effects estimates are biased, since the tenure effect is likely to be underestimated among individuals who just switched industry.

To avoid the problems encountered with first-difference estimates, Björklund et al. (2007) examined the role of unobserved ability in explaining inter-industry wage differentials using data on siblings (brothers). The authors argue that industry wage premia computed from data on siblings are more accurate than those estimated on the basis of individuals switching industry because they do not depend on the exogenous job mobility assumption. Their results show that unobserved ability accounts for approximately 50 per cent of the industry wage dispersion in the US and for between 11 and 24 per cent in the Scandinavian countries. Furthermore, in contrast to virtually all previous studies, the authors find that the contribution of industry wage differentials to the overall wage variation is not significantly larger in the US than in the Scandinavian countries, after controlling for unobserved factors common to brothers.

The unobserved quality explanation has also been tested by Martins (2004) with Portuguese matched employer–employee data from 1995. His empirical strategy, developed for cross-sectional data, boils down to estimate extended quantile wage regressions, controlling for a large number of variables, at the mean and at the 10th and 90th percentiles of the wage distribution. It is based on the following reasoning. On the one hand, workers with better unobserved characteristics (e.g. ability, motivation, industry-specific skills) are likely to be found at the top of the conditional wage distribution. On the other hand, according to the unobserved quality explanation, workers with better unmeasured characteristics are over-represented in high-wage sectors. As a result, if the unobserved quality explanation is valid, we should expect: (i) industry wage differentials to be larger at the top end of the wage distribution, (ii) a bigger difference in industry wage premia across the wage distribution in high-wage sectors than in low-wage sectors, and (iii) a highly positive correlation between industry wage differentials computed at the mean and at the 90th percentile of the wage distribution (or, equivalently, a strong positive correlation between the mean premia and the difference between the premia at the top and bottom percentiles).

Martin's results for Portugal reject the hypothesis that high-wage industries draw disproportionately more on high-ability workers. Therefore, he concludes that non-competitive forces may play an important role in the wage determination process. Using the same methodology, Plasman et al. (2006) end up with a different conclusion for the Belgian economy. Their findings, based on matched employer–employee data from 1995 and 2002, suggest that unobserved ability is partially responsible for the observed wage differentials across sectors. Yet, these results should be interpreted with caution given that Martin's test for unobserved ability relies on quite restrictive assumptions regarding, for example, the choice of industries by the agents, the behaviour of low-skilled workers (they are implicitly assumed to be present in all industries) and the return to unobserved ability (it is implicitly supposed to be invariant across industries). Therefore, as a robustness check, it would be interesting to verify whether the conclusions for the Belgian and Portuguese economies hold when adopting a more standard approach, that is, when estimating a fixed effects model.

All in all, there is no consensus regarding the exact scale of the industry wage premia. Moreover, while studies on industry wage premia offer some evidence against the perfectly competitive model, they hardly allow discrimination among alternative models supporting the existence of an effect of the employer's characteristics on wages (Benito, 2000; Krueger and Summers, 1988; Lindbeck and Snower, 1990; Thaler, 1989; Walsh, 1999).

5.3 The role of employer's characteristics

Prima facie, wage disparities observed between sectors militate in favour of the efficiency wage theory. Indeed, the latter shows that, if the incentive conditions for effort vary between sectors, then two workers with identical productive characteristics, placed in the same working conditions, are likely to earn different wages. For instance, according to the effort version of the efficiency wage theory, big companies would find it in their interests to offer relatively higher wages to their employees because they face higher costs in order to monitor the effort of the latter. However, this theory does not make it clear why the scale of the inter-industry wage differentials varies between countries and appears to be more compressed in corporatist countries. The constraints encouraging companies to pay efficient wages, that is, wages above the competitive level, actually seem to be similar among the industrialized countries.

Therefore, some authors (Hartog et al., 1997) believe that the justification put forward by Holmlund and Zetterberg (1991), based upon the rent-sharing theory, is more compelling.[4] The latter showed that the influence of the sectoral conditions (variations in prices and productivity) on wages is strong in the US, moderate in Germany and low in the Scandinavian countries. The elasticity between the sectoral environment and wages would thus be more pronounced in the non-corporatist countries. To put it another way, the determination of wages would depend more on the general macroeconomic conditions in the corporatist countries.

This result might be explained by the fact that the explicit or implicit coordination of the wage bargaining in the corporatist countries restricts the insider power of the workers, in other words their ability to capture part of the sectoral rents. In addition, it is argued that the policy of 'wage solidarity' pursued by unions in most of the corporatist countries reinforces this phenomenon.[5] For instance, Vainiomäki and Laaksonen (1995: 172) emphasize that 'the difference [in the dispersion of inter-industry wage differentials] between Sweden and Finland [may derive from] the less successful implementation of solidarity wage policy and more flexibility in industry level agreements in Finland'. In sum, this strand of the literature suggests that rent-sharing is partly responsible for the observed sectoral wage premia and for their apparently higher dispersion in non-corporatist countries.

This conclusion should, however, be made with care for at least two reasons. First, the hypothesis that the dispersion of industry wage differentials is significantly lower in corporatist countries has been challenged by Björklund et al. (2007). Using data on siblings, the latter find that industry wage differentials are, indeed, not significantly larger in the US than in Scandinavian countries, after controlling for unobserved factors common to brothers.

Second, more convincing evidence on the existence and magnitude of rent-sharing is provided by studies estimating directly the elasticity between wages and profits (or value-added) with firm-level or matched employer–employee (panel) data (Abowd and Lemieux, 1993; Araï, 2003; Blanchflower et al., 1996; Christofides and Oswald, 1992; Fakhfakh and FitzRoy, 2004; Goos and Konings, 2001; Gürtzgen, 2005; Hildreth and Oswald, 1997; Margolis and Salvanes, 2001; Rycx and Tojerow, 2004; Teal, 1996; Van Reenen, 1996). The theoretical approach in these studies is a bargaining framework (often the right-to-manage or the efficient bargaining model) in which insiders (not necessarily a union) bargain over wages and eventually employment.

Findings from this literature show that profitable firms pay higher wages even when controlling for detailed personal and firm characteristics. Nevertheless, it is still unclear whether the magnitude of the pay–profit elasticity is larger in countries with little centralization or corporatism. Moreover, the evidence regarding the contribution of rent-sharing to the estimated industry wage differentials is very limited.

Yet, several papers support the hypothesis that industry wage premia result from intersectoral variations in 'ability to pay', that is, profits. For example, Kouwenberg and van Opstal (1999) show that industry wage differentials in the Netherlands are positively and significantly correlated with industry profits. A similar result is reported for the UK by Benito (2000) and for six member states of the European Union by Gannon et al. (2007). Genre et al. (2005), on the opposite, find no significant relationship between industry wage premia and sectoral profits in the euro area. However, this may be due to some data restrictions.

A more explicit test of the contribution of rent-sharing to the observed industry wage differentials is provided by Du Caju et al. (2008). Using matched employer–employee data from Belgium for 1999–2005, they find that the magnitude, dispersion and significance of industry wage differentials decreases sharply when controlling for (instrumented) profits in an individual wage regression including many covariates. Therefore, they conclude that rent-sharing accounts for a large fraction of the estimated industry wage premia. Yet, caution is required as their (repeated) cross-sectional data do not really make it possible to control for the fact that more profitable firms may employ workers with better unobserved characteristics.

5.4 The impact of international trade

Another trend of the literature has been focusing on the impact of international trade on industry wage premia. Trade effects on industry wage differentials can pass through different channels. First, strong import growth or trade liberalization reforms may involve pro-competitive effects in the product market that may influence industry rents and therefore the industry wage structure (Dutta, 2007). Borjas and Ramey (1995) show, for example, that wages are sensitive to net imports in an open economy version of Abowd and Lemieux's (1993) rent-sharing model in which market structures vary across sectors. Moreover, trade changes may have an impact on industry- or firm-level productivity, thereby changing industry relative wages (Dutta, 2007). Also noteworthy is that growth in the import penetration level may be considered as a shock to labour demand that affects the industry wage structure in the presence of imperfect labour mobility across sectors (Dutta, 2007).

Regarding the export side, Schank et al. (2007) suggest that high-export sectors offer high wages as the result of relatively favourable foreign demand shocks. They also put forward that the wage premium in exporting sectors is compatible with the turnover version of the efficiency wage theory. The point is that high-export industries succeed thanks to their product quality advantage and the associated highly qualified workforce. Since this kind of workforce is relatively rare and involves higher turnover costs, it is argued that firms in these sectors offer wages above the market level to secure their competitive advantage in the global market. Lundin and Yun (2004) propose another argument to explain why exporting industries pay higher wages. They suggest that exports increase profits and stimulate expansion. In the short run, this situation causes firms to compete more for the same workforce, and as a result wages increase in the whole industry.

The empirical literature regarding the impact of trade openness on industry wage premia is still relatively scarce (Borjas and Ramey, 1995; Gaston and Trefler, 1994; Jean and Nicoletti, 2002; Lundin and Yun, 2004). However, results are quite compelling. For example, Grey (1993) and Katz et al. (1989) show for Canada and the US, respectively, that workers in import-intensive industries have lower wage premia, while workers in export-intensive industries receive higher wage premia. Using US data, Borjas and Ramey (1995) report a negative impact of import penetration on wages of low-skilled workers in concentrated industries. For Norway, Salvanes et al. (1998) find a positive relationship between the degree of openness and wage premia. Lundin and Yun (2004) examined the situation in the Swedish manufacturing sector. Their results indicate that industries that face intensive import competition from low-wage countries have lower wage premia. In contrast, export intensities are not found to have a significant impact on workers' wages. Also noteworthy is that, according to Abowd and Kramarz (1999), imports at the firm level have negative effects on wages in France.

Researchers have also investigated how trade reforms affect inter-industry wage differentials essentially in developing countries (Dutta, 2007; Feliciano, 2001; Goldberg and Pavcnik, 2005; Hasan and Chen, 2003; Pavcnik et al., 2004; Robertson, 2000). For example, Dutta (2007) examines the link between tariff reduction and industry wage premia in India. He finds that high-tariff industries offer higher wage premia. A similar result is found for Colombia by Goldberg and Pavcnik (2005), when industry fixed effects are included in the analysis. Jean and Nicoletti (2002) also report a positive impact of tariffs on wages using panel data for 12 OECD countries. In contrast, Pavcnik et al. (2004) obtain no significant effect between changes in industry wage premia and changes in trade policy in Brazil.

5.5 Implications for gender and other types of inequalities

Another important question is how inter-industry wage differentials contribute to gender and other types of inequalities. The empirical evidence in this field is still limited. However, several papers document the interplay between industry wage premia and the gender wage gap. Using the 1988 US Current Population Survey, Fields and Wolff (1995) find significant industry wage differentials for women and men, after controlling for productivity-related individual characteristics. These differentials are highly correlated and their dispersion is of the same order of magnitude for both sexes. In spite of these similarities, the authors report significant gender wage gaps within industries. Moreover, their results suggest that around one-third of the overall gender wage gap is explained by industry effects. A similar study has been undertaken for six European countries (i.e. Belgium, Denmark, Italy, Ireland, Spain and the UK) by Gannon et al. (2007).[6] Using the 1995 European Structure of Earnings Survey, the authors report significant inter-industry wage differentials in all countries for both sexes. They also find for most countries that a significant part of the gender wage gap can be explained by the segregation of women in lower-paying industries. This part is estimated at around 16 per cent in Italy, between 7 and 8 per cent in Ireland, Spain and the UK, and less than 3 per cent in Belgium and Denmark. Differences in industry wage premia for male and female workers significantly affect the gender wage gap in Denmark and Ireland only. In these countries, gender differences in industry wage premia account for respectively 14 and 20 per cent of the gender wage gap. To sum up, findings of Gannon et al. (2007) show that combined industry effects explain around 29 per cent of the gender wage gap in Ireland, 14 and 16 per cent in Denmark and Italy respectively, around 7 per cent in the UK and almost nothing in Belgium and Spain.

5.6 Conclusion

This review of the literature has shown that industry wage differentials have been intensively studied since the end of the 1980s. Nevertheless, their existence remains a complex and unresolved puzzle. Indeed, it has been emphasized that:

a. The role of unmeasured abilities in explaining inter-industry wage differentials is still unsettled. To put it differently, there is no consensus in the literature on whether high-wage sectors employ a larger fraction of workers with better unobserved abilities.
b. Studies on inter-industry wage differentials offer some evidence against the perfectly competitive wage determination model. However, they hardly allow discrimination between alternative models supporting the existence of an effect of the employer's characteristics on wages (e.g. rent-sharing or efficiency wage models).
c. Empirical findings regarding the effects of international trade, product market regulation and collective bargaining institutions on industry wage premia are still relatively scarce and/or mixed.
d. International comparisons of inter-industry wage differentials must be considered with caution. The point is that results obtained for different countries are seldom strictly comparable because of cross-country differences in: (i) the characteristics of the data used, and (ii) the specification of the wage equation. Another issue is that the contribution of unobserved abilities to the dispersion of industry wage premia may vary across countries.
e. The evidence regarding the implications of industry wage differentials for gender and other types of inequality is quite limited and would deserve more attention.
f. The economic consequences of inter-industry wage differentials are not easy to determine. This is principally due to the fact that their theoretical interpretation is still disputed.

To sum up, it appears that the existence and consequences of inter-industry wage differentials are still not clearly understood. Therefore additional research is needed, particularly on the basis of matched employer–employee data. The European Structure of Earnings Survey (ESES), for instance, has unique features (e.g. harmonized setting, international coverage, reliability and preciseness of information on wages, detailed sectoral nomenclature) to improve our comprehension of this phenomenon in a cross-national perspective. However, research based on matched employer–employee panel data and on data sets containing more information on workers' (e.g. actual years of labour market experience, occupation at the ISCO 4-digit level) and firms' characteristics (e.g. type of market on which the firm operates, value-added, profits) than in the ESES is also needed.

Notes

1. Among the best-paying sectors, we generally find the extraction of crude petroleum and natural gas industry, the coking, refining and nuclear industry, the chemical industry, the production and distribution of electricity, gas, steam and hot water, the air transport sector, the financial sector and computer activities. At the bottom of the wage distribution, we usually find traditional sectors, including the clothing and fur industry, the leather and footwear industry, woodwork and the manufacture of articles in wood, retail trade, and hotels and restaurants.
2. Cross-country comparisons of inter-industry wage differentials must, however, be considered with caution. The point is that results obtained for different countries are seldom strictly comparable because of differences in the specification of the wage equation, the sectoral nomenclature used, the field covered by the data, or the period under investigation.
3. The concept of corporatism, borrowed from political science, resembles the level of centralization of collective bargaining as well as the degree of coordination between the social partners. However, as this concept has not been defined in one single way, there are differences in opinion as to the relative position of the industrialized countries on the scale of corporatism (OECD, 1997, 2004). The Scandinavian countries and Austria are nevertheless always in the category of strongly corporatist countries, whereas the US and Canada are invariably at the bottom of the ranking.
4. For a review of the literature on rent-sharing see Chapter 6 in this book.
5. A survey of the literature regarding the effects of trade unions on wages is provided in Chapter 7 of this book.
6. Other studies on this issue include, for example, Edin and Richardson (2002), Horrace and Oaxaca (2001) and Rycx and Tojerow (2002).

References

Abowd, J. and Kramarz, F. (1999) 'Econometrics Analysis of Linked Employer-Employee Data', *Labour Economics*, 6: 53–74.

Abowd, J. and Lemieux, T. (1993) 'The Effect of Product Market Competition on Collective Bargaining Agreements: The Case of Foreign Competition in Canada', *Quarterly Journal of Economics*, 108(4): 983–1014.

Abowd, J., Kramarz, F. and Margolis, D. (1999) 'High Wage Workers and High Wage Firms', *Econometrica*, 67(2): 251–333.

Araï, M. (2003) 'Wages, Profits and Capital Intensity: Evidence from Matched Worker-Firm Data', *Journal of Labor Economics*, 21(3): 593–618.

Araï, M., Ballot, G. and Skalli, A. (1996) 'Différentiels intersectoriels de salaire et caractéristiques des employeurs en France', *Economie et Statistique*, 299: 37–58.

Benito, A. (2000) 'Inter-Industry Wage Differentials in Great Britain', *Oxford Bulletin of Economics and Statistics*, 62(0): 727–46.

Björklund, A., Bratsberg, B., Eriksson, T., Jäntti, M. and Raaum, O. (2007) 'Inter-Industry Wage Differentials and Unobserved Ability: Siblings Evidence from Five Countries', *Industrial Relations*, 46(1): 171–202.

Blanchflower, D., Oswald, A. and Sanfey, P. (1996) 'Wages, Profits and Rent-Sharing', *Quarterly Journal of Economics*, 111(1): 227–51.

Borjas, G. and Ramey, V. (1995) 'Foreign Competition, Market Power and Wage Inequality', *Quarterly Journal of Economics*, 110: 1075–110.

Carruth, A., Collier, W. and Dickerson, A. (2004) 'Inter-Industry Wage Differences and Individual Heterogeneity', *Oxford Bulletin of Economics and Statistics*, 55(5): 811–46.

Christofides, L. and Oswald, A. (1992) 'Real Wage Determination and Rent-Sharing in Collective Bargaining Agreements', *Quarterly Journal of Economics*, 107(3): 985–1002.

Dickens, W. and Katz, L. (1987) 'Inter-Industry Wage Differences and Industry Characteristics', in Lang, K. and Leonard, J. (eds) *Unemployment and the Structure of Labour Market*, Oxford: Basil Blackwell.

Du Caju, P., Rycx, F. and Tojerow, I. (2008) 'Rent-Sharing and the Cyclicality of Wage Differentials', IZA Discussion Paper no. 3844, Bonn.

Dutta, P. (2007) 'Trade Protection and Industry Wages in India', *Industrial and Labor Relations Review*, 60(2): 268–86.

Edin, P.-A. and Richardson, K. (2002) 'Swimming with the Tide: Solidary Wage Policy and the Gender Earnings Gap', *Scandinavian Journal of Economics*, 104(1): 49–97.

Edin, P.-A. and Zetterberg, J. (1992) 'Interindustry Wage Differentials: Evidence from Sweden and a Comparison with the USA', *American Economic Review*, 82(5): 1341–9.

Fakhfakh, F. and FitzRoy, F. (2004) 'Basic Wages and Firm Characteristics: Rent-sharing in French Manufacturing', *Labour*, 18(4): 615–31.

Feliciano, Z. (2001) 'Workers and Trade Liberalization: The Impact of Trade Reforms in Mexico on Wages and Employment', *Industrial and Labor Relations Review*, 55(1): 95–115.

Ferro-Luzzi, G. (1994) 'Inter-Industry Wage Differentials in Switzerland', *Swiss Journal of Economics and Statistics*, 130(3): 421–43.

Fields, J. and Wolff, E. (1995) 'Interindustry Wage Differentials and the Gender Wage Gap', *Industrial and Labor Relations Review*, 49(1): 105–20.

Gannon, B., Plasman, R., Rycx, F. and Tojerow, I. (2007) 'Inter-Industry Wage Differentials and the Gender Wage Gap: Evidence from European Countries', *Economic and Social Review*, 38(1): 135–55.

Gaston, N. and Trefler, D. (1994) 'Protection, Trade and Wages: Evidence from U.S. Manufacturing', *Industrial and Labor Relations Review*, 47(4): 574–93.

Genre, V., Momferatou, D. and Mourre, G. (2005) 'Wage Diversity in the Euro Area, an Overview of Labour Cost Differentials across Industries', *ECB Occasional Paper* no. 24, Frankfurt.

Gibbons, R. and Katz, L. (1992) 'Does Unmeasured Ability Explain Interindustry Wage Differentials?', *Review of Economic Studies*, 59(3): 515–35.

Goldberg, P. and Pavcnik, N. (2005) 'Trade, Wages and the Political Economy of Trade Protection: Evidence from the Colombian Trade Reforms', *Journal of International Economics*, 66: 75–105.

Goos, M. and Konings, J. (2001) 'Does Rent-Sharing Exist in Belgium? An Empirical Analysis Using Firm Level Data', *Reflets et Perspectives de la vie économique*, XL(1/2): 65–79.

Goux, D. and Maurin, E. (1999) 'Persistence of Inter-Industry Wage Differentials: A Reexamination Using Matched Worker-Firm Panel Data', *Journal of Labor Economics*, 17(3): 492–533.

Grey, A. (1993) 'Interindustry Wage Differentials in Manufacturing: Rents and Industrial Structure', *Canadian Journal of Economics*, 26: 525–35.
Gürtzgen, N. (2005) 'Rent-sharing: Does the Bargaining Regime Make a Difference? Theory and Empirical Evidence', *ZEW Discussion Paper* no. 05-15, Mannheim.
Hartog, J., Pereira, P. and Vieira, J. (2000) 'Inter-Industry Wage Dispersion in Portugal', *Empirica*, 27(4): 353–64.
Hartog, J., Van Opstal, R. and Teulings, C. (1997) 'Inter-Industry Wage Differentials and Tenure Effects in the Netherlands and the U.S.', *De Economist*, 145(1): 91–9.
Hasan, R. and Chen, L. (2003) 'Trade and Workers: Evidence from the Philippines', East-West Center Working Paper (Economic Series) no. 61, Honolulu.
Helwege, J. (1992) 'Sectoral Shifts and Interindustry Wage Differentials', *Journal of Labor Economics*, 10(1): 55–84.
Hildreth, A. and Oswald, A. (1997) 'Rent-Sharing and Wages: Evidence from Company and Establishment Panels', *Journal of Labor Economics*, 15(2): 318–37.
Holmlund, B. and Zetterberg, J. (1991) 'Insider Effects in Wage Determination: Evidence from Five Countries', *European Economic Review*, 35(5): 1009–34.
Horrace, W. and Oaxaca, R. (2001) 'Inter-Industry Wage Differentials and the Gender Wage Gap: An Identification Problem', *Industrial and Labor Relations Review*, 54(3): 611–18.
Jean, S. and Nicoletti, G. (2002) 'Product Market regulation and Wage Premia in Europe and North America: An Empirical Investigation', *OECD Economics Department Working Paper* no. 318, Paris.
Kahn, L. (1998) 'Collective Bargaining and Interindustry Wage Structure: International Evidence', *Economica*, 65(260): 507–34.
Katz, L., Summers, L., Hall, R., Schultze, C. and Topel, R. (1989) 'Industry Rents: Evidence and Implications', *Brookings Papers on Economic Activity. Microeconomics*, 1989: 209–90.
Kouwenberg, J. and van Opstal, R. (1999) 'Inter-industry Wage Differentials: Evidence from Micro Data', *CPB Report 1999/3*, The Hague.
Krueger, A. and Summers, L. (1987) 'Reflection on the Inter-Industry Wage Structure', in Lang, K. and Leonard, J. (eds) *Unemployment and the Structure of Labour Markets*, Oxford: Basil Blackwell.
Krueger, A. and Summers, L. (1988) 'Efficiency Wages and Inter-Industry Wage Structure', *Econometrica*, 56(2): 259–93.
Lindbeck, A. and Snower, D. (1990) 'Interindustry Wage Structure and the Power of Incumbent Workers', in Brunetta, R. and Dell' Aringa, C. (eds) *Labour Relations and Economic Performance*, London: Macmillan, 378–90.
Lucifora, C. (1993) 'Inter-Industry and Occupational Wage Differentials in Italy', *Applied Economics*, 25(8): 1113–24.
Lundin, N. and Yun, L. (2004) 'International Trade and Inter-Industry Wage Structure in Swedish Manufacturing: Evidence from Matched Employer-Employee Data', *FIEF Working Paper* no. 196, Stockholm (forthcoming in *Review of International Economics*).
Magda, I., Rycx, F., Tojerow, I. and Valsamis, D. (2008) 'Wage Differentials across Sectors in Europe: An East-West Comparison', IZA Discussion Paper no. 3830, Bonn.
Margolis, D. and Salvanes, K. (2001) 'Do Firms Really Share Rents with their Workers?', CREST Working Paper no. 2001-16, Paris.
Martins, P. (2004) 'Industry Wage Premia: Evidence from the Wage Distribution', *Economics Letters*, 83: 157–63.
Murphy, K. and Topel, R. (1990) 'Efficiency Wages Reconsidered: Theory and Evidence', in Weiss, Y. and Fishelson, G. (eds) *Advances in the Theory and Measurement of Unemployment*, London: Macmillan, 204–40.
OECD (1997) *Employment Outlook*, Paris.
OECD (2004) *Employment Outlook*, Paris.
Pavcnik, N., Blom, A., Goldberg, P. and Schady, N. (2004) 'Trade Liberalization and Industry Wage Structure: Evidence from Brazil', *World Bank Economic Review*, 18(3): 319–44.

Plasman, R., Rycx, F. and Tojerow, I. (2006) 'Industry Wage Differentials, Unobserved Ability, and Rent-Sharing: Evidence from Matched Worker-Firm Data, 1995–2002', IZA Discussion Paper no. 2387, Bonn.

Robertson, R. (2000) 'Trade Liberalization and Wage Inequality: Lessons from the Mexican Experience', *World Economy*, 23(6): 827–49.

Rycx, F. (2002) 'Inter-Industry Wage Differentials: Evidence from Belgium in a Cross-National Perspective', *De Economist*, 150(5): 555–68.

Rycx, F. (2003) 'Industry Wage Differentials and the Bargaining Regime in a Corporatist Country', *International Journal of Manpower*, 24(4): 347–66.

Rycx, F. and Tojerow, I. (2002) 'Inter-Industry Wage Differentials and the Gender Wage Gap in Belgium', *Brussels Economic Review*, 45(2): 119–41.

Rycx, F. and Tojerow, I. (2004) 'Rent Sharing and the Gender Wage Gap in Belgium', *International Journal of Manpower*, 25(3/4): 279–99.

Salvanes, K., Burgess, S. and Lane, J. (1998) 'Source of Earnings Dispersion in Linked Employer-Employee Data: Evidence from Norway', Department of Economics, University of Bergen, mimeo.

Schank, T., Schnabel, C. and Wagner, J. (2007) 'Do Exporters Really Pay Higher Wages? First Evidence from German Linked Employer-Employee Data', Journal of International Economics, 72: 52–74.

Slichter, S. (1950) 'Notes on the Structure of Wages', *Review of Economics and Statistics*, 32: 80–91.

Teal, F. (1996) 'The Size and Sources of Economic Rents in a Developing Country Manufacturing Labour Market', *Economic Journal*, 106(437): 963–76.

Teulings, C. and Hartog, J. (1998) *Corporatism or Competition? Labour Contracts, Institutions and Wage Structures in International Comparison*, Cambridge: Cambridge University Press.

Thaler, R. (1989) 'Anomalies: Interindustry Wage Differentials', *Journal of Economic Perspectives*, 3(2): 181–93.

Vainiomäki, J. and Laaksonen, S. (1995) 'Interindustry Wage Differentials in Finland: Evidence from Longitudinal Census Data for 1975–85', *Labour Economics*, 2(2): 161–73.

Van Reenen, J. (1996) 'The Creation and Capture of Rents: Wages and Innovation in a Panel of U.K. Companies', *Quarterly Journal of Economics*, 111(1): 195–226.

Walsh, F. (1999) 'A Multisector Model of Efficiency Wages', *Journal of Labor Economics*, 17(2): 351–76.

Zanchi, L. (1992) 'Inter-Industry Wage Structure: Empirical Evidence for Germany and a Comparison with the US and Sweden', European University Institute Working Paper no. ECO 76, Florence.

Zweimüller, J. and Barth, E. (1994) 'Bargaining Structure, Wage Determination and Wage Dispersion in 6 OECD Countries', *Kyklos*, 47(1): 81–93.

6
Rent Sharing: A Survey of Methodologies and Results

Pedro S. Martins

6.1 Introduction

A large body of research has established that different workers are paid different wage rates, even after controlling for many of their observable differences. One specific dimension of such differences across workers that has attracted particular interest concerns the role of the firms in which workers are employed and, in particular, the role of firms' profitability – the subject of this paper.

From the point of view of the simplest competitive labour-market model, one would not expect that profitability differences across firms would lead to differences in wage rates of similar workers. After all, under the competitive model, supply and demand for each worker type would lead to a single price (i.e. a single wage rate) paid to all workers with the same set of characteristics. The only exceptions to this rule in the context of a competitive model would arise because of compensating differentials – for instance, if some firms offer worse working conditions, their workers would demand a premium to compensate them for that.

However, there are alternative, non-competitive models of the labour market that have very different implications as to the existence of wage differentials and rent-sharing. Three important examples are the equilibrium unemployment theory, efficiency-wages models and 'fairness' models. For instance, a core assumption of equilibrium unemployment models is that matches between employers and employees involve frictions that generate rents which are then shared between the two parties. To the extent that an employer cannot fill a vacancy instantaneously and that an unemployed worker cannot immediately find a job, wages will tend to be somewhere in between the value of the marginal product of the worker (the relevant threshold from the point of view of the employer) and the worker's outside option (the unemployment benefit or a minimum wage, for instance – the relevant threshold from the point of view of the employee). The difference between the wage and each party's outside option would then depend on their bargaining powers.

Given these ambiguous theoretical predictions, a considerable body of empirical literature has emerged, typically presenting strong positive correlations between different measures of profitability and wages and using different econometrics methods. This finding strengthens the view that rent-sharing is an important component of the functioning of labour markets. 'Rent-sharing' is thus defined as when rents (profits above the level that results from paying all factors their market rates) are shared, at least in some part, with employees.

6.2 Research methodologies[1]

Many empirical studies consider as their theoretical motivation a bargaining model in which workers and their employers decide how to split profits by choosing over wages and employment:

$$\text{Max}_{w,N} \left[\phi \log \{(w-x)N\} + (1-\phi) \log \pi \right], \tag{1}$$

where w represents the wage rate, N the employment level, x is the alternative wage and ϕ the bargaining power of workers, π are profits, equal to $\theta F(N,K) - wN - rK$, in which θ is a demand shifter, $F(.)$ the production function (assumed to depend only on labour and capital), r the interest rate, and K the capital stock.

As in other cases, some assumptions also need to be made here in order to simplify the theoretical model. For instance, it is assumed that the outside option of employers is zero profit. Possibly more importantly, particularly from the point of view of Europe (as opposed to the US), it is also assumed that employers can freely adjust their employment levels, disregarding the considerable adjustment costs faced in a large number of European countries.

Adopting these assumptions and after some algebra, one obtains an empirically testable wage equation that results from the above-described bargaining process:

$$w = x + \frac{\phi}{1-\phi} \frac{\theta F(N,K) - rK - wN}{N}. \tag{2}$$

Transition from the theoretical relationship in equation (2) to empirical analysis is not always smooth. For instance, for econometric convenience, authors typically estimate the equation above using the logarithm of wages, although the model indicates the use of wage levels. More importantly, the concept of rent-sharing is particularly challenging to measure. For instance, one needs to know the opportunity cost of all factors used by the firm, including those of labour.

After addressing (or not) such issues, one finally arrives at a wage equation that can be estimated with data sets available in an increasing number of countries:

$$y_{it} = X_{it}\beta_1 + F_{it}\beta_2 + \beta_3 \pi_{j(i,t),t} + \varepsilon_{it}, \tag{3}$$

where y_{it} denotes the logarithm of real hourly wages of worker i in period t, X_{it} will be a set of human capital variables (schooling, tenure, occupation, gender, etc.) that will allow one to control for the differences in the workers' outside options, and F_{it} will be a set of firm characteristics (industry, size, age, region, ownership type, etc.) that will similarly control for differences across firms (and their workers) in terms of their likely level of profitability and/or differences in terms of compensating differentials. Finally, $\pi_{j(i,t),t}$ will denote some measure of rents (typically profits per worker) in period t at the firm (j) of worker i in period t. Finally, ε_{it} is an error term following the standard assumptions.

As mentioned below, depending on the richness of the data, one can also include more sophisticated controls for differences across workers and their firms, such as in the following specification:

$$y_{it} = X_{it}\beta_1 + F_{it}\beta_2 + \beta_3 \pi_{j(i,t),t} + v_{ij} + \varepsilon_{it}, \tag{4}$$

where v_{ij} denotes a worker–firm spell fixed effect, that is, a dummy variable for each worker observed in the same firm. Under this approach, the estimation of the β_3 coefficient, the key result from the analysis, will be unbiased, under the assumption that variation of profits within a worker–firm match is exogenous (not simply within a worker over time, not to mention across workers).

However, even such a rich specification as the one above can still be misleading, to the extent that it may not warrant a causal interpretation of the link between profits and wages. For instance, it may be the case that other (missing) variables are simultaneously driving profits and wages, so that there is not a direct impact of profits upon wages. Among other possible examples, if the demand of the products of an industry is expanding, the value of their workers' marginal product will increase and their firms will also enjoy higher rents, at least until the industry moves back to a long-run equilibrium. Nonetheless, although wages and profits increase simultaneously, there is no causality from profits to wages.

In order to rule out this type of events, it will be necessary to find instrumental variables – variables that are correlated with profits but do not have any direct impact on wages. One example is exchange rates: it can be argued that changes in exchange rates will affect profits of firms that export and/or import, and it can also be argued that there are no additional channels whereby exchange rates affect wages (the exclusion restriction).

A related methodological issue is about the presentation and comparison of estimates of rent-sharing. A relatively popular approach involves the use of the Lester range (Lester, 1952). This range, defined as the elasticity of wages with respect to profits multiplied by four times the ratio between the standard deviation of profits and mean profits, can be interpreted as indicating the degree to which wages would change if a worker were hypothetically to move from a low- to a high-rents firm. More specifically, the range considers a worker who keeps all characteristics unchanged except that he or she switches jobs from a firm whose profits are two standard deviations below the mean level of profits to another firm whose profits are two standard deviations above that mean level. Of course, this range is not necessarily a measure easily comparable across countries, as the dispersion of profits across firms may also vary from economy to economy, not to mention across samples that cover different subsets of firms.

6.3 Data used and their relative merits

Studies of rent-sharing have used data measured at the industry, firm or worker level. Obviously, the more disaggregated the data, the better, as the quality of the test is much higher if one can specifically relate the wages, say, of each worker to the profits of his/her firm than if one can only relate the average wages of an entire industry to the profits of that same industry. Alternative explanations that may also affect the correlation between profits and wages (e.g. unobservable differences across workers) tend to be much more difficult to control when using more aggregated data.

In this context, the recent emergence of matched employer–employee (longitudinal) data sets is a major step towards more sophisticated analyses of rent-sharing. Having access to information about the same worker over time and simultaneously about the characteristics of that worker's firm, one is able to assess whether changes in the profitability of the firm are systematically related to changes in the worker's wages. However, as mentioned above, one needs to acknowledge the fact that even data of such quality and complexity may not be enough to adequately estimate rent-sharing effects. Good instruments may also be fundamental for the identification of the rent-sharing effect.

Moreover, even if endogeneity of this type is not a concern, as it may be wiped out by within-differencing, it is still true that many countries do not have such matched data available. Currently, they only exist in some European countries, in some states of the US and in a few other countries in the world.[2] In the European Union, the best known matched employer–employee panel data sets are those of Denmark, Finland, Portugal, and Sweden (France, Germany, Switzerland and Austria are also important examples). Each data set covers all firms in each country and all employees of each firm in each year over a relatively long period (typically at least since the early 1980s).

6.4 Some main empirical results

One may argue that there are three main strands in the empirical literature. The first set of results focuses on the control for firm or firm/worker fixed effects, exploiting the longitudinal nature of their data. This literature includes Blanchflower, Oswald and Sanfey (1996), Bronars and Famulari (2001) and Hildreth and Oswald (1997). All papers present significant estimates of rent-sharing for the countries covered (US, UK and US again, respectively); the first uses industry-level data, while the latter two use firm-level panels.

A second stream focuses on the endogeneity of profits and the role of instruments in achieving identification of the bargaining models. Some instruments are based on international trade, such as Abowd and Lemieux (1993), who use prices of imports and exports, and Teal (1996), who uses exchange-rate variation. Different instruments include past technological innovations – Van Reenen (1996) – and output movements in the sector to which an industry sells – Estevão and Tevlin (2003). Again all papers find evidence of rent-sharing.

A third and most recent stream of the empirical literature combines controls for unobserved variables and the instrumentation of profits. To the best of our knowledge there are only four contributions here: Arai (2003), Kramarz (2003), Margolis and Salvanes (2001), and Martins (2009a). Overall, these papers have documented smaller estimates of rent-sharing than those typically obtained in the literature that focuses on the endogeneity of profits, and results either smaller than or similar to those of the stream of the literature that controls for time-invariant characteristics.

In Margolis and Salvanes (2001), the authors examine the degree of rent-sharing in France and Norway, using large matched employer–employee panel data sets and progressively adding further controls to the wage equations. In their final specification, which includes controls for industries, business cycle effects, fixed worker and firm effects and an instrument, Margolis and Salvanes eliminate the rent-sharing coefficient in France but not in Norway. However, one concern about the results of Margolis and Salvanes (2001) is that they use what they consider to be 'weak' instruments (sales). This could explain their insignificant results for the case of France.

Swedish data is used in Arai (2003), who examines a panel of workers and finds Lester ranges of between 12 and 24 per cent. Arai's results support bargaining interpretations of the wages–profits correlations rather than those based on supervision efficiency-wages models or short-run demand frictions. In a related paper, Arai and Heyman (2001), a large Swedish matched panel with information for 1991 and 1995 is used and robust evidence of rent-sharing is found. As in the other papers that use IV referred to above, rent-sharing estimates increase substantially when profits are instrumented (with survey evidence on the degree of product–market competition faced by each firm): Lester ranges go up from 14 to 50 per cent.

Kramarz (2003) considers French matched data. Special attention is placed on the twofold impact of imports: decreasing the workers' outside options (due to outsourcing decisions) but improving workers' bargaining outcomes (due to the hold-up that can arise after firms invest in importing schemes). Rents are instrumented with lagged prices of US exports. The results indicate that, for most workers, the effect of deteriorating outside options is stronger than that of the import investments hold-up. The bargaining power parameter is estimated at 0.20.

Finally, Martins (2009a) finds that estimates using instrumental variables tend to overestimate the amount of rent-sharing if controls for firm or worker characteristics are missing. This upward bias also occurs if the measure of rent-sharing used (typically net profits) is less correlated with the instrument than an alternative measure (gross profits). Evidence is found of a significant and substantial amount of rent-sharing in our data, leading to a Lester range of 56 per cent.[3]

6.5 Consequences for economic policy

Rent-sharing may have important macroeconomic implications, as it may prevent an efficient allocation of labour across firms. If firms that are successful in their product market are forced to pay higher wages than other firms, then those more profitable firms will necessarily hire fewer workers than if they were not subject to rent-sharing. This phenomenon may be particularly important if constraints to pay discrimination force the successful firms to pay higher wages not only to current workers but also to new hires. This will also contribute to involuntary unemployment and labour-market segmentation: there will be workers willing to be employed at wage rates paid in such firms.

A related possibility is that employment fluctuations will also be lower than otherwise, particularly if in periods of lower profits firms are able to cut back on the rents shared with workers during periods of greater prosperity. In other words, economic fluctuations will lead to wage changes and relatively small employment adjustments. However, given the evidence of (nominal) downward wage rigidity for many countries, more complex models of wage bargaining may be warranted: firms may anticipate that any wage increases due to profit-sharing will not be recovered in periods of low profits, leading to levels of rent-sharing lower than otherwise.

Rent-sharing will also affect the division of surplus between capital and labour, favouring the latter at the expense of the former. From a normative point of view, if it is deemed desirable to redress the 'imbalance' between the remuneration of the two factors of production so that labour earns an increasing share of surplus (however distributed across workers), then 'promoting' rent-sharing may be a good way to achieve such a goal.

6.6 Tracks for future research

There are several avenues in which rent-sharing raises important questions which have, as yet, received limited attention. One of them concerns the increasing internationalization of production, as globalization becomes a more important phenomenon. One consequence of globalization is that the outside options of employers – and thus their bargaining power – are enhanced, as offshoring and outsourcing become easier to implement. As this leads to the erosion of the relative bargaining power of workers, if rent-sharing is indeed an important component of wage determination, lower wages will follow.

However, there is also recent evidence that multinational firms may also engage in rent-sharing across their affiliates in different countries: Budd and Slaughter (2004) and Budd et al. (2005). This important area of analysis also presents considerable challenges that will need to be tackled: for instance, the practice of transfer pricing makes it difficult to compare profits of foreign firms across countries. (See also Martins and Yang, 2009).

Another topic for further research may be the differences across specific groups of workers in terms of how much they benefit from rent-sharing. Current estimates suggest that workers who tend to benefit the most from rent-sharing are also those who are perceived to have more bargaining power: men, more tenured workers, more qualified workers, etc. (Black and Strahan, 2001; Fakhfakh and FitzRoy, 2002; Gartner, 2006; Martins, 2009a; Nekby, 2003; Rycx and Tojerow, 2004). In this context, rent-sharing may have important implications for gender and other types of inequality. Moreover, to the extent that such specific groups of workers are indeed better able to extract wage increases out of their firms' rents, lack of competition in the labour market can be seen as a source of such wage differentials.

However, a related question is whether product-market deregulation will necessarily generate less rent-sharing. This is a matter that can also be considered from the point of view of how firms adjust the structure of incentives faced by their workers when product-market competition evolves. For instance, Cuñat and

Guadalupe (2005), using UK data, find evidence that a higher level of product-market competition increases the performance–pay sensitivity of compensation schemes, in particular for executives. If this result were to hold also in the context of rent-sharing, then one might predict that, on average, while rents to be shared fall, the sensitivity of wages with respect to rents increases. Depending on how rent-sharing is measured, rent-sharing could even increase with increasing competition.

Another important point concerns the differences between rent and risk-sharing. While most correlations between profits and wages are perceived as evidence of rent-sharing, some recent research (Oyer, 2004) suggests that firms may instead be splitting the risks of their business, so that wages go up when profits increase, but wages can also go down if firms have losses (or, more generally, if their profits fall).[4]

Notes

Email: p.martins@qmul.ac.uk. Web: http://webspace.qmul.ac.uk/pmartins. Address: School of Business and Management, Queen Mary, University of London, Mile End Road, London E1 4NS, United Kingdom. Phone: +44 (0) 2078827472. Fax: +44 (0) 2078823615.

1. See Abowd et al. (1999) and Oswald (1996) for additional details.
2. The Nordic countries' data sets tend to stand out, as, unlike most other countries which also have matched data, they include not only detailed information on all workers (and their firms) in each economy; household and unemployment information are typically also available. Such a wealth of data allows researchers to control for many variables that would be unobservable (and potentially correlated with the variable of interest, rents or profits) with less detailed data sets.
3. In a very recent paper, Martins and Esteves (2006), matched panel data from Brazil is used, following a similar methodology than that of Martins (2009a). Interestingly, no evidence is found of rent-sharing, with zero Lester ranges across many different specifications and estimation methods. This result may suggest that rent-sharing is a practice that only arises in labour markets developed economies. See also Gürtzgen (2009 and forthcoming).
4. Some authors have attempted to address this alternative interpretation by checking for any asymmetries as to how wages change when profits increase or decrease. However, Arai (2003) and Martins (2009a) find evidence that risk-sharing may not be important, at least to the extent that, when focusing only on firms whose profits increase, the estimates of rent-sharing increase substantially with respect to the case when considering all firms. This suggests an asymmetry in which wages increase with rents but do not fall with losses. See also Martins (2009b) for preliminary evidence on the relationship between employment protection and wages.

References

Abowd, J. and Lemieux, T. (1993) 'The Effects of Product Market Competition on Collective Bargaining Agreements: The Case of Foreign Competition in Canada', *Quarterly Journal of Economics*, 108: 983–1014.

Abowd, J., Kramarz, F. and Margolis, D. (1999) 'High-Wage Workers and High-Wage Firms', *Econometrica*, 67: 251–333.

Arai, M. (2003) 'Wages, Profits and Capital Intensity: Evidence from Matched Worker-Firm Data', *Journal of Labor Economics*, 21: 593–618.

Arai, M. and Heyman, F. (2001) 'Wages, Profits and Individual Unemployment Risk: Evidence from Matched Worker-Firm Data', FIEF Working Paper 172.

Black, S. and Strahan, P. (2001) 'The Division of Spoils: Rent Sharing and Discrimination in a Regulated Industry', *American Economic Review*, 91: 814–31.

Blanchflower, D., Oswald, A. and Sanfey, P. (1996) 'Wages, Profits and Rent-Sharing', *Quarterly Journal of Economics*, 111: 227–52.

Bronars, S. and Famulari, M. (2001) 'Shareholder Wealth and Wages: Evidence for White-Collar Workers', *Journal of Political Economy*, 109: 328–54.

Budd, J., Konings, J. and Slaughter, M. (2005) 'International Profit Sharing in Multinational Firms', *Review of Economics and Statistics*, 87: 73–84.

Budd, J. and Slaughter, M. (2004) 'Are Profits Shared Across Borders? Evidence on International Rent Sharing', *Journal of Labor Economics*, 22: 525–52.

Cuñat, V. and Guadalupe, M. (2005) 'How Does Product Market Competition Shape Incentive Contracts?', *Journal of the European Economic Association*, 3: 1058–82.

Estevão, M. and Tevlin, S. (2003) 'Do Firms Share their Success with Workers? The Response of Wages to Product Market Conditions', *Economica*, 70: 597–617.

Fakhfakh, F. and FitzRoy, F. (2004) 'Basic Wages and Firm Characteristics: Rent-Sharing in French Manufacturing', *Labour*, 18: 615–31.

Gartner, H. (2006) 'Gender Wage Inequality and Rent-Sharing', in B. Mahy, R. Plasman and F. Rycx (eds) *Gender Pay Differentials: Cross-National Evidence from Micro-Data*, Applied Econometrics Association Series, Palgrave Macmillan, 118–31.

Gürtzgen, N. (2009) 'Rent-Sharing and Collective Bargaining Coverage – Evidence from Linked Employer-Employee Data', *Scandinavian Journal of Economics*, 111: 323–49.

Gürtzgen, N. (forthcoming) 'Rent-Sharing and Collective Wage Contracts – Evidence from German Establishment-Level Data', *Applied Economics*.

Hildreth, A. and Oswald, A. (1997) 'Rent Sharing and Wages: Evidence from Company and Establishment Panels', *Journal of Labor Economics*, 15: 318–37.

Kramarz, F. (2003) 'Wages and International Trade', CREST, mimeo.

Lester, R. (1952) 'A Range Theory of Wage Differentials', *Industrial and Labor Relations Review*, 5: 483–500.

Margolis, D. and Salvanes, K. (2001) 'Do Firms Really Share Rents With Their Workers?', University of Paris I, mimeo.

Martins, P. (2009a) 'Rent Sharing Before and After the Wage Bill', *Applied Economics*, 41(17): 2133–51.

Martins, P. (2009b) 'Dismissals for Cause: The Difference that Just Eight Paragraphs Can Make', *Journal of Labor Economics*, 27(2): 257–79.

Martins, P. and Esteves, L. (2006) 'Is There Rent Sharing in Developing Countries? Matched-Panel Evidence from Brazil', IZA DP 2317.

Martins, P. and Yang, Y. (2009) 'International Rent Sharing: Evidence from 50 Countries', Queen Mary, University of London, mimeo.

Nekby, L. (2003) 'Gender Differences in Rent Sharing and its Implications for the Gender Wage Gap. Evidence from Sweden', *Economics Letters*, 81: 403–10.

Oswald, A. (1996) 'Rent-Sharing in the Labor Market', Warwick Economics Research Papers 474.

Oyer, P. (2004) 'Why Do Firms Use Incentives that Have No Incentive Effects?', *Journal of Finance*, 59: 1619–50.

Rycx, F. and Tojerow, I. (2004) 'Rent Sharing and the Gender Wage Gap in Belgium', *International Journal of Manpower*, 25(3/4): 279–99.

Staiger, D. and Stock, J. (1997) 'Instrumental Variable Regression with Weak Instruments', *Econometrica*, 65: 557–86.

Teal, F. (1996) 'The Size and Sources of Economic Rents in a Developing Country Manufacturing Labour Market', *Economic Journal*, 106: 963–76.

Van Reenen, J. (1996) 'The Creation and Capture of Rents: Wages and Innovation in a Panel of U.K. Companies', *Quarterly Journal of Economics*, 111: 195–226.

7
Union Effects on Wages
Alex Bryson

7.1 Introduction

A primary goal of trade unions is to maintain and improve workers' terms and conditions, particularly workers who are members of the union, through collective bargaining with employers. Whether unions are successful depends, in large part, on their bargaining strength – which is based on their ability to restrict the supply of labour to the employer – and the ability of employers to concede above-market wages (Freeman and Medoff, 1984). In an era of decline in union density such as the one experienced over the past two decades (Blaschke, 2000) it is frequently assumed that unions are marginalized and will have less influence on wage setting. This chapter reviews the processes by which unions affect pay levels, discusses the difficulties analysts face when seeking to identify the causal impact of unions on wages, and then reviews evidence to date on union wage effects before concluding with some suggestions for future research.

7.2 How might unions affect wages?

Unions' bargaining strength, which ultimately derives from their ability to disrupt the supply of labour to employers, is enhanced by the percentage of all workers they represent and leads to a higher union wage premium (Forth and Millward, 2002; Freeman and Medoff, 1981; Lewis, 1986; Schumacher, 1999; Stewart, 1987). Where the vast majority of workers in a given industry are covered by collective bargaining, union-negotiated wages have less impact on the employer's cost competitiveness than in instances in which competing employers have ready access to non-union labour. This is because above-market wage costs are faced by all competitors. Unions' success in raising wages is further enhanced if the price elasticity of demand for products or services in the industry is low, as might be the case where there is a monopoly or oligopolistic production, since employers are able to meet additional costs from above-normal profits or pass the additional costs onto consumers without undue fear of being undercut by other producers.

It is normally assumed that the mechanism by which unions create a union wage premium is through their direct impact on covered workers' wages through pay bargaining. However, there are a variety of ways in which a union–non-union wage differential can emerge. The first is unions' ability to limit downward wage flexibility in times of hardship relative to their uncovered counterparts: this shows up as a counter-cyclical rise in the premium (Blanchflower and Bryson, 2002). A second is the possibility that union-induced wage hikes limit worker entry to the union sector, or result in job cuts that increase the supply of labour to the non-union sector, thus lowering wages relative to those paid in the covered sector. A third union wage effect, which may compress union–non-union wage differentials, is the 'threat' effect whereby non-union employers raise their wages to avoid the threat of unionization (Farber, 2003; Freeman and Medoff, 1981; Rosen, 1969).

Union wage policies are also traditionally guided by the principle of a 'fair day's pay for a fair day's work', such that wages are attached to jobs rather than individuals' attributes. This wage standardization policy, coupled with concerns to tackle wage discrimination on grounds of race, gender and disability, often acts to compress wage differentials (Blau and Kahn, 2002).[1] Whether unions actually compress wage differentials depends on the position of unionized workers in the pay distribution, the union premium attached to different types of worker, and the degree of centralization and coordination in collective bargaining.

Unions may also have more indirect effects on wages. For instance, their 'voice' face lengthens job tenure, which is itself often correlated with higher wages, and alters the incentives employers and workers face when investing in their human capital.[2]

7.3 Difficulties identifying the causal impact of unions on wages

The discussion above highlights the potential causal effect that unions may have on wages, in both the covered and uncovered sectors. However, there are serious difficulties in being able to isolate the causal impact of unions on wages because of the difficulties identifying the counterfactual, that is, what wages would look like in the absence of unions. The presence of unions in the economy can change the level and distribution of wages generally. In theory, these general equilibrium effects may both raise and reduce the level of aggregate wages in the economy (Farber, 2001). Since it is not possible to observe wages in the absence of unions the effect is very difficult to estimate. Instead, estimates of union wage effects assume a partial equilibrium framework.[3] Even then, the fact that unionization is not randomly assigned means that it is very difficult to isolate the true causal impact of unions on wages. Biased estimates are likely to occur because factors unobserved by the analyst that affect wages may also affect worker and employer selection into the covered sector. Thus union status is endogenous with respect to wages. Selection into union status is likely to be a function of both worker and employer choices (Abowd and Farber, 1982). The wage standardization policy of trade unions is well known to workers and will be most appealing to those workers with low underlying earnings potential, since they have most to gain through unionization. However, not all workers who desire union employment can find union jobs (Bryson and Freeman, 2006). This affords employers the opportunity to pick workers from the queue and since, unlike the analyst, they are able to observe the quality of workers in the queue, they will choose the best in the queue. As Farber (2001: 19) notes, the two selection processes appear to have offsetting effects on the estimated wage gap, with the worker selection implying negative bias and the employer selection implying positive bias. However, the effect of double selection on ordinary least squares (OLS) estimates of the union wage gap is uncertain a priori since it depends on the relative size of the two biases.

This is not the only selection issue that may affect estimates of union wage effects. A second is unions' choice of employer for organizing, a choice that is likely to be influenced by the cost of organizing, the benefits of organizing – and, in particular, the availability of surplus profits – and working conditions conducive to worker desire for union solutions (such as low or unfair pay).[4] Third, employers may have some choice as to whether they are in the covered or uncovered sector, or the type of collective agreement they adhere to.

For these reasons analysts have experimented with alternative methods in identifying the effect of unions on wages. Ever since H. Gregg Lewis's pioneering research (1963, 1986), in which he argued that OLS estimates were the least biased estimator of union wage effects, most analysts have contented themselves with estimates of a union *membership* wage premium based on OLS. However, OLS only returns an unbiased union impact where all factors influencing both unionization and wages are accounted for. This 'selection on observables' assumption, known as the conditional independence assumption in the treatment literature, requires a very rich set of covariates. In practice, most analysts rely on cross-sectional individual or household-level data. These contain only a small number of workplace characteristics. Recent empirical research indicates that, at least in the case of Britain, the paucity of employer controls tends to result in an upward bias in union wage effects. This is because unionized workplaces tend to be better paying than non-union workplaces for reasons that are not directly attributable to membership (Blanchflower and Bryson, 2004).[5] The linkage of employees to employer data is thus likely to reduce the bias in estimating union wage effects.[6]

OLS estimation also assumes a functional form for the wage equation, which means that union effects may be recovered for workers for whom there is no true counterfactual in the non-unionized sample. In the treatment literature this is referred to as extrapolating beyond the 'common support', which is the range of probabilities for treatment (in this case union membership or coverage) where one can find both members and non-members. This limitation of OLS can be overcome using propensity score matching (PSM), though as yet there are few PSM estimates of the union wage premium (Bryson, 2002; Eren, 2007).

Both OLS and PSM rely on the assumption that selection into unionization is captured with observable data. However, there are good reasons to suspect that, even with rich linked employer–employee cross-sectional data, there are likely to be factors determining both unionization and wages which are not observable to the researcher. These include worker motivation which may lead workers to become union members – if, for instance, they wish to have a voice in workplace organization or job design – as well as affecting their wages (for instance, through the effort they devote to their job). This has led researchers to explore methods of tackling selection on unobservables. With cross-sectional data this entails the simultaneous estimation of union status and earnings to account for the simultaneity. The approach relies on arbitrary assumptions regarding functional form and the use of instrumental variables which affect the probability of union status but do not have a direct bearing on wages. These instruments are hard to find and it is generally difficult to design them into surveys. Furthermore, they often lead to unstable estimates, which are frequently much larger than those obtained through other methods (Lewis, 1986).[7]

Additional identification opportunities arise when the analyst has longitudinal data. Analysts have identified union effects on wages by looking at wage changes among workers who switch in or out of union membership (Freeman, 1984). Misclassification of union status and measurement error tend to downwardly bias panel estimates (Freeman, 1984). Furthermore, union switching may be endogenous, that is, whether or not a worker enters or leaves membership may itself be a function of wages. However, observations on workers (workplaces) over time allow the analyst to net out time-invariant factors associated with the worker (workplace) that may influence unionization and wages, thus permitting an estimate of union effects on wages net of the fixed differences between workers (workplaces). If one combines matching, as described in the case of PSM above, with longitudinal data, one can recover matched difference-in-difference estimates of union wage effects which account for observable and fixed unobservable differences between union and non-union workers.[8] Union wage effects might also be captured where natural experiments occur which provide exogenous variation in union status. This technique has been used in the USA, where identification is based on changes in state laws governing union organizing. Unfortunately for the analyst, these occur relatively infrequently.

Perhaps one of the best-known recent examples of recovering union wage effects is that by DiNardo and Lee (2004), in which they used a regression discontinuity design to estimate the effects of being in a unionized environment relative to a non-unionized environment using the narrow margin between union success and failure in the vote for representation. Whilst ingenious, these data are rarely available. Furthermore, this sort of regression discontinuity design captures union effects only at the margin of 'just' being union or non-union.

7.4 Union coverage and union membership

The form that union pay bargaining takes differs a great deal across countries, such that what is meant by 'union effects' on wages differs markedly with the institutions in place. The bulk of the early literature on union effects was conducted in Anglo-American countries, where most pay bargaining occurs at company or workplace level.[9] Analyses relied on individual and household surveys, where measures of coverage were treated with suspicion, such that analysts focused on union membership as the preferred union measure. This is a reasonable proxy for coverage in the United States since, once organized, employees in a workplace tend to join the union even in right-to-work states (Bryson and Freeman, 2006). It is less appropriate in the UK since the correlation between union membership and coverage is not strong (Andrews et al., 1998).

This tradition of focusing on union membership effects is not helpful in the European context, since in most Continental European countries (Belgium, France, Germany, Italy, the Scandinavian countries and Spain) the vast majority of workers are covered by collective labour agreements, whether they are union members or not.[10] Bargaining may occur at national, sectoral, regional or company level, with many workers covered by bargaining occurring at more than one level. Abowd and Farber's (1982) queuing model and Lee's (1978) 'worker choice' model may be less relevant in this instance. Instead, it often makes sense to estimate the effects of different types of collective bargaining. The level at which collective bargaining occurs and the degree of coordination between bargaining levels may affect both the level and distribution of wages.

7.5 Evidence on union wage effects

In the empirical literature for the Anglo-American world, what is usually estimated is the difference between the ceteris paribus earnings of union members and those of non-members. That is, how much would wages change if an individual moved from non-union to union status or vice versa, holding constant their individual and workplace characteristics? Using the International Social Survey Program (ISSP) data for 1994–9, Table 7.1 shows the union wage premium in 17 countries. There are five countries – France, Germany, Italy, the Netherlands and Sweden – where the union wage premium is zero. According to Blanchflower and Bryson (2003: 211), this is 'primarily due to the fact that unions are also able to control wage outcomes in the non-union sector' by extension of collectively bargained rates.

Where most workers are covered by a collective bargaining agreement, focusing on union membership effects is not particularly valuable. Instead exploration of union wage effects should address the question: what effect do combinations of different forms of bargaining have on wages? This is the approach adopted by Dell'Aringa and Pagani (2007) and Plasman et al. (2007). Both studies use the European Structure of Earnings Survey for 1995. Plasman et al. concentrate on the role of company-level agreements in manufacturing in Belgium, Spain and Denmark. They find that in Belgium and Denmark company-level collective agreements raise average wages and increase wage dispersion compared with multi-employer agreements. In Spain, company-level agreements also raise average wages but wage dispersion is actually lower under company-level agreements.[11] The authors suggest their results are consistent with employers in Belgium and Denmark using company agreements to adapt the pay structure to specific needs of the firm whereas, in Spain, they are used by unions to compress the wage distribution. In their analyses of pay compression in Belgium, Spain and Italy, Dell'Aringa and Pagani consider the pay compression effects of single-employer and multi-employer collective bargaining combined relative to the 'default' case of multi-employer bargaining. They find pay is no more compressed among workers

Table 7.1 Union membership wage premium from around the world

Country	Years	Union % increase
Australia	1994, 1998–9	12
Austria	1994, 1995, 1998–9	15
Brazil	1999	34
Canada	1997–9	8
Chile	1998–9	16
Cyprus	1996–8	14
Denmark	1997–8	16
France	1996–8	3 (ns)
Germany	1994–9	4 (ns)
Italy	1994, 1998	0
Japan	1994–6, 1998–9	26
Netherlands	1994–5	0
New Zealand	1994–9	10
Norway	1994–9	7
Portugal	1998–9	18
Spain	1995, 1997–9	7
Sweden	1994–9	0
UK	1993–2002	10
USA	1973–2002	17

Notes: Dependent variable log of earnings variously defined. * indicates statistically significantly different from zero. Controls are age, age squared, years of schooling, private sector, hours and union status. Sample restricted to employees. Germany includes East and West. Dependent variable defined as follows:

Australia	Yearly income in Australian $
Austria	R's personal net income per month in shilling
Canada	In what range would your own personal income fall in Canadian $
Chile	R's monthly net income in CLP
Cyprus	Monthly gross earnings before taxes in Cyprus Pounds
Denmark	R's earnings per year before taxes in Dkr
France	R's monthly earnings in Francs
Germany	R's net earnings per month after taxes and social insurance in DM
Italy	R's net income per month in thousands of Lire
Japan	How much did you earn yourself last year before taxes in thousands of Yen
Netherlands	R's income after taxes in Gld
New Zealand	Yearly income from all sources before tax in N.Z.$
Norway	Personal gross income before taxes and allowances in 1997 include retirement benefits etc
Portugal	R's monthly average net income in escudos
Southern Ireland	Weekly gross income before taxes and social insurance
Spain	R's monthly earnings in pts
Sweden	Approximate income per month before taxes in SEK

Source: ISSP, 1994–9. Based on Blanchflower and Bryson (2003).

covered by multi-employer bargaining alone, suggesting that any increase in dispersion arising from the addition of single-employer bargaining is mirrored in 'wage drift' in the multi-employer bargaining only sector.[12] Taken together, these results indicate that both the level at which bargaining occurs and the degree of coordination between bargaining levels can affect wage levels and wage dispersion. However, effects differ across studies. Furthermore, only some of these studies account for endogenous selection of bargaining regime by employers, an issue to which Corneo and Lucifora (1997) have drawn attention.

There is substantial evidence to suggest that union wage effects differ across workers and workplaces.[13] Where union wage effects are heterogeneous the effects of unionization on covered workers (relative to their counterfactual non-coverage status) are liable to differ systematically from the estimated effects of coverage for those who are currently uncovered. Thus, the effects of unionization on covered workers are likely to differ from estimates of unionization effects for the average worker, or indeed for the worker close to the margins of coverage. Since different estimation techniques recover different parameters it is important to bear this in mind when comparing union wage effects across studies.[14]

7.6 Change over time in the union wage premium

Changes in unions' monopoly power may bring about changes in the level of the union wage premium. Stewart (1995) suggests that the demise of the closed shop in Britain has reduced the union wage premium. More generally, one might have anticipated a secular decline in the union premium arising from increased opportunities for union employers to substitute non-union for union labour. These opportunities arise with declining union density in developed countries and the ability to outsource production to non-unionized labour in less developed countries. In fact, there is little empirical evidence in support of a secular decline in the union wage premium in Britain and the US (Blanchflower and Bryson, 2004). The small reduction in the union membership wage premium in the USA over the past two decades is largely confined to women (Blackburn, 2008). There is also no evidence that increased competition induced by higher import penetration has lowered union wage premiums. In fact, quite the reverse: Bratsberg and Ragan (2002) and Blanchflower and Bryson (2003) show that higher import penetration raises the premium, perhaps because organized workers are more able to resist downward wage pressures that this induces, at least in the short term.

7.7 Future research and policy implications of existing research on union wage effects

Investigations of union wage effects need to adopt theoretical frameworks that are pertinent to the countries at hand and their institutional arrangements. In countries where bargaining coverage is near-universal, studies focus on the levels at which bargaining occurs and the degree of coordination between them. Where company or workplace-level bargaining occurs it is also important to take account of local union bargaining power. In Anglo-American countries, most of which are characterized by more fragmented bargaining occurring predominantly at workplace or company level, it is relevant to consider the effects of both union coverage and membership.

Although economists have devoted much attention to the analysis of union wage effects in the USA and the UK, the literature on union effects elsewhere – including Continental Europe – is small. Consequently, little is known about union effects beyond the USA and the UK.

For the purpose of policy formation it is not enough to know the size of union wage effects. One needs to know where the above-market wages come from. One also needs to know whether unions' propensity to compress pay is useful or harmful from both economic and welfare perspectives. To the extent that unions challenge employer payment of wages below marginal product (e.g. due to monopsony power), unions may perform social good (tackling discrimination and low pay) with no economic harm – and even some benefits (e.g. in the form of greater purchasing power). Similarly, if above-market wages derive primarily from surplus profits, these may be diverted to workers with minimal economic costs.[15] From a theory perspective, it may be unsustainable to pay workers above their market wage. However, efficiency wages can induce greater worker effort, as can perceptions of fairer pay. It is also unclear from a theoretical perspective whether union-induced pay compression is good or bad for firms. Whereas a more dispersed wage structure may create incentives for workers to increase effort, recent results from laboratory experiments suggest that incentives decline above a certain level of inequality (Freeman and Gelber, 2006).

Notes

1. There are a number of possible reasons as to why unions prefer wage standardization. One is that worker solidarity benefits from a uniform wage distribution (Freeman, 1980a). Another is the prediction under the median worker model that, once the mean exceeds the median, the majority of workers will favour redistribution in favour of the lower-paid (Freeman, 1980b).
2. Unions are also known to have effects on fringe benefits and non-wage labour costs, as well as methods of payment, but these are not discussed here.
3. Where union wage setting affects a large percentage of the working population and union effects are sizeable, general equilibrium effects are likely to be substantial. For an example of such a study see Sanner (2003).
4. Brown et al. (2009: 39) find union presence in Britain in the last quarter century has declined least in industries with high rents, suggesting unions have targeted their organizing resources on high-rent sectors.
5. Other studies (e.g. Farber, 2001; Robinson, 1989) have shown that biases in OLS cross-sectional estimates due to unobserved heterogeneity may both upwardly and downwardly bias the 'true' impact.
6. Where covered and uncovered workers are present in the same workplace, multiple employee observations linked to workplace data make it possible to estimate the within-workplace effect of coverage. However, when interpreting such estimates one needs to bear in mind the 'spillover' effect of coverage in pay setting for non-covered workers. Forth and Millward (2002) present evidence of this spillover effect. Booth and

Bryan (2004) use multiple worker observations per workplace to estimate the union membership wage premium among covered workers.
7. Reasons why IV impacts differ so much have recently been discussed in Heckman et al. (2006). They show that IV estimates vary where returns to treatment are heterogeneous and individuals select into treatment with partial knowledge of idiosyncratic returns.
8. This design remains vulnerable to trend effects over time that impact on union and non-union workers differently, as well as potential compositional differences in the union and non-union workers over time.
9. The demise of sector-level pay bargaining in the UK means that this is even more the case today (Kersley et al., 2006; Millward et al., 2000).
10. Furthermore, in many cases EU states mandate the extension of collectively agreed terms and conditions to uncovered workers.
11. Most other studies for Europe indicate that company agreements raise average wages. See Dell'Aringa and Lucifora (1994a) for the Italian metal/mechanical industry; Hartog et al. (2002) for the Netherlands' private sector; Rycx (2003) for the Belgian private sector; and Cardoso and Portugal (2003) for the Portuguese private sector.
12. The effects of company-level bargaining agreements on pay dispersion differ across studies and countries. As noted above, Dell'Aringa and Pagani (2007) find no effects relative to multi-employer only bargaining; Dell'Aringa and Lucifora (1994b) find company agreements reduce pay dispersion between firms in the Italian metal–mechanical industry; Checchi and Pagani (2004) find they reduce wage inequality in the Italian private sector; Rycx (2003) finds they increase inter-industry pay differentials; but Dominguez and Rodriguez-Gutierez (2004) show that they reduce dispersion in wages within firms in the Spanish private sector. Dell'Aringa et al. (2004) find no stable results in their study of within-firm wage dispersion in Belgium, Spain, Italy and Ireland.
13. For a review of this literature with particular emphasis on the USA and the UK see Blanchflower and Bryson (2003).
14. For more information on the relationship between different treatment effects and how they can be reconciled see Heckman et al. (2006).
15. Of course, any wage-induced profit reduction may result in shareholder responses that affect the financial health of the company, such as a lower propensity to invest.

References

Abowd, J. and Farber, H. (1982) 'Job Queues and the Union Status of Workers', *Industrial and Labor Relations Review*, 36: 354–67.
Andrews, M.J., Stewart, M.B., Swaffield, J.K. and Upward, R. (1998) 'The Estimation of Union Wage Differentials and the Impact of Methodological Choices', *Labour Economics*, 5: 449–74.
Blackburn, M. (2008) 'Are Union Wage Differentials in the United States Falling?' *Industrial Relations*, 47(3): 390–418.
Blanchflower, D.G. and Bryson, A. (2002) 'Changes Over Time in Union Relative Wage Effects in the UK and the US Revisited', NBER Working Paper #9395.
Blanchflower, D. and Bryson, A. (2003) 'What Effect Do Unions Have on Wages Now and Would "What Do Unions Do?" Be Surprised', NBER Working Paper #9973.
Blanchflower, D. and Bryson, A. (2004) 'The Union Wage Premium in the US and the UK', Centre for Economic Performance Discussion Paper #612, London School of Economics.
Blaschke, S. (2000) 'Union Density and European Integration: Diverging Convergence', *European Journal of Industrial Relations*, 6: 217–36.
Blau, F. and Kahn, L.M. (2002) *At Home and Abroad: US Labor Market Performance in International Perspective*, New York: Russell Sage.
Booth, A.L. and Bryan, M. (2004) 'The Union Membership Wage-Premium Puzzle: Is There a Free Rider Problem', *Industrial and Labor Relations Review*, 57: 402–21.

Bratsberg, B. and Ragan, J.F. (2002) 'Changes in the Union Wage Premium by Industry', *Industrial and Labor Relations Review*, 56(1): 65–83.

Brown, W., Bryson, A. and Forth, J. (2009) 'Competition and the Retreat from Collective Bargaining', in W. Brown, A. Bryson, J. Forth and K. Whitfield (eds) *The Evolution of the Modern Workplace*, Cambridge: Cambridge University Press.

Bryson, A. (2002) 'The Union Membership Wage Premium: An Analysis Using Propensity Score Matching', Centre for Economic Performance Discussion Paper No. 530, London School of Economics.

Bryson, A. and Freeman, R. (2006) 'Worker Needs and Voice in the US and the UK', NBER Working Paper #12310, Cambridge, MA.

Cardoso, A.R. and Portugal, P. (2003) 'Bargained Wages, Wage Drift and the Design of the Wage Setting System', IZA Discussion Paper #914.

Checchi, D. and Pagani, L. (2004) 'The Effects of Unions on Wage Inequality. The Italian Case in the Nineties', PIEP Working Paper, Centre for Economic Performance, LSE.

Corneo, G. and Lucifora, C. (1997) 'Wage Formation Under Union Threat Effects: Theory and Empirical Evidence', *Labour Economics*, 4: 265–92.

Dell'Aringa, C. and Lucifora, C. (1994a) 'Collective Bargaining and Relative Earnings in Italy', *European Journal of Political Economy*, 10: 727–47.

Dell'Aringa, C. and Lucifora, C. (1994b) 'Wage Dispersion and Unionism: Do Unions Protect Low Pay?' *International Journal of Manpower*, 15(2,3): 150–70.

Dell'Aringa, C., Lucifora, C., Orlando, N. and Cottini, E. (2004) 'Bargaining Structure and Intra-Establishment Pay Inequality in Four European Countries. Evidence from Matched Employer-Employee Data', PIEP Working Paper, Centre for Economic Performance, London School of Economics.

Dell'Aringa, C. and Pagani, L. (2007) 'Collective Bargaining and Wage Dispersion In Europe', *British Journal of Industrial Relations*, 45(1): 29–54.

DiNardo, J. and Lee, D.S. (2004) 'Economic Impacts of New Unionization on Private Sector Employers: 1984–2001', *Quarterly Journal of Economics*, 119(4): 1383–442.

Dominguez, J.F.C. and Rodriguez-Gutierez, C. (2004) 'Collective Bargaining and Within Firm Wage Dispersion in Spain', *British Journal of Industrial Relations*, 42(3): 481–506.

Eren, O. (2007) 'Measuring the Union-Nonunion Wage Gap Using Propensity Score Matching', *Industrial Relations*, 46(4): 766–80.

Farber, H. (2001) 'Notes on the Economics of Labor Unions', Princeton University Industrial Relations Section Working Paper #452.

Farber, H. (2003) 'Nonunion Wage Rates and the Threat of Unionization', NBER Working Paper #9705.

Forth, J. and Millward, N. (2002) 'Union Effects on Pay Levels in Britain', *Labour Economics*, 9: 547–61.

Freeman, R.B. (1980a) 'The Exit-Voice Trade-Off in the Labour Market: Unionism, Job Tenure, Quits and Separations', *Quarterly Journal of Economics*, 94: 643–73.

Freeman, R.B. (1980b) 'Unionism and the Dispersion of Wages', *Industrial and Labor Relations Review*, 34(1): 3–23.

Freeman, R.B. (1984) 'Longitudinal Analyses of the Effects of Trade Unions', *Journal of Labor Economics*, 2(1): 1–26.

Freeman, R.B. and Gelber, A.M. (2006) 'Optimal Inequality. Evidence from a Tournament', Harvard mimeo.

Freeman, R.B. and Medoff, J.L. (1981) 'The Impact of the Percentage Organized on Union and Nonunion Wages', *Review of Economics and Statistics*, 63: 561–72.

Freeman, R.B. and Medoff, J.L. (1984) *What Do Unions Do?* New York: Basic Books.

Hartog, J., Leuven, E. and Teulings, C. (2002) 'Wages and the Bargaining Regime in a Corporatist Setting: The Netherlands', *European Journal of Political Economy*, 18: 317–31.

Heckman, J.J., Urzua, S. and Vytlacil, E. (2006) 'Understanding Instrumental Variables in Models with Essential Heterogeneity', paper to the Comparative Analysis of Enterprise Data Conference, Chicago.

Kersley, B., Alpin, C., Forth, J., Bryson, A., Bewley, H., Dix, G. and Oxenbridge, S. (2006) *Inside the Workplace: Findings from the 2004 Workplace Employment Relations Survey*, London: Routledge.

Lee, L. (1978) 'Unionism and Wage Rates: A Simultaneous Equations Model with Qualitative and Limited Dependent Variables', *International Economic Review*, 19: 415–34.

Lewis, H.G. (1963) *Unionism and Relative Wages in the United States: An Empirical Inquiry*, Chicago, IL: University of Chicago Press.

Lewis, H.G. (1986) *Union Relative Wage Effects: A Survey*, Chicago, IL: University of Chicago Press.

Millward, N., Bryson, A. and Forth, J. (2000) *All Change at Work? British Employment Relations, 1980–98, as portrayed by the Workplace Industrial Relations Survey Series*, London: Routledge.

Plasman, R., Rusinek, M. and Rycx, F. (2007) 'Wages and the Bargaining Regime Under Multi-level Bargaining: Belgium, Denmark and Spain', *European Journal of Industrial Relations*, 13(2): 161–80.

Robinson, C. (1989) 'The Joint Determination of Union Status and Union Wage Effects: Some Tests of Alternative Models', *Journal of Political Economy*, 97: 639–67.

Rosen, S. (1969) 'Trade Union Power, Threat Effects and the Extent of Organization', *Review of Economic Studies*, 36: 185–96.

Rycx, F. (2003) 'Industry Wage Differentials and the Bargaining Regime in a Corporatist Country', *International Journal of Manpower*, 24(4): 347–66.

Sanner, H. (2003) 'Imperfect Goods and Labour Markets and the Union Wage Gap', Potsdam University Discussion Paper #55.

Schumacher, E.J. (1999) 'What Explains Wage Differences Between Union Members and Covered Nonmembers?' *Southern Economic Journal*, 65(3): 493–512.

Stewart, M.B. (1987) 'Collective Bargaining Arrangements, Closed Shops and Relative Pay', *Economic Journal*, 97(385): 140–56.

Stewart, M.B. (1995) 'Union Wage Differentials in an Era of Declining Unionisation', *Oxford Bulletin of Economics and Statistics*, 57: 143–66.

8
Low-Wage Employment and the Role of the Firm: An Agenda for Data and Research

Wiemer Salverda

8.1 Background

Many important issues of labour-market analysis, such as inter-industry differentials, union and employer behaviour, the effects of institutions and rent-sharing or the absence of it, come together in the (both theoretically and empirically) extremely interesting slice of employment that is situated at the lower end of the wage distribution, be it at the very end, where the minimum wage, if any, is found, or higher up to the low-wage threshold, which we will discuss below.

The fortunes of low-wage employment have been receiving increased attention from researchers and policymakers since the early 1990s, triggered by the question of whether or not minimum wages are harming employment. For a long time there had been no doubt among economic analysts that there was a harmful relationship indeed. It was the a priori of the received wisdom, and only the magnitude of the harm could vary. The fresh approach developed in David Card and Alan Krueger's (1995) *Myth and Measurement* book, preceded by various journal contributions, provided a turning point in this debate. Since then a new strand of literature has developed based on a novel, much broader view of monopsony in the labour market. Replacing the traditional view of the 'company town', the new idea is that employers in general may have an edge over their employees, basically because they cannot and will not all leave overnight. The approach culminated in Alan Manning's (2003) *Monopsony in Motion* book, which was also preceded by various contributions, by himself, Stephen Machin, Richard Dickens and others, concerning low-wage employment in Britain. Without this change in the profession's thinking it would plausibly have been more difficult to introduce a national minimum wage in the UK in 1999 after Margaret Thatcher's government had abolished the last remains of the Wage Council system of (narrowly targeted) minimum wages in 1993.

A natural implication of this change for the analysis of low-wage employment is that progressively more attention is now being paid to the role of the firm. Recently, the type of matched employer–employee data that are essential for such analysis is increasingly becoming available, though the situation is still far from satisfactory, especially at the European level. Several projects, European and American,[1] are witness to this increased interest and provide a good opportunity to take another step at the European level regarding both analysis and data collection, which is an important aim of this contribution.

Given the nature of this contribution, we focus on the workings of the labour market and leave the relations between low pay and (household) poverty aside, in spite of their potential role for labour supply and their political importance.[2]

8.2 Relevant empirical results

The focus on the low-pay segment of employment is empirical by nature and throws up several questions that need to be answered first. Foremost, a proper demarcation and description of low-wage employment is needed to enable a correct focus on this part of the economy. In principle, a definition of low pay can be absolute or relative (OECD, 1996: 69). The former is difficult to interpret in international comparison, in contrast to the latter. This seems obvious for amounts chosen in national currencies with the help of nominal exchange rates. However, it is also the case when an equal level would be chosen in terms of purchasing power parities (PPPs) that correct for diverging price levels. PPPs still cannot take away gross international differences in levels of economic development, as minimum wages in the EU may illustrate. In 2008 the 14-fold variation in their nominal values, from €112 (Bulgaria) to €1,610 (Luxembourg) per month, is only halved to a ratio of almost 7:1 if measured by PPPs, from 232 in Romania to 1,532 in Luxembourg (see also Table 8A.2). To bridge the gap the Luxembourg minimum wage should be reduced to a seventh of its present value, which obviously does not make sense.

A relative approach can be defined in different ways: either, first, as all wages in a share of the wage distribution itself, that is, a fixed quantile such as, for example, the bottom 10 per cent, 20 per cent or 30 per cent; or, second, as all wages below a threshold defined relative to an anchoring point in the country's wage distribution, for example, as a percentage of the median wage. In the first case the incidence of low pay among a country's employees cannot change by definition,[3] but the incidence among different categories of employees can change and so can the *composition* of low-wage employment as a result.[4] In the second case the aggregate incidence can also change, in addition to the composition. This is the approach now mostly taken, usually with the threshold chosen at two-thirds of the median wage. One caveat, in a dynamic perspective, is that for an individual in a wider earnings distribution a relative measure may be more difficult to exceed in a process of earnings mobility; this is often thought to be the case for the American distribution in comparison to that of European countries, but not yet convincingly demonstrated.

Note that such a threshold can help to discuss low pay also for countries that do not have a statutory minimum wage. Where there is one, the low-pay threshold may deviate from it to a smaller or larger extent, and such deviation is an interesting topic of study in itself. Studies of the minimum wage can also provide valuable insights into the workings of the low-wage labour market, if only because a lower relative level of the minimum to average or median pay in the economy often seems to go together with a lower employment share of those earning the minimum wage – contrary to what textbook economics would lead one to expect, on the common assumption that a lower minimum wage will increase labour demand and include in employment less productive individuals whom a higher minimum wage tends to exclude.

Even with such a straightforward definition, the measurement of low-wage employment across countries is not trivial. First, the concept still needs further refinement for adequate application, as we will see below, especially the basic time frame chosen for defining the relevant wage (hourly, monthly, etc.). Second, no single adequate internationally comparative data set is available, as we will also discuss below. Unfortunately, the many studies of low pay have not led to the establishment of an international statistic of low-wage employment, however desirable it may be. As a result, the precise levels and compositions depend on specific studies and the data they use. Thus the updating of existing comparisons to more recent years, which is needed to uncover trends, requires a renewed treatment of the data each time. These statistical problems may hamper a proper analysis of the mechanisms at work in the low-wage labour market – relative levels, trends and the firm side are not unequivocally established. Nevertheless, there are some stylized facts that allow several conclusions for both analysis and policymaking. These facts primarily concern the individuals on low pay, not the behaviour of firms, given the current state of the data and the research.

Given the definition of low pay, the important questions to pose are:

- Who are the low-paid?
- How did their numbers develop?
- Where in the economy do we find the low-paid?
- What is the extent of low-pay persistence over individual life courses?
- On what do these depend?
- What are the differences between the European countries?
- Is the situation different internationally, especially between the EU and the US?

Such questions started to be asked in the early 1990s. The European Commission studied low wages (CERC, 1991) in preparation of its *Opinion on an Equitable Wage* of September 1993. The OECD studied the incidence of low pay and earnings mobility out of low pay in the mid-1990s (Keese et al., 1998). The European Low-wage Employment Research network LoWER has made it the focus of its activities since 1996 (www.uva-aias.net/lower), financially supported by the Commission's research funding (Asplund et al., 1998; Blázquez Cuesta and Salverda, 2006). Naturally, many individual researchers are also contributing. The main emphasis is still on the individual employees in low pay, though increasing attention is now being paid to the firm side, as we will stress here.

This is not the place for a comprehensive presentation and comparison of results. Much can be found in publications by the European Commission, the PIEP project (esp. Fernandez et al., 2004) and the LoWER network (esp. Bazen et al., 1998; Lucifora et al., 2005; Lucifora and Salverda, 2009; Salverda et al., 2001), and the international research project undertaken by the Russell Sage Foundation.[5] Results from the latter two are brought together in Salverda and Mayhew (2009). These works draw on two European data sets, the European Community Household Panel (ECHP) and the European Structure of Earnings Survey (ESES)[6] (to which we will come back below), and various national data sets.[7] Some results have been brought together in Appendices 3 and 4.

Before we start considering low-wage employment in some detail, it is interesting to see (Table 8A.2) that a statutory minimum wages exists within EU in a majority of 18 countries and across the US, where many states have slightly higher minimum wages. As a percentage of average earnings this varies from 34 per cent in the US to 49–50 per cent in Luxembourg and Malta. For the share of employees earning the minimum wage, data are scarce. What is available dates back to 2004, concerns full-time workers only and is aggregated for the economy as a whole without further compositional detail. The shares diverge substantially, and do not seem to be correlated with the minimum wages' relative levels in the earnings distributions. The employment incidence is very small in many countries (0.8–2 per cent), relatively high (12–18 per cent) in Lithuania, France and Luxembourg, and in between (3–8 per cent) in Ireland, the Czech Republic, Estonia, Hungary, Poland and Portugal.

8.2.1 Who are they? Where do we find the low-paid? How did their numbers develop? Does the incidence of low-wage employment vary within EU countries? Is the situation different in the EU and the US?

Regarding *personal characteristics*, invariably – over time and cross-country – young workers, women and minorities are found to be over-represented in low-wage employment. This is found with both straightforward descriptives and elaborate estimations that control for personal and job characteristics. Contrary to what many would perhaps expect, low pay and low skill are not necessarily identical. On the one hand, better-skilled persons are increasingly found in low-paid employment. In many countries the role of students is growing, and therewith the overlap between educational participation and labour-market activity. On the other hand, low-skilled persons who are seeking employment more and more have no alternative to low pay – the low-skilled tend to become an increasingly negatively selected group, while in the past many left education in spite of their talents and developed these on the job, unrecognized by educational classifications.

As to *where* low-wage jobs are found, it seems to be another universal feature that these are concentrated in retail trade, hotels and catering, agriculture and personal services. The same four industries usually trail the hierarchy of inter-industry differentials in many countries and are unaffected by the passing of time.[8] In general, low-wage jobs are also increasingly part-time jobs and flexible or temporary jobs. An important question is whether the distinction between low-wage employment and the rest of the economy is a matter of degree – the level of pay being lower than elsewhere – or a matter of principle – being embedded in a labour market that works differently. The latter view may get support from several features such as the high concentration in specific industries that mainly depend on consumer demand, the importance of exits and entries to the labour market, the role of small enterprise, and the role of job characteristics such as flexible contracts and working part-time. Fundamentally, the 'where' question points to the role of the firm, about which we know very little for both practical (lack of data) and theoretical reasons (the neoclassical framework leaves little room for the role of the firm), as pointed out by Holzer (2005). There is good reason to think that on the demand side specific types of firm operate here that are prone to pay low wages. In the most relevant industry, retail trade, we find 20 per cent of all firms, only 8 per cent of value added and 14 per cent of employment.[9] The size distribution of these firms is strongly polarized. Large firms (>250 employees) are relatively fewer in number but are as important in the industry in terms of value added (33 per cent) and employment (35 per cent) as in the aggregate economy; at the same time very small ('micro') enterprises (<10 employees) play a larger role in terms of numbers (96 per cent) than in any other industry. It is not unlikely that large retail firms feel the competition from the many small ones.[10]

Internationally, there seems to be systematic *variation*; there is no single European level of low-wage employment, nor is it the same in the US. Generally speaking, the incidence of low pay is higher in Anglo-Saxon countries, including the UK and Ireland within the EU. Nevertheless, the current level in Germany is around 20 per cent of all employees, similar to the UK. Denmark is the only EU country with an incidence that is still clearly less than 10 per cent; other countries such as France and the Netherlands are between 10 and 20 per cent. Thus major differences occur within the European Union. In recent years the incidence in several Continental countries has been increasing, while that in the US has remained roughly stable at about 25 per cent of all employees since the 1970s.[11]

8.2.2 How do earnings of low-paid workers evolve over the life cycle? Are there important differences in earnings mobility between countries? Is earnings mobility increasing over time?

These questions concerning the dynamics of low pay are equally interesting. However, we only touch upon them as the focus is on the firm and examining these dynamics in relation to firms is still a bridge too far.

Real long-term, life-cycle studies across countries are few (e.g. Buchinsky et al., 2003; Eriksson, 1998; Gregory and Elias, 1994; Lucifora et al., 2005; McKnight, 1998) as they can only be performed on long-run panel data (or work histories). Most studies cover only a modest number of years (e.g. OECD, 1996) or have to pool years – thus disregarding the evolution – to obtain a sufficient number of observations (Salverda and Mayhew, 2009). International comparison[12] is mostly ex post and therefore rather limited and mainly restricted to aggregate mobility patterns without paying much attention to the determinants of mobility. One pattern is, unsurprisingly, that youths generally have higher chances of escaping low pay. Another stylized fact is that, though substantial shares of the low-paid manage to move to higher-paid jobs, they may also exit from employment more frequently than the better-paid.

8.3 Main underlying research questions

Given the above demarcation of low-wage employment, a first layer of analytical questions for research is:

- What determines the individuals' chances of being in low-paid jobs?
- What determines the duration of this being in low pay or, phrased differently, the chances of escaping it, by moving to either a higher-wage job or non-employment?
- What determines the amount of low-wage employment available?
- Is the outcome competitive?

These questions seem obvious to pose and for a long time seemed also relatively easy to answer, given the limited nature of the theoretical approach. Answers have been sought and given primarily in the perspective of an individual employee's behaviour in the labour market, that is, primarily in the perspective of reservation wages and schooling and training. From there the role of institutions was brought forward as an important subject of study, as reservation wages, for example, may depend on the unemployment-insurance system. The new, post-Card and Krueger approach and the perspective of the firm side make approaches and analyses more complex.

8.3.1 What are the determinants of low-wage employment? What is the role of labour market institutions (minimum wages, collective bargaining, etc.)?

The research on individual determinants of being in low pay largely confirms what is found in the descriptives: higher risks for youth, women, the low-skilled and those on temporary contracts or with low tenure, and often, but not always, for part-time workers. In the dynamic perspective (earnings mobility) of escaping low pay, results and comparisons are less clear-cut but also less relevant in the present framework.

The role of institutions in the comparative analysis of low-wage employment, and earnings inequality in general, is aptly summarized in Lucifora et al. (2005). This type of analysis is hampered in a narrow sense, first, by the limited number of country-level observations,[13] and second, by the way institutions are often taken at face value instead of by their 'bite' (which would necessitate meticulous research).[14] In a broader sense it is hampered where it 'neglects the role that market forces or other factors may play' (Lucifora et al., 2005: 274). In this sense an exclusive focus on institutions risks covering only half the story and coming up with misleading results. The role of the economy and internationally diverging structures of (consumer) demand in explaining low-paid service employment is developed in, for example, Glyn et al. (2007).

The existing analyses risk becoming outmoded also in the light of the attention that is increasingly paid to the role of the firm. It has become clear that, in addition to personal and job characteristics, firm characteristics play an essential role. The upshot is the enormous heterogeneity among firms in relation to their employees (e.g. Abowd et al., 2006; Bingley and Lanot, 2003). Being first developed at the aggregate level (e.g. Abowd et al., 1999, 2006; Cardoso, 2005; Hellerstein and Neumark, 2005), the application of the analysis of firm behaviour to the low-wage segment was only a matter of time.

Particularly, a group of US scholars has recently made important advances in using matched panel data for the analysis of low pay. Julia Lane (2006)[15] summarizes the state of the art, underlining its importance by stating that 'traditional surveys of workers that measure the "kitchen sink" of demographic characteristics...are typically able to explain some 30% of earnings variation. Longitudinal data on workers and firms explain about 85% of earnings variation'.[16] There is a hint of a high road and a low road in firm behaviour vis-à-vis its workers. Lane also notes the heterogeneity and advocates a stronger industry-by-industry focus and a linking to qualitative research (see e.g. Grimshaw, 2005). Last but not least, she draws attention to the atheoretical and descriptive nature of the research. This type of firm-focused research is only just beginning, and that warrants the conclusion that 'despite decades of empirical research, we know surprisingly little about the low-wage labor market along certain dimensions' (Andersson et al., 2005: 2). In the end, questions such as whether or not the low-wage outcomes are competitive, or what is the role of rent-sharing (or, better, its absence in comparison with workers higher up the earnings distribution) in the low-wage labour market, may in due course find a better answer with the help of data that include the firm. Bolvig (2005, 2006) also clearly demonstrates the importance of accounting for the firm, as she can link the likelihood of escaping low pay to the sector/firm in which the low-paid person is employed. Another illustration, pertaining directly to the analysis of institutions, is given by Lam et al. (2006), who examine the way the UK minimum wage affects the pay structure of relevant companies, by compressing wages or a broader uplifting of wages above the minimum wage. New analyses focus on the role of a firm's wage bill and the significant effects on this of the pay of employees leaving and joining the firm (Duhautois and Kramarz, 2006).

A direct analysis of firms operating low pay and minimum wages seems an important avenue for research to pursue. There is virtually no information on the frequency in the universe of firms paying low wages or minimum wages to one or more of their employees or about the specific characteristics of firms that do or the frequency with which they do so. A specific category of firms seems to operate here, and it will be important to consider their characteristics and possible uniformity or heterogeneity across European countries. Unsurprisingly, how firms react in this respect to the general economic situation and labour-market developments is also largely uncharted territory. Even simple straightforward questions have no answer. For example, depending on the economic cycle, does the frequency of low or minimum pay among firms change or do the same firms vary the frequency among their personnel? This firm perspective will not alter the relevance of the underlying questions mentioned at the beginning of this section, but it potentially affects the answers, giving firm characteristics a role that may otherwise be attributed to the characteristics of individual workers.

8.4 Data used and their relative merits in view of the underlying questions

Though there is a wealth of individual data on employment and pay, there are particular problems precisely when it comes to studying low wages.

First, the observation of low pay in the data sources may be imprecise.[17] In this part of the earnings distribution, informal, if not illegal, employment and small jobs play a much more important role than higher up, and also jobs and job occupancy are more volatile due to a higher turnover of individuals and jobs. So not all relevant units may be observed. In addition, the observation of the wage itself may be hampered as, for instance, tips (in cash) may be more important and (annual) bonuses less. It is also here that part-time jobs are over-represented, implying the desirability of examining earnings inequalities on the basis of hourly earnings so as not to confound low pay with the choice of working fewer hours[18] – be it voluntary or involuntary. This is changing rapidly over time and differs significantly between countries and is also, as we have seen, particularly important for low-wage employment. It means that an adequate measurement of (hourly) low pay will frequently depend also on the correct observation of hours of work, which is often difficult.

Second, data may come from different types of sources, which have different strengths and weaknesses. Administrative data and firm survey data (e.g. ESES) may register (gross) pay and formal hours of work more adequately, while household surveys (e.g. ELFS, ECHP) may be better at observing personal characteristics, such as the educational level attained as well as net pay and actual hours of work.

Third, the individual data sets are often small (e.g. ECHP, EU-SILC) and may not allow detailed analyses. Or they (e.g. ESES) may not fully cover the economy, and particularly not important parts of low-wage employment. A traditional problem of ECHP for determining hourly earnings is that hours of work are not covered for persons working fewer than 15 hours per week.[19] However, Blázquez and Salverda (2009) show that a slightly different variable offers a solution. The new EU-SILC database that has succeeded the ECHP, which ran up to the year 2001, seems to be particularly unpromising in this respect. For more than half the 26 EU countries covered by the waves of 2005 and 2006, wage earnings information is entirely missing.[20] ESES leaves out certain parts of the economy, though this has improved between the 1995 and 2002 surveys. An important remaining problem of ESES for low pay, however, is that small firms are not covered (compare percentages of data coverage in Table 8A.4) and that many of these operate in low-wage industries.

Generally, data relating to the firm side are few, though matched employer–employee data are gradually becoming available at the national level and are used for research. Evidently, these are in principle the best type of data for enabling research. As argued by Galindo-Rueda and Pereira (2004: 96), the firms' payroll data need to be complete and data must also enable looking at firm demography in relation to the minimum wage, or low pay for that matter, as part of the effect of improving pay may actually reside in replacing low-paying low-productivity firms by new ones with enhanced attributes. However, for a truly good analysis the data should be on a panel basis for the firms too, to permit a proper accounting for firm characteristics and policies. The American LEHD project is a big step in that direction (Abowd et al., 2004). The ESES 2006 is still a far cry from that situation, even apart from the very fact that is not a panel. Within employer–employee data sets the range of firm characteristics is evidently important. Preferably, it should stretch outside the labour market to include the product market as well as the productive performance of the firm. Unfortunately, this range is very limited in the ESES and entirely confined to labour-market characteristics, as is the case in many other data sets.

Though the different types of data have their own merits for the analysis (for example, household data cannot be missed for an analysis of in-work poverty, but, as already said, that is outside the scope of this chapter), the present state of the art requires matched panel data for all levels of analysis, be it the individual employee or the firm. The relevance of both sides for the outcome has been demonstrated convincingly. Increasingly it is considered that the analysis of individual determinants of low pay and earnings mobility cannot be fully grasped without taking the firm side into account. Working with ESES may help to come closer to that ideal situation. Advocating that a sufficiently large and regular European matched panel data set be started as soon as possible is equally important.

However, even if such matched panel data come about they will have clear limitations. Evidently, they would be inadequate on their own for grasping the interactions between low-wage employment and non-employment (such as, e.g., the low-pay-no-pay cycle which is one of the stylized facts of the analysis of low pay), because of their restriction to firms and people in employment. Proper information about the origin of new hires and destination of leavers from the firm is vital in this respect, as is firm demography.

8.5 Statistical methodologies

A simple but increasingly important methodological requirement is to distinguish between the two dimensions of persons (or head count) on the one hand and full-time equivalents (or hours worked) on the other. This is not only because of the growing, and in many respects diverging, incidence of part-time work, but also for direct analytical reasons, as firms and employees may trade off wages and employment also along the dimension of hours of work (Dickens et al., 2009; Stewart and Swaffield, 2004), and may do so differently across the earnings distribution and across the economic cycle.

As we have seen, the analysis of employer behaviour is still an infant industry, and the theory to guide this is not very well developed. Often there is still a lot to be learned from simple descriptives. At the same time, the two levels of the firm and the employee that are available in the data may incite the use of different analytical tools, such as hierarchical linear modelling (compare Mühlau and Salverda, 2000).

8.6 Consequences for economic policy and future research

In labour-market policymaking there are two main worries, which may conflict with each other: a lack of (low-wage) jobs for the low-skilled on the one hand and the risk of poverty-in-work on the other hand. The latter was left out of account here. On the former a valuable contribution may be made if employer behaviour is included in the analysis. A very first step could be taken by enabling comparison between different editions of the ESES (1995, 2002, 2006) and adapting future ESES to that requirement. So far this has not been possible. However, even if it were possible it would be grossly inadequate for a proper analysis. Starting a sufficiently large and regular European matched employer–employee panel data set is of the utmost importance – the sooner the better. Only that will bring us close to the answer to the question of how low pay relates to the European economy and its social model.[21]

Appendix

Table 8A.1 Data sets to analyse low-wage employment

ASHE	Annual Survey of Hours and Earnings (UK) replacing NES in 2004
CCP/IDA	Centre for Corporate Performance Århus School of Business IDA database
CPS	Current Population Survey (US) going back to 1940 (with limited coverage)
ECHP	European Community Household Panel 1994–2001, EU15 at best
EE	Enquête Emploi (France) with precise earnings available since 1990, strong series break in 2003
ELFS	European Labour Force Survey since 1983 depending on country, no earnings data
ESES	European Structure of Earnings Survey 1995, 2002, EU15 at best
EU-SILC	European Union Statistics on Income and Living Conditions First wave in 2003, but not in all EU25 countries; full swing only in 2007
GSOEP	German SocioEconomic Panel (Germany) since 1984 in West and 1990 also in East
LEHD	Longitudinal Employer-Household Dynamics (US) Increasingly covering most of the 1990s and beyond, and most of the states
LIAB	Longitudinal employer–employee data set combines BA employment register and IAB establishment panel, no full detail available before 2002
LSO	Loonstructuuronderzoek (Netherlands) (1979, 1989, 1996, 2002)
NES	New Earnings Survey (UK)

Note: Compare LoWER (1997) for a more detailed view of relevant data sets.

Table 8A.2 Minimum wages in July 2008 and minimum-wage employment in 2004, 18 EU countries (nine EU15 and nine new member states) and the US

	Euro*	PPS*	% of average monthly earnings 2007	% of full-time employees receiving the minimum wage 2004
Belgium	1,336	1,268	46*	
Bulgaria	112	245	43	
Czech Republic	329	460	38	2.0
Estonia	278	390	33**	5.7
Greece**	681	768		
Spain	700	753	42	0.8
France	1,321	1,239		15.6
Ireland	1,462	1,160	43	3.1
Latvia	228	351	32	
Lithuania	232	388	33	12.1
Luxembourg	1,610	1,532	51	18.0
Hungary	285	418	36	8.0
Malta	612	837	49	1.5
Netherlands****	1,357	1,316	46**	2.1
Poland	334	469	35	4.5
Portugal	497	588	42	5.5
Romania	137	232	29	
Slovenia	567	736	44	2.0
Slovakia	267	381	47	1.9
United Kingdom	1,148	1,183	38	1.4
United States	652	882	34	1.4

Note: As figures refer to statutory minimum wages applicable on 1 January, the average exchange rate for December 2005 has been used to convert to euros. The conversion rates for PPS are provisional. * 2002, **2005, ***Minimum wage for non-manual workers. A different rate applies to manual workers. **** Adult minimum wage (at age 23) only; there is a long tail of youth minimum wages starting at age 15 at 30 per cent of the adult rate. The weighted average minimum wage including youth wages is an estimated 87 per cent of this, implying a percentage of average earnings of 40 per cent.

Source: Eurostat, Statistics-in-Focus 2008/105, November 2008 and website Minimum-wage database.

Table 8A.3 Incidence of low pay (%) by year, 13 EU15 countries 1996–2000

	1995	1996	1997	1998	1999	2000
Germany	14.3	13.9	13.8	13.9	15.0	15.7
Denmark	9.0	8.6	8.9	8.6	8.8	8.6
Netherlands	13.3	14.4	15.4	15.6	15.8	16.6
Belgium	13.4	12.9	13.2	12.9	12.4	12.2
France	15.8	15.5	15.4	15.5	16.2	15.6
United Kingdom	20.9	20.6	20.0	19.4	19.4	19.4
Ireland	21.8	21.7	21.6	21.2	20.2	18.7
Italy	10.4	10.1	9.9	10.0	9.8	9.7
Greece	16.1	15.4	15.7	15.5	15.8	16.0
Spain	18.9	18.5	17.8	16.9	16.0	15.6
Portugal	14.4	13.6	12.9	12.7	11.8	10.9
Austria	–	13.9	12.4	12.2	11.5	11.2
Finland	–	–	11.3	11.4	11.0	10.8

Notes: Calculated from ECHP UDB version December 2003; data for SE and LU are not available.
Three-year moving averages.
The low-pay threshold is defined as two-thirds of the median hourly gross salary and it is country-specific. The low-pay incidence is computed for paid employees working more than 15 hours per week, excluding those in paid apprenticeship and in training under special schemes related to employment. Only those working 15 or more hours per week have been considered because of data reliability.

Source: Employment in Europe 2004, Table 51, p. 168.

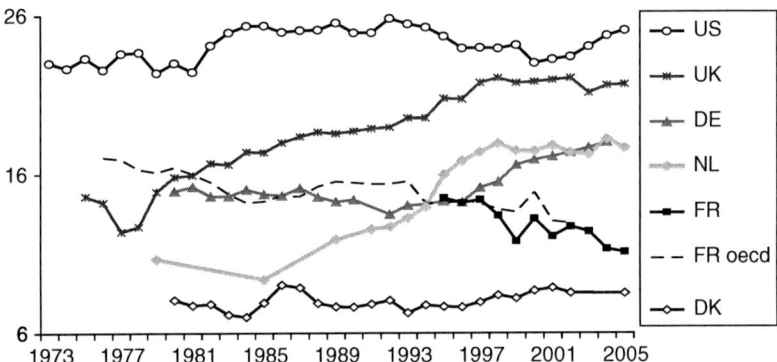

Figure 8A.1 Incidence of low pay (%) with comprehensive coverage, five EU countries and US, 1973–2005

Source: Salverda and Mayhew (2009), Figure 2.

Table 8A.4 Incidence of low pay (%) with varying coverage in different data sets, four EU15 countries, 1996* #

	Total economy		Excluding agriculture and fishery, public administration, education, health care and other community services (Sectors C-K)						
			All**		≥10 employees		≥10 employees, ≥15 hours		
							Comparison sample		
	Full micro survey***	Full ECHP	Micro sample	Micro sample	Full ESES	Micro	ESES	ECHP
France								
Incidence	8.4 (8.9)	16.0	6.1	9.0	7.3	9.1	8.2	12.1
Data coverage	100%		71%	58%		57%		
Germany****								
Incidence	13.7 (12.6)	n.a.	12.0	10.5	n.a.	10.0	n.a.	n.a.
Data coverage	100%		68%	64%		62%		
Netherlands								
Incidence	16.6 (14.4)	n.a.	17.9 (15.2)	17.1 (14.4)	n.a.	14.5 (13.0)	n.a.	n.a.
Data coverage	100%		67 (70)%	55 (57)%		48 (56)%		
United Kingdom								
Incidence	23.9 (22.7)	20.8	22.3	23.1	20.8	22.7	20.0	19.0
Data coverage	100%		6%	53%		51%		
United States								
Incidence	25.2 (25.5)							

Notes: ECHP: European Community Household Panel
ESES: European Structure of Earnings Survey 1995
* UK 1995
\# Headcount results (full-time equivalent employment in brackets)
** Also more than four employees for Germany
*** Full micro surveys: France: Enquête Emploi, Germany: GSOEP, Netherlands: Loonstructuuronderzoek 1996; UK: BHPS; US: CPS ORG
**** West Germany only
n.a., not applicable

Source: Salverda et al. (2001), Tables 35, 36 and 49.

Notes

1. For example, the Linked Employer–Employee Data (LEED) project for the European Commission as a follow-up to the PIEP project (http://cep.lse.ac.uk/piep/query.asp?id=8) or the massive Longitudinal Employer–Household Dynamics Programme (LEHD) of the US Census Bureau.
2. For more see, for example, European Foundation (2004), Cooke and Lawton (2008). Note that US poverty-wages cover a range extending to twice the low-wage threshold applied here, depending on household composition.
3. However, the incidence of low pay among the *population* as a whole will change when the employment rate alters.
4. For example, with a demographic decline among youth the composition may shift to adults, potentially implying a growing problem of poverty-in-work.
5. Compare Gautié and Schmitt (2009) and the five underlying country studies for Denmark, Germany, France, the Netherlands and the UK: Westergård-Nielsen (2008), Bosch and Weinkopf (2008), Caroli and Gautié (2008), Salverda et al. (2008) and Lloyd et al. (2008).
6. For PIEP 1995. The LEED project managed to use ESES 2002 but only for a few countries. Some tabulations of ESES 2006 are available at Eurostat's website.
7. For more details about these data sets and their acronyms see Table 8A.1.
8. At the high-wage end no such uniform industry pattern is found across countries by Salverda et al. (2001).
9. Eurostat, Structural Business Statistics. These and the following figures relate to the non-financial business economy (excluding agriculture).
10. A problem for research is posed by the sheer number of small firms involved; witness the extremely low 7 per cent response rate to the UK Low Pay Commission's survey of employers in low-paying sectors (LPC, 2009: 6).
11. Salverda and Mayhew (2009).
12. European Commission (2004), Chapter 4, compares one-year transitions rates only, averaged over seven pooled waves of ECHP (1994–2001), and unfortunately lumps all available EU countries together for an analysis of the determinants of mobility.
13. The country level itself may be problematic for conducting the analysis (Marsden, 2005b).
14. Compare Salverda (2008b). Institutions may also be too complex to be reduced to a single dimension used for comparative indicators (Marsden, 2005b: 6).
15. Compare also Golan et al. (2007).
16. The effect may be smaller in (European) countries where traditional personal and job characteristics explain a larger percentage of the variation.
17. For an example of the nitty-gritty detail see the ASHE-LFS comparison of Griffiths et al. (2007).
18. Contributions focused on full-time workers (e.g. OECD, 1996) miss out on an increasingly important part of employment, especially at the lower end, while those using monthly earnings (e.g. Marlier and Ponthieux, 2000) mix up the effects of wage and hours. Salverda (2008a, 48ff.) shows for the Netherlands that low pay among full-timers has remained steady since the end of the 1970s (10 per cent) while that among part-timers has increased strongly (17 per cent–27 per cent).
19. In the Netherlands this fraction amounts to 14 per cent of all employed persons, in other countries to between 1 and 6 per cent.
20. Private communication, Bertrand Maître (ESRI, Dublin).
21. Salverda (2006) draws the implications of the research reported in Gregory et al. (2007).

References

Abowd, J.M., Haltiwanger, J. and Lane, J. (2004) 'Integrated Longitudinal Employee-Employer Data for the United States', *American Economic Review*, 94(2): 224–9.

Abowd, J.M. and Kramarz, F. (1999) 'The Analysis of Labor Markets Using Matched Employer-Employee Data', in O. Ashenfelter and D. Card (eds) *Handbook of Labor Economics*, Vol. 3, Part B, North Holland: Elsevier, 2629–710.

Abowd, J.M., Kramarz, F. and Margolis, D.N. (1999) 'High-Wage Workers and High-Wage Firms', *Econometrica*, 67(2): 251–333.

Abowd, J.M., Kramarz, F. and Roux, S. (2006) 'Wages, Mobility, and Firm Performance: An Analysis Using Matched Employee and Employer Data from France', *Economic Journal*, 116(June): F245–F285.

Andersson, F., Holzer, H. and Lane, J. (2005) *Moving Up or Moving On: Who Advances in the Low-Wage Labor Market?* NY: Russell Sage.

Asplund, R., Sloane, P.J. and Theodossiou, I. (eds) (1998) *Low Pay and Earnings Mobility in Europe*, Edward Elgar.

Bazen, S., Gregory, M. and Salverda, W. (eds) (1998) *Low-Wage Employment in Europe*, Edward Elgar.

Bazen, S., Lucifora, C. and Salverda, W. (eds) (2005) *Job Quality and Employer Behaviour*, Palgrave Macmillan.

Bingley, P. and Lanot, G. (2003) 'Starting Wages, Hires and Separations', paper presented at CAED Conference on Comparative Analysis of Enterprise (Micro)Data, London.

Blázquez Cuesta, M.T. and Salverda, W. (2006) 'Low-Pay Incidence and Mobility in the Netherlands – Exploring the Role of Personal, Job and Employer Characteristics', AIAS Working Paper No 46, University of Amsterdam.

Blázquez Cuesta, M.T. and Salverda, W. (2009) 'Low-Wage Employment and the Role of Education and On-the-job Training', *Labour*, 23(Special Issue 'Training and Job Insecurity'): 5–35.

Bolvig, I. (2005) Within- and between-firm mobility in the low-wage labour market, in Bazen, Lucifora and Salverda (eds), 132–56.

Bolvig, I. (2006) 'Starting Wages and the Return to Seniority: Firm Strategies towards Unskilled Labour Market Entrants', paper presented at CAFE Conference on the Analysis of Firms and Employees, IAB, Nuremberg.

Bosch, G. and Weinkopf, C. (eds) (2008) *Low-Wage Work in Germany*, New York: Russell Sage.

Buchinsky, M., Fields, G., Fougère, D. and Kramarz, F. (2003) 'Francs or Ranks? Earnings Mobility in France, 1967–1999', unpublished paper, March.

Card, D. and Krueger, A.B. (1995) *Myth and Measurement. The New Economics of the Minimum Wage*, Princeton, NJ: Princeton University Press.

Cardoso, A.R. (2005) 'Big Fish in Small Pond or Small Fish in Big Pond? An Analysis of Job Mobility', Discussion Paper 1900, IZA, Bonn.

Caroli, E. and Gautié, J. (eds) (2008) *Low-Wage Work in France*, New York: Russell Sage.

CERC (1991) *Les Bas Salaires dans les Pays de la Communauté Européenne*, La documentation française, no 101, Paris.

Cooke, G. and Lawton, K. (2008). *Working Out of Poverty. A Study of the Low Paid and the 'Working Poor'*, London: Institute for Public Policy Research.

Dickens, R., Riley, R. and Wilkinson, D. (2009) *The Employment and Hours of Work Effects of the Changing National Minimum Wage*, Research Report for the Low Pay Commission, UK.

Duhautois, R. and Kramarz, F. (2006) 'Wage Bill Creation and Destruction', paper presented at CAED Conference on Comparative Analysis of Enterprise (Micro)Data, Chicago.

Eriksson, T. (1998) 'Long-Term Earnings Mobility of Low-Paid Workers in Finland', in Asplund, Sloane and Theodossiou (eds), 32–46.

European Commission (2004) *Employment in Europe 2004*, Brussels.

European Foundation for the Improvement of Working and Living Conditions (2004), *Working Poor in the European Union*, Dublin/Luxembourg.

Eurostat (2006) 'Minimum Wages 2006', *Statistics in Focus – Population and Social Conditions Series No 9*, Luxembourg.

Fernandez, M., Meixide, A., Nolan, B. and Simon, H. (2004) *Low-Wage Employment in Europe*, PIEP Working paper.

Galindo-Rueda, F. and Pereira, S. *The Impact of the National Minimum Wage on British Firms: Final Report to the Low Pay Commission on the Econometric Evidence from the Annual Respondents Database*, Low Pay Commission, UK.

Gautié, Jérôme and John, Schmitt (2009) *Low-Wage Work in Wealthy Countries*, New York: Russell Sage (forthcoming).

Glyn, A., Möller, J., Salverda, W., Schmitt, J. and Sollogoub, M. (2007) 'Employment Differences in Distribution: Wages, Productivity and Demand', in Gregory, Salverda and Schettkat (eds), 141–75.

Golan, A., Lane, J. and McEntarfer, E. (2007) 'The Dynamics of Worker Reallocation within and across Industries', *Economica*, 74: 1–20.

Gregory, M. and Elias, P. (1994) 'Earnings Transitions of the Low-paid in Britain, 1976–91: A Longitudinal Study', *International Journal of Manpower*, 15(2/3): 170–88.

Gregory, M., Salverda, W. and Bazen, S. (eds) (2000) *Labour Market Inequalities: Problems and Policies of Low-Wage Employment in International Perspective*, Oxford University Press.

Gregory, M., Salverda, W. and Schettkat, R. (eds) (2007) *Services and Employment: Explaining the US-European Gap*, Princeton, NJ: Princeton University Press.

Griffiths, C., Ormerod, C. and Ritchie, F. (2007) *Measuring Low Pay: Method and Precision*, Office for National Statistics, UK.

Grimshaw, D. (2005) 'Using Qualitative Data to Understand Employer Behaviour in Low-Wage Labour Markets', in Bazen, Lucifora and Salverda (eds), 111–31.

Hellerstein, J.K. and Neumark, D. (2005) 'Using Matched Employer-Employee Data to Study Labor Market Discrimination', IZA Discussion Paper No. 1555.

Holzer, H.J. (2005) 'Employers in the Low-Wage Labour Market: Is Their Role Important?', in Bazen, Lucifora and Salverda (eds), 87–110.

Keese, M., Puymoyen, A. and Swaim, P. (1998) 'The Incidence and Dynamics of Low-Paid Employment in OECD Countries', in Asplund, Sloane and Theodossiou (eds), 223–65.

Lam, K.H., Ormerod, C., Ritchie, F. and Vaze, P. (2006) 'Do Company Wage Policies Persist in the Face of Minimum Wages?' paper presented at CAFE Conference on the Analysis of Firms and Employees, IAB, Nuremberg.

Lane, J. (2006) *The Impact of Employers on the Outcomes of Low-wage Workers*, LoWER Working paper no. 12, www.uva-aias.net/lower.asp (forthcoming).

Lloyd, C., Mason, G. and Mayhew, K. (eds) (2008) *Low-Wage Work in the United Kingdom*, New York: Russell Sage.

LoWER (European Low-wage Employment Research network) (1997) *Statistical Data Available on Low-Wage Employment in the European Union and Its Member States*, Special Report (www.uva-aias.net/files/lower/1997lowerstatdata.pdf).

LPC (Low Pay Commission, UK) (2009) *National Minimum Wage. Low Pay Commission Report 2009*, Norwich: The Stationery Office.

Lucifora, C., McKnight, A. and Salverda, W. (2005) 'Low-Wage Employment in Europe: A Review of the Evidence', *Socio-Economic Review*, 3: 259–92.

Lucifora, C. and Salverda, W. (2009) 'Low Pay', in W. Salverda, B. Nolan and T. Smeeding (eds) *Oxford Handbook of Economic Inequality*, Oxford University Press, 257–83.

Mcknight, A. (1998) 'Low-Wage Mobility in a Working-Life Perspective', in Asplund, Sloane and Theodossiou (eds), 47–76.

Manning, A. (2003) *Monopsony in Motion, Imperfect Competition in Labour Markets*, Princeton, NJ: Princeton University Press.

Marlier, E. and Ponthieux, S. (2000) 'Low-Wage Employees in EU Countries', *Statistics in Focus*, Theme 3–11, Eurostat, Luxembourg.

Marsden, D. (2005a) *Pay Inequalities and Economic Performance*, Project report V5, CEP at LSE.

Marsden, D. (2005b) 'The End of National Models? The Future of Comparative Institutional Analysis', Paper for the German Industrial relations Association Meeting, Trier.

Mühlau, P. and Salverda, W. (2000) 'Effects of Low-Wage Subsidies: The Example of 'SPAK' in the Netherlands', in Salverda, Nolan and Lucifora (eds), 67–92.

OECD (1996) *Employment Outlook 1996*, Paris.
Salverda, W. (2006) 'Employment and Pay in Europe and the US, Food for Thought about Flexibility and the European Social Model', in M. Jepsen and A. Serrano (eds) *Unwrapping the European Social Model*, Bristol: Policy Press, 71–92.
Salverda, W. (2008a) 'Low-Wage Work and the Economy', in W. Salverda, M. van Klaveren and M. van der Meer (eds), *Low-Wage Work in the Netherlands*, New York: Russell Sage, 32–62.
Salverda, W. (2008b) 'Labor Market Institutions, Low-Wage Work, and Job Quality', in W. Salverda, M. van Klaveren and M. van der Meer (eds), *Low-Wage Work in the Netherlands*, New York: Russell Sage, 63–131.
Salverda, W. and Mayhew, K. (2009) 'Capitalist Economies and Wage Inequality', *Oxford Review of Economic Policy*, 25(1): 126–54.
Salverda, W., Nolan, B. and Lucifora, C. (eds) (2000) *Policy Measures for Low-Wage Employment in Europe*, Edward Elgar.
Salverda, W., Nolan, B., Maitre, B. and Mühlau, P. (2001) *Benchmarking Low-Wage and High-Wage Employment in Europe and the United States*, Report to the European Commission DG Employment and Social Affairs (http://ec.europa.eu/employment_social/docs/study.pdf)
Salverda, W., van Klaveren, M. and van der Meer, M. (eds) (2008) *Low-Wage Work in the Netherlands: Labor-Market Developments and the Role of Labor-market Institutions, with a Focus on Five Industries and Occupations*, New York: Russell Sage.
Stewart, M.B. and Swaffield, J.K. (2004) *The Other Margin: Do Minimum Wages Cause Working Hours Adjustments for Low-wage Workers?* Report to the UK Low Pay Commission, London.
Westergård-Nielsen, N. (ed.) (2008) *Low-Wage Work in Denmark*, New York: Russell Sage.

9
Do Firms Compress the Wage Distribution?

Ana Rute Cardoso

9.1 Introduction

'Too many theories, too few facts.' This title, chosen by Baker and Holmstrom (1995) for their overview of the analysis of labour markets internal to the firm, remains today particularly suited to describe the work so far undertaken on the topic of the current chapter: do firms compress the wage distribution relative to the distribution of worker productivities? If so, what is the impact of such compression on worker and firm performance and on labour turnover? A profusion of theories has not been matched by empirical testing, constrained as the analysis has been for a long time by data limitations. 'Unfortunately, an appropriate data base with both worker and firm characteristics does not yet exist. A more complete understanding of the relationship between [...] productivity, and wage dispersion may have to await better sources of data' (Levine, 1991: 251). In the meantime, a long path has been tracked in the production and analysis of linked employer–employee data.

Early work on employer wages policies relied on extensive fieldwork on American companies. Interestingly, it called attention to the remarkable diversity in wage rates across firms, even when located in narrowly defined local labour markets, and the uniformity of wages inside the firm. Examples of this literature include Lester (1952), Dunlop (1957), Reynolds (1951) or, using econometric analysis on microdata on workers, Rees and Shultz (1970); an overview is provided by Kerr (1994). Ever since, the theoretical reasoning on why firms might have an incentive to compress the wage distribution relative to the distribution of worker productivities has been refined, and some empirical testing using linked employer–employee data (henceforth LEED) has been undertaken.

This chapter starts with an overview of theoretical reasoning on the compression of wages by the firm. It aims, on one hand, to prepare the stage for the review of the empirical literature that follows and, on the other hand, to help define the setting for future empirical work, by getting into some detail on similarities and contrasts among the alternative theories. It then reviews empirical work that has used LEED to test theoretical predictions on the existence of a firm wage-compression effect and its implications on worker and firm productivity and labour turnover.

The chapter focuses on intra-firm wage-dispersion, leaving out issues such as decomposition of inequality into its within- and between-firm components, differences between high- and low-wage firms or overall inequality in the labour market, to the extent that they are not directly linked to the level of wage inequality within the firm. The terms dispersion and inequality will be used interchangeably.

9.2 Theoretical framework on wage-compression within the firm: A profusion of models

A clarification of what is meant by compression of the wage distribution by the firm is in order. In a perfectly competitive labour market, workers' pay would be attached to their productivity and a single wage would hold for workers of the same quality, no matter which firm they worked for; on the contrary, workers of different quality would receive different wages, even if working for the same firm. However, the distribution of wages paid by each firm does not necessarily mirror the distribution of workers' productivities. To the extent that the distribution of workers' productivities within the firm is more stretched than that of workers' wages, we refer to the existence of a firm wage-compression effect.

The key factors explaining the existence of an employer wage-compression effect range from workers' preferences to the production technology or the information structure and frictions in the labour market, depending on the theoretical line considered.

Efficiency wage models in general are set in a framework of market frictions, such as hiring, training, firing and moving costs. Wages above the market clearing level would operate as a device to stimulate effort and prevent workers from shirking, discourage quitting, which is costly to the firm given the existence of hiring, training and firing costs, or attract the more able workers, when they are heterogeneous in their ability and the wage the worker is willing to accept signals his or her ability. A positive link between the wage and worker effort therefore follows. The fairness or morale version of efficiency wages further brings into the analysis the level of dispersion of wages within the firm or the equity of its wage distribution. The assumption in this case is that there is interdependence of preferences and that the behaviour of the worker, in particular his or her effort, will depend on the norms of the group where he or she belongs and will drop if the wage level is perceived to be unfair. That would arguably be the reason why firms would adopt a consistent pay standard across their labour force – that is what is considered fair, and thus induces effort, when the utility of the worker is shaped also by equity and fairness considerations. It therefore follows that more unequal firm wage distributions would threaten the morale or the cohesiveness of the group and reduce productivity. Hamermesh (1975) introduced for the first time interdependencies among workers when modelling labour demand and labour supply, as individual effort and productivity would depend not just on the worker's own wage, but also on a comparison wage, for example, the average wage in the firm. Solow (1979) referred to adverse selection, shirking and morale considerations as keys to establish a link between wages and worker productivity, which would contribute to explaining the slow adjustment of wages when the macroeconomic conditions change. Akerlof (1982) and Akerlof and Yellen (1990) are widely quoted as the initial formulation of the morale efficiency wage theory in the economics literature. Levine (1991) stressed the mechanisms linking wage-compression to worker cohesiveness (workers sharing and behaving by group norms) and its impact on firm performance. Alexopoulos and Cohen (2004) contribute to the morale efficiency wage literature by discussing the choice of comparison groups and modelling the inclusion of workers below the worker's own wage level in his or her comparison group, to conclude that a firm's output and profits will decline if wage-compression from below is imposed, since the level of effort of the better-paid workers will decline. Skott (2005) highlights that norms change endogenously, as past events shape what is considered a fair – in other words, a normal – wage, which therefore adjusts to fit actual outcomes,[1] leading in turn to a sluggish adjustment of wages to labour market shocks.[2]

A different setting of interdependencies among preferences is assumed by Frank's (1984, 1985) theory on the quest for status – individuals care for their position in a hierarchy, comparing their own standing with the standing of others. Given distaste for being ranked low in a comparison group, and given the assumption that individuals are free to choose the groups they join, in particular the firm they work for (the neighbourhood they live in, etc.), they would presumably choose to associate with those who are similar to them and would sort into homogeneous groups. This is not the standard situation in the labour market, because some individuals are willing to pay for status, and heterogeneity in willingness to pay renders status within one's hierarchy a tradable good like any other. Heterogeneous associations will thus form, as status seekers transfer resources to those who care less about status. The relevant comparison group would be the firm, a local hierarchy of co-workers, and the wage of workers of equal productivity would vary depending on the rank position: those occupying a high rank in a firm would have given up part of their wage (relative to their marginal productivity) to pay for status, while those occupying a low rank in a firm would be compensated with a wage premium (relative to their marginal productivity). This compensating differential would prevent workers at the bottom from moving to join a new firm, where the productivities and wages of co-workers would be closer to their own.[3] This trade-off between wage and status would be the key to explaining the observed compression of the distribution of wages within firms, when compared with the distribution of worker productivities (Frank, 1984: 552).

An apparent contrast with the tournament theory is worth noting. Whereas, according to Frank, rank position within one's hierarchy matters and workers are willing to pay for it, some versions of tournament theory establish, on the contrary, a convex relationship between pay and hierarchical level – as one moves up to the top of the firm hierarchy, pay differences increase. In Lazear and Rosen (1981), such convexity of the pay scale would work as an incentive mechanism to elicit investment in skills and effort from the workers. Rosen (1986) introduces the option to move further up as an additional benefit to those who are promoted (beyond the immediate monetary gain) and as such, at the top of the hierarchy, an extra wage differential would be required to compensate for the lack of option to move further up. Nevertheless, Lazear (1989) considers the disruptive effects that tournaments may have on firm performance if workers can engage in counterproductive activities (such as sabotage of colleagues' work). In this case, he predicts some pay equality in profit-maximizing firms, to avoid disruptive behaviour by 'hawks' in a system of pay for performance. One should, however, note that the type of pay equality Lazear refers to does not necessarily match that predicted by Frank. Frank's model considers the dispersion of the wage distribution relative to the dispersion of productivities, whereas in Lazear's model differences in productivity matter to the extent that the winner (the highest-productivity worker) gets the predefined higher wage; as such, what matters in terms of productivity is just workers' ranking, and wage differences could be larger or smaller than realized productivity differences (see Lazear, 1984).

A model with interdependence of preferences and labour market frictions was proposed by Cabrales et al. (2008), extending the dynamic setting of contract theory where, in the presence of uncertainty, risk-neutral firms offer contracts to their risk-averse workers. The model assumes that workers are heterogeneous, but perfect substitutes, and, moreover, that their true ability is unobserved, being revealed after the start of an employment spell. A particular type of inequity-aversion is considered – workers dislike inequality when they are the low-wage earners, but have no concern when they are the high earners. Their reference group includes colleagues in the same firm with similar skill (more precisely, those with 'a similar career history within the firm'). As such, the comparison group changes endogenously, as workers enter and leave the group, due to job turnover. Interesting predictions emerge concerning the link between productivity and wages and worker segregation across firms. First of all, frictions in the labour market tend to reduce worker segregation across firms. Indeed, in the presence of moving or hiring costs, flows of workers across firms will be lower and, once the productivity of a worker inside a firm is revealed to be high, his or her wage does not increase as much – labour market frictions shield the employer from the competitive or outside wage rate – but nevertheless he or she may stay with the firm. Within the firm, low and high-skill workers will therefore coexist. Second, workers' preference for equity will operate in the opposite direction, towards increasing segregation, simply because lower-ability workers will suffer disutility from working with more skilled and higher-paid colleagues and would prefer to join a firm with a more homogeneous workforce. The relative importance of these two factors and the actual degree of segregation will depend on the extent of the moving costs. Thirdly, either factor operates to compress the wage distribution inside the firm relative to workers' productivities: labour market frictions enable the firm to appropriate part of the productivity gains from higher-skilled workers, even though it is subject to outside competitive pressure when setting its wages; lower-skilled workers will require a compensation for the disutility of working with higher-paid colleagues and will thus receive productivity-unrelated wage increases.[4] Fourthly, the firm will use its personnel policy to manipulate the comparison group (for example, promoting some workers out of the comparison group and gradually increasing their salary, to reduce the costs of envy) and minimize the productivity-unrelated wage increases. The dynamic nature of the model is a major accomplishment with respect to previous models.

Fehr and Schmidt (2001) and Sobel (2005) provide a very complete overview of models that assume the existence of interdependent preferences, distinguishing between stable preferences, when individuals care about the distribution of income or other payoffs at stake – they have 'social preferences', such as inequity-aversion or altruism – and context-specific preferences, when the individuals also care about the intentions behind the actions, the process or the environment – such as reciprocity models. Tests aimed at discriminating among these models have so far almost invariably relied on laboratory experiments and, less often, on field experiments.

Away from interdependent preferences, the model by Kremer (1993) assumes that technological reasons could induce each employer to systematically choose employees with certain homogeneous characteristics. In this case, interdependence of workers' skills is the crucial assumption. The skill of the worker is defined as the probability of successfully fulfilling his or her task and the basic idea is that the production process is made up of a series of complementary tasks, each of which can be performed perfectly or with errors. Only if all the tasks are completed perfectly will the product keep all its value and, in case of mistakes, the output will proportionately lose value – an analogy with the space shuttle *Challenger* is presented, where a small component among thousands of other ones, the O-rings, ruined the whole project. The output of a worker depends, therefore, not just on his or her own skill, but also on that of his or her co-workers. As such, the firm will have an incentive to combine workers of similar skill into the productive process: 'firms with high q workers in the first $(n-1)$ tasks place the highest value on having high-skill workers in the nth task, so they bid the most for these workers. Thus, in equilibrium, workers of the same skill are matched together in firms' (Kremer, 1993: 554). Each firm is predicted to build a homogeneous labour force, producing goods with corresponding quality, instead of hiring workers of different qualities and paying them the marginal product. The sorting of workers into firms according to their observed and unobserved ability would explain the wage differences among firms. Wages for different occupations would be correlated within firms due to the interactions among workers' skill or 'multiplicative quality effects'. Further developing the model generates the prediction that small differences in skill lead to sharp differences in wages and productivity across firms. Note, however, that in this case firms adopt a compressed wage distribution that reflects workers' ability (observed and unobserved) and their productivity, augmented by the presence of skill externalities.

Still other models allow for market imperfections as the key factor explaining the compression of wages but, unlike models previously described, they make no assumption concerning interdependence of preferences. Acemoglu and Pischke (1999) explicitly consider labour market frictions that compress the distribution of wages relative to the distribution of productivities: collective bargaining wage floors, national minimum wages, asymmetric information between current and prospective employers, or job search and other mobility costs. Under any of these mechanisms, the outside wage option of an employed worker is lower than his or her productivity. For example, the worker may have to incur a mobility cost, such that, even if he or she were paid his or her marginal product in the new firm, the net benefit from changing firms would be lower; the possibility of an intervening period of unemployment also lowers the net benefit from job changing; prospective employers cannot fully observe the worker's skill and therefore the wage offer may not fully reflect it. Any of these frictions gives the current employer some monopsony power, that is, the ability to pay the worker a wage below his or her marginal productivity, as it takes into account the worker outside option. Moreover, most of these frictions mean that the rents the firm extracts from skilled workers are larger than those it extracts from the unskilled – if the cost of unemployment is larger for the skilled, in particular when the unemployment benefit system is progressive; when higher skills are harder to observe by prospective employers; or when minimum wages are enforced. Having pinpointed the reasons leading to wage-compression inside the firm, these authors' core analysis is devoted to showing why firms may have an interest in investing in worker training – as a result of training, the worker's productivity will increase but, given the compression of the wage distribution, the firm does not have to fully pay the worker for the productivity improvement.[5]

Manning (2003) provides a thorough discussion of monopsony models and several of their implications. In particular: the firm wage-setting policy may detach wages from worker productivity, for example, if the firm reacts to outside wage offers the worker may receive; worker turnover may be reduced if the firm matches outside wage offers, therefore resulting in lower turnover at the expense of higher internal wage-dispersion; firms may be willing to provide and pay for training, in a type of reasoning with similarities to Acemoglu and Pischke (1999).

A few other bodies of theory were considered beyond the scope of this chapter. Insurance models per se, without any assumption on interdependent preferences, relate more directly to the reaction of wages to shocks and can explain why wages do not adjust as much as predicted by spot market theory. It is, therefore, more appropriate to analyse wage changes than wage levels. Incentives and delayed payment contracts, on the other hand, would lead one to expect the dispersion of wages to be larger than the dispersion of productivities, to the extent that young workers are paid below their marginal productivity and older workers are paid above their marginal productivity. Rent-sharing could explain wage differences across firms, as workers benefit from the good performance of their firm, but it does not provide an explanation of why wage differentials inside the firm would be muted.[6]

9.3 Do firms compress the wage distribution?

The challenge involved in testing the type of theories just described has been eloquently synthesized by Raff and Summers, even though they were focusing on efficiency wage theories alone: 'The very impediments to evaluating workers' ability, motivation and stability that might lead employers to pay efficiency wages make conventional testing of efficiency wage theories difficult. If the information needed to test these theories were available, there might be no need to pay efficiency wages. Econometric tests of efficiency wage theories also face the problem that variations in wages across firms or workers are unlikely to be exogenous, complicating considerably the problem of identification' (Raff and Summers, 1987: S59). As such, tests on theories that assume interdependence of preferences have in the recent past often been conducted in laboratory experiments, which are not the scope of the current book. Instead, this chapter overviews empirical work using LEED that has aimed at testing theories that predict firm wage-compression and, in some cases, attempted to disentangle explanations based on preferences, technology or market frictions.[7]

Machin and Manning (2004) concentrated on a narrowly defined occupation in a narrow geographic labour market (care assistants in elderly residential homes in a region in the UK), arguing that in this market one should find competitive wages, given the large number of firms delivering a homogeneous good and the lack of union influence or minimum wage enforcement.[8] However, analysis of variance of wages indicates that wage-dispersion across firms is large, while wage-dispersion within the firm is small. That contrasts with the results on worker observable attributes (age, tenure and hours worked), for which the within-firm component of dispersion is very relevant. Corroborating evidence follows from the comparison of the determinants of wages and of the price of the product, taken as an indicator of performance, in two different samples: those firms that pay a flat wage to all their workers, and those firms whose wage distribution has some degree of dispersion. Machin and Manning find that, while the determinants of the product price are similar across the two groups of firms, the determinants of wages are not, concluding that worker attributes that are related to productivity are not the ones shaping wage differentials and, moreover, that worker unobservable quality cannot account for the differences in wages. Overall, they interpret their results as evidence against the competitive wage-setting model, possibly linked to the existence of labour market frictions that grant employers some freedom when setting wages, combined with workers' preference for equity.

A narrow set of workers and firms has also been considered in Bishop's (1987) study. He relies on interviews with leaders of approximately 500 US firms, who provided information on two workers recently hired. The author runs regressions of the wage difference between these two workers on their productivity difference (as judged by supervisor rating) and a set of control variables. He concludes that relative wages inside the firm adjust to relative productivity, though by no means completely (as the elasticity is always below one). Larger firms adjust their relative wages less to productivity differences, which is interpreted as a result of higher monitoring costs, whereas firms in large markets adjust more, to avoid losing their more productive workers.

O'Reilly et al. (1988) also relied on a narrow set of workers in approximately 100 US firms, using the wages of CEOs to explicitly test social comparison theories against tournament theory. They found that comparisons with a reference group outside the firm would lead, in this case, to increased inequality within the firm. In fact, they interpret the increasing wage differentials at the top of the hierarchy as evidence in favour of a social comparison model, after finding that the wages of CEOs were positively linked to the wages of outside directors in the board or the compensation committee. Members of the compensation committee would thus set wages having in mind social comparisons, with their own wages as a benchmark.

9.4 Does wage-compression lead to higher productivity and improved firm performance?

Evidence on the impact of wage-compression inside the firm on worker and firm performance is rather mixed, with results ranging from a positive impact to a negative one, and including a hump-shaped relationship or no significant relationship altogether.

Several studies on particular occupations and industries concluded that wage-dispersion inside the firm leads to lower performance.

DeBrock et al. (2004) used longitudinal linked employer–employee data to study the impact of wage-dispersion on firm-level outcomes in a single industry – baseball teams. Though a particular sector, it enables a clearer observation of worker productivity and firm performance than most other sectors. Several measures of firm performance are considered, from won-lost records and attendance of games to the value of the franchise, revenue and profits, but the first two are analysed, given the more reliable information available. The authors compute the expected or market wage for a particular worker, by regressing the salary on several worker attributes, from his age to statistics of his performance in the previous year and throughout his career. They then compute two measures of wage-dispersion inside the firm using the Herfindahl index: the dispersion of expected wages, to capture the degree of heterogeneity in workers' observable quality; and the dispersion in actual wages beyond the expected wage (residual wages), as an indicator of 'unexplained' wage heterogeneity inside the firm. They find that wage-dispersion has a negative impact on firm performance – teams with more homogenous worker observable quality fare better and teams with less 'unexplained' inequality also fare better.[9] Even though fairness considerations could play a role explaining the results, they interpret their evidence as more compellingly pointing to the relevance of matching workers with similar quality, given that the 'technology' in this industry dictates a high degree of interdependence among workers' skills. The matching of workers with similar quality would yield better outcomes, in a reasoning similar to that proposed by Kremer (1993).

Similarly, Bloom (1999) analysed the performance of baseball teams using longitudinal data on both players and teams. The dispersion measures are computed on raw wages and he considers different indicators of the team sportive and financial performance, as well as individual player performance. Results indicate that, after controlling for team effects and a wide set of worker attributes, higher dispersion of salaries within the team has a negative impact on team performance and on most measures of individual performance. Interdependencies among workers' skill are again pointed out as the crucial factor leading to this outcome.

Another particular sector, that of academics, was analysed by Pfeffer and Langton (1993), relying on cross-section data on a wide sample of colleges and universities in the US. Despite the main focus on satisfaction, their work also deals with the impact of raw salary dispersion within a department on research productivity, measured as the number of publications authored.[10] They find that individual research productivity declines with salary dispersion within a given academic department.

The quality of the product, as perceived by the customers, has been used by Cowherd and Levine (1992) as an indicator of performance for approximately 100 firms, mostly from the UK and the US. They check the impact of inequality between the salary of top managers and lower-level workers (hourly paid employees, as well as lower-rank managers) on performance. The inequality measure basically compares the firm's wage distribution with the outside market wage distribution: first, the relative position that top managers in the firm occupy in the wage distribution of top managers in the same region or industry is computed; similarly, for lower-level workers, their pay ranking in the outside market is computed; subsequently, the ratio of the two provides an indication of the degree of inequity internal to the firm, when compared with the surrounding economy. After controlling for factors that may influence the pay of lower-level workers or pay equity inside the firm, such as worker unionization, firm size and its market share, or the complexity of the production technology, the authors find that higher wage-dispersion inside the firm leads to lower performance. The results are interpreted as evidence showing that pay equity boosts motivation and induces worker commitment to the firm's goals.

Studies relying on broader sets of occupations and industries, though controlling to different extents for these variables in their analyses, tend to find the opposite result, with a positive impact of wage-dispersion on firm performance.

Swedish white-collar workers were the target of analysis of Heyman (2005), using longitudinal linked employer–employee data. Both the raw wage-dispersion within the firm and unexplained wage-dispersion are considered, the second one computed on the residuals of a wage regression run separately for each firm and year with the worker observable attributes (gender, education, experience, tenure) as explanatory variables. Similarly to DeBrock et al. (2004), this measure captures wage-dispersion persisting after taking into account observable dimensions of the human capital of the workers. In a second-stage regression, the firm performance is regressed on the first stage alternative measures of wage-dispersion and control variables (such as composition of the workforce, industry, and firm size). Some versions of the analysis account for firm unobserved heterogeneity to address the problem of omitted variables (which may be correlated with wage-dispersion) and instrument wage-dispersion using its lagged values from four years earlier, to address the potential endogeneity problem. The author finds that wage-dispersion among white-collars in the firm has a positive impact on firm performance.

Belfield and Marsden (2003) study performance-related pay and aim at judging on its relative merits, given that two opposite mechanisms may operate: an incentive mechanism, if it stimulates worker productivity; a disincentive mechanism, if equity is a matter of concern for workers. They use cross-section linked employer–employee data on the UK to check the impact of performance-related pay on both intra-firm wage inequality and firm performance.[11] The financial performance of the firm is a self-reported measure, with establishment leaders asked to classify the establishment performance with respect to that of the other establishments in the same industry, from 'much better' to 'much worse' than average. The authors find that performance-related payment schemes are associated with both higher intra-firm inequality and better firm performance. They conclude, therefore, that any potential disincentive effects of performance-related pay are compensated by the incentive effects, resulting in a positive overall impact on firm performance. That is particularly true for firms that adopt the 'right' kind of payment system (performance-related or input-related), as predicted by a wide set of variables characterizing their production regime, nature of jobs, degree of supervision, etc.

Lallemand et al. (2004) also used cross-sectional linked employer–employee data, but on the Belgian economy. They run separate wage regressions for each firm and year and use the standard error of each regression as the measure of wage-dispersion inside the firm for similar workers. This is the explanatory variable of interest in a second-stage regression explaining firm performance (value added per employee). Since wage-dispersion may be endogenous, to the extent that good firm performance may lead to the award of wage premiums to some workers, they instrument the dispersion of total salary with the dispersion of income taxes on salary excluding bonuses. Results indicate a positive impact of wage inequality inside the firm on firm productivity.[12]

Hibbs and Locking (2000) identify 'good' and 'bad' wage-compression. Their reasoning departs from the changes that took place after the mid-1980s in the Swedish economy, as its wage-setting system moved away from centralized collective bargaining with strong equity concerns, and both the economy's wage distribution and firms' wage distributions grew more unequal. The authors estimate Cobb-Douglas production functions and labour productivity functions, either one augmented with the inclusion of two terms on wage-dispersion: dispersion within- and between-firms. Using OLS to estimate the production functions and instrumental variables to estimate the productivity functions,[13] they reach two contrasting results: wage-compression within the firm has an adverse effect on productive efficiency, reducing worker productivity and firm output, due to its (dis)incentive effects, whereas wage-compression across firms has a favourable impact on productive efficiency, as it provides an incentive for capital and labour to flow from less to more efficient firms. Though actually running their analysis at a rather aggregate level, these authors rely on variables computed from micro-data on workers and firms.

An additional flavour to the results is brought by studies finding a hump-shaped relationship between firm wage-dispersion and its performance.

Winter-Ebmer and Zweimuller (1999) use Austrian longitudinal linked employer–employee data and, lacking information on worker or firm performance, infer workers' productivity from their wages. From a wage regression run separately for each firm and year, they retrieve: the estimated wage for a representative worker, which is taken as the indicator of firm productivity; the standard error of the regression, taken as the measure of wage-dispersion inside the firm for similar workers.[14] Subsequently, they run regressions of the proxy for productivity on a quadratic term on wage-dispersion and control variables,[15] finding a hump-shaped pattern in the relationship – some inequality inside the firm would improve productivity, but too much inequality would be detrimental. Nevertheless, assuming that firms pay their workers their marginal product (to justify the use of wages as a proxy for productivity) excludes the possibility that wages can be determined by equity or similar types of considerations. Under this setting, it is not clear why wage-dispersion would have an impact on productivity, and the capacity of the procedure to ascertain the relationship under testing is limited.

Linked employer–employee data on the Danish economy has been used by Bingley and Eriksson (2001), who similarly find, for white-collar workers, a hump-shaped relationship between wage-dispersion and firm productivity – some inequality inside the firm improves performance, but too much inequality is counterproductive. They depart from a different methodology, though: firm performance is measured as total factor productivity (the Solow residual in a Cobb-Douglas production function);[16] wage-dispersion is computed as the standard deviation of residual wages (after controlling for worker observables); the equation of interest, estimated in the second-stage, relates firm performance to wage-dispersion. Also here instrumental variables are used, since good firm performance may be associated with the payment of wage premiums to some types of workers (such as managers), thus increasing wage-dispersion inside the firm. The study takes advantage of the variation in the tax rates according to the workers' municipality of residence, which impacts the dispersion of after-tax wages inside the firm but is assumed to have no direct impact on firm performance.

Finally, still another group of studies finds no significant relationship. Arguing that wage increases, rather than wage levels, are judged by workers in terms of fairness and have a more direct impact on morale, Grund and Westergaard-Nielsen (2008) analyse Danish data on both wage levels and wage changes, limiting their analysis to workers who remain with the same firm for at least two periods. Their indicator of firm performance is value added per employee, and wage-dispersion is measured as the lagged coefficient of variation of wages. Relying initially on OLS regressions with several controls for the composition of the workforce, they find a hump-shaped relationship between the dispersion of wages inside the firm and its performance, consistent with the results of Winter-Ebmer and Zweimuller (1999). However, that impact vanishes once unobservable differences across firms are accounted for by including firm fixed-effects in the regression.[17]

It is curious that studies considering a very narrow set of occupations tend to find a negative impact of inequality on performance, whereas studies relying on broader occupational groups tend to find a positive impact of inequality on performance. Under a setting of interdependent preferences, could it be that workers indeed adopt narrow comparison groups such as the specific occupation? Under a setting of interdependence of skills, could it be that studies using a broader set of occupations are picking up positive externalities that may result from combining workers of different occupations within the firm?

Pfeffer and Langton's comment remains pertinent: 'One of the more useful avenues for research on pay systems may be precisely this task of determining not which pay scheme is best but, rather, under what conditions salary dispersion has positive effects and under what conditions it has negative effects' (Pfeffer and Langton, 1993: 383).

9.5 Does wage-compression reduce worker turnover?

Evidence on the implications of firm wage-compression on worker and job flows is rather scarce, but already divergent. In general, on theoretical grounds, morale and equity type of models would suggest that firms with higher inequality would have higher worker flows, whereas labour market frictions and the monopsony type of models would lead to lower flows, also because employers would have more freedom to manipulate wages trying to retain certain workers.

The Slovenian economy is analysed by Haltiwanger and Vodopivec (2003) using longitudinal matched employer–employee data. They rely on several indicators of wage-dispersion within the firm: i) raw wage-dispersion; ii) residual wage-dispersion, after controlling for worker observable attributes (education, experience and tenure); iii) similar residual wage-dispersion, but further controlling for firm fixed effects; and finally iv) difference in wage-dispersion between a model with firm and worker observable attributes plus their interaction, and a model with just worker observables. The aim is to pin down the dispersion resulting from idiosyncratic worker wage effects within the firm, given that: specification (ii) controls for the influence of collective bargaining that sets base wages relying on worker observable attributes; specification (iii) further controls for firm-wide wage policies that affect every worker in the firm in the same way; specification (iv) retrieves wage-dispersion within similar firms and within groups of workers with similar observable attributes, beyond the inequality existing in the overall economy within this group of workers. Subsequently, alternative measures of job and worker flows are regressed on these alternative indicators of wage-dispersion (plus controls for the firm average residual wage and the industry). Results show that higher wage-dispersion inside the firm[18] leads to less employment volatility, that is, less job creation and destruction, which the authors interpret as an indication that, in the presence of more flexible wages, when shocks occur quantities do not need to adjust as much. However, results are less clear-cut once the analysis focuses on worker reallocation, since two opposing forces play a role. Note that excess worker reallocation, the major indicator commented upon, evaluates the flow of workers over and above what is strictly needed to account for the employment change in the firm, reflecting worker separations that are not due to job destruction and worker accessions that are not due to the need to fill a newly created job. Excess reallocation, therefore, quantifies worker-firm matches that are destroyed and replaced by another match, with no change in the overall employment level. Interestingly, the authors find that, in firms with higher wage-dispersion, excess worker separations come predominantly from worse matches (workers from the lower part of the residual wage distribution), and less so from better matches (workers from the higher part of the residual wage distribution). In other words, firms with high wage-dispersion are able to retain their best workers, while inducing the worst ones to leave. As such, wage-dispersion would work as a device used by firms to promote better job matches.

A comparable result is reached by Pfeffer and Davis-Blake (1992), though concentrating on a narrow occupational group, that of college and university administrators in the US. They find that a higher dispersion of the salary distribution is negatively associated with turnover for administrators with high salaries and positively associated with turnover for those with low salaries. Public knowledge of the salary distribution, either within the firm or in the external labour market, contributes to strengthening this relationship. In their analysis, the authors control for several other factors, both at the firm and the individual level, that may have an impact on turnover, such as the firm's size and financial resources, the type of institution and its funding source, the tenure structure of its workforce and the worker's gender and tenure.

A method to compute wage-dispersion within the firm similar to Haltiwanger and Vodopivec (2003) had been used by Powell, Montgomery and Cosgrove (1994), as they relied on the residual wages retrieved from a regression of wages on worker observable attributes (in particular, education and experience) and establishment fixed-effects. Unlike Haltiwanger and Vodopivec, though, they concentrate on one single industry – childcare centres in the US. They estimate tobit models on quit and fire rates at the establishment level,[19] finding that wage-dispersion within the firm has no significant impact on worker turnover.[20]

Mixed results are also reported by Heyman (2008), who uses Swedish longitudinal linked employer–employee data but nevertheless runs his analysis on industry-level aggregates. Wage-dispersion is computed as the coefficient of variation of raw wages within the industry. Alternative indicators of job flows – job reallocation and its separate components, job creation and job destruction – are regressed on the wage-dispersion measure. Industry unobservable heterogeneity is accounted for and the potential endogeneity of wage-dispersion is handled by using its lagged values as instruments. Results show that, in manufacturing, subindustries with higher wage-dispersion have lower job reallocation, in particular job destruction.[21] Again this author interprets the finding as suggesting that wage-compression limits the extent of wage adjustments and therefore calls for employment adjustments once shocks hit an industry. However, in the services, the opposite effect is detected, as subindustries with higher wage-dispersion have higher job reallocation.[22] Differences in the technology used and the possibly higher costs of job reallocation in the manufacturing sector may play a role in explaining this difference in patterns between manufacturing and the services, but the exact mechanism in operation does not seem to have yet been pinpointed.

9.7 Conclusion

Having in the late 1980s asked the question 'Does the new generation of labor economists know more than the older generation?', Freeman asserted: 'the main conclusion I reach is that while labor economists are more knowledgeable of labor supply issues, we do not know more about firm behavior, labor demand and the overall functioning of the markets' (Freeman, 1989: 319). The empirical discussion on the existence of a firm wage-compression effect and some of its implications is an example of the use of linked employer–employee data by the research community during the last couple of decades to gear research in the direction suggested by Freeman.

However, alongside with the potential of LEED, the difficulties involved in testing for the existence of a firm wage-compression effect and its implications have been exposed. In fact, the margin of consensual results seems rather small: there is some degree of uniformity in wages within a firm, more so the narrower the set of occupations considered.

Once the aim is to explore the reasons and implications of an employer wage-compression effect, we find all shades of results. Several reasons can justify this outcome: the data sets used have quite different characteristics, from coverage of a narrow set of occupations in a narrow set of firms, to coverage of the population of firms and workers in an economy; the measures used, in particular on worker and firm performance, have also diverged widely; the empirical methods so far used are equally far apart in their capacity to tackle the issue and address the potential empirical problems. This strand of literature is probably still in its infancy (or teenagehood).

Identification of a test that would enable disentangling theories that often lead to similar predictions on this issue remains a challenge. One of the aims of this chapter has been to show some of the way that the empirical literature has covered and to highlight some of the major theories that could guide future empirical research on this topic.

Notes

1. Though it may also suffer exogenous shocks.
2. This model is more concerned with wage changes than with wage levels.
3. Frank assumes a competitive labour market and argues that on average it would still hold that workers in each firm would be paid their marginal productivity.
4. Moreover, in this setting of contract theory, insurance provision may further increase wage-compression inside the firm.
5. Booth and Zoega (2004) further highlight that the firm may have an incentive to provide training even in situations usually associated with competitive wages and no market distortions, such as piece-rate payments, as long as the worker does not receive fully the benefits of the increase in productivity.
6. Rent-sharing is subject to detailed analysis in other chapters of this book.

7. Away from the focus of this chapter on LEED, several studies provide a lively overview of the role of fairness in wage determination, based on real-life situations and interviews with firm leaders.
8. At the time the analysis was undertaken, there was no minimum wage in the UK.
9. Though this last result is not always significant.
10. Normalized by dividing by the average in the scientific field.
11. Note that workers can be rewarded according to their performance and still the distribution of wages can exhibit lower dispersion than the distribution of productivities, if the premium on productivity increases less than proportionally.
12. A positive impact of salary dispersion on firm performance tends to be found in other studies that concentrate only on the salary of managers and aim to test tournament theories (see, for instance, Eriksson (1999) and Main et al. (1993)). Leonard's (1990) work points to no significant relationship.
13. Output is an endogenous variable in the productivity regression, being instrumented with its own lagged values and the Swedish exports to OECD countries.
14. They estimate tobit regressions, given the top-coding of wages, and include as independent variables age, gender, tenure, blue-collar and foreigner status, but not education, which is not available.
15. Using OLS regressions on the contemporaneous levels of the dependent and independent variables and models with firm-specific effects, in a reasoning aimed at capturing longer-term relationships.
16. They also proxy worker effort by the inverse of sickness absence (averaged for the firm level).
17. When considering the dispersion of wage increases, instead, they find that for the bulk of firms, and for white-collars in particular, fairness considerations dominate, with an increase in the dispersion of wage changes being associated with worse firm performance.
18. Lagged one period.
19. Instrumenting the wage level of the establishment, which is also included in the regression, with indicators of the cost of living and the wages in the area, as well as the fees charged by the school.
20. The analysis by Galizzi (2001) of the duration of employment spells, aimed at detecting contrasts in the behaviour of men and women, included among the explanatory variables the interaction of the worker's own wage with the average wage in the firm for the worker's broad occupation and gender. This measure of 'relative wages' matches more closely an indicator of the firm wage level, rather than a measure of wage-dispersion inside the firm.
21. With no significant effect detected on job creation.
22. With no significant impact on job creation and job destruction separately.

References

Acemoglu, D. and Pischke, J.S. (1999) 'The Structure of Wages and Investment in General Training', *Journal of Political Economy*, 107(3): 539–72.

Akerlof, G.A. (1982) 'Labor Contracts as Partial Gift Exchange', *Quarterly Journal of Economics*, 97(4): 543–67.

Akerlof, G.A. and Yellen, J.L. (1990) 'The Fair Wage-Effort Hypothesis and Unemployment', *Quarterly Journal of Economics*, 105(2): 255–83.

Alexopoulos, M. and Cohen, J. (2004) 'What's Wrong with Forced Wage Compression? The Fair Wage Hypothesis Redux', *Economics Letters*, 83: 391–8.

Baker, G. and Holmstrom, B. (1995) 'Internal Labor Markets: Too Many Theories, Too Few Facts', *American Economic Review*, 85(2): 255–9.

Belfield, R. and Marsden, D. (2003) 'Performance Pay, Monitoring Environments, and Establishment Performance', *International Journal of Manpower*, 24(4): 452–71.

Bingley, P. and Eriksson, T. (2001) 'Pay Spread and Skewness, Employee Effort and Firm Productivity', Mimeo, University of Aarhus.
Bishop, J. (1987) 'The Recognition and Reward of Employee Performance', *Journal of Labor Economics*, 59(4): S36–S56.
Bloom, M. (1999) 'The Performance Effects of Pay Dispersion on Individuals and Organizations', *Academy of Management Journal*, 42(1): 25–40.
Booth, A.L. and Zoega, G. (2004) 'Is Wage Compression a Necessary Condition for Firm-Financed General Training?' *Oxford Economic Papers*, 56: 88–97.
Cabrales, A., Calvó-Armengol, A. and Pavoni, N. (2008) 'Social Preferences, Skill Segregation, and Wage Dynamics', *Review of Economic Studies*, 75: 65–98.
Cowherd, D.M. and Levine, D.I. (1992) 'Product Quality and Pay Equity between Lower-Level Employees and Top Management: An Investigation of Distributive Justice Theory', *Administrative Science Quarterly*, 37: 302–20.
DeBrock, L., Hendricks, W. and Koenker, R. (2004) 'Pay and Performance: The Impact of Salary Distribution on Firm-Level Outcomes in Baseball', *Journal of Sports Economics*, 5: 243–61.
Dunlop, J.T. (ed.) (1957) 'The Task of Contemporary Wage Theory', *The Theory of Wage Determination*, London: MacMillan, 3–27.
Eriksson, T. (1999) 'Executive Compensation and Tournament Theory: Empirical Tests on Danish Data', *Journal of Labor Economics*, 17(2): 262–80.
Fehr, E. and Schmidt, K. (2001) 'Theories of Fairness and Reciprocity – Evidence and Economic Implications', CEPR discussion paper 2703, London: Centre for Economic Policy Research.
Frank, R.H. (1984) 'Are Workers Paid their Marginal Products?' *American Economic Review*, 74(4): 549–71.
Frank, R.H. (1985) *Choosing the Right Pond: Human Behaviour and the Quest for Status*, Oxford: Oxford University Press.
Freeman, R.B. (ed.) (1989) 'Does the New Generation of Labor Economists Know More than the Older Generation?' *Labour Markets in Action: Essays in Empirical Economics*, New York: Harvester Wheatsheaf, 317–42.
Galizzi, M. (2001) 'Gender and Labor Attachment: Do Within-Firms's Relative Wages Matter?' *Industrial Relations*, 40(4): 591–619.
Grund, C. and Westergaard-Nielsen, N. (2008) 'The Dispersion of Employees' Wage Increases and Firm Performance', *Industrial and Labor Relations Review*, 61(4): 485–501.
Haltiwanger, J. and Vodopivec, M. (2003) 'Worker Flows, Job Flows and Firm Policies', *Economics of Transition*, 11(2): 253–90.
Hamermesh, D.S. (1975) 'Interdependence in the Labor Market', *Economica*, 42(168): 420–9.
Heyman, F. (2005) 'Pay Inequality and Firm Performance: Evidence from Matched Employer-Employee Data', *Applied Economics*, 37: 1313–27.
Heyman, F. (2008) 'How Wage Compression Affects Job Turnover', *Journal of Labor Research*, 29(1): 11–26.
Hibbs, D.A. and Locking, H. (2000) 'Wage Dispersion and Productive Efficiency: Evidence for Sweden', *Journal of Labor Economics*, 18(4): 755–82.
Kerr, C. (1994) 'The Social Economics Revisionists: The "Real World" of Labor Markets and Institutions', in C. Kerr and P.D. Staudohar (eds) *Labor Economics and Industrial Relations: Markets and Institutions*, Cambridge, MA: Harvard University Press, 66–108.
Kremer, M. (1993) 'The O-Ring Theory of Economic Development', *Quarterly Journal of Economics*, 108(3): 551–75.
Lallemand, T., Plasman, R. and Rycx, F. (2004) 'Intra-Firm Wage Dispersion and Firm Performance: Evidence from Linked Employer-Employee Data', *Kyklos*, 57(4): 451–566.
Lazear, E.P. (1984) 'Incentives and Wage Rigidity', *American Economic Review*, 74(2): 339–44.
Lazear, E.P. (1989) 'Pay Equality and Industrial Politics', *Journal of Political Economy*, 97(3): 561–80.
Lazear, E.P. and Rosen, S. (1981) 'Rank-Order Tournaments as Optimal Labor Contracts', *Journal of Political Economy*, 89: 841–64.

Leonard, J.S. (1990) 'Executive Pay and Firm Performance', *Industrial and Labor Relations Review*, 43(3): 13S–29S.
Lester, R.A. (1952) 'A Range Theory of Wage Differentials', *Industrial and Labor Relations Review*, 5: 483–500.
Levine, D.I. (1991) 'Cohesiveness, Productivity, and Wage Dispersion', *Journal of Economic Behavior and Organization*, 15: 237–55.
Machin, S. and Manning, A. (2004) 'A Test of Competitive Labor Market Theory: The Wage Structure among Care Assistants in the South of England', *Industrial and Labor Relations Review*, 57(3): 371–85.
Main, B.G.M., O'Reilly III, C.A. and Wade, J. (1993) 'Top Executive Pay: Tournament or Teamwork?' *Journal of Labor Economics*, 11(4): 606–28.
Manning, A. (2003) *Monopsony in Motion*, Princeton, NJ: Princeton University Press.
O'Reilly III, C.A., Main, B.G. and Crystal, G.S. (1988) 'CEO Compensation as Tournament and Social Comparison: A Tale of Two Theories', *Administrative Science Quarterly*, 33: 257–74.
Pfeffer, J. and Davis-Blake, A. (1992) 'Salary Dispersion, Location in the Salary Distribution, and Turnover among College Administrators', *Industrial and Labor Relations Review*, 45(4): 753–63.
Pfeffer, J. and Langton, N. (1993) 'The Effect of Wage Dispersion on Satisfaction, Productivity, and Working Collaboratively: Evidence from College and University Faculty', *Administrative Science Quarterly*, 38(3): 382–407.
Powell, I., Montgomery, M. and Cosgrove, J. (1994) 'Compensation Structure and Establishment Quit and Fire Rates', *Industrial Relations*, 33(2): 229–48.
Raff, D.M.G. and Summers, L.H. (1987) 'Did Henry Ford Pay Efficiency Wages?' *Journal of Labor Economics*, 5(4): S57–S86.
Rees, A. and Shultz, G.P. (1970) *Workers and Wages in an Urban Labor Market*, Chicago, IL: University of Chicago Press.
Reynolds, L.G. (1951) *The Structure of Labor Markets*, Westport, CT: Greenwood Press, 155–229.
Rosen, S. (1986) 'Prizes and Incentives in Elimination Tournaments', *American Economic Review*, 76(4): 701–15.
Skott, P. (2005) 'Fairness as a Source of Hysteresis in Employment and Relative Wages', *Journal of Economic Behavior & Organization*, 57: 305–31.
Sobel, J. (2005) 'Interdependent Preferences and Reciprocity', *Journal of Economic Literature*, 43(2): 392–436.
Solow, R.M. (1979) 'Another Possible Source of Wage Stickiness', *Journal of Macroeconomics*, 1(1): 79–82.
Winter-Ebmer, R. and Zweimuller, J. (1999) 'Intra-Firm Wage Dispersion and Firm Performance', *Kyklos*, 52: 555–72.

Part III

Consequences of Globalization and Data Challenges

10
Labour Market Outcomes of Internationalization – What Have We Learnt from Analyses of Microdata on Firms and Their Employees?

Tor Eriksson

10.1 Introduction and background

Internationalization and globalization have become buzzwords in the societal discussion in recent years. Europe is in a process towards a further integration of its economies simultaneously with a strong growth in the integration of the East Asian economies in the world economy. Globalization is not, however, only enlarged trade and increased foreign direct investments, but also intensified and deepened cooperation between countries. The mechanisms behind internationalization are mobility of goods and services, financial capital and technology transfers. Notably, mobility of labour is not one of the drivers of globalization; with the exception of some rare and rather small occupations, we cannot say that there is a global labour market.

Given the enormous international differences in wages, it is actually something of a mystery why international labour mobility is so low; see Borjas (2002). Thus, as Richard Freeman, very much to the point, has expressed it, our 'wages are not set in Beijing' (Freeman, 1995). However, as Freeman 10 years later has emphasized (Freeman, 2005), the huge increase in global labour supply – Freeman's estimate is that as a consequence of China's entry to the WTO alone supply increased by about a third of the OECD labour force, and on top of that there is a substantial increase from the introduction of market capitalism to India and Eastern Europe – cannot be without consequences for Western labour markets. Consequently, what happens in other parts of the world currently has, probably, a considerably stronger impact on wages and employment conditions of workers in individual European countries than before.

So far the effects of increasing integration have been largest in the manufacturing sector, but, as the developments during recent years have clearly demonstrated, the new information and communication technologies also make it possible to move or outsource several of firms' service activities to remote countries. Some economists have argued, however, that only a fairly small portion of activities in the service sector are likely to be moved, as many transactions typically require that both the supplier and the buyer are physically present or that the language used in the communication between the parties is that of the buyer; see Baghwati et al. (2005). This view, which is quite common among economists but differs quite a lot from the common perception, has been increasingly questioned; see, for example, Amiti and Wei (2005, 2009), who warn against drawing this conclusion on the basis of a few data points only. Blinder (2006, 2007) assesses that as many as half of all service jobs in the United States are such that they do not require face-to-face contact between providers and buyers and that electronic transmission of the tasks involved can be carried out without considerable reduction in their quality. Moreover, the current holders of these jobs are not from the lower end of the skills and wage range, but rather in middle-class jobs (Blinder, 2007). In another attempt to put numbers on the magnitude of service jobs that potentially can be offshored, Jensen and Kletzer (2006) exploit information on the geographical concentration of service activities in the US to identify services that can only be traded domestically. The key assumption they make is that domestically traded activities are not potentially tradable internationally. This method gives an estimate of the share of employees of total service employment that is in potentially tradable activities (jobs) of about 39 per cent.[1]

Thus, the labour market consequences of internationalization may very well extend far beyond the manufacturing sector, which in most advanced capitalist countries accounts for only around 15 per cent of GDP. Despite all the discussions about internationalization, location of manufacturing is primarily determined by the availability and location of natural resources. Comparative advantages in the services sector and the new economy reflect to a much higher extent human decisions and effort. Therefore, there is less persistence in the service industries, and developments therein are less predictable. Moreover, it is important to notice that when service jobs are offshored they are, unlike in manufacturing, not only limited to low-skill tasks. Some examples of jobs that have been offshored in recent years are those of computer programmers, radiologists and accountants. These are not only high-skill jobs but also examples of jobs held by people who are likely to be able to organize a stronger resistance against these developments if they occur on a larger scale.

The relatively large and rapid changes in the geographical location of the world's manufacturing production and in the international pattern of foreign direct investments have spawned an intensive debate about the consequences of these changes, and increasing efforts have been devoted to providing empirical evidence. In Section 10.4 below, a review of the stock of research-based knowledge on these issues is provided.

Considerably less attention has been paid to the fact that integration is not a one-way street. As a consequence of the liberalization of financial markets, continued European integration and further deregulation of international trade, the more advanced economies are also becoming more international in the sense that a growing proportion of the firms operating in them are foreign-owned.

Some examples from Northern Europe, where international ownership before the mid-1980s was very uncommon, illustrate the ongoing change. Today, about one out of five private sector employees in Denmark and Sweden is employed in a foreign-owned firm, and the share is increasing. In Finland, the number of foreign-owned firms has tripled since 1990 and the proportion of workers employed in foreign-owned firms increased from 9 to 18 per cent between the years 1994 and 2002. The trend towards increased foreign ownership has been particularly pronounced in the manufacturing sector. But increasing foreign ownership is a feature found not only in the more advanced old EU member states. Foreign direct investments have been large in some of the Central and Eastern European countries, such as the Czech Republic, Hungary and the Baltic states. A natural question to ask is: can these changes occur without leaving any traces in the labour markets, and in the structure of employment and wages in particular? This is the topic of Section 10.5 below.

10.2 Theory – very briefly

Although it is a commonplace to think that increased competition from low-wage countries implies an increased risk for low-skilled and unqualified workers to lose their jobs, standard economic theory does not yield such straightforward conclusions. In fact, static general equilibrium models of trade do not give unambiguous predictions; see, for example, Markusen (2002). Note, however, that standard international trade theory is about trade of finished goods, whereas the nature of international trade today is quite different and involves to a considerable extent also trade of tasks – manufacturing tasks as well as other business functions.

Economic theorists have in recent years started to build models that capture some of the features of the new international trade in tasks. One part of this literature deals with the classic question in the theory of the firm: firms' choices of organizational form (make-or-buy).[2] Another part models the fragmentation and asks questions about how this affects trade, welfare and factor prices. As firms' decisions in these models are discrete, not marginal, it has proven difficult to generate general predictions. A recent paper by Grossman and Rossi-Hansberg (2008) proposes a conceptualization of production processes which addresses some of these problems, and produces, for instance, unambiguous predictions concerning wage effects of offshoring. Nevertheless, theoretical work on the new international trade is likely to remain an area of considerable development for several years.

10.3 Data and measurement issues

Although the discussion about globalization and outsourcing of production has been lively for several years, hard facts which would help to inform the debates are still relatively rare. Consequently, applied research speaking to the discussion is also rather scant. This state of affairs is basically due to the fact that conventional statistics and data sources mainly produced by the national statistical offices are, save trade statistics, not international.[3] Statistics and the underlying data sources on production and employment of firms only describe what firms do within their national borders.[4] As a result of this, data for research as well as for monitoring of changes in the areas of internationalization of firms and their outsourcing/offshoring activities are not readily available from conventional sources.[5] Non-conventional sources, such as the information on Swedish multinational companies (see, e.g. Ekholm and Hakkala (2006)) and the German MIDI-USTAN database at Deutsche Bundesbank, are quite rare. It would be unfair, however, not to also mention the extensive efforts made by the OECD in recent years to construct indicators of globalization, which are now part of the regular statistics published by the organization. Nevertheless, most empirical analyses of the consequences of internationalization of firms have so far made use of trade statistics to construct surrogate measures of outsourcing and offshoring. With a few exceptions, these trade statistics-based measures are available only at the industry level.

An oft-used measure of internationalization, following Feenstra and Hanson (1996, 1999), is the value of imported intermediate products. This can be computed at the industry level from the input–output tables in the national accounts.[6] The measure is broad in the sense that it also encompasses situations where a firm stops producing an intermediate good itself and instead buys from an independent, foreign or domestic, supplier. Hence, this measure captures the fragmentation of production processes that has characterized manufacturing industries during the last two decades. Hummels et al. (2001) used trade data from 10 OECD countries and showed that in the 1990s trade in intermediate goods accounted for about 30 per cent of these countries' total exports. Moreover, they demonstrate that this trade in intermediate products has increased strongly in recent times.

Increased imports of intermediate goods are likely to have a negative effect on demand for labour in the industries competing with these imports. If the imported intermediate goods are produced in low-wage countries, the low-skilled workers in particular will be affected most. But labour demand in industries using these imported intermediate goods is also likely to be affected. Note that the low-skilled workers are affected in a similar way as when they are substituted for by robots or automation. Hence, distinguishing between the impacts of increased outsourcing of intermediate inputs and of non-neutral technological change is not straightforward; see the arguments in Feenstra and Hanson (2003) and Katz and Autor (1999). See also the study by Faggio et al. (2006), which exploits matched employer–employee data from the United Kingdom and shows that the increase in between-firm wage inequality has been accompanied by an increase in the firm-level productivity dispersion.

Now, 'the man in the street' does not associate the words outsourcing and offshoring with increased trade in intermediate input factors but rather with the relocation of the firm's own activities, and in particular with production of final goods being moved to other countries. This form of internationalization of firms and labour markets, oftentimes called in-house offshoring, is not picked up by the imports of intermediate inputs measure, which therefore clearly underestimates the extent of globalization. Obtaining data on the outsourcing of production of final goods is a big challenge and can only be done in the rare cases where the firm statistics also include information about production and employment in foreign subsidiaries or when these pieces of information are derived from other sources such as questionnaires, registers, company accounts, etc.

A second common characteristic of many studies is the high level of aggregation of the analysis. The unit of analysis is typically industries, whereas firm-level analyses are considerably less common. And yet, the point of departure of the debate as well as the economic theories is the behaviour of firms. In this respect it is important to distinguish between dependent and independent variables. In the latter case we are concerned with the internationalization or outsourcing/offshoring variable. In this context aggregate-level analysis is unproblematic as long as industry averages mimic well what is taking place at the firm level. We know, however, that, due to considerable heterogeneity, this is not the case for many economic phenomena, not even when industries are quite narrowly defined. As there are no a priori reasons why there would be less heterogeneity with respect to outsourcing and internalization, aggregate analyses are likely to be misleading. A related concern is that changes at the level of an industry refer to changes at both the intensive and the extensive margin and we cannot tell which kind of changes (within existing firms or changes due to exit and entry of old and new firms, respectively) are driving the results.

So, are aggregate-level dependent variables problematic as well? What was said above applies to them, too. However, they have some potential advantages relative to firm-level measures that are worth pointing out. Many firm-level analyses use data on multinational firms, and the sample analysed often consists of firms that were multinational prior to the date of analysis.[7] From a policy perspective it is not the effect of foreign direct investments, outsourcing or offshoring of a firm on the firm itself that is the most interesting piece of information, but rather the effects on the region the multinational enterprise is located in. Multinational firms may be affected differently from other firms because their activities may be associated with externalities. In other words, findings that outsourcing of activities reduces employment in the multinational firm may not carry over to domestic firms. An example of a negative externality in connection with outsourcing is replacement of local with foreign suppliers, and an example of a positive externality is increased demand for intermediate inputs from local suppliers in connection with offshoring of production. To capture these externalities and spillover effects you need a dependent variable at a more aggregate level than the firm. Note, however, that use of industry-level data is not very helpful in this respect, as the externalities and spillover effects are not likely to occur within an industry, but rather within the regional labour market.

A potential problem which has been pointed out in connection with the industry studies, but which is present also in firm-level investigations, is that firms choose to outsource, offshore or move production, and hence internationalization cannot be considered as exogenous in the empirical analyses. A related criticism is that demand for different types of labour is determined simultaneously with decisions regarding location of production or fragmentation of the value chain. While there is something in these objections, it should also be noticed that internationalization and fragmentation are not exclusively driven by changes in relative prices of imported inputs. Examples of other factors are liberalization of world trade, China's entrance into the WTO, peaceful transitions from communism, and new information and communication technologies, all of which enable firms to use more efficient communication systems and modern supply management methods and to exploit absolute price differences between countries. These changes can be considered as exogenous shifts in production technology, which in turn affect demand for different types of labour and other factors of production.

10.4 The evidence

10.4.1 Industry-level analyses

Until recently, there were relatively more US studies of the consequences of globalization. This is somewhat surprising, as the American economy is much more a closed economy in comparison with Europe. The US discussion is to a large extent focused on China and East Asia, whereas the European discussion and research are concerned both with East Asia and with the enlargement of the European Union.

In the main, the American studies find that import competition, and international outsourcing in particular, hurts unskilled workers in form of considerable reductions in their relative wages; see Feenstra and Hanson (1996, 1997, 2003) and studies cited therein. Several studies have demonstrated that increased internationalization has had an impact on the structure of employment. In industries characterized by both higher levels of, and growth rates in, foreign direct investment or imports of intermediate inputs, the proportion of unskilled workers is lower. Furthermore, for the unskilled employees who keep their jobs, the relative wage is lower.

Following Feenstra and Hanson (1996), a frequently used vehicle of econometric analysis is a cost share of labour equation, which is based on a translog cost function and was first introduced for analysis of trade and skills demand by Berman et al. (1994). In the short run, capital is considered a quasi-fixed, and hence the industry's (firm's) employment share of labour belonging to a certain skill group becomes a function of its wage share, the outsourcing variable, the capital stock, value added and factors that pick up factor-biased technological change. These employment share equations are typically estimated as a system of seemingly unrelated regressions.

Corresponding analyses for major European countries such as the UK (Hijzen et al., 2005), Germany (Falk and Kobel, 2002) and France (Strauss-Kahn, 2004) show similar effects to the US studies on the employment structure and relative wages. The magnitudes of the estimated effects are smaller, though. The results for the United Kingdom are perhaps less surprising, as the British labour market has since the early 1990s been characterized by considerable wage flexibility and has experienced a marked drop in demand for unskilled labour in the manufacturing sector.[8] France and Germany are more interesting and surprising cases. In the 1980s and 1990s (Western) Germany has, in contrast to many other countries, had unchanged relative wages and, as a consequence, a quite stable income and wage development. In view of that, the findings that foreign outsourcing has had similar impacts, although not of the same magnitude, on wages and employment as in the US are quite noteworthy. Moreover, these results have been corroborated by evidence from an analysis using individual-level data for employment and wages and industry-level variables for outsourcing; see Geishecker and Görg (2008).

Since the late 1980s France has experienced a strong increase in the unemployment differential between skilled and unskilled employees. The study by Strauss-Kahn (2004) shows that international outsourcing has contributed to the decline in employment of unskilled workers in French manufacturing. However, the bulk (75–85 per cent) of the decline is, according to the study, explained by other factors, notably skill-biased technological change.

Similar studies for some other European countries have produced somewhat more mixed evidence. For Denmark, Sørensen and Skaksen (2005) estimate a Feenstra and Hanson type of model and find that outsourcing (measured as proportion of imported intermediates of total imports) has had a negative impact on employment in the textiles industry and a positive effect in the chemical, IT and electronics industries. They also find a positive effect on wages for employees in the chemical industry and a negative effect in glass and cement industries. Munch and Skaksen (2005) make use of individual-level information on wages and industry-level outsourcing variables. Regarding the latter, they distinguish between domestic and foreign outsourcing of intermediate inputs. They find that foreign outsourcing benefits skilled employees but hurts unskilled workers' wages. Domestic outsourcing gives rise to higher wages for both groups of employees. Interestingly, the results are similar to those in Geishecker and Görg's (2008) study for Germany.

In a more recent paper, Geischecker et al. (2007) estimate the same specification on similar data sets from three countries – Denmark, Germany and UK – and distinguish between outsourcing (at the industry level) to CEEC and non-CEEC regions. They find pronounced differences in the effects on wages between the three countries: Danish wages are only slightly affected by outsourcing, whereas UK wages are reduced by outsourcing to CEEC countries. The pattern for Germany is more mixed. The authors interpret the results as reflecting differences in labour market institutions, especially wage-setting and employment protection.

For Sweden, Hansson (2005) examines the effects of transfer of production within multinational companies on demand for production and non-production workers, respectively. His main finding is that expansion of production in countries outside the OECD has a negative impact on demand for production workers. Recently, Ekholm and Hakkala (2006) have estimated the effects of offshoring of intermediate inputs on the structure of labour demand in Sweden (note, not only manufacturing). Their main result is that offshoring to low-wage economies shifts demand away from workers with secondary education.[9] This negative effect is chiefly due to offshoring to Central and Eastern Europe.

To the best of my knowledge there is so far only one study that attempts to capture (some of) the regional externalities associated with internationalization of firms. Federico and Minerva (2008) carry out a panel data analysis of outward foreign direct investment and local employment for 103 administrative provinces in Italy. The key result, which is robust to inclusion of controls for industrial structure and area fixed effects, is that foreign direct investment has a positive effect on employment growth in the region, implying that foreign direct investment does not have detrimental effects on the labour market of the home region. Clearly, this is an avenue of research one would like to see being followed by additional studies.

A central argument against the notion that competition from countries with substantially lower wage costs would have significant negative employment and wage effects in advanced capitalist countries is that the trade flows between the low and the high wage-cost countries are too small to play an important role. Although this argument neglects the strong growth in trade of intermediate goods, it may still have some merits, especially in a short-term perspective. With further integration the effects may become bigger, but then there will also be counteracting effects in the longer run arising from increasing wage levels in the low-wage economies. At any rate, it is of some interest to consider the experiences from countries that have had substantially larger foreign direct investment than European countries have had so far.

One, admittedly somewhat extreme, example is Hong Kong, from which comes a large part of the Chinese diaspora investing in mainland China. Hsie and Woo (2004) have examined the effects on the employment structure in the Hong Kong manufacturing sector during the last decades of the twentieth century. The share of production workers in the sector fell dramatically from 88 per cent in 1976 to 52 per cent in 1996. According to the econometric analysis, half of this decline can be attributed to outsourcing to China. To set these findings in perspective, one should notice that the influence of trade unions in Hong Kong is quite limited and minimum wage laws or other arrangements to protect low-paid workers do not exist. These features are shared with another East Asian economy that has also invested heavily in its neighbouring countries, namely Taiwan. Taiwanese firms make large foreign direct investments in China and other Southeast Asian countries. While investments are shown to have significant and positive effects on product quality and technology, and hence skill upgrading, they also have sizeable negative effects on home production and home employment; see Yeh and Lin (2006). Thus, the impact of the strong growth and competition from China and India is stronger and more profound in the neighbouring countries and the Pacific Rim.

10.4.2 Firm-level analyses

As mentioned above, there are fewer studies based on information at the level of firms. A main advantage of these studies is that they measure more precisely than industry-level studies the foreign activities of individual firms, either the amount of production in foreign plants or employment at them. Firm-level data enable researchers to examine empirically the mechanisms at work more precisely. A drawback is that they typically do not account for outsourcing of intermediate inputs. But, on the other hand, they capture outsourcing of final production, which industry-level studies do not.

As a matter of fact, this literature is somewhat older and emanates from interest in how home employment of American multinationals was affected by expanded production and sales in their foreign subsidiaries. The first generation of studies from the 1960s and 1970s were case studies. Early studies utilizing more representative data sources, such as Kravis and Lipsey (1988, 1994), find (like the majority of the case studies) that foreign activities increase employment in the home company.

More recent studies have arrived at different conclusions, however. Blomström et al. (1997) examine the impact of foreign production on home employment (controlling for home production), using data on US and Swedish firms. The authors find that, for the American firms, larger foreign production decreases home employment when production is outsourced to developing countries. But the results for the Swedish firms differ and are also somewhat puzzling. First of all, the employment effects are positive, and particularly large for production in developing countries. Even more surprisingly, when the authors distinguish between production and non-production workers they find that the positive effect is more pronounced for production workers. They point out that the data mainly come from a period, the 1970s, when Swedish firms' foreign investments were predominantly directed to other OECD countries, and do not include recent periods with investments in the former Communist Baltic states, East Asia or Southern America. However, a panel analysis based on essentially the same data set carried out by Braconier and Ekholm (2000) finds a negative effect of foreign production in high-wage countries, but no effects of production in low-wage countries.

Eriksson and Li (2006) make use of linked employer–employee data for Denmark, which are merged with two questionnaires directed to firms concerning their foreign operations. The authors find that, up to the mid-1990s, home employment is increased as a consequence of increases in operations in foreign subsidiaries, but that this effect becomes quantitatively smaller over time. Distinguishing between regions of the foreign operations reveals that operations in developed countries are associated with positive home employment effects for all types of employees, whereas operations in developing countries, and Central and Eastern European countries in particular, are negatively correlated with home employment for production workers especially.

US studies using firm panels – Brainard and Riker (1997), Slaughter (1995, 2000) – report relatively small negative effects on home employment. Slaughter distinguishes between skilled and unskilled workers and finds that for the latter, too, the negative effects are of modest magnitude. The negative employment effects are especially small relative to those found in the studies that used the industry-level measures for foreign outsourcing. It should be recalled that these two types of studies capture different forms of internationalization of the firms' production. A recent American study by Harrison et al. (2007), which distinguishes between subsidiaries in high and low wage countries, finds that the relationship between employment in mother and daughter firms is complementary when the subsidiaries are located in a high-wage country and negative when they are in a low-wage country. However, given the large magnitude of the reduction in US manufacturing jobs during the period under study – 1977 to 1999 – the estimated substitution effect appears to be rather modest.

Two important studies (Biscourp and Kramarz, 2006; Kramarz, 2006) use French linked employer–employee data and firm-level measures of imports from the years 1986 to 1992. This is a period when French manufacturing, which was previously protected from competition, gradually faced increasing competition, in particular as a consequence of the European Union's Single Market Programme. The first paper looks at how outsourcing to low-wage countries affects employment of skilled and unskilled workers in different types of firms. A notable finding is that the origins of imports do not seem to be important for the impact on wages. The second paper takes a more detailed look at how the increased international competition affects wages. For this purpose the author builds a bargaining model which captures key features of the French wage-setting institutions, and in particular models carefully how firms' ability to pay, as well as trade unions' bargaining position, is affected. Key results are that workers' wages deteriorate as a consequence of competitive pressures. This is mainly due to their employers' decreased ability to pay. When competitors to the employing firm import goods, workers' wages are hurt, but workers benefit when their own employer is importing goods.

During the last two decades, Japanese firms, in particular in the electronics industry, have moved an increasing portion of their production to low as well as high-wage countries. Head and Ries (2002) analyse the home employment consequences of these changes, making use of a panel of Japanese firms followed over the period 1965–90. They find clear evidence of skill-upgrading of the home companies in Japan. As the proportion of a firm's employees in low-wage countries increases, the wage share of non-production workers in the home company increases. The share of employees in high-wage countries is not found to be systematically related to the wage shares in Japan.

The studies of the consequences of the EU enlargement have mainly dealt with the impacts on worker mobility, whereas there are considerably fewer investigations of the employment effects of the investment made by firms from the old member states in the new member countries. In connection with the enlargement, it was frequently argued that the investments in the new member states were in industries that are not producing for exports, such as the communication, energy industries and the services sector in general. Thus, the main purpose of the investments has been claimed to be to locate production closer to the new markets, and not to exploit opportunities to produce at lower costs. And so, the argument goes, there would at most be only minor negative effects on employment in EU15 countries.

Two studies have examined this conjecture: Cuvyers et al. (2002) and Konings and Murphy (2006). Both studies find some substitution between the mother company and the foreign subsidiaries, but Konings and Murphy do not find traces of substitution when the foreign investments are made in Central or Eastern

Europe (but rather for investments in other old member states). Note, however, that single country studies that distinguish between destination countries of offshoring activities (e.g. Ekholm and Hakkala (2006), Eriksson and Li (2006)) do find negative employment effects from CEE countries on home employment in the offshoring firms.

A problem in investigations of the consequences of outsourcing is to assess what would have happened if the outsourcing had not occurred. Another problem is that most studies cannot distinguish between firms that are outsourcing activities for the first time and those that have done it numerous times before. Two recent exceptions look at manufacturing firms that have not earlier carried out international direct investments, and examine their choice of whether to continue as before or move production to another country. Both studies make use of propensity-score matching methods and are therefore explicitly showing their assumptions regarding the counterfactual developments. Both also make a distinction between high and low-wage countries as destinations for the foreign direct investments.

In the first study, Barba Navaretti et al. (2006) exploit two panel data sets, one for French firms with more than 20 employees during 1995–2000, and another with corresponding information from Italian firms in the period 1993–2001. The authors find that the foreign direct investments have had a positive influence on home employment for both the French and the Italian firms. No differences in effects between direct investments in low and high-wage countries were found.

The counterfactual in the second study by Debaere et al. (2006) is also that the firm continues to produce solely in the home country, which in their analysis is South Korea. The panel data include listed companies during the years 1980 to 1999. During this period, South Korean firms' foreign direct investments to low-wage countries have predominantly been to China. These turn out to have had a negative impact on the company's home employment growth, whereas investments in high-wage countries have not left any traces in the development of home employment. This is consistent with different motives for investing in low and high-wage countries; investment in the former is primarily to save costs, whereas investment in the latter aims to search for new and expanding markets. The findings from these two studies differ markedly from each other, although the studies are quite similar with respect to design, data and choice of methods.

As is clear from this and the previous section, almost all studies concerned with the impact of internationalization on the structure of employment apply a distinction either between production and non-production workers or between skilled and unskilled employees. These are the traditional distinctions used in labour market research. But they are not necessarily the most relevant ones in an increasingly internationalized world. As emphasized by Blinder (2007) and Jensen and Kletzer (2006) in their papers, the key distinction is between tradable and non-tradable jobs (or tasks), and that distinction is not likely to coincide with the skilled/unskilled or production/non-production classifications.[10] In particular, they argue that the jobs/tasks which have a higher offshoring potential are from the middle of the skill/wage distribution.

The bulk of the literature on the effects of outsourcing is concerned with the consequences for the home countries of the outsourcing firms or the firms themselves. Substantially less research sheds light on how the labour markets of the countries where the outsourced production takes place are affected. (However, as we will see in the next section, there is a somewhat larger literature on labour outcomes of international firms operating in advanced countries.) Moving out jobs that in rich countries are considered as work requiring few qualifications may well lead to a significant skill-upgrading in the receiving country.

Feenstra and Hanson (1997) examine the consequences for the Mexican labour market of the establishment of the NAFTA in the early 1980s and the subsequent waves of outsourcing of US manufacturing firms' assembly line tasks to the border regions of Northern Mexico. Their study shows that about half of the growth in the wage share of Mexican non-production workers during the period 1975–88 was due to outsourcing of activities from Northern America. This is quite a large impact, and it would be most interesting to have similar assessments for new EU member states and East Asian regions.

10.5 Internationalization of advanced economies

As mentioned in the Introduction, the labour markets in the EU member states have also become increasingly internationalized in recent years as a consequence of growing inward foreign direct investments in most European countries. This has been facilitated by continuous deregulation of foreign ownership; see Golub (2003) for a description and analysis. Removals of restrictions on foreign ownership, on procedures for approval of foreign owners, and other restrictions such as, for instance, those concerning representation of foreign owners on corporate boards have been especially widespread in the 1990s. As a consequence, there are no longer significant differences in restrictions on foreign ownership between European countries and the rest of the OECD.

10.5.1 Foreign versus domestic firms

Studies of the consequences of foreign ownership of firms are relatively scarce. This is somewhat surprising in view of the fact that, in several countries, many regions actively try to attract foreign direct investments and multinational firms to locate their plants there by means of lower taxes or subsidies. The purpose is to improve local employment conditions and to obtain an injection of new technological knowledge into the local business community. This is not only true for regions; countries also have pursued this strategy, and occasionally, as in the case of Ireland, quite successfully, too. What research there is has typically been inspired by the economics of multinational enterprises and their localization decisions; see Driffield and Taylor (2000) and Markusen (2002) for two recent surveys.

A growing empirical literature is comparing wages (and productivity levels) in domestic and foreign-owned firms; for evidence of higher productivity in foreign-owned firms see, for example, Conyon et al. (2002) and Girma and Görg (2007), and for corresponding evidence regarding wages see, for example, Aitken et al. (1995), Doms and Jensen (1998) and Lipsey and Sjöholm (2004). A frequent interpretation of these findings is that multinational companies enter industries with higher profits and higher wages.[11] This cannot be the whole story, however, because the same pattern – higher productivity and higher wages in the foreign-owned firms – is also observed in quite narrowly defined industries (as in Lipsey and Sjöholm (2004)). Furthermore, it should be noticed that the analyses mentioned above are in most cases carried out using firm-level data; that is, comparing average wages in firms with different types of owners. A higher average wage does not necessarily imply that the wages will rise in domestic firms after they have been acquired by a foreign investor. Nor does it mean that newly started foreign-owned firms pay higher wages than domestic firms. This is because the differences in average wages may reflect systematic differences in the employees' human capital (education, training and experience). As has been demonstrated by studies using matched employer–employee data (Heyman et al., 2007 and Martins, 2004), employees in foreign-owned firms possess higher qualifications and are rewarded accordingly. Thus, these employees do not necessarily enjoy a premium for working in a foreign-owned company. Martins's study contains a careful investigation of a host of alternative interpretations of the observed differences in wages between foreign and domestically owned firms. Heyman et al. (2007) make the important point that there is a wage differential between multinationals and domestic firms (also after catering for employees' qualifications) but no difference between domestically owned (Swedish) multinationals and foreign-owned multinational enterprises.

The reasoning above, of course, applies exclusively to advanced countries, and in particular to Northern European countries, where skilled labour is relatively cheap. In these countries increased foreign ownership may increase demand for skilled labour, which in turn may give rise to an increase in wage inequality. Another reason why multinationals may contribute to increased wage dispersion is the so-called spillover effects hypothesis, according to which the success of multinational companies emanates from their development of more firm-specific human capital. In order to retain their workers and not to lose these human capital investments, multinational firms have to pay their employees a wage premium. It should be pointed out that an increase of foreign acquisitions of human capital-intensive firms does not automatically lead to an increase in skilled labour. In order to secure scale and scope economies in their R&D activities, many multinational companies, usually with some time-lag, move the more knowledge-intensive parts of the acquired firms to the mother firm. In other words, a risk associated with a strategy based exclusively on investments in advanced technology and high technological research is that the highly skilled workforce and their employers can become targets of foreign acquisitions.

10.5.2 Foreign acquisitions

It should be noted that our discussion has so far been concerned with differences between foreign and domestically owned firms. A considerable proportion of foreign-owned firms have not been established as so-called Greenfield births, but have rather been acquired through acquisitions of firms which originally had domestic owners.[12] The public debate about the labour market consequences of foreign ownership is primarily about the jobs and wages in firms acquired by multinational enterprises. There are two opposite strands in this debate. On the one side, commentators frequently express fears that the multinational owners have a considerably lower threshold than domestic owners for taking decisions to move parts of or the whole production to other locales. Or, in economic terms, labour demand becomes more elastic, which for the employees implies that uncertainty about employment increases.

On the other hand, decision-makers are often interested in attracting foreign owners because the foreign-owned firms are expected to have positive spillover effects on the local companies. The spillover effects can arise as employees learn new skills (related to technology, marketing, management, etc.) which they take with them when they move to work in the domestic firms. Another mechanism is that domestic firms acting as suppliers or customers learn new useful practices from the multinational firms and hence become more productive. It should be noted, however, that the foreign investors may not necessarily be interested in contributing to such knowledge spillover, as this will lead to increased competition from the local firms. Thus, whether or not spillover effects are significant is an empirical matter.

In view of how often these arguments are repeated in the debate, it is somewhat surprising how little research-based evidence there is to inform the discussion. The existing evidence is predominantly based on either case studies, a key weakness of which is that their results are hard to generalize, and industry-level studies, which frequently suffer from the problem that one cannot exclude reverse causality. A third and more informative type of investigation makes use of panels on firm-level data. Most of these studies focus on developing countries (see, e.g. Aitken and Harrison (1999) and Haddad and Harrison (1993)) and typically fail to find positive spillover effects. Studies of industrialized countries, such as Haskel et al.'s (2007) study of the UK, do find evidence of positive effects on the domestic firms.

The new EU member states are good laboratories for examining these issues as they were, up to the transition, completely closed for foreign investors. Moreover, they have, in contrast to the developing countries studied, a relatively skilled labour force, and so it is more likely that knowledge spillovers will be observed in these countries. But Konings (2001), who examined spillover effects in Poland, Bulgaria and Romania, did not find traces of them. Javorcik (2004), who studied another transition economy, Lithuania, did find positive spillover effects, but between industries, not within the same industry, and, moreover, only for firms with shared (foreign and domestic) ownership. Kosova (2009) finds that foreign firms in the Czech Republic have had technology spillovers and short-term crowding-out effects. In the longer term, however, the sales growth of foreign firms has a positive impact on the survival of domestic firms (via a domestic demand creation effect).

Linked employer–employee data are valuable for obtaining a better understanding of what occurs within firms when there is a change in the presence of foreign firms in an industry or region. Four recent studies have used this type of data to look at what happens to the wages of employees who work in a foreign-owned firm when they move to a domestically owned firm. Andrews et al. (2007) examine this question for Germany and find that moves to foreign-owned employers lead to higher wages, whereas moves from foreign to domestic firms are not associated with changes in wages in any direction. Martins (2006) addresses the same issue for Portugal and finds that employees who move from multinational to domestic companies on average experience a reduction in their wages.[13] Balsvik's (2006) analysis, which is based on Norwegian data, shows that mobility from foreign to domestically owned firms is associated with an increase in the employee's wage. Moreover, she demonstrates that mobility between the two types of firms within the same industry has a positive impact on productivity in the domestic firms. A Finnish study by Pesola (2007b) accounts for the fact that the employee's educational background may affect his or her possibilities to learn and transfer new knowledge from the multinational to the domestic firm. Like Balsvik, she also finds that previous experience of work in a multinational firm has a positive impact on the worker's wage when he or she subsequently becomes employed in a domestic firm. This positive wage effect is, however, statistically significant only for employees with higher education.

All in all, the evidence on the existence of positive spillover effects remains rather mixed. It may be too strong to call it a pattern, but it is interesting to note that positive spillover effects are found in more advanced industrialized countries, while they are absent or even negative in other countries.

Turning next to the consequences of foreign acquisitions for the elasticity of labour demand, it can again be noted that the limited existing evidence is of very recent date. A study which has received considerable attention is Barba Navaretti et al. (2003), in which the authors compare adjustment of labour demand between multinational and domestically owned companies in a sample of European firms. Thus, the analysis is not based on observed changes in ownership. At any rate, the key result is that foreign-owned subsidiaries display a less elastic demand for labour. The interpretation of this finding, which contradicts the oft-made claim in the public debate that foreign ownership increases job insecurity, is that it reflects the fact that the employees' skill levels in multinational enterprises are higher than in domestic firms. A substantial body of earlier research has documented that demand for skilled workers is clearly less elastic than for unskilled employees. But the results of the study have also been questioned. Görg et al. (2009) use data from Ireland and find a considerably higher elasticity in the international companies. These markedly contrasting results could, however, be due to the very different firm structure in Ireland.

Two recent studies based on data from the Norwegian manufacturing sector lend some support for Barba Navaretti et al. (2003). According to Balsvik and Haller's (2007) analysis, which is based on a firm panel covering the 1990s, foreign acquisitions have a positive impact on local productivity, whereas foreign Greenfield establishments are associated with a negative effect. In their other study (Balsvik and Haller, 2006), which also includes the 1980s, the same authors find that foreign investors, contrary to what is frequently claimed, do not acquire highly productive domestic firms to next lay off a considerable portion of their employees. In fact, the foreign takeover contributes to a reversal of the negative trend in employment and productivity.

A study from Sweden, Hakkala et al. (2007), differs from previous analyses in two important respects. First, it distinguishes between the effects on the labour demand elasticity of foreign ownership and foreign acquisition, respectively. Second, it compares multinational companies with non-multinational companies and foreign-owned firms with domestically owned firms. As the authors make use of linked employer–employee data, this allows them to distinguish between different groups of employees, in particular with respect to education. The results of the analysis can be summarized quite briefly: there are no significant differences in the elasticity of labour demand between the different ownership types.

A handful of studies have examined more directly the employment consequences in the acquired firms, exploiting panel data to track changes subsequent to takeovers.[14] They typically find negative effects of foreign acquisitions; see Girma and Görg (2004) for an analysis based on British data and Böckerman and Lehto (2008) and Pesola (2007a) for analyses of employment consequences at the workplace and individual levels, respectively, using Finnish linked employer–employee data. It should be noted, however, that most studies only track the firms during a relatively short period after the ownership change and that the counterfactual is not always well defined.

Three investigations have focused on whether foreign acquisitions give rise to changes in composition of the acquired firms' workforces. Two opposite effects can be expected. One is that, since multinationals in general have a more qualified workforce, a foreign acquisition would generate an upgrading of the workforce in the acquired firm. Another is that an acquisition (foreign as well as domestic) leads to a reduction in administrative and managerial employment and hence less demand for highly educated employees. As the net effect is ambiguous, it is not surprising that researchers have arrived at rather different results: Almeida (2003) observes no changes in the qualification structure in acquired Portuguese firms, whereas Lipsey and Sjöholm (2004) find evidence of strong upgrading in acquired Indonesian companies. Huttunen (2007) uses propensity-score matching techniques to construct the control group for comparisons (i.e. accounting for the fact that acquired firms represent a selected group of firms). Her analysis, which is based on linked Finnish data from a relatively long period (1988–2001), gives evidence of a small but statistically significant reduction in the share of highly educated workers in the acquired firms.

Huttunen's (2007) study also sheds some light on the effect of the foreign acquisition on the employees' wages. She finds a gradual, positive effect on wages which is larger the higher the employee's level of education. Hence, the foreign acquisition is followed by increased within-firm wage dispersion. This result is corroborated by Heyman et al. (2006), who also find that wage differentials within Swedish firms grow after having been acquired by foreign investors. Notably, dispersion in the upper part of the within-firm wage distribution widens, indicating that in particular managerial employees gain (in terms of higher wages) from the acquisition. Earle and Telegdy (2008) examine the wage consequences of foreign acquisition of Hungarian firms. They find that foreign investors systematically acquire firms that are already paying higher wages. Accounting for this leads to a substantial decline (from 40 to 7 per cent) in the estimated foreign ownership wage premium.

10.6 Trade and employment structure

In addition to relocation of production, changes in international trade also affect employment and the employment structure through other mechanisms. Increased international competition in product markets could, for instance, create pressures on domestic firms to change their product mix, and hence lead to skill-upgrading. Some earlier studies, Berman et al. (1994) and Autor et al. (1998), did not, however, find strong evidence in support of such conjectures. Rather, they find that skill-upgrading is predominantly a within-industry phenomenon, whereas between-industry effects, which are thought of as triggered by trade, play only a minor role.

A more recent study sheds some new light on this issue. Bernard et al. (2006) show that firms do adjust their product composition especially in response to increased import penetration from low-wage countries. Thus, in contrast to previous studies, they attribute a large share of the skill-upgrading to within-industry shifts.

The studies mentioned so far are based on American data. In the United States increased import competition is likely to affect wages and hence have less strong impact on employment than in Europe, where the more rigid wage structures could result in employment adjustments to sharper international competition. Two studies provide some evidence on this. Salvanes and Førre (2003) make use of linked employer–employee data from the Norwegian manufacturing sector to examine the impact of international competition in the product markets on demand for different types of labour. A key finding is that demand for qualified labour is unaffected whereas the number of jobs for less skilled workers has been adversely affected.

The other study, which uses a French data set constructed by linking data on firms' trade transactions to a panel of manufacturing firms covering the years 1986 to 1992 (Biscourp and Kramarz, 2007), also obtains results that in part differ from those using American data. This study applies distinctions between finished and intermediate goods, between countries of origin for import and between skilled/unskilled and production/non-production workers, respectively. The authors find that firms importing finished goods destroy more employment than those importing intermediate goods. Imports from low-wage countries have only a slightly more negative effect than imports from other countries. As for the skill-upgrading, this is found to take place mainly within firms.

10.7 Summary and concluding remarks

In brief, we have seen that:

- There have been large changes in international trade in recent decades. From a European perspective the two important changes are the integration of the large economies in East Asia and the EU enlargement. But foreign ownership of firms has increased also within European countries. Trade in intermediate inputs has grown rapidly, reflecting increased outsourcing.
- The impact (so far) is largest in the manufacturing sector, but this may well extend to services.
- International trade theory is being renovated to accommodate for changes in international trade.
- Research and monitoring of the internationalization of firms and labour markets are severely hampered by lack of data, due to the predominantly national focus of statistical information produced. Measurement issues are also considerable.
- Empirical evidence so far is mainly based on aggregate, industry-level indicators for offshoring or outsourcing. Several studies show that these give rise to skill-upgrading of employment (i.e. hurting employment prospects of unskilled workers) and increase the wage differentials between skilled and unskilled labour. Findings are similar on both sides of the Atlantic, but magnitudes larger in the US.
- There are remarkably few studies of the impacts of the marketization of Central and Eastern Europe and the enlargement of the EU.
- Firm-level studies paint a more varied picture. Earlier studies found positive home employment effects, but investigations based on data from more recent periods find less positive and even negative effects.
- Foreign-owned firms in advanced economies do not seem to pay large wage premiums to their employees, but are, rather, employing workers with higher qualifications and skills than domestic firms.
- How increased foreign ownership affects labour markets is largely an open question. There are some indications that wage dispersion within firms acquired by foreign investors increases, but whether this spills over to non-acquired firms is not known. There is no consensus about whether or not foreign acquisitions make labour demand more elastic. The same is true for the tiny literature on the consequences of foreign acquisitions on the structure of firms' workforces.

Notes

This chapter was originally written as a report included in the Final report of the LEED project submitted to European Commission's DG of Employment in March 2008. It should be pointed out that the purpose of the report was not primarily to provide a comprehensive survey of existing research, but rather to demonstrate how micro data sets at the level of firms and/or employees can be used to answer important questions related to employment policy. Another aim was to identify major improvements in the data needed for employment research. In the current version I have included some new references, updated some old ones, and slightly edited the text. I am grateful to colleagues who participated in the LEED project and to participants at meetings and workshops organised by the DG of Employment for comments and discussions on earlier drafts.

1. The authors do not, of course, claim that all these activities will be offshored, but a large number tell us that the potential is greater than normally assumed. See also van Welsum and Reif (2006).
2. See, for example, Antràs (2003) and Grossman and Helpman (2002, 2005).
3. For a detailed discussion of the measurement issues related to offshoring and outsourcing activities and their employment consequences, see Hatzichronoglou (2005).
4. International statistical agencies such as Eurostat primarily collect data from the national statistical agencies, but seldom carry out data collection themselves.
5. In 2004 the Bureau of Labor Statistics at the US Department of Labor began recording data on job loss related to movement of work as part of its Mass Layoffs Statistics programme. An oft-used method of estimating the magnitude of the changes involved is media tracking. The European Restructuring Monitor programme, which began recording outsourcing as a form of restructuring as from 2002, also uses this methodology.
6. Hijzen et al. (2005) go one step further and distinguish between purchases from domestic and foreign suppliers and between different groups of countries.
7. This means that these studies do not capture effects of the first offshoring decisions of firms, which naturally is a limitation in times when first-time offshoring is spreading rapidly among firms.
8. Amiti and Wei (2005) show, however, that the negative effects are not detected when they adopt a relatively broad definition of sectors, indicating that the negative effects are small and not widespread across sectors.
9. Demand for workers with primary education is, according to the results, not affected.
10. For very interesting ongoing research adopting an alternative classification of jobs, see Becker et al. (2008).
11. Another factor that is important for international investors' location decisions is that there is a large enough pool of specialists in the region. Increasing economic integration leads to further specialisation, and hence firms in high tech-industries gather in clusters in specific geographical areas (such as Northern Italy and Southern France).
12. Thus, for instance, in Sweden about 60 per cent of the foreign-owned companies have been established through acquisitions (ITPS, 2006).
13. Martins and Esteves (2008) obtain the same result for Brazil.
14. There are more studies that look at the employment consequences of acquisitions but do not distinguish between foreign and domestic new owners. One example is Margolis (2006), which shows that the likelihood of unemployment and mobility increases as a consequence of the new ownership conditions.

References

Aitken, B. and Harrison, A. (1999) 'Do Domestic Firms Benefit from Direct Foreign Investment? Evidence from Venezuela', *American Economic Review*, 89: 605–17.
Aitken, B., Harrison, A. and Lipsey, R. (1995) 'Wages and Foreign Ownership: A Comparative Study of Mexico, Venezuela and the United States', NBER Working Paper 510.
Almeida, R. (2003) 'The Effects of Foreign Owned Firms in the Labor Market', IZA Discussion Paper No. 785.
Amiti, M. and Wei, S-J. (2005) 'Fear of Service Outsourcing', *Economic Policy*, April: 307–47.
Amiti, M. and Wei, S-J. (2009) 'Does Service Offshoring Lead to Job Losses? Evidence from the United States', forthcoming in M. Reinsdorf and M.J. Slaughter (eds) *International Trade in Services and Intangibles in the Era of Globalization*, University of Chicago Press.

Andrews, M., Bellman, L., Schank, T. and Upward, R. (2007) 'The Takeover and Selection Effects of Foreign Ownership in Germany: An Analysis Using Linked Worker-Firm Data', forthcoming in *Review of World Economics*.

Antràs, P. (2003) 'Firms, Contracts, and Trade Structure', *Quarterly Journal of Economics*, 118: 1375–418.

Autor, D., Katz, L. and Krueger, A. (1998) 'Computing Inequality: Have Computers Changed the Labor Market?' *Quarterly Journal of Economics*, 113: 1169–213.

Baghwati, J., Panagariya, A. and Srinivasan, T. (2005) 'The Muddles over Outsourcing', *Journal of Economic Perspectives*, 18: 93–114.

Balsvik, R. (2006) 'Is Mobility of Labour a Channel for Spillovers from Multinationals to Local Domestic Firms?' NHH, Department of Economics DP No. 25/06.

Balsvik, R. and Haller, S. (2006) 'The Contribution of Foreign Entrants to Employment and Productivity Growth', ESRI Discussion Paper 26/2006.

Balsvik, R. and Haller, S. (2007) 'Foreign Firms and Host-Country Productivity: Does the Mode of Entry Matter?' NHH Discussion Paper SAM 2, 2006.

Barba Navaretti, G., Checchi, D. and Turini, A. (2003) 'Adjusting Labor Demand: Multinational versus National Firms: A Cross-European Analysis', *Journal of the European Economic Association*, 1: 708–19.

Barba Navaretti, G., Castellani, D. and Disdier, A.-C. (2006) 'How Does Investing in Cheap Labour Countries Affect Performance at Home? France and Italy', Centro Studi Luca D'Agliano Working paper 215.

Becker, S., Ekholm, K. and Muendler, M.-A. (2008) 'Offshoring and the Onshore Composition of Tasks and Skills', Mimeo.

Berman, E., Bound, J. and Griliches, Z. (1994) 'Changes in the Demand for Skilled Labor within U.S. Manufacturing: Evidence from the Annual Survey of Manufactures', *Quarterly Journal of Economics*, 104: 367–98.

Bernard, A., Jensen, J. and Schott, P. (2006) 'Survival of the Best Fit: Exposure to Low-Wage Countries and the (Uneven) Growth of US Manufacturing Plants', *Journal of International Economics*, 68: 219–37.

Biscourp, P. and Kramarz, F. (2007) 'Employment, Skill Structure and International Trade: Firm-Level Evidence for France', *Journal of International Economics*, 72: 22–51.

Blinder, A. (2006) 'Fear of Offshoring', *Foreign Affairs*, March/April.

Blinder, A. (2007) 'How Many U.S. Jobs Might Be Offshorable?' Princeton, NJ: Princeton University, CEPS Working Paper No. 142.

Blomström, M., Fors, G. and Lipsey, R. (1997) 'Foreign Direct Investment and Employment: Home Country Experience in the United States and Sweden', *Economic Journal*, 107: 1787–97.

Böckerman, P. and Lehto, E. (2008) 'Analysing the Employment Effects of Mergers and Acquisitions', *Journal of Economic Behavior & Organization*, 68: 112–24.

Borjas, G. (2002) 'Puzzles in Economics of Immigration', EALE Lecture.

Braconier, J. and Ekholm, K. (2000) 'Swedish Multinationals and Competition from High- and Low-wage Locations', *Review of International Economics*, 8: 448–61.

Brainard, L. and Riker, D. (1997) 'Are U.S. Multinationals Exporting U.S. Jobs?' NBER Working Paper 5958.

Conyon, M., Girma, S., Thompson, S. and Wright, P. (2002) 'The Productivity and Wage Effects of Foreign Acquisition in the United Kingdom', *Journal of Industrial Economics*, L: 85–10.

Cuvyers, L., Dumont, M., Rayp, G. and Stevens, K. (2002) 'Home Employment Effects of EU Firms' Activities in Central and Eastern European Countries', University of Gent, Working Paper 158.

Debaere, P., Lee, H. and Lee, J. (2006) 'Does Where You Go Matter? The Impact of Outward Foreign Direct Investment on Multinationals' Employment at Home', CEPR Discussion Paper No. 5737.

Doms, M. and Jensen, B. (1998) 'Comparing Wages, Skills, and Productivity between Domestically and Foreign-Owned Manufacturing Establishments in the United States', in R. Baldwin, R. Lipsey and D. Richardson (eds) *Geography and Ownership as Bases for Economic Accounting*, Chicago, IL: University of Chicago Press.

Driffield, N. and Taylor, K. (2000) 'FDI and the Labour Market: A Review of the Evidence and Policy Implications', *Oxford Review of Economic Policy*, 16: 90–103.

Earle, J. and Telegdy, A. (2008) 'Ownership and Wages: Estimating Public-Private and Foreign-Domestic Differentials with LEED from Hungary, 1986–2003', in S. Bender et al. (eds) *The Analysis of Firms and Employees: Quantitative and Qualitative Approaches*, Chicago, IL: University of Chicago Press, 135–62.

Ekholm, K. and Hakkala, K. (2006) 'The Effect of Offshoring on Labour Demand: Evidence from Sweden', CEPR Discussion Paper No. 5648.

Eriksson, T. and Li, J. (2006) 'The Effects of the Internationalization of Danish Enterprises on Home Employment and Wages: Analysis of Firm Data', ASB working paper.

Faggio, G., Salvanes, K. and van Reenen, J. (2006) 'The Evolution of Inequality in Productivity and Wages: Panel Data Evidence', NBER Working Paper No. 13351.

Falk, M. and Kobel, B. (2002) 'Outsourcing, Imports and Labour Demand', *Scandinavian Journal of Economics*, 104: 567–86.

Federico, S. and Minerva, G. (2008) 'Outward FDI and Local Employment Growth in Italy', *Review of World Economics*, 144: 295–324.

Feenstra, R. and Hanson, G. (1996) 'Foreign Investment, Outsourcing and Relative Wages', in R. Feenstra, G. Grossman and D. Irwin (eds) *The Political Economy of Trade Policy*, Papers in Honor of Jagdish Bhagwati, MIT Press.

Feenstra, R. and Hanson, G. (1997) 'Foreign Direct Investment and Relative Wages: Evidence from Mexico's Maquiladoras', *Journal of International Economics*, 42: 371–94.

Feenstra, R. and Hanson, G. (1999) 'Productivity Measurement and the Impact of Trade and Technology on Wage Estimates for the U.S., 1972–1990', *Quarterly Journal of Economics*, 114: 907–40.

Feenstra, R. and Hanson, G. (2003) 'Global Production Sharing and Rising Inequality. A Survey of Trade and Wages', in E. Choi and J. Harrigan (eds) *Handbook of International Trade*, London: Blackwell.

Freeman, R. (1995) 'Are Your Wages Set in Beijing?' *Journal of Economic Perspectives*, 9: 15–32.

Freeman, R. (2005) 'China, India and the Doubling of the Global Labor Force', *The Globalist*, June.

Geischecker, I. and Görg, H. (2008) 'Winners and Losers: Fragmentation, Trade and Wages Revisited', *Canadian Journal of Economics*, 41: 243–70.

Geischecker, I., Görg, H. and Munch, J. (2007) 'Do Labour Market Institutions Matter? Micro-Level Wage Effects of International Outsourcing in Three European Countries', IZA Discussion Paper No. 3212.

Girma, S. and Görg, H. (2004) 'Blessing or Curse? Domestic Plants' Employment and Survival Prospects after Foreign Acquisition', *Applied Economics Quarterly*, 50: 89–110.

Girma, S. and Görg, H. (2007) 'Evaluating the Causal Effects of Foreign Acquisitions on Domestic Skilled and Unskilled Wages', *Journal of International Economics*, 72: 97–112.

Golub, S. (2003) 'Measures of Restrictions on Inward Foreign Direct Investment for OECD Countries', *OECD Economic Studies* No. 36, 85–116.

Grossman, G. and Helpman, E. (2002) 'Integration versus Outsourcing in Industry Equilibrium', *Quarterly Journal of Economics*, 117: 85–120.

Grossman, G. and Helpman, E. (2005) 'Outsourcing in a Global Economy', *Review of Economic Studies*, 72: 135–59.

Grossman, G. and Rossi-Hansberg, E. (2008) 'Trading Tasks: A Simple Theory of Offshoring', *American Economic Review*, 98: 1978–97.

Haddad, M. and Harrison, A. (1993) 'Are There Positive Spillovers from FDI? Evidence from Panel Data for Marocco', *Journal of Development Economics*, 42: 51–74.

Hakkala, K., Heyman, F. and Sjöholm, F. (2007) 'Cross-Border Acquisitions, Multinationals and Wage Elasticities', IFN, Stockholm, Working Paper No. 709.

Hansson, P. (2005) 'Skill Upgrading and Production Transfer within Swedish Multinationals', *Scandinavian Journal of Economics*, 107: 673–92.

Harrison, A., McMillan, M. and Null, C. (2007) 'U.S. Multinational Activity Abroad and U.S. Jobs: Substitutes or Complements?', *Industrial Relations*, 46: 347–65.

Haskel, J., Pereira, S. and Slaughter, M. (2007) 'Does Inward Foreign Direct Investment Boost the Productivity of Domestic Firms?' *Review of Economics and Statistics*, 89: 482–96.

Hatzichronoglou, T. (2005) *The Impact of Offshoring on Employment: Measurement Issues and Implications*. Paris: OECD.

Head, K. and Ries, J. (2002) 'Offshore Production and Skill Upgrading by Japanese Manufacturing Firms', *Journal of International Economics*, 58: 81–105.

Heyman, F., Sjöholm, F. and Gustafsson Tingvall, P. (2006) 'Acquisitions, Multinationals and Wage Dispersion', Research Institute of Industrial Economics, Working Paper No. 675.

Heyman, F., Sjöholm, F. and Gustafsson Tingvall, P. (2007) 'Is There Really a Foreign Ownership Wage Premium: Evidence from Matched Employer-Employee Data', *Journal of International Economics*, 73: 355–76.

Hijzen, A., Görg, H. and Hine, R. (2005) 'International Outsourcing and the Skill Structure of Labour Demand in the United Kingdom', *Economic Journal*, 115: 860–78.

Hsie, C-T. and Woo, K. (2004) 'The Impact of Outsourcing to China on Hong Kong's Labor Market', *American Economic Review*, 95: 1673–87.

Hummels, D., Ishii, J. and Yi, K.-J. (2001) 'The Nature and Growth of Vertical Specialization in World Trade', *Journal of International Economics*, 54: 75–96.

Huttunen, K. (2007) 'The Effect of Foreign Acquisition on Employment and Wages: Evidence from Finnish Manufacturing', *Review of Economics and Statistics*, 89: 497–509.

Javorcik, B. (2004) 'Does Foreign Direct Investment Increase the Productivity of Domestic Firms? In Search for Spillovers through Backward Linkages', *American Economic Review*, 94: 605–27.

Jensen, B. and Kletzer, L. (2006) 'Tradable Services: Understanding the Scope and Impact of Services Offshoring', in L. Brainard and S. Collins (eds) Brookings Trade Forum 2005, *Offshoring White-Collar Work – The Issues and the Implications*, Brookings Institution.

Katz, L. and Autor, D. (1999) 'Changes in the Wage Structure and Earnings Inequality', in O. Ashenfelter and D. Card (eds) *Handbook of Labor Economics*, Vol 3A, 1463–558.

Konings, J. (2001) 'The Effects of Foreign Direct Investment on Domestic Firms', *Economics of Transition*, 9: 619–33.

Konings, J. and Murphy, A. (2006) 'Do Multinational Enterprises Relocate Employment to Low-wage Regions? Evidence from European Multinationals', *Review of World Economics*, 142: 1–20.

Kosova, R. (2009) 'Do Foreign Firms Crowd Out Domestic Firms? Evidence from the Czech Republic', forthcoming in *Review of Economics and Statistics*.

Kramarz, F. (2006) 'Offshoring, Unions, and Wages: Evidence from Data Matching Imports, Firms, and Workers', CREST-INSEE Working Paper.

Kravis, I. and Lipsey, R. (1988) 'The Effect of Multinational Firms' Foreign Operations on their Domestic Employment', NBER Working Paper 2760.

Lipsey, R. (1994) 'Foreign-Owned Firms and U.S. Wages', NBER Working Paper 4927.

Lipsey, R. and Sjöholm, F. (2004) 'FDI and Wage Spillovers in Indonesian Manufacturing', *Journal of Development Economics*, 73: 415–22.

Margolis, D. (2006) 'Should Employment Authorities Worry About Mergers and Acquisitions?', *Portuguese Economic Journal*, 5: 1–40.

Markusen, J. (2002) *Multinational Firms and the Theory of International Trade*, Cambridge: MIT Press.

Martins, P. (2004) 'Do Foreign Firms Really Pay Higher Wages? Evidence from Different Estimators', IZA Discussion Paper No. 1388.

Martins, P. (2006) 'Inter-firm Mobility, Displacement, and Foreign Direct Investment Spillovers', Queen Mary College, Working paper.

Martins, P. and Esteves, L. (2008) 'Foreign Ownership, Employment and Wages in Brazil: Evidence from Acquisitions, Divestments and Job Movers', IZA Discussion Paper No. 3542.

Munch, J. and Skaksen, J. (2005) 'Specialization, Outsourcing and Wages', IZA Discussion Paper No. 1907.

Pesola, H. (2007a) 'Individual Level Employment Effects of Foreign Acquisitions', Helsinki School of Economics, working paper.

Pesola, H. (2007b) 'Foreign Ownership, Labour Mobility and Wages', HECER Discussion Paper No. 175.

Salvanes, K. and Førre, S. (2003) 'Effects on Employment of Trade and Technical Change: Evidence from Norway', *Economica*, 70: 293–329.

Skaksen, J. and Sørensen, A. (2002) 'Capital-Skill Complementarity and Rigid Relative Wages: Inference from the Business Cycle', CEBR Working paper.

Slaughter, M. (1995) 'Multinational Corporations, Outsourcing, and American Wage Divergence', NBER Working Paper 5253.

Slaughter, M. (2000) 'Production Transfer within Multinational Enterprises and American Wages', *Journal of International Economics*, 50: 449–72.

Sørensen, A. and Rose Skaksen, J. (2005) 'Capital-Skill Complementarity and Rigid Relative Wages: Inference from the Business Cycle', *Contributions to Macroeconomics*, Vol. 5.

Strauss-Kahn, V. (2004) 'The Role of Globalization in the Within-Industry Shift Away from Unskilled Workers in France', in R. Baldwin and A. Winters (eds) *Challenges to Globalization: Analyzing the Economics*, NBER and University of Chicago Press.

Van Welsum, D. and Reif, X. (2006) 'Potential Offshoring: Evidence from Selected OEVD Countries', in L. Brainard and S. Collins (eds) *Offshoring White-Collar Work – The Issues and the Implications*, Brookings Institution.

Yeh, R. and Lin, H. (2006) 'The Effects of FDI Location Choices on the Home Economy: A Firm Level Analysis', National Chi-Nan University Working paper.

11
Development of Linked Employer–Employee Data for EU Labour Market and Social Policy Analysis

Tanvi Desai

11.1 Introduction

This book has looked at a range of research questions using evidence from business microdata. In order to produce evidence-based research, good-quality, accessible data resources are vital. This chapter presents research into the current situation with regard to linked employer–employee data resources, and examines strategies by which they could be more fully exploited.

European economic and social policy benefits greatly from being underpinned by high-quality research and evaluation. In order for policy-oriented research to be effective, accurate data resources are necessary, along with an infrastructure that makes them conveniently accessible, while maintaining respondent confidentiality.

At present governments and other data providers may expend significant sums on the collection and preparation of data sources that get little use beyond the publication of aggregate tables. Full exploitation of data resources not only enables a wider range of research and policy questions to be answered more accurately, but also improves data quality (through identification of errors, and advice on suitability of data for research purposes), delivers better value for money to bodies that fund data collection, and minimizes the number of independent data collection projects undertaken by researchers.

A survey for European Commission DG for Employment and Social Affairs (Desai, 2008) has shown that there is a rich collection of linked employer–employee data within Europe, including data that already exist at a national level and data that can be created from administrative and other sources. However, these sources are still relatively underused compared with labour force and household survey data. This is partly due to the perceived increased risk of disclosure for business data compared with household or individual data, which has meant that infrastructure for access has developed more slowly than for other data sources.

Consequently, business microdata are less accessible to researchers, and as a result the research methodology and culture surrounding linked employer–employee data are underdeveloped.

While the previous chapters of this book are concerned with specific research questions in the fields of (i) labour turnover flows and mobility, (ii) wages, human resource strategies and institutions, and (iii) labour market outcomes of internationalization, this chapter examines the situation with regard to availability and access to the resources needed for research in these areas to be successful.

The first section will look at the legislation governing access to business microdata in the EU, and the availability of Linked Employer–employee Data (LEED) resources. It will also outline some of the barriers to accessing LEED, and to using national sources for comparative research. The second section looks at strategies for secure access to confidential microdata, and discusses their strengths and weaknesses from an academic researcher's point of view. The third section will give an overview of the experience of developing a remote solution for secure access to European Structure of Earnings Survey data, and examine how well the solution met member states' needs for the dissemination of business microdata. Finally this paper will make some recommendations to improve the use of linked employer–employee data for comparative research.

11.2 Linked employer–employee data within the EU and beyond

Many countries have some form of linked employer–employee data that could potentially be used for research purposes. These data mainly take one of three forms:

- A dedicated linked employer–employee survey, designed specifically for the task. These are almost always administered by the National Statistical Institute (NSI) or the Ministry for Labour (sometimes with the cooperation of academic experts).
- A linked survey generated by matching existing data sources to create the resource needed. These are usually developed by academic researchers to address specific questions.
- Register data, which in this case refers to administrative sources covering whole populations, primarily found in the Nordic countries.

The first and third options are obviously preferable because matched data sets are usually created when there is an absence of an official source, and there will always be some methodological compromises to be made in generating matched data resources. In addition, the sources used to create matched data sets are often administrative data with limited access to which only experts, with good contacts in governments or Statistical Institutes, can negotiate access in special circumstances. Therefore there may be no transparent access route for the average researcher.

In addition to these first three types of data, a fourth form of LEED is becoming more common as NSIs realize the need for resources of this type: an official linked data set developed by government from administrative data. Though these data suffer from the weaknesses of matched data, government officials have access to a wider range of data sources, containing more detail than would be available to the average researcher, potentially allowing construction of data sets with larger populations and fewer biases. These sources are very welcome to the research community, as NSIs and governments are often able to dedicate more time and resources to developing higher-quality reusable sources than academics; for example, Denmark's IDA database, developed by matching administrative sources, took 10 years to develop. Additionally, access to an officially constructed source is usually far more transparent and straightforward than to one developed by independent researchers.

In this section we will look at the common ground in data release legislation, the availability of LEED resources in Europe, and the barriers to access and cross-national research using linked employer–employee microdata.

11.2.1 Conventions governing access to microdata

Legislation governing the release of microdata varies from country to country; however, for most countries there are some common principles, which include:

- The overarching requirement to protect the identity of the individual respondent
- That the data be used for 'statistical purposes only' (a term which is open to differing interpretations)
- That the individual granted access to the data be a 'bona fide' researcher (this sometimes requires an institutional guarantee)
- That the data are not passed to a third party
- That the individual signs an undertaking/licence agreeing to abide by the conditions of release.

It is also quite common to require:

- That the microdata are not matched to other sources
- That the microdata are destroyed or returned to the provider on completion of the project.

This final rule is often a problem for academic researchers due to the time it takes to publish research results. It takes at least a year (sometimes up to five years) following the end of a project to get a publication accepted by a journal. If the editor asks for revisions that the researcher is not able to provide due to lack of data access, then the publication is rejected. This is a major concern to academic researchers, as publication in a refereed journal is usually the primary goal of any research project. Academic researchers may choose not to use a data source rather than risk not being able to publish.

In the case of business microdata, laws governing release are more variable due to the potential for disclosure, as a business (in particular a large business or one that dominates a sector) is often more easily identified than an individual or a household. Because of this, procedures for releasing firm-level data are far less developed than those for household or individual data, and for some countries, even where legislation allows for release of business data, concerns about the ability to ensure confidentiality mean there is no formal process that allows researchers to gain access. However, more and more countries are accepting the need for research access to microdata, and methods of dissemination are discussed in more detail in Section 11.3 below.

11.2.2 Availability of LEED

A survey of linked employer–employee data sets for the European Commission DG for Employment and Social Affairs [DGEmp] (Desai, 2008) showed a high potential for the creation and use of resources of this type within the EU. Of the 27 member states, the survey was able to obtain information on LEED resources for 19. Of these 19 countries only Poland appeared to have no ability to develop and release these data. Of the remaining 18 countries, 12 had some form of official (usually government-collected or commissioned) LEED resource, for three there was evidence of a LEED resource created by academic researchers from administrative data (for example, researcher-created subsets of Italian Social Security data are publicly available in various forms), and three more countries had the potential to create LEED resources from existing administrative or register data.

However, despite this potentially rich collection of resources, there are still significant barriers to access at the national level, let alone to using the data for cross-national comparative research.

11.2.3 Barriers to access

The first challenge for many researchers is just identifying the existence of a suitable data set. Even when a source has been found, for example referenced in an academic paper, discovering how to access it is often far from straightforward. While many countries are very willing to provide information about data resources, finding that information, and gaining access to the resources, can be challenging. Either countries may not have well-established business data access procedures, or these procedures are very difficult to discover or to comply with.

The EROHS (Blueprint for the European Resource Observatory for the Humanities and Social Sciences) finding that 'Researchers in humanities and social sciences still spend a disproportionate amount of time searching for relevant information, whether text or data and then negotiating arcane and antiquated access arrangements in order to extract value from these resources' (Christiansen, 2004: 12) still holds true, though significant advances have been made in many countries in the last five years.

Access to matched data sets poses particular problems, as in order to generate a high-quality matched data set it is usually necessary to use data that is considered disclosive. The need for highly detailed sources presents a significant challenge to data providers, who may want to support research, but whose primary responsibility is to protect their respondents. One outcome is that only researchers with personal contacts are able to establish an adequate level of trust to access these resources. This creates a situation of privileged access for the few and it may delay junior researchers' acquisition of skills, if they have not built up the necessary contacts to acquire the resources they need.

Another consideration is that the incentive for researchers to make these matched data sets available to others is low. Creation of a matched data set is a significant investment of time and resources for most researchers and it is in their interest to protect the source for their own use, particularly when the main route to career development for academic researchers is via publication. It is rare for credit to be given for development of research infrastructure and resources. It would be advantageous to the wider research community to consider incentives to encourage researchers to share resources.

The increase in the number of countries developing Research Data Centres (RDCs) and secure remote access solutions (see Section 11.3) will give more researchers the opportunity of creating matched data sets. RDCs provide a secure environment where researchers can undertake manipulations of confidential data under the supervision of staff authorized to oversee data security. However, RDCs are not easily accessible to everyone (see below).

A programme to support and encourage member states in the development of transparent access procedures would significantly increase the range and quality of research that can be carried out using linked employer–employee data. A starting point for such a programme is the UN's 'Principles for Managing the Confidentiality of Microdata'. The fourth of the document's Core Principles states: 'The procedures for researcher access to microdata, as well as the uses and users of microdata, should be transparent and publicly available' (UNECE CES, 2007: 6).

A centralized resource providing up-to-date details of the linked employer–employee and firm-level data sets available, with information on access procedures, would further increase the user community and the quality of research produced using these resources.

11.2.4 Barriers to comparative research

So far comparative European research has usually been carried out by international teams with members working on their own national data, as many countries allow access to national data only within their borders, or restrict access to nationals. This not only limits the quality and range of analyses that can be carried out, but skews international research towards countries with more accessible data resources.

Data sources designed to be comparative across a number of countries are rare. In the case of linked employer–employee data, the only comparative source covering the whole EU is the European Structure of Earnings Survey, and even that is not strictly comparable, as member states choose their own survey methods, and in some cases definitions and interpretations of required variables. Furthermore there is currently no format in which microdata for all member states can be accessed.

For a researcher or group of researchers wishing to undertake comparative analysis of national LEED sources, the challenge in securing permission to bring together a number of national data sources is considerable. In 2008, only five member states allowing access to LEED microdata for non-nationals beyond national boundaries could be identified, two via remote access (the Netherlands, Sweden), three via anonymized microdata files (France, Italy, the UK) (Desai, 2008). This fragmentation of data sources inevitably affects researchers' ability to do high-quality international research. The need to preselect a model that can be run separately on a number of national data sets severely limits the range of analysis, and so reduces the quality and value of the research. 'The fact that we can't pool data render them second rate...we can't really do good statistical tests' (Markus Jäntti, quoted in Desai and Cowell, 2006: 14). There is an urgent need for a research infrastructure, such as a remote system or a network of secure labs, that allows data from different countries to be brought together in one place for the purpose of comparative research.

Further problems of inadequate documentation, and incompatible definitions and classifications, add another level of difficulty. At the most basic level, the definition of the survey unit varies; for example, there is no universal (or even European) agreement on the definition of a firm, or an establishment. This means that data sources that look similar may actually contain different units of observation. Research for ERHOS found that:

> European research based at European level often falls below the standards applied at a national level as data are not immediately comparable due to differences in standards and documentation – sampling collection, variables, size formats. In conducting European research one has to frequently rely on post harmonisation of national data at the lowest common denominator. As a result, quality and detail are both compromised. (Christiansen, 2004: 6)

Recent discussions at events such as European Government Industrial Relations Research Forum (Paris, 11 September 2008) on the possibility of a European-wide linked employer–employee data set along the lines of the European Social Survey (http://www.europeansocialsurvey.org) may open up new possibilities. Though a cross-national survey is some way off, the willingness among producers of the official LEED resources for France (REPONSE), the UK (WERS) and Estonia to investigate the possibility of harmonizing questions and definitions is a very positive start.

11.3 Methods of secure data access

National Statistical Institutes are increasingly making efforts to provide access to data resources to allow bona fide researchers to undertake statistical research. This is in response to a growth in demand from researchers, but also a growing acknowledgement that there are advantages to making data available for this purpose. Full exploitation of data resources provides benefits to the NSIs: increased support for, and justification of, funding for data collection; feedback from researchers on data quality issues; and high-quality policy analysis. Provision of official statistics for research purposes also minimizes the need for researchers to carry out their own surveys. This is an advantage, as such surveys are expensive, increase the national response burden, and lead to publication of results from data which are inferior to those available from official government sources.

The methods used by NSIs to disseminate data are varied depending on the country and the level of detail in the data. The next section will present an overview of the most common methods of data dissemination. It will briefly touch on anonymized data in the form of static tables, and public use microdata files (PUM), but will concentrate primarily on data of a more sensitive nature, ranging from anonymized licensed files to full microdata. It is not within the scope of this chapter to comment on the application and validity of statistical disclosure control methods (SDC) applied to data releases, but a short list of references on the subject can be found in the Appendix.

11.3.1 Anonymized data

The most familiar form of anonymized data is a static table. These tables provide aggregate statistics with disclosure controls applied in advance of dissemination to ensure that no confidential information is released. Static tables have long been disseminated in hard copy publications, and are the most common form of data found online. Many countries, among them Denmark and Finland, also provide a service where researchers can request bespoke tables that are generated by the NSI for a fee; these tables are checked for confidentiality before being released.

Online utilities enabling generation of interactive tables such as those offered by (among others) the UK Census (CASWEB) and the US Census (American Factfinder) provide researchers with more flexibility. However, though this method is used for the dissemination of household and census data, no firm-level data has been identified as being disseminated in this way.

The next level of complexity is the public use microdata file (PUM). These are microdata files that have been anonymized to a level where they are considered safe for general dissemination. These files cannot be used to identify individuals even if matched with other data sources. PUMs are a valuable commodity to the research community due to the freedom they offer to analyse data at the desktop. However, in order to reach an acceptable level of confidentiality, detail is often reduced to a point where the data are inappropriate for complex research questions. This problem is particularly pronounced for firm-level data, as the variables that are often of most interest to researchers, such as economic activity, enterprise size and geographic position, are also the most sensitive (similarly, for linked employer–employee data the variables of interest on the employee side, such as gender, age, education level and occupation, are also vital for research but sensitive to disclosure). To address this problem many countries have made licensed anonymized microdata files (LM) available. These files require an undertaking by the researcher to safeguard the data (common conditions are listed in Section 11.2.1 above). While this additional licence is, in many cases, enough for individual and household data to be released to researchers for desktop use, in the case of business microdata even LMs are rarely accessible to researchers without some additional form of confidentiality protection due to the sensitivity of the data. Some of the release strategies used by member states and the international community are examined below.

11.3.2 Data Laboratories and Research Data Centres

Recent years have seen a proliferation of 'Research Data Centres' (or safe centres, secure labs, etc.) as a way of providing secure access to confidential data. Research Data Centres (RDCs) are typically located on the premises of the NSI initially, and provide licensed researchers with an interface to detailed microdata that would otherwise be too sensitive to release. This interface is usually a 'thin client' (or dumb terminal), where the computer the researcher is using has no processing capacity, software or links to the outside world, only a connection to a central server where the data are stored, and where all processing takes place. Researchers are allowed access to the full data set with no restrictions on analyses within the confines of the RDC. Any output they wish to remove must be submitted to NSI staff for disclosure control, and will only be released to users once it is confirmed that it contains no confidential information. The DGEmp project identified seven member states with established RDCs: Finland, Germany, Ireland, Netherlands and the UK; access to the Czech Republic and Slovakian LEED provided by the company TREXIMA via an RDC (Desai, 2008); and INSEE France is now in the process of developing one.

While RDCs have a very high level of security, the criticism from academic researchers is that travelling to a specific location for data access can be difficult and creates inequitable access to resources. Travel to the location, and accommodation for the duration of the analysis period, can be prohibitively expensive, even before taking access fees into account. Researchers who are carers or who cannot spend extended periods away from home are effectively denied access via this method. To ease the burden on both the researchers and the RDCs, some NSIs, such as Statistics Netherlands and the German Statistical Office, provide synthetic data sets of simulated data with the same structure as the confidential data set, from which researchers can develop programs before travelling to the RDC. However, creating effective synthetic files is not a trivial undertaking and few NSIs have provided them so far.

The next stage in addressing the accessibility of RDCs is to allow their establishment in 'trusted' research environments, as has been the case in North America, with Statistics Canada's Research Data Centres Program (part of the Data Liberation Initiative) and the US Census Bureau RDCs. RDCs based in research environments (usually a university) consist of a secure remote terminal room with a link to the central data server on the data providers' premises. Data analysis and disclosure control of output are the same as if the researcher were using an RDC at the Statistical Institute. In the case of the US Census Bureau RDCs, an employee of the US Census must be on site at the RDC to ensure data security. A major drawback of RDCs is the expense not just for users, but also for NSIs, as Ritchie states in relation to the UK Office for National Statistics (ONS) RDC (VML):

> The VML is a last-resort solution for situations where the data cannot be released. ONS uses a variety of distribution channels (such as the UK Data

Archive), and the default is to anonymise and release data if possible; running any kind of lab is expensive and inconvenient for all concerned. (Ritchie, 2006: 5)

11.3.3 Remote access and execution

To alleviate the burden on researchers of travelling to RDCs, and on NSIs of providing a physical location, countries are increasingly looking to develop remote solutions. Remote solutions come in two forms: remote access and remote execution. The UNECE Glossary on Statistical Disclosure Control (http://neon.vb.cbs.nl/CASC/Glossary.htm#D) defines these processes as:

> **Remote access:** On-line access to protected microdata
>
> **Remote execution:** Submitting scripts on-line for execution on disclosive microdata stored within an institute's protected network. If the results are regarded safe data, they are sent to the submitter of the script. Otherwise, the submitter is informed that the request cannot be acquiesced. Remote execution may either work through submitting scripts for a particular statistical package such as SAS, SPSS or STATA which runs on the remote server, or via a tailor made client system which sits on the user's desk top.

Specifically, remote access systems give direct access to microdata in much the same way as in an RDC, but operate from the researcher's desktop. While logged on, a researcher can access the full data set and the full range of analyses; however, any results he or she wishes to download must be checked for statistical disclosure by the data provider before being released to the researcher. Practically speaking, most remote access systems need additional security over and above the standard username and password in order to guarantee that the person accessing the data is the person licensed to do so. Statistics Netherlands use a fingerprint recognition system, while the Danish Statistical Institute uses a physical token (RSASecurID card) that generates a unique ID number that changes every minute.

Disclosure control for remote execution systems can work via input checking or output checking. Output checking is as described above. An example of a system that can use either output or input checking is the PiEP-LISSY system developed to provide access to the European Structure of Earnings Survey microdata (ESES) (see Section 11.4 below). For ESES data the PiEP-LISSY system uses input checking in an effort to prevent analyses with the potential to output disclosive results from ever reaching the data. This method is less secure than output checking, as it is impossible to establish in advance all potentially disclosive analyses. However, the main aim of input checking is to make it impossible for a researcher to mistakenly output confidential information, and to create an environment that will expose any attempt to breach security. Input checking also makes the generation and transmission of sensitive output a far rarer event than output checking. From a researcher point of view, an advantage of input checking is the speed with which results are returned. Unlike output checking, where researchers must wait until the NSI has checked their output before it can be returned, researchers using an input checking system can see little difference in time taken to generate results compared with working with the data and software locally. However, in order for security to be maintained, analyses that are considered likely to output sensitive data are often blocked altogether, which can be frustrating for researchers.

A significant problem with output checking in all the above systems is the need for staff with sufficient statistical knowledge to understand the analyses run by the most sophisticated of users. As noted by Felix Ritchie:

> Manual SDC checking requires a level of statistical expertise on the part of the checker. Even for those with a statistical background, this requires some time to develop. For dealing with advanced queries on releasable outputs (is a Herfindahl index safe? A Gini coefficient?), statistical knowledge needs to be similarly developed. However, it is likely that those with a sufficiently developed statistical knowledge would not find SDC of other people's work particularly interesting or motivating. It may be difficult to fill and fund posts. (Ritchie, 2005: 9)

This is likely to become a problem increasingly faced by data providers as the proliferation of systems using manual output checking compete for the few qualified staff available. One way to minimize this problem would be to develop automatic checks. However, before this can be done effectively there is an urgent need for more research into potentially disclosive analyses. The focus up until now has been primarily on tabular data, but research is needed on ways of controlling for more complex statistical methods.

In reality, no single method of data dissemination covers all researchers' needs. Whereas, for some, tabular data will not contain enough detail to answer their research questions, for others, the time and expertise necessary to analyse microdata make it impractical to use. The best possible strategy is a range of solutions, fit for a range of purposes and levels of expertise. For example, to disseminate the European Structure of Earnings Survey, Eurostat plan a range of solutions, including:

- Static tabular data release via the Data Portal (previously NewCronos)
- Anonymized microdata released on CDRom
- Access to full microdata via the Eurostat SAFE centre (an RDC).

Almost all NSIs use a range of methods to release data of some sort, but not all EU member states have a strategy for releasing business microdata, for which the investment in infrastructure is significant, and the legal barriers formidable.

In cases where the cost of developing an infrastructure is the barrier, member states might consider agreements with countries that already have a remote access infrastructure. Legislative frameworks permitting, countries with established infrastructures could provide access to microdata from other member states. Software which supports distributed systems, as does PiEP-LISSY, could even be used to facilitate output checking in the home country, thus allowing member states to maintain control of outputs of their national data. Alternatively, the experience of developing the PiEP-LISSY system shows that there is scope for collaborative projects between academic researchers and NSIs, particularly if the service is provided free to NSIs and researchers (see below).

11.4 The PiEP-LISSY system and the European Structure of Earnings Survey

The development of the PiEP-LISSY system for access to the European Structure of Earnings Survey microdata is an example of what can be achieved given cooperation between NSIs, academic researchers and Eurostat, and a relatively small amount of funding. It demonstrates that for many countries remote access is an acceptable way to make business microdata available.

11.4.1 A history of PiEP-LISSY

The PiEP-LISSY system was originally developed for the Pay Inequalities and Economic Performance project (PiEP) (for more details of the project, and copies of papers produced using ESES 1995 data, see http://cep.lse.ac.uk/piep/). The PiEP project began in 2000, and was funded under the European Commission's Fifth Framework Programme.

The aim of the PiEP project was to make use of the European Structure of Earnings Survey microdata (ESES), as this valuable resource had never been adequately exploited by researchers for cross-country comparisons. The project originally approached Eurostat, the holders of the ESES, for access to the data. However, they did not have the authority to grant access, and referred us to the individual member states.

It soon became clear that those countries that were willing to allow access to data would, or could, not let the data be stored anywhere but Eurostat. Some countries have laws that prevent microdata leaving the country with an exception solely for Eurostat. The need to hold the data at Eurostat, while managing access from London for an international research team, made a remote access solution essential.

The main priorities when choosing the remote access system were:

- Security capable of safeguarding confidential microdata to the satisfaction of the NSIs
- An environment that allowed users to feel, as far as possible, as if they were working at their own PCs
- A system compatible with the Eurostat network that could be managed from London.

After having looked at a number of options we chose the LISSY system developed by HAL computing. The advantages of this system were significant; they included the fact that LISSY had been used successfully by the Luxembourg Income Study (http://www.lisproject.org) for 20 years to provide secure remote access to household income study microdata. At the time that negotiations for providing access to ESES via PiEP-LISSY were taking place, the LIS project was providing access to data for 25 countries, including all EU member states except Greece and Portugal, meaning that the LISSY system was familiar to the member states, and tried and trusted in providing secure access to microdata.

Many NSIs were, however, concerned that the LISSY system, while suitable for household and labour force data, did not provide adequate security for business microdata. Working together with the LISSY System Consultant and the NSIs, we were able to add an additional layer of security; thus the PiEP-LISSY system was developed (for more information on the PiEP-LISSY system see Marsden et al. (2008), chapter 5).

The security system for PiEP-LISSY is fully flexible, allowing the configuration of country (variable or user)-specific controls. Security can also be updated and changed according to the needs of member states at any time with minimal interruption to the system.

The process of negotiation, system development and testing took just over two years, and the PiEP-LISSY system was finally configured and opened to users in 2002. The system provided access to 1995 ESES data for six member states (Belgium, Denmark, Ireland, Italy, Spain and the United Kingdom) for three years until February 2005, when the system was forced to close due to lack of funding.

The PiEP-LISSY system was reinstated for the DGEmp-sponsored LEED project in 2007. The project secured access to 2002 Structure of Earnings Survey microdata for 11 countries: Czech Republic, Hungary, Italy, Latvia, Lithuania, Luxembourg, Netherlands, Portugal, Slovak Republic, Spain and Norway. Access to 1995 data for Spain and Italy was retained and 1995 data for Luxembourg added.

11.4.4 Does LISSY meet member states' needs?

In any discussion of the LISSY system's ability to meet member states' needs for a secure method of disseminating microdata it makes sense to take into account all organizations making use of LISSY to provide access to microdata.

The largest collection of data accessible via LISSY is from the Luxembourg Income Study, which currently has two ongoing data harmonization projects: the Luxembourg Income Study (LIS) and the Luxembourg Wealth Study (LWS) (data are also available for the Luxembourg Employment Study, though this is no longer updated). Between them these databases contain microdata for 37 countries including all but five EU member states (see Table 11A.1). The DIW Berlin uses LISSY to make Socio-Economic Panel data available. Both the LIS and DIW data sets are household surveys and therefore have different disclosure control requirements from business data. However, both DIW and LIS use the original version of LISSY without additional security.

The PiEP-LISSY software, with additional security, has recently been successfully trialled by Banca d'Italia as a way of disseminating the Survey of Industrial and Service Firms. This demonstrates the confidence that a major national institution has in a remote solution as a method for providing secure access to business microdata.

Feedback from NSIs about making ESES data available via PiEP-LISSY has been mixed. In many cases no feedback at all was received, giving no indication whether the barriers were legal, political, technical or otherwise. Fifteen member states gave positive feedback during the process of negotiating access to ESES, agreeing to disseminate data via PiEP-LISSY, though data for only 11 countries were eventually released. Feedback from the A8 countries involved in the project was particularly positive: the Czech Republic, Latvia, Lithuania, and the Slovak Republic all welcomed the system on the condition that there was no cost to their NSIs. The project is also very grateful for the significant support of Netherlands Central Bureau for Statistics, who, as part of their promotion of remote access solutions, not only allowed their ESES data to be accessed through PiEP-LISSY, but also recommended the system in Eurostat Working Groups and other international forums.

Three of the four countries that explicitly refused permission did so because the London School of Economics was to manage the system: Denmark and Greece both stated that they were happy with the ability of the PiEP-LISSY system to provide safe access to the data, but only provided the administration of the system was handled by Eurostat. Poland also refused access due to LSE management, but did not express support for a remote access system. Finally, Ireland originally agreed to get involved in the project, but withdrew permission following system testing (see below).

A weakness of the LISSY system is that there is no way to control for the number of observations per cell in complex analyses. For tabulations, the LISSY web-tabulation utility allows interactive generation of tabular analyses subject to a predefined set of conditions which prevent potentially disclosive output being displayed. However, the interface with the Eurostat network is not compatible with this utility, so it is not available for the ESES data. For analyses that are more complex than tabulations there is no way for to control for cell size in LISSY.

This was a potential problem for three of the member states interested in providing access to their ESES microdata via PiEP-LISSY: Ireland, Latvia and Lithuania all have legal restrictions on the cell sizes that can be reported, as follows:

- a minimum threshold for number of respondents in a cell
- a restriction on reporting cells where one respondent (two for Ireland) accounts for a significant portion of the cell's value
- a requirement to protect sensitive cells by suppressing complementary cells.

However, the stage at which this law must be applied varies between countries, affecting the suitability of the LISSY system. For Ireland, data not conforming to the legal guidelines on cell size cannot be released into the public domain. The LEED project offered to set up a fully integrated 'Review Queue', so that any analysis run on Irish data was automatically forwarded to the Irish Central Statistical Institute (CSO) for output checking, before being returned to the researcher. However, understandably, CSO were not able to provide the manpower to undertake this, and therefore the Irish data were withdrawn.

In both the Lithuanian and Latvian cases the law refers to the 'publication' of sensitive data, providing more flexibility than in the Irish case. In the case of Lithuania, the Statistical Institute felt confident that the contractual requirement to make all publications available for them to check before they enter the public domain was sufficient to ensure protection of sensitive data. In the case of Latvia, researchers are required to sign an additional form agreeing to abide by Latvian law in generating their outputs. Copies of all outputs that researchers wish to publish must first be submitted to the Latvian Statistical Institute for checking before being included in a publication, then all publications must further be submitted for checking according to the standard contractual agreement.

The PiEP-LISSY system has advantages in a cross-national context, as the different components of the system, such as data management, review queues and data storage, can be distributed across different countries. Also, the flexibility of the security system means that protection can be tailored to each country's needs, and, where necessary, to the needs of different user groups.

All EU member states except Bulgaria and Malta disseminate some form of microdata through a LISSY system. That 15 member states expressed an interest in providing access to structure of earnings survey data via PiEP-LISSY, and two more were confident in the system (though not LSE management of the system), strongly indicates that PiEP-LISSY and other remote access systems could become effective and economical methods of disseminating business microdata, at least in the European context.

11.5 Future developments

As can be seen from the chapters in this book, a wide range of research questions can be investigated using linked employer–employee data, many of which are key to understanding the effect of economic and labour market policies both within and across countries.

A major challenge to the development of resources for the use of business microdata is the lack of funding for infrastructure projects that are not directly linked to research questions, in particular in the cross-national context. This means that the responsibility for providing long-term established infrastructures falls entirely on National Statistical Institutes, National Data Archives and international organizations such as Eurostat, as researchers can only develop infrastructures for the duration of a research project (usually a maximum of five years). An increase in funding and in the incentives for the development of research infrastructures is essential in order to fully exploit the range of interest and expertise available in the academic community.

The section below sets out some developments that would improve the quality and usefulness of linked employer–employee data.

11.5.1 Exploit expertise in the academic research community

The expertise available in the research community is currently underexploited. There is a wealth of experience among data users but they are given little incentive to share information beyond their immediate colleagues.

Researcher expertise can help data providers uncover inaccuracies and weaknesses in data that only come to light through thorough use. Data users are also able to advise on how different survey methodologies affect data utility, and the suitability of survey questions for answering research problems, and can even indicate emerging research questions for which evidence will be needed. Additionally, researchers have the knowledge to reduce the support burden on data providers, provided the mechanisms and incentives are in place for them to do this.

EU-funded initiatives such as EPUNet (http://epunet.essex.ac.uk/), which was developed to act as a focus for information relating to the European Community Household Panel Survey and as a provider of value added support, have proved how much can be achieved in information-sharing with even a small amount of funding.

To make full use of the resources available to the data community as a whole, data users' knowledge and expertise should be fully exploited. The most straightforward way of doing this is to improve and encourage networks. A longer-term plan would be a change in the research culture to reward contributions to research infrastructure.

11.5.2 Develop networks

Formal networks that bring together expertise in data use and support, data collection and provision, and policymaking are still relatively rare, particularly in an international context. International networks are vital for cross-national research, as legal, cultural and structural differences between countries mean that, even in surveys designed to be comparable, variables cannot be accurately understood without some national expertise.

One sign of progress is the COST Action ISO701, established to enhance linked employer–employee data, which had a first meeting in February 2008. However, this network is not open to the wider research community and has not yet made any recommendations public.

There is a need for networks that act as regular open forums for data users, providers and policymakers to discuss strategies for improving data access and quality; as a focus for fund-raising and lobbying for standards in linked employer–employee data; and as sources of expertise for policymakers to draw on. Such networks would increase the level and quality of use of LEED, as well as improving communication and the sharing of expertise across the data community.

11.5.3 Improve existing national resources

Some form of LEED has been identified in 18 EU member states and in seven countries outside the EU. This represents a significant potential resource for researchers and policymakers. However, even where formal dissemination policies exist at the national level, these can be relatively difficult to discover and activate, so the data are generally underexploited. Areas that can be addressed to improve existing national LEED resources include provision of information, access procedures, data linking and data structure.

Locating data resources can be a challenge. Information on content, structure, sampling, questionnaire design and access procedures for linked employer–employee data sets need to be more visible. Ideally this would be as part of a centralized international resource, as mentioned above (p. 258) but more visible information at the individual country level should also be encouraged.

Straightforward access procedures not only increase the use of data, but also increase the security of data, as researchers are less likely to try to circumvent a registration process that is easy to understand and carry out.

Due to confidentiality considerations, it can be difficult for researchers to obtain permission to link LEED to other sources. Many linked employer–employee data sets lack information needed to answer key research questions. For example, data on output and performance would assist analysis of the interactions between the demand and supply sides of the labour market. If NSIs were to provide linked data sets containing key variables that would not otherwise be available together, it would increase the policy-relevant research that could be undertaken using LEED resources. In the absence of such official linked resources, the infrastructure necessary to allow researchers to carry out the linking themselves should be developed.

Data users would also welcome more panel or, at least, longitudinal linked employer–employee data. These elements are important for studying trends, and the effect of individual events, making them particularly important for policy-oriented research.

11.5.4 Facilitate international comparative research

Comparative research is becoming increasingly important in a European context, and also worldwide, as globalization means that labour market and economic policy decisions taken in one country impact not only on that country's neighbours, but, in some cases, on the wider international community. This creates a need for good-quality international comparative data, or at least policies that allow national data sources from a number of countries to be analysed side by side.

At present, disparities in methods and classification at the national level make it difficult for researchers to be confident that results of analyses showing differences between countries are genuine, rather than the result of differences in survey methodology. Encouraging harmonization would greatly enhance the quality of cross-national research and increase the range of analyses that can be undertaken.

Information on survey methodology, questionnaire design, definitions etc. in documentation provided for national sources is frequently not detailed enough to assess the comparability of data sets with any great level of accuracy. Improving this information would enable researchers to make more informed decisions on whether to use or combine data sources.

The common requirement that a country's data remain within its national borders is a significant barrier to international comparative research. There is an urgent need to develop policies and infrastructure that enable data from different countries to be brought together for high-quality cross-national research, at least at the European level if not internationally.

The ideal LEED resource for international comparative research would be a high-quality cross-national data set with a uniform methodology and common definitions. This, however, is an expensive long-term solution. A harmonization of methods is also a longer-term goal (though creation of an international survey may act as a driver to harmonization). In the shorter term, an improvement in documentation standards would enhance cross-national research. However, taking into account the issues raised above, the one resource that would, in the present conditions, have the greatest effect on researchers' ability to carry out high-quality comparative international research would be an infrastructure in which microdata sources from different countries could be stored and accessed side by side. This would ideally be a remote facility to ensure access for the largest possible number of researchers, but at the very least a distributed network of safe centres across countries is required.

11.5.5 European Structure of Earnings Survey

The European Structure of Earnings Survey is the only comparable linked employer–employee survey currently available in Europe. The research opportunities offered by this data set are wide–ranging, as can be seen from earlier chapters. However, ESES is far from fulfilling its potential at the present time. There are a number of initiatives that could improve the utility of the data.

For example, access to both the microdata and tabulations could be improved. There is currently no access to the full collection of microdata for all countries. No anonymized licensed microdata files have been released on CD-ROM, and, though some data are available via the Eurostat SAFE centre, this is only a subset of countries, and is very expensive to access. A method for releasing the full microdata at low cost to researchers would increase the opportunities to use ESES for cross-national research. For tabulations, a secure online interactive tool to allow researchers to exploit the full range of possible tabulations available would be welcomed by data users, particularly following the problems with comparability between 1995 and 2002 tables made available via NewCronos.

Individual countries are allowed discretion in data collection methods provided that the resulting data meet an agreed common specification. Improved harmonization of data collection methods, definitions of variables, etc. would raise the quality of the data. However, it is unlikely that member states would be able to make these changes without some funding support.

An area where greater harmonization is not required is in the release of anonymized licensed microdata files. At present, the principle for the release of licensed microdata is that if a variable is potentially disclosive for one member state it is anonymized, that is, removed or aggregated, for all member states. This leads to a data set of 'lowest common denominators'. The ESES licensed microdata will be more valuable to researchers if as much detail is preserved as possible. Therefore, if a country has concerns about a variable, it should be anonymized only for the affected country, thus preserving as much detail as possible.

Finally, two initiatives to add to the data already available for ESES would be linked resources and the digitization of old waves. Links with data such as the Structural Business Statistics (http://epp.eurostat.ec.europa.eu/portal/page/portal/european_business/introduction) would increase the range of questions that could be researched using ESES. Digitization of old hard copy data from ESES going back as far as 1966 would preserve an irreplaceable resource, and add a valuable time series component. This last initiative is particularly urgent as much of this early data is in danger of being lost.

11.5.6 Remote access

Remote access to data is the method of secure access most favoured by academic researchers. It allows them to analyse data at their desktops in the comfort of their own offices. It is a relatively inexpensive method of dissemination when compared with Research Data Centres. Provided the charge for access is low or non-existent, remote access is an equitable form of data dissemination, removing the need to travel to Research Data Centres, and enabling both data and users to be distributed internationally.

National remote solutions should be accessible to data users from other countries. However, more importantly, an international remote solution for linked employer–employee data would significantly improve access, leading to an increased user group, better-quality international research covering a wider range of countries, and an improvement in LEED resources internationally.

11.5.7 Research on potentially disclosive analyses

There has been a proliferation of data access systems that require disclosure control of output (or more rarely input). However, while research into disclosure control for tabulations is relatively advanced, understanding of the potential for more complex statistical analyses to output sensitive data is less so.

As data providers increasingly turn to disclosure control of output, competition for and cost of staff with the experience to undertake this role will necessitate the automation of output checking. Therefore, research into potentially disclosive analyses is needed, not just for confidence in the effectiveness of manual disclosure control, but also to enable the development of automatic disclosure control systems.

11.6 Conclusions

As can be seen from this book, there is a wealth of policy-oriented research that can be carried out using linked employer–employee data in areas that in the past have been subject to little analysis. The chapters in this book give an indication of the linked employer–employee data resources that are potentially available for academic research. However, as outlined in this chapter, there is much that can be done to improve the quality, availability and level of use of these LEED resources.

A primary reason why access procedures for linked employer–employee data and other business data resources are less developed than for other data resources is the concern over confidentiality. Businesses, in particular large businesses and those that dominate an industrial sector, are more easily identified than households or individuals, making data providers reluctant to release business data as licensed anonymized microdata files, the format that most researchers use to analyse less sensitive data at their desktop, without additional security measures.

In recent years, secure access solutions, such as research data centres and remote access systems, have become more commonplace, and these infrastructures could be used to provide access to business microdata with minimal, if any, adjustments. In addition, projects such as PiEP/LEED and procedures developed by individual member states are beginning to establish a basis for providing secure access to business microdata.

While research data centres are the most secure method of data dissemination, they are expensive to set up, maintain and use. The need to travel to an RDC for the period of data analysis limits who can use the resource. Remote access systems are much cheaper to maintain, and, provided the cost of using them is low or non-existent, they are a secure and equitable way to disseminate data.

The problems faced in accessing data from a number of countries for comparative research are even more of a challenge. Many countries do not allow data to be taken outside national borders, and few countries allow access for non-nationals. Currently, comparative research usually requires an international team with each member working on his or her own national data, with members from countries that have accessible data more likely to be included, thus skewing both the research opportunities and output in favour of countries with accessible data.

A key challenge internationally, and for EU member states in particular, is to develop a framework that allows high-quality comparative research to be carried out across national sources. Whether this is via convergence of statistical legislation, or through the development of a European data infrastructure, or most likely a combination of the two, full exploitation of the wealth of national sources for comparative research will not be possible until changes have been made.

There are some relatively straightforward measures that could be taken to improve both the quality and the availability of LEED. The establishment of networks of users, some purely technical and others that bring together researchers, data providers and policymakers, is a proven way of enhancing data. Improved data documentation to allow more accurate comparison of national sources would enhance the quality of research output. Research into new ways of maintaining confidentiality, especially for advanced statistical analyses, would increase data security.

More radical improvement depends on a change in funding policy to include funding for work on infrastructure, on specific aspects of data harmonization, and, ideally, on the development of high-quality genuinely comparable cross-national surveys for Europe and beyond.

Acknowledgements

I would like to thank Josep Domingo-Ferrer and Gail Wilson for their advice.

Appendix

Table 11A.1 Microdata disseminated via LISSY (and other remote access systems) by EU member states

	Data in LIS	Data in LWS	SES via PfEP-LISSY	Comments	National data released via a LISSY system	Remote access to business microdata via other systems
Austria	X	X			X	
Belgium	X				X	
Bulgaria						
Cyprus		X				
Czech Republic	X		X		X	
Denmark	X			LISSY OK, but only if managed by Eurostat	X	X
Estonia	X				X	
Finland	X	X			X	
France	X				x	X
Germany	X	X		DIW Berlin providing access to household panel	X	X
Greece	X			LISSY OK, but only if managed by Eurostat	X	
Hungary	X		X		X	
Ireland	X		X		X	
Italy	X	X	X	Banca d'Italia providing access to enterprise survey	X	
Latvia			X		X	
Lithuania			X		X	

Continued

Table 11A.1 Continued

	Data in LIS	Data in LWS	SES via PiEP-LISSY	Comments	National data released via a LISSY system	Remote access to business microdata via other systems
Luxembourg	X				X	
Malta						
Netherlands	X		X		X	
Poland	X			Eurostat responsible for data access and security	X	X
Portugal			X		X	
Romania	X					
Slovak Republic	X		X		X	X
Slovenia	X				X	
Spain	X		X		X	
Sweden	X	X			X	
UK	X	X			X	X
Norway	X	X	X		X	

Note: X = yes.

References

Abowd, J.M. and Lane, J.I. (2004) 'New Approaches to Confidentiality Protection Synthetic Data, Remote Access and Research Data Centers', LEHD Technical paper No. TP-2004–03. http://lehd.did.census.gov/led/library/techpapers/tp-2004–03.pdf

Bryson, A., Forth, J. and Barber, C. (eds) (2006) 'Making Linked Employer–Employee Data Relevant to Policy', DTI Occasional Paper no 4. http://www.berr.gov.uk/files/file28176.pdf

Christiansen, L. (2004) *Blueprint for the European Research Observatory for the Humanities and Social Sciences*, Draft proposal from the Working Group on Research Infrastructure in the Humanities and the Social Sciences. http://www.nessie-essex.co.uk/roundtable_4docs/RISSH.pdf

COST Action ISO701 (2007) Comparative Analysis of Enterprise Data: Industry Dynamics, Firm Performance and Worker Outcomes: Memorandum of Understanding. http://w3.cost.esf.org/typo3conf/ext/bzb_securelink/pushFile.php?cuid=253&file=fileadmin/domain_files/ISCH/Action_IS0701/mou/IS0701-e.pdf

Desai, T. (2003) *Providing Remote Access to Data: The Academic Perspective*, Invited Paper, UNECE/Eurostat Work Session on Statistical Data Confidentiality, Luxembourg, 7–9 April 2003. http://www.unece.org/stats/documents/2003/04/confidentiality/wp.9.s.e.pdf

Desai, T. (2008) *A Guide to Linked Employer-Employee Data Sources in Europe and Beyond*. Report to the European Commission, DG Employment and Social Affairs. http://cep.lse.ac.uk/leed/docs/public/LEEDEU_GUIDE1.doc

Desai, T. and Cowell, F. (2006) *ESRC Review of International Data Resources and Needs*.

Eriksson, T. (2003) *The Potential of Firm-Level Panel Data and Linked Employer-Employee Microdata for Employment Analysis*. Report to the European Commission, DG Employment and Social Affairs.

Kooiman, P. and Kroese, A.H. (2001) *Restructuring Statistical Processes at Statistics Netherlands*. http://isi.cbs.nl/iamamember/CD2/pdf/395.PDF

Marsden, D. Cardoso, A R., Eriksson, T., Desai, T. and Rycx, F. (2008) *Study and Conference on European Labour Market Analysis using Firm-level Panel Data and Linked Employer–Employee Data: Final report*. http://cep.lse.ac.uk/leed/docs/public/ch1-5.pdf

MEADOW project: Measuring the Dynamics of Organisations and Work. http://www.meadow-project.eu/

Nas, S.O. and Ekeland, A. (2009) *Take the LEED: Existing Surveys and Administrative Data to Analyse the Role of Human Resources for Science and Technology in Innovation and Economic Performance*, Report to OECD Working Party of National Experts on Science and Technology Indicators, DSTI/EAS/STP/NESTI(2009)12.

Ritchie, F.J. (2005) *Statistical Disclosure Control in a Research Environment*, mimeo, Office for National Statistics, London.

Ritchie, F.J. (2006) *Access to Business Microdata in the UK: Dealing with the Irreducible Risks*, UN.

UNECE CES (2007) *Managing Statistical Confidentiality and Microdata Access: Principles and Guidelines of Good Practice*. http://www.unece.org/stats/publications/Managing.statistical.confidentiality.and.microdata.access.pdf

WORKS project: Work Organisation and Restructuring in the Knowledge Society: FP6. http://www.worksproject.be/

Links

CBS statline (access to statistical data cubes for Netherlands) http://statline.cbs.nl

Eurostat Data Portal (previously NewCronos) http://epp.eurostat.ec.europa.eu/portal/page/portal/statistics/search_database

Statistics Canada Research Data Centres http://www.statcan.ca/english/rdc/index.htm

US Census Bureau State Data Center Program http://www.census.gov/sdc/www/

References for statistical disclosure control methods

Papers

Domingo-Ferrer, J. (2009) *Inference Control in Statistical Databases*, entry for the Encyclopedia of Database Systems, in Ling Liu and Tamer Özsu (eds), New York: Springer-Verlag. http://www.informatik.uni-trier.de/~ley/db/reference/db/i.html#Domingo-Ferrer09b

Domingo-Ferrer, J. (2009) *Statistical Databases*, entry for the Wiley Encyclopedia of Computer Science and Engineering, in Benjamin Wah (ed.), Hoboken NJ: Wiley.

Elliot, M. and Smith, D. (2008) *A Measure of Disclosure Risk for Tables of Counts*. Transactions on Data Privacy 1: 34–52. http://www.tdp.cat/issues/tdp.a003a08.pdf

Hundepool, A., Domingo-Ferrer, J., Franconi, L., Giessing, S., Lenz, R., Longhurst, J., Schulte Nordholt, E., Seri, G. and de Wolf, P.P. (2006) *Handbook on Statistical Disclosure Control*. Eurostat (CENEX SDC Project Deliverable). http://neon.vb.cbs.nl/casc/handbook.htm#handbook

Hundepool, A., van de Wetering, A., Ramaswamy, R., de Wolf, P.P., Giessing, S., Fischetti, M., Salazar, J.J., Castro, J. and Lowthian, P. (2007) *τ-ARGUS v. 3.2 Software and User's Manual*. Eurostat (CENEX SDC Project Deliverable). http://neon.vb.cbs.nl/casc/tau.htm

Ritchie, F.J. (2005) *Statistical Disclosure Control in a Research Environment*, mimeo, Office for National Statistics, London.

Schulte Nordholt, E. (2002) 'Applications of Statistical Disclosure Control Methods', Statistics Netherlands research paper 1495-02-SOO. (Abbreviated version available at http://neon.vb.cbs.nl/CASC/ISIBerlin/SchulteNordholt.pdf)

Web Resources

Computational aspects of statistical confidentiality (2004) European project IST-2000-25069 CASC, 5th FP, 2001–2004, http://neon.vb.cbs.nl/casc/cascindex.htm.

The Confidentiality and Privacy Group (CAPRI) http://www.ccsr.ac.uk/capri/publications/

τ-Argus: Statistical Disclosure Control Software for tabular data http://neon.vb.cbs.nl/CASC/TAU.html

UNECE/ Eurostat Worksession on Statistical Data Confidentiality (2005) http://www.unece.org/stats/documents/2005.11.confidentiality.htm

UNECE/ Eurostat Worksession on Statistical Data Confidentiality (2007) http://www.unece.org/stats/documents/2007.12.confidentiality.htm

US Census Bureau, Statistical Disclosure Control Resources http://www.census.gov/srd/sdc/

Glossaries

OECD Glossary of Statistical Terms http://stats.oecd.org/glossary/index.htm

UNECE Glossary on Statistical Disclosure Control http://neon.vb.cbs.nl/CASC/Glossary.htm

Index

academic research community, 257–8
acquisitions, foreign, 233–7
administrative data, 192
adverse selection, 203–4
aggregate shocks, 48
allocation shocks, 48
anonymized data, 250–1
Argentina, 51
assignment theory, 127
Austria, 29
automotive repair industry, 53

bargaining model, 167–8
bargaining power
 globalization and, 171
 of unions, 174–5, 180–1
Belgium, 178
benefits, 2–3
Brazil, 51
British Household Panel Survey (BHPS), 20
business cycles, 47–9
business microdata, 13, 211, 244–5
 see also linked employer-employee data (LEED)
 access to, 13
 analyses of, 221–39
 conventions governing access to, 246–7
 longitudinal, 17–18

Central Europe, 223
centralised bargaining, 3, 52
China, 221, 226, 228
churning flow, 38–9, 44–5
collective bargaining, 8–9, 174, 178
comparative research
 barriers to, 248–9
 international, 259–60
compensation
 see also wages
 worker flows and, 45–7
competition
 barriers to, 6
 import, 160, 180, 226, 237
 international, 12, 237
 from low-wage countries, 221–3, 228
 perfect, 25
 product market, 3, 51, 56, 57, 170, 171–2
competitive hypothesis, 6

contract theory, 205, 215n4
corporatism, 159, 162n3
COST Action ISO701, 258
Croatia, job and worker flows in, 56
cross-country comparisons, in job and worker flows, 40–4
Current Population Survey, 64
Czech Republic
 educational mismatch in, 137–9, 141–2, 145–6
 job and worker flows in, 55
 skill mismatch in, 123

data
 see also business microdata; linked employer-employee data (LEED)
 access to, 13
 administrative, 192
 anonymized, 250–1
 comparative, 12–13
 on low-wage employment, 192–3, 194–7
 methods to secure access to, 249–54
 remote access and execution, 252–4, 261
 on turnover and mobility, 31
data laboratories, 251–2
data resources, 258–9
decentralisation, within firms, 53
Denmark, 178
 consequences of globalisation in, 227
 job flows in, 37
deregulation, 222–3
difference-in-difference estimators, 32
disclosive analyses, 261
dismissal costs, 2, 27
Displaced Worker Survey (DWS), 4, 64, 72
displaced workers, 3–4, 64–6, 70, 72, 80, 95
 see also job displacement
domestic firms, 232–3
duration models, of unemployment, 21–2, 32

earnings losses, 80
 measuring cost of, 67–8
earnings mobility, 189
East Asia, 228
Eastern Europe, 221
 foreign direct investment in, 223
 labour market flows in, 54–6

economic policy
  low-wage employment and, 194
  rent-sharing and, 170–1
educational mismatch, 137–46
  see also overeducation; skill mismatches; undereducation
  empirical strategy for study of, 133–7
educational requirements, measurement of, 124–5
efficiency wage policies, 7
efficiency wage theories, 158, 166, 203–4, 207
employers
  see also firms
  characteristics of, and wage disparities, 157–9
  wage policies of, 202
employers' associations, 9
employment contracts, 27–8
employment dynamics, 21–2
employment protection legislation (EPL), 3, 29, 49–51, 57
employment structure, international trade and, 237
equilibrium unemployment theory, 166
equilibrium wage, 155
Estonia, job and worker flows in, 56
Europe
  consequences of globalisation in, 226–8
  displaced workers in, 64
  job loss data for, 104–15
  job loss estimates, 80–92
  minimum wages in, 195
  skill mismatches in, 122–54
  union membership in, 178
European Central Bank, 12
European Restructuring Monitor programme, 239n5
European Structure of Earnings Survey (ESES), 13, 131, 178, 192, 254–7, 260–1
European Union (EU)
  expansion of, 230–1
  internationalization in, 232–7
excess job reallocation, 38
exchange mobility, 18
exchange rate, 51–2

fairness models, 166
financial markets, liberalization of, 222–3
finished goods, 10, 224–5
firm survey data, 192
firms
  domestic, 232–3
  foreign-owned, 222–3, 232–7
  life cycle, 45
  wage compression by, 202–16
  worker flows and size of, 44–5
foreign acquisitions, 233–7
foreign direct investment, 231, 232
foreign subsidiaries, 228–32
foreign-owned firms, 222–3, 232–7
France
  consequences of globalisation in, 227
  skill mismatch in, 123
fringe benefits, 46

gender differences
  in wages, 160–1
  in worker flows, 45
  in worker turnover, 46
Generalized Method of Moments (GMM), 20
German Socio-Economic Panel (GSOEP), 24
Germany
  consequences of globalisation in, 227
  educational mismatch within, 131
  foreign-owned firms in, 235
  skill mismatch in, 123
globalization, 10–13, 171, 221
  see also internationalization
Greenfield births, 233–4
gross job creation, 38
gross job flow, 38

Health and Retirement Study, 115n7
hierarchy, 204–5
high-skilled workers
  demand for, 122–3, 124, 138, 140
  supply of, 122
hiring policies, 58
  worker flows and, 46–7
home employment, impact of foreign production on, 228–32
Hong Kong, 228
human capital theory, 126, 130

import competition, 160, 180, 226, 237
India, 221, 228
industry wage differentials, 155–62
inequity-aversion, 205, 206
institutions
  impact on job and worker flows, 49–52, 57
  low-wage employment and, 190
  wage mobility and, 25–6
insurance models, 207
interdependencies, among workers, 203, 205–6

interest rates, 12
inter-industry wage differentials, 7, 155–62
intermediate goods, 11, 224
international comparative research, 259–60
international competition, 12, 237
International Social Survey Program (ISSP), 178
international trade, 10–12
  employment structure and, 237
  wage differentials and, 159–60
international trade theory, 223–6
internationalization, 10–13
  of advanced economies, 232–7
  data and measurement issues, 223–6
  firm-level analyses, 228–32
  industry-level analysis, 226–8
  labour market outcomes of, 221–39
  theory, 223–6
  trade and employment structure and, 237
Italy, 28, 178

Japan, 230
job and worker flows, 3, 37–63
  Baltic countries, 55
  business cycles and, 47–9
  cross-country differences, 40–4
  data issues, 39–40
  employment protection legislation and, 49–51
  impact of institutions on, 49–52, 57
  measures, 38–9
  research on, 37–8
  technological and organisational changes and, 52–4
  in transition economies, 54–6
  trends in, 49, 57–8
  wage compression and, 213–14
job competition model, 126, 127
job creation/destruction, 3
  business cycles and, 47–9
  gross, 38
job displacement, 1, 3–4
  costs of, 68–72
  literature on, 64–7
job loss
  costs of, 72–80
  data sets, EU, 104–15
  data sets, US, 98–103
  earnings effects of, 68–72
  estimation methods for, 93
  EU estimates, 80–92
  firm-level estimates, 94–6

  heterogeneous effects of, 97, 103
  introduction to, 64–7
  measurement error in, 96
  methodology and threats to validity of estimating effects of, 92–103
  short and long-term effects of, 64–6
  US estimates, 72–80
job matching processes, 5
job mobility, 1–6, 22–4
job satisfaction, 23–4
job security regulations, 49–51
job stability, wages and, 3

labour demand
  foreign acquisitions and, 234, 235, 236, 238
  hiring and, 58
  interdependencies among workers and, 203
  international trade and, 12, 159
  internationalization and, 224
  minimum wage and, 187
  offshoring and, 227
labour force, unobserved quality of, 156–7
labour market flows
  technological and organisational changes and, 52–4
  in transition economies, 54–6
labour market institutions, 24–30
  labour turnover and, 26–30
  research on, 32–3
  wage mobility and, 25–6
labour market laws, impact of, 24–30
labour market reforms, 32
  in Colombia, 27
  in Italy, 28
labour markets
  competitive model of, 6, 7, 166
  data on, 12–13
  dynamics, 17
  frictions in, 206–7
  functions of, 2
  impact of temporary employment on, 28–9
  interdependence of European, 12
  internationalization of, 221–39
  linked employer-employee data for, 244–62
  research on dynamics of, 32–3
  Walrasian (competitive) model of, 155
labour mobility, 221
labour motility, 2
labour productivity, of MNCs, 11–12

270 *Index*

labour turnover, 1–6, 21–4
  defined, 21
  employment dynamics, 21–2
  high rates of, 2
  impact of labour market laws on, 24–30
  institutional settings and, 26–30
  life cycle aspects, 31
  low levels of, 2
  measures of, 30–1
  wage mobility and, 24
Latin America, trade liberalisation in, 51
Lester range, 168
licensed anonymized microdata
  (LM) files, 250–1
lifetime earnings, job loss and, 65
linked employer-employee data
  (LEED), 1, 13, 169, 198n1
  anonymized, 250–1
  availability of, 13, 247
  barriers to access to, 247–8
  barriers to comparative research
    and, 248–9
  conventions governing access to, 246–7
  development of, for EU labour market
    and social policy analysis, 244–62
  within EU, 245–9
  on foreign firms, 234–5, 236
  forms of, 245–6
  future developments, 257–61
  from governments, 245–6
  methods to secure access to, 249–54
  PiEP-LISSY system, 253–7
  remote access and execution, 252–4, 261
  on wage compression, 202, 209,
    212, 213–14
Lisbon Strategy, 30, 140
Lisbon treaty, 12
LISSY system, 254–7, 263–4
longitudinal microdata, 17–18
low-wage countries
  competition from, 221–3, 228
  impact of outsourcing on, 232
  offshoring to, 227
low-wage employment, 9
  characteristics of persons in, 188
  concentration of, 188
  consequences of, for economic policy, 194
  data on, 192–3, 194–7
  determinants of, 190–1
  dynamics of, 189
  empirical results on, 186–9
  incidence of, 188–9, 196–7
  research questions on, 190–1
  role of firm and, 185–98

statistical methodologies for research
  on, 193

make or buy decisions, 11
manufacturing, globalization and, 10–11,
  221–2
market imperfections, wage compression
  and, 206–7
Markovian models, of employment
  dynamics, 22
Mass Layoffs Statistics programme, 239n5
measurement error, in job loss and
  earnings, 96
merger and acquisitions, 58
Mexico, 232
microdata, *see* business microdata
minimum wage, 185, 186–7, 188, 195, 207
minimum-wage legislation, 52
monopsony models, 207
multinational companies (MNCs)
  labour demand elasticity and, 236
  labour productivity of, 11–12
  outsourcing and, 225
  rent-sharing by, 171
  studies on, 233

National Longitudinal Survey of Youth
  (NLSY), 19, 24, 115n7
national resources, 258–9
National Statistical Institutes (NSIs),
  249–50, 251, 252–4
net job flow, 38
Netherlands, 37
networks, 258
Nordic countries, 57
North American Free Trade Agreement
  (NAFTA), 232
Norway, 37, 57, 235–6

offshoring, 171, 224–5
  effects of, 227
  of service jobs, 221–2
ordinary least squares (OLS)
  estimation, 176
organisational structure, labor market
  flows and, 52–4
outsourcing, 171, 221–2, 224–5
  impact on home employment of,
    228–32
  intermediate goods and, 224
  unskilled workers and, 226–7
overeducation, 122–5
  see also skill mismatches
  reasons for, 128–31

Panel Study of Income Dynamics (PSID), 20, 115n7
Pay Inequalities and Economic Performance project (PiEP), 254
performance, wage compression and, 209–13
PiEP-LISSY system, 253–7
Poland
  distribution of employees by skill level, 141
  educational mismatch in, 143–4, 147–8
  employment data from, 132
  job and worker flows in, 55
  skill mismatch in, 123, 139
Polish Structure of Earnings Survey, 132
Portugal
  foreign-owned firms in, 235
  minimum wage in, 52
problem of initial conditions, 19–20
product market competition, 3, 51, 56, 57, 170–2
productivity
  labour market flows and, 53
  resource reallocation and, 53–4
  wage compression and, 209–13
  wage differentials and, 9–10
  wages and, 203–4
product-market deregulation, 171–2
professional organizations, 6–7
profitability, wage differentials and, 166–7
propensity score marching (PSM), 176
public policy, 6–7
public use microdata (PUM), 250
purchase power parities (PPPs), 186

recessions, job flows in, 48–9
Reder, Melvin, 6
relative wages, 2
remote access, 252–4, 261
remote execution, 252–4
rent-sharing, 7, 12, 158–9, 166–73, 207, 215n6
  consequences of, for economic policy, 170–1
  data on, 168–9
  empirical results, 169–70
  future research on, 171–2
  research methodologies, 167–8
research community, 257–8
Research Data Centres (RDCs), 251–2
retirement age, 52
risk sharing, 172
Russia, job and worker flows in, 54–5

sectoral effects, on wages, 155–62
services
  globalization and, 11
  outsourcing of, 221–2
shocks, 48–9
Single European Market, 10, 230
skill levels, 206
skill mismatches, 1, 4–5
  data on, 131–3
  empirical evidence on, 127–8
  empirical strategy for study of, 133–7
  in Europe, 122–54
  firm-level analyses, 138–40
  measurement of, 124–5
  reasons for, 128–31
  wage effects of, 123–31
skilled labour
  demand for, 122–3, 124, 138, 140
  supply of, 122
skill-upgrading, 237
Slovenia, job and worker flows in, 56
social comparison theories, 208–9
social policy analysis, 244–5
social preferences, 206
Southeast Asia, 228
Spain
  educational mismatch in, 141–2, 145–6
  labour markets in, 28
  skill mismatch in, 123, 138
  union wage effects in, 178
starting wages, 3
static tables, 250
status, 204
structural estimation, 32
structural mobility, 18
supply chains, international, 10–11
Survey of Income and Program Participation (SIPP), 23
Survey on Households Income and Wealth (SHIW), 20
Sweden, 57
  consequences of globalisation in, 227
  foreign-owned firms in, 236

Taiwan, 228
technological change, 52–4, 227
temporary jobs, 2
  growth of, 27–8
  impact of, on labour market, 28–9
tournament theory, 9, 204–5, 209, 216n12
trade liberalisation, 3, 51
  see also international trade
trade unions, see unions
trade-off hypothesis, 129–30

training, for unemployed, 30
transition economies, 3
  job and worker flows in, 54–6
transition matrices, 19
turnover costs, 58

UK Census, 250
Ukraine, job and worker flows in, 56
undereducation, 122–5
  see also skill mismatches
  reasons for, 128–31
unemployed persons, training of, 30
unemployment
  labour turnover flows and, 2
  low pay and, 2
unemployment benefits, 29–30, 207
  job flows and, 52
unemployment duration, 21–2, 32
union wage premium, 180
unions, 6–7, 25, 158
  bargaining power of, 174–5, 180–1
  coverage and membership, 177–8
  effects on wages of, 174–82
  wage mobility and, 25–6
United Kingdom
  consequences of globalisation in, 226–7
  minimum wage in, 185
  skill mismatch in, 124, 141
  union membership in, 178
United States
  consequences of globalisation in, 226
  educational mismatch within, 131
  import competition in, 237
  job flows in, 37
  job loss data for, 72–80, 98–103
  job loss in, 64
  skill mismatch in, 124
  unions in, 177–8
unobserved ability hypothesis, 156–7
unskilled workers, outsourcing and, 226–7
US Census, 250
U.S. manufacturing sector, 47, 229–30

wage adjustments, 2
wage compression, 9–10, 52, 202–16
  firm performance and, 209–13
  by firms, 207–9
  productivity and, 209–13
  research on, 207–9
  theoretical framework on, 203–7
  worker turnover and, 213–14
Wage Council system, 185
wage determination process, 155

wage differentials, 7, 166
  compressed, 175
  gender and other types of inequalities and, 160–1
  impact of international trade on, 159–60
  performance and, 9–10
wage distribution, compression of, *see* wage compression
wage dynamics, 20
wage effects, of educational mismatch, 129–30
wage function, 125–6
wage inequalities
  between countries, 11
  role of employer's characteristics, 157–9
wage levels, job stability and, 3
wage mobility, 1, 3, 18–21
  analysis of, using transition matrices, 19
  defined, 18
  econometric models of, 19–20
  impact of labour market laws on, 24–30
  institutional settings and, 25–6, 32–3
  labour turnover and, 24
  life cycle aspects, 31
  measures of, 30–1
  measuring, 18–19
  sources of, 20
wage solidarity, 158
wage standardization policy, 175, 181n1
wage variability, across sectors, 155–62
wage-bargaining systems, centralisation in, 3, 52
wages
  collective bargaining and, 8–9
  data on, 8
  efficiency, 7, 158, 166, 203–4, 207
  equilibrium, 155
  foreign acquisitions and, 236–7
  in foreign vs. domestic firms, 233
  job mobility and, 23–4
  minimum, 185, 186–7, 188, 195, 207
  productivity and, 203–4
  relative, 2
  rent-sharing and, 7
  skill mismatches and, 123–31
  starting, 3
  status and, 204
  union effects on, 174–82
  worker flows and, 45–7
welfare reform, 29
West Germany, unemployment benefits in, 29

women
  gender wage gap and, 160–1
  skill mismatches and, 139
  turnover of, and wages, 46
work contracts, 27–8
worker displacement, *see* job displacement
worker flows, 3
  see also job and worker flows
  compensation and, 45–7
  defined, 38
  firm and workers characteristics, 44–7

worker stability, wages and, 3
worker turnover
  costs of, 58
  wage compression and, 213–14
  wages and, 45–7
workers
  displaced, 3–4, 64–6, 70, 72, 80, 95
  high-skilled, 122–4, 138, 140
  interdependencies among, 203, 205–6
workforce demographics, worker
    flows and, 44–5